EURIPIDES

IPHIGENIA IN TAURIS

EDITED WITH

INTRODUCTION AND COMMENTARY

BY

M. PLATNAUER

FELLOW OF BRASENOSE COLLEGE
UNIVERSITY LECTURER IN GREEK AND LATIN
LANGUAGES AND LITERATURE

OXFORD
AT THE CLARENDON PRESS

Oxford University Press, Amen House, London E.C.4
GLASGOW NEW YORK TORONTO MELBOURNE WELLINGTON
BOMBAY CALCUTTA MADRAS KARACHI KUALA LUMPUR
CAPE TOWN IBADAN NAIROBI ACCRA

FIRST EDITION 1938
REPRINTED 1952, 1956, 1960

PRINTED IN GREAT BRITAIN

PREFACE

THE text and critical apparatus of this edition are those of Professor Murray as published in the series of Oxford Classical Texts, second edition, 1913.

The foundation of a text is a difficult business, and in being allowed to take over this one ready-made I cannot but express relief at being spared a long and responsible task. Nevertheless, the writing of a commentary on a given text has its disadvantages, for, although in ninety-nine cases out of a hundred I should subscribe to Professor Murray's readings, the hundredth case does occur. This means that in some passages I seem, as it were, to offer a thing with one hand and take it away with the other. It also means that there is a great deal more 'critical' annotation than is usually found in notes mainly exegetical.

For this, however, I offer no apology. The usual habit of segregating critical notes merely results in the student's not reading them, and so leaves him to enjoy a 'dogmatic slumber' in which he dreams of a text transmitted direct from heaven. My own faith, too, is not sufficiently robust to make me believe that in any given passage one reading or emendation is necessarily right and all the rest wrong; I have, therefore, nearly always given a good many suggestions (some may think too many), merely indicating my own preference where I have one. 'In the elucidation of corrupt texts,' as Professor A. C. Pearson once wrote (and what text is not to some extent corrupt?), 'criticism and interpretation are complementary of each other.'

For the critical part of this edition I have relied, as any editor of any of Euripides' plays must, on the exhaustive compilation of Prinz-Wecklein. In matters of exegesis I owe much to the editions of England, Wecklein, and Weil, and something to older editors such as Hermann and Badham. The constant references to Kühner-Gerth's *Griechische Grammatik* and Mr. J. D. Denniston's *Greek Particles* attest my indebtedness to those invaluable works. In matters of *Metrik* I have mainly used and referred to Descroix's *Le trimètre iambique* and Wilamowitz's *Griechische Verskunst*, and on points of orthography I have had recourse to Meisterhans's *Grammatik der attischen Inschriften*.

A word of explanation is perhaps needed apropos of a few citations from the *marginalia* of the late Professor Housman. These come from his copy (now in my possession) of England's edition, and some of them subsequently saw the light in the pages of the *Classical Review*. Though Housman himself deprecated the publication of what he described as 'the mere guesses which we all jot down in our margins simply to help us take up the thread of thought to-morrow where we drop it to-day', I have ventured to quote a few on the ground that nothing emanating from such a source can be without interest and value.

I should like to take this opportunity of acknowledging my obligations and expressing my thanks to Mr. J. D. Denniston for much valuable advice on points of metre, and to Mr. A. S. Owen for his careful reading of the revises—above all to Mr. Alan Ker for his critical scrutiny of the commentary while still in manuscript, and to Mr. Denys Page for his reading of the page proofs.

OXFORD,
September 1937.

NOTE

Abbreviations are in general those used in the new edition of Liddell & Scott's *Greek-English Lexicon*.

INTRODUCTION

THE *Iphigenia in Tauris*[1] has never been ranked as among its author's greatest plays. It has neither the moving pathos of the *Hecuba* nor the stark tragedy of the *Hippolytus*, nor can its heroine compare as a dramatic character with Alcestis or Medea. But it is a bad type of criticism which complains that *As You Like It* is an inferior play to *Hamlet*; we have no business to weigh in the balance against one another dramas of different quality and find some wanting.

To begin with, the *Iphigenia* is not a tragedy at all. There is no violence—if we except the uneven and slightly ludicrous struggle which leads to the capture of Orestes and Pylades and the subsequent attempt to prevent their escape—no one is killed and the play ends happily for every one, for even Thoas, the only 'sufferer', is, we are given to understand, finally reconciled to the loss of his priestess. If there is tragedy in it at all it is, as Professor Murray suggests[2] 'the tragedy not of death, but of home-sickness', and that is no tragedy at all where, as in this play, the home-sick are restored to home. Like the *Helen* and the *Andromache* the *Iphigenia* is not so much a tragedy as a romance—a romance, it may be added, with some of the elements of a 'thriller'. The *mise-en-scène*—no well-known or easily imagined city of Hellas, but the wild and almost fabulous coast of the Crimea—the furtive arrival of Orestes and Pylades, the story of their

[1] Custom has sanctioned this title in English. Strictly speaking, there being no place actually called Tauris, we should speak of 'Iphigenia among the Taurians' (Ἰφιγένεια ἡ ἐν Ταύροις). Several writers of antiquity quote from the play, though most of them, e.g. Aristotle, Plutarch, Longinus, and Lucian, do not mention it by name. Stobaeus gives quotations as simply ἐν Ἰφιγενείᾳ, not distinguishing the Tauric Iph. from Iph. in Aulis. But such authors as give a *provenance* to their citations, e.g. Eustathius, Hesychius, and a few scholiasts, always quote as ἐν τῇ Ἰφιγενείᾳ τῇ ἐν Ταύροις. The correct English title *Iphigenia in Aulis* has no doubt strengthened, by false analogy, the incorrect *Iphigenia in Tauris*.

[2] *Euripides and his age*, p. 146.

capture, their recognition of Iphigenia (surely one of the most effective of such scenes in the whole range of Greek drama), the ingenious plot for the removal of the image, the highly dramatic yet wholly natural meeting of Iphigenia, as she is carrying it away, with Thoas, so effectively deceived as to her motives, the final escape, which the fugitives' own resourcefulness and not merely the intervention of Athena made possible—all these things must have gripped an audience, or at least an audience in certain moods, perhaps more powerfully than the slow-moving tragedy of the *Troades* or the subtle intricacies of the *Ion.*

A few words may be said about the characters. Thoas, it must be admitted, is little more than a figure; a simple-minded barbarian king misled to believe Iphigenia's trick by a religiosity which subsequently causes him to lend a ready ear to Athena's command to spare the chorus. Orestes and Pylades are complementary characters: of the two one feels that the neurotic Orestes was the greater; he is the leader, his is alike the determination to act and the resourcefulness in action. Yet it is Pylades who in Orestes' initial moments of misgiving, not to say cowardice, steels his friend to the obeying of those commands of Apollo which look so like involving both in certain destruction. The character of Iphigenia, the chief personage of the play, can scarcely be understood unless we realize that she is a woman with an *idée fixe.*[1] She can never forget the horror of her all but sacrifice at Aulis—*κακῶν γὰρ τῶν τότ' οὐκ ἀμνημονῶ*, as she says. It is the constant thought of this that enables her to overcome the scruples natural to a civilized Greek woman and to take her part in those human sacrifices from which one less hardly treated by fortune would inevitably have shrunk. Still more, after her

[1] The 'madness' of Iphigenia is well brought out in an 'epigram' (*APl.* 128) evidently composed for a picture or statue of her:

Μαίνεται Ἰφιγένεια· πάλιν δέ μιν εἶδος Ὀρέστου
ἐς γλυκερὴν ἀνάγει μνῆστιν ὁμαιμοσύνης·
τῆς δὲ χολωομένης καὶ ἀδελφεὸν εἰσοροώσης
οἴκτῳ καὶ μανίῃ βλέμμα συνεξάγεται.

dream has convinced her that Orestes, all that she has to live for, is dead, is her mind hardened against those whom she believes to have been the cause of all her miseries—νῦν δ' ἐξ ὀνείρων . . . δοκοῦσ' Ὀρέστην μηκέθ' ἥλιον βλέπειν, δύσνουν με λήψεσθ', οἵτινές ποθ' ἥκετε. Yet Iphigenia is at heart a normal, kindly-natured woman who realizes in her saner moments that human sacrifice, though seemingly ordained by the gods, is nevertheless a crime, and who does not hesitate to deny the divinity of such as have ordained it (ll. 378–91). Once, too, she discovers that Orestes is still alive and realizes that but for the inscrutable workings of destiny she herself might have been his murderer, the spell is broken, her hatred of Greece and the Greeks disappears, and Iphigenia is ready to forget her old wrongs and to return to Argos with the brother she so dearly loves.

THE LEGEND OF IPHIGENIA

The story of Iphigenia, as told in the two plays of Euripides which bear her name, is so well known that it is hard to believe that it is in fact a piece of mythological syncretism which, in all probability, only received its final form at the hands of Euripides himself.

We have to distinguish in Iphigenia three elements, which we may call respectively (1) the Attic goddess; (2) the Tauric goddess; (3) the human Iphigenia.

(1) We find many traces in Attica of the worship of a goddess referred to indifferently at various times as Artemis, Artemis-Tauropolos, Iphigenia, and Artemis-Iphigenia. Two places connected with this worship are mentioned in our play (*a*) Halae Araphenides (on the SE. coast of Attica—the modern Rafina), where, according to Strabo,[1] was a temple of Artemis-Tauropolos containing the wooden image (ξόανον) which was supposed to have been brought from Tauris (cf. l. 1453); (*b*) Brauron (a few miles south of Halae—the

[1] 9. 1. 22; cf. Call. *Dian.* 173.

modern Vraôna), one of the twelve cities in the συνοικισμός of Attica, where, according to Pausanias,[1] a goddess, Iphigenia. was worshipped, and to which, as another story tells, the Tauric ξόανον was brought (cf. l. 1463). It was from Brauron that the Persians took a (or the) ξόανον to Susa at the time of the Persian wars.[2] We have in the *Lysistrata* of Aristophanes[3] an interesting reference to this worship in the chorus' remark κᾆτ' ἔχουσα τὸν κροκωτὸν ἄρκτος ἦ Βραυρωνίοις, 'and then wearing the yellow garment I was a "Bear" at the Festival ⟨of Iphigenia⟩ at Brauron.' From the scholiast on the passage we learn of a festival held at Brauron every five years in which Athenian girls of between five and ten years old took part. These girls were known as ἄρκτοι, or Bears, and no Athenian girl who had not been an ἄρκτος was allowed to marry. At this festival goats were sacrificed to the goddess, the story being that in the old days a certain Embarus, commanded by the goddess to sacrifice his daughter for the purpose of stopping a famine, had dressed up a goat to resemble her and sacrificed it in her place—a clear reference to a primitive ritual involving human sacrifice.[4]

At Athens Pausanias again[5] tells us of a shrine of the Brauronian Artemis as standing on the Acropolis and containing a statue by Praxiteles.

Outside Attica itself we find traces of this worship at Aegira (in Achaea) where there seems to have been a temple of Artemis with a ξόανον; at Hermione, on the coast south of Troezen where, according to Pausanias,[6] was a shrine of Artemis 'surnamed Iphigenia' (Ἀρτέμιδος ἐπίκλησιν Ἰφιγενείας); and at Megara where stood a ἡρῷον Ἰφιγενείας and where, according to one tradition, the mortal Iphigenia died.[7]

For the nature of the Attic goddess Iphigenia we need not look further than her name 'the Strong in Birth'. This

[1] 1. 33. 1. [2] Paus. 3. 16. 6. [3] l. 645.
[4] Cf. E. *IA*. 1524, 5 θύμασιν βροτησίοις | χαρεῖσα of Artemis.
[5] 1. 23. 9. [6] 2. 35. 1. [7] Paus. 1. 43. 1.

function of hers is mentioned in our play where we read (ll. 1464 sqq.) that to her were dedicated the clothes of such women as died in child-birth. Looking at it in another way we may say that Artemis-Iphigenia is Artemis in her capacity of birth-helper, the name Iphigenia being originally little more than an epithet of Artemis, in much the same way as Callisto materialized as a person out of Artemis καλλίστη.[1]

It is possible, though not, I think, likely, that the goddess, for all her Hellenic name, is not Greek but Phoenician, being introduced into Attica by some early Phoenician settlers and being identical with the Phoenician goddess, Astarte. Astarte being a Moon-goddess, this theory would give some explanation of the otherwise strange epithet Tauropolos, for Tauropolos might mean 'bull-rider' and be used with reference to the horned moon. If, however, we accept it we must also accept the more than dubious equation Iphigenia-Artemis = Astarte-Aphrodite, and suppose that the Porphyrion, who is said to have introduced the latter into Attica, was not a native king at all who 'reigned before Actaeus',[2] but = 'the Purple Man', i. e. the Phoenician who, conquering the eponymous hero of the Attic coast (Actaeus, from ἀκτή), brought with him the Phoenician goddess.[3]

(2) For the Tauric goddess we have the testimony of Herodotus.[4] She is called the Maiden (ἡ Παρθένος) and to her men sacrifice τούς τε ναυηγοὺς καὶ τοὺς ἂν λάβωσι Ἑλλήνων 'The goddess to whom they sacrifice', Herodotus adds, 'the Tauri themselves call Iphigenia, daughter of Agamemnon'. This goddess, of whose existence we need have no doubts, must have been for the Greeks of a more civilized age a most useful peg whereon to hang the barbarities of the similarly natured Attic Iphigenia, in much the same way as they in all

[1] Paus. I. 29. 2 : 8. 35. 7.

[2] Paus. I. 14. 6.

[3] On this theory Theseus' victory over the Amazons and his killing of the Marathonian bull = the Ionians' victory over the Phoenicians in Attica.

[4] 4. 103.

probability used the Colchian Medea, the murderess of her children, as a screen for Medea, the Phoenician Moon-goddess of Corinth to whom in earlier times children were sacrificed.

(3) Of the human Iphigenia there appear to have been two traditions. According to the older one (which seems to have gone down before the later, and only to have been dug up by the Alexandrine savants) Iphigenia was the daughter not of Agamemnon but of Theseus. Her mother was Helen, raped not by Paris but by Theseus, and she was born at Aphidna (in Attica) or at Argos on the return journey of Helen to Sparta. According to this story the scene of the attempted sacrifice was Brauron, and Artemis was said to have saved her protégée by causing to be sacrificed in her stead not a deer but a bear. Pausanias, who gives us this information,[1] attributes it to Stesichorus and Euphorion, and this latter attribution is vouched for by a line of Euphorion found in the above-mentioned *scholium* to Ar. *Lys.* 645: ἀγχίαλον Βραυρῶνα, κενήριον ('cenotaph') Ἰφιγενείης.[2] This points to a tradition according to which the Greek fleet sailed from Brauron rather than from Aulis, and connects up with the Attic goddess Iphigenia.

In the passage mentioned Pausanias goes on to say that the baby Iphigenia was *given* by Helen to Clytemnestra and Agamemnon. In the (probably) later and certainly better known story Iphigenia is the daughter of Agamemnon and Clytemnestra. Of this story, however, Homer knows, or at least says, nothing. He takes the story of the House of Tantalus only down to Orestes' murder of Aegisthus, not even mentioning the murder of Clytemnestra. According to him,[3] too, Agamemnon's daughters are Chrysothemis, Laodice, and Iphianassa, and there is no real justification for identifying the latter with Iphigenia.

[1] 2. 22. 7.

[2] Euph. fr. 91 (in Powell's *Coll. Alex.*). Nonnus borrowed the line (13. 186).

[3] Il. 9. 145; cf. (for Iphianassa) S. *El.* 158.

Which of the two versions Hesiod accepted we do not know for certain, our only information on the subject coming again from Pausanias[1] and being to the effect that in the Κατάλογος γυναικῶν Hesiod made Iphigenia *οὐκ ἀποθανεῖν, γνώμῃ δὲ Ἀρτέμιδος Ἑκάτην εἶναι.*

The earliest account of the story in its later form comes from Proclus' *Chrestomathia.*[2] Proclus cites the *Cypria* of Stasinus (? *circ.* 700 B.C.) to the effect that when the Greek fleet was gathered at Aulis Artemis, in consequence of a boast of Agamemnon's that he, when hunting, shot better than the goddess could have done,[3] sent upon the Greeks contrary winds which prevented their sailing. Calchas, when consulted, advised the sacrifice of Agamemnon's daughter Iphigenia; but the goddess, repenting of the evil, sent her off to Tauris and made her immortal (*εἰς Ταύρους μετακομίζει καὶ ἀθάνατον ποιεῖ*). Pindar also[4] seems to accept this later version of the story.

The fusion of these three personages, the Attic goddess, the Tauric goddess, and the human Iphigenia is not hard to understand when we remember that the early Greek colonists must have known the story in the *Cypria* and may well have identified with the deified Iphigenia the Παρθένος whom they found worshipped on the coast of the Crimea with much the same rites as those accorded to the Attic goddess.

We see, then, that long before Euripides' time the story of the attempted sacrifice of Iphigenia at Aulis by her father was generally accepted. It is likely moreover that Iphigenia's bringing of the *ξόανον* to Attica was in the poet's day a recognized tradition. Euripides himself seems to have modified the saga in two ways: first he seems to have eliminated the

[1] 1. 43. 1; cf. Hes. *fr.* 100.

[2] Proclus, himself an epitomizer of the fifth century A.D., has only survived in the epitome of the ninth-century Photius. The account may be read in the O.C.T. Homer (vol. v, p. 104).

[3] Cf. Schol. E. *Or.* 658 *διὰ τὰς καυχήσεις Ἀγαμέμνονος τοξεύσαντος τὴν ἔλαφον καὶ εἰπόντος μηδ' ἂν τὴν Ἄρτεμιν οὕτω βαλεῖν.* This matter is obscurely referred to at S. *El.* 569

[4] *P.* 11. 22.

jealousy of Artemis as an at least partial cause of the trouble at Aulis, thus throwing the whole blame on the seer Calchas; secondly it is likely that he introduced Orestes into the story. According to the older tradition, as found in the *Eumenides* of Aeschylus, the Furies were reconciled with Orestes after his acquittal in the court of the Areopagus by the casting vote of Athena. According to Euripides those of the Furies who had voted against Orestes still harboured their resentment and continued to plague their victim. As a result of this Orestes goes for advice to the oracle of Delphi, by which he is told that he must bring back from Tauris the image of the goddess before he can finally free himself from the Furies' pursuit. Obedient to this command Orestes (with Pylades) goes to Tauris, where we find him when the play opens.

The story of Iphigenia, in some form or another, seems to have engaged the attention of other dramatists besides Euripides. Aeschylus, over and above the constant references to her in the *Agamemnon*, wrote a play of that name,[1] as did Sophocles.[2] Of Aeschylus' *Iphigenia* only a single line remains, and it is one which gives no indication of the nature of the play. The fragments of Sophocles' play, on the other hand, are sufficiently clear to make it plain that the plot resembled that of Euripides' *Iphigenia in Aulis*.

Another play of Sophocles, the *Chryses*, offers a problem of interest to the student of Euripides' *Iphigenia in Tauris*. Two views have been put forward as to its plot: (1) that this is to be found in Hyginus' fables 120 and 121 and is as follows:

Orestes, Pylades, and Iphigenia arrive with the image on their return journey at the island of Sminthe, the home of Chryses, priest of Apollo. This Chryses was in reality the son of Agamemnon and Chryseis, but his mother pretended that Apollo was his father, and in that theory of his parentage Chryses believed. When the fugitives arrived pursued by

[1] Schol. S. *Aj.* 722 and Schol. Ar. *Ra.* 1270.
[2] *frr.* 305–13.

Thoas, Chryses was inclined to surrender them and was only dissuaded from doing so by Chryseis who, discovering the identity of Orestes and Iphigenia, confessed to her son that he too was a child of Agamemnon. Thereupon Chryses helped Orestes to kill Thoas and the three fugitives made good their escape to Greece.

Now one fragment of this play (no. 727) was parodied by Aristophanes in the *Birds*,[1] a fact which dates it to before 414 B.C. If, as we shall have reason to believe, Euripides' *Iphigenia* was subsequent to this, it follows that Orestes' part in the rescue of Iphigenia and the image was not the invention of Euripides. But another view has been put forward.[2] According to this (2) the plot of Sophocles' play is concerned rather with the wanderings of Chryses in search of Iphigenia after the murder of Agamemnon, and the founding of the city Chrysopolis where Chryses died. It is difficult to decide between the two views, nor is the evidence from Pacuvius' tragedy of the same name of much, or indeed of any, value. The scene in one of his plays,[3] in which Orestes and Pylades disputed over their identity in order that each might save the other from death, is not definitely attributable to the *Chryses*, nor, even if it were, would it follow that Pacuvius' *Chryses* was derived from Sophocles'. It is equally possible that the Roman dramatist made use of the work of some post-Euripidean tragedian who dealt with the story of Iphigenia. Such might be Polyidus, 'the Sophist', who seems to have written a play on much the same lines as the *Iphigenia in Tauris*. The ἀναγνώρισις of this tragedy is twice mentioned with approval by Aristotle.[4] It is brought about not by means of a letter as in Euripides' *Iphigenia* but by Orestes' remark, 'So I too was fated to be sacrificed, like my sister'.

[1] l. 1240. [2] Wilamowitz in *Hermes*, xviii, pp. 249-63.
[3] See Cic. *de amicit.* 7. 24.
[4] *Po.* 1455 a and b. It is possible that Ovid knew Polyidus' play and referred to it in *Trist.* 4. 4. 79 'cum *vice sermonis* fratrem cognovit'.

DATE, SCENERY, AND CONSTRUCTION OF THE PLAY

It is unfortunate that the short and fragmentary hypothesis of our play gives no information as to its date. A few indications, however, point to a late, rather than an early, date of composition.

(1) Euripides does not seem to use trochaic tetrameters in his earlier plays.[1] The earliest definitely dateable play in which they are found is the *Troades* which was produced in 415 B.C. The presence, therefore, of these tetrameters in the *Iphigenia* suggests that this play was not written before, or not long before, 415 B.C.

(2) Euripides seems to have employed an increasing number of resolved feet in his iambic senarians. In the *Alcestis* (438 B.C.) we get only 6·3 per cent.,[2] in his latest plays we find six times this amount: in the *Orestes* (408 B.C.) 40·2 per cent., in the *Bacchae* (after 406 B.C.) 37·3 per cent. Our play contains 26·5 per cent., a percentage nearer the late *Troades* (415 B.C.) with its 23·6 per cent. than the middle period *Supplices* (? 421 B.C.) with its 16·7 per cent.

(3) Thucydides[3] tells us that after the failure of the Sicilian expedition the Athenians were especially bitter against the soothsayers and oracle-mongers who had encouraged them to their ruin. It may have been a similar feeling that caused Euripides not only to lay the entire blame for Iphigenia's 'sacrifice' on the seer Calchas but also to put such lines as 570–5 into Orestes' mouth. If this is so the play may be dated to about 414–13 B.C.

(4) The concluding lines (1490, 1) *ἴτ' ἐπ' εὐτυχίᾳ τῆς σῳζομένης | μοίρας εὐδαίμονες ὄντες* read not unlike a pathetic prayer for the salvation of the city faced with some overwhelming

[1] This argument, adduced by Wecklein (introd. p. 18), is considerably weakened by the fact that trochaic tetrameters occur in the *H. F.* (ll. 855 sqq.)—a play which most authorities assign to 423–420 B.C.

[2] J. Descroix, *Le trimètre iambique*, Macon, 1931.

[3] 8. 1. 1 *ὠργίζοντο δὲ καὶ τοῖς χρησμολόγοις τε καὶ μάντεσι καὶ ὁπόσοι τι τότε αὐτοὺς θειάσαντες ἐπήλπισαν ὡς λήψονται Σικελίαν.*

disaster, and would sound particularly appropriate if published, say, in the spring of 413 B.C., by which time the failure of the expedition must have been a foregone conclusion.

(5) The extraordinary similarity between our play and the *Helen* cannot be a mere accident. This will become clear if we tabulate the contents of both side by side.

IT.	*Hel.*
Prologue by the expatriated Iphigenia.	Prologue by the expatriated Helen.
θρῆνος in the form of a dialogue between Iphigenia and the chorus on the death of Orestes.	θρῆνος in the form of a dialogue between Helen and the chorus on the death of Menelaus.
Dialogue between Iphigenia and Orestes on the fate of the Greeks and especially of the house of Atreus.	Dialogue between Teucer and Helen on the same subject.
ἀναγνώρισις of Iphigenia.	ἀναγνώρισις of Helen.
Stichomythia between Iphigenia and Orestes who arrange the plan of escape.	Distichomythia between Helen and Menelaus who arrange a similar plan.

This similarity, as we have said, cannot be accidental. Euripides is, in one of the two plays, definitely copying the other. But which is the original and which the copy? There are, I think, at least two reasons for regarding the *Iphigenia* as the earlier:

(*a*) According to tradition, as exemplified by, e.g., Herodotus, the king of Egypt at the dramatic date of the *Helen* was the kindly Proteus. In his place we find in Euripides' play the cruel Theoclymenus. It looks, then, as though Euripides had banished Proteus and introduced in his place a character copied from Thoas in the *Iphigenia*.

(*b*) Theoclymenus seems in all respects a caricature of

Thoas. While Thoas is stern and reasonably credulous, Theoclymenus can scarcely be restrained from killing his own sister whom he suspects of complicity in the fugitives' escape, and that though he himself has supplied the ship and provisions which alone made that escape possible. If this is so it is reasonable to suppose that Thoas is the earlier character and therefore *Iphigenia* the earlier play.

This would date our play to before 412, the year of the production of the *Helen*.

Professor Murray would date the play 414–412 B.C., placing it before the *Helen*[1] and perhaps before the *Electra*. If we commit ourselves to a definite year perhaps 413 B.C. is the most likely.

Mention should perhaps be made of Markland's now discredited theory that the play was produced shortly after 422 B.C. In 422 B.C. the Athenians forcibly ejected the Delians from their island,[2] and Markland, arguing from ll. 1098 sqq. that the chorus consisted of women of Delos, supposed that the poet intended a reference to this recent fact of history. There is, however, no proof that the chorus is composed entirely of Delian women—indeed it is almost certain that this is not the case, and therefore the theory falls to the ground.

We have no definite information about the scenic arrangements of the *Iphigenia*, but it is clear that, as in so many cases in Tragedy, the back scene would represent a temple—here the temple of the goddess with a blood-stained altar in front. The temple was presumably approached by steps (see ll. 97 sqq., and notes). From reading Herodotus' account[3] of the actual temple in Tauris we should suppose that it faced out to sea, but on the stage it probably faced inland, the sea being

[1] In an article in *Stud. it. Fil. Class.*, 1928, pp. 5–53, G. Perotta argues that there is nothing to show the priority of the *IT.* to the *Helen* (412 B.C.).

[2] Thuc. 5. 1.

[3] 4. 103.

imagined as behind it. In accordance with the usual conventions the town of the Tauri and the palace of Thoas would have been imagined as being on the right from the audience's point of view, so that from the right-hand parodos would enter the chorus and Thoas. The parodos on the spectators' left would be supposed to lead to the cliffs and sea. Through it would enter Orestes and Pylades and the herdsman who announces their capture, and through it would exit Iphigenia with the lustral procession.

The number of regular actors being by a well-known convention limited to three, their parts would be distributed as follows:

Protagonist: Iphigenia and Athena.
Deuteragonist: Orestes, the herdsman, and the messenger.
Tritagonist: Pylades and Thoas.

The play is from a structural point of view divisible into eleven[1] sections:

I. Prologos.
Scene 1 (ll. 1–66). Monologue of Iphigenia.
Scene 2 (ll. 67–122). Orestes and Pylades.

II. Parodos of the Chorus and funeral dirge in which Iphigenia joins (ll. 123–235).

III. First Epeisodion.
Scene 1 (ll. 236–343). Iphigenia and herdsman.
Scene 2 (ll. 344–91). Monologue of Iphigenia.

IV. First Stasimon (ll. 392–466).

V. Second Epeisodion.
In one scene (ll. 467–642). Iphigenia and Orestes.[2]

VI. Kommos.
Sung by Orestes and Pylades and portions (or single members) of the chorus (ll. 643–657).

[1] I follow Wecklein and England in regarding the *κόμμος* as equal to a *στάσιμον* and the play as therefore containing four (not three) ἐπεισόδια.

[2] Some editors include Pylades as more than a *muta persona* in this scene. See crit. note on l. 494.

VII. Third Epeisodion.

Scene 1 (ll. 658–724). Orestes and Pylades.

Scene 2 (ll. 725–1088). Orestes, Pylades, and Iphigenia.

[This is the main scene of the play and contains the ἀναγνώρισις].

VIII. Second Stasimon (ll. 1089–1152).

IX. Fourth Epeisodion.

In one scene (ll. 1153–1233). Iphigenia and Thoas.

X. Third Stasimon (ll. 1234–83).

XI. Exodos.

Scene 1 (ll. 1284–1306). Messenger and Chorus.

Scene 2 (ll. 1307–1434). Messenger and Thoas.

Scene 3 (ll. 1435–99). Thoas and Athena, with final short choric song.

This last scene, like almost all others which contain a *deus* (or *dea*) *ex machina*, has given offence to critics ancient and modern, and it must be confessed that this conventional type of ending does not accord with present-day ideas. In this instance, however, it may be urged that Euripides had on any showing some justification. In the first place, had the three fugitives been allowed to make good their escape without divine intervention the fate of the chorus would have been certain and unenviable. Thoas realized their complicity in the fraud (ll. 1431–3) and would, if we may argue from his character as depicted in the play, have without doubt put them all to death. Indeed only Athena's express command (ll. 1467 sqq.) saved them from this treatment. In the second place, it was reasonable in the playwright to introduce the eponymous and tutelary goddess of Athens as ordainer of the Attic cult and ritual the aetiology of which he desired to explain. From a moral point of view, too, Athena is useful as giving, as it were, a heavenly *imprimatur* to an action which, viewed from a human standpoint, could only be characterized as one of lying, fraud, and theft. And lastly, as England points out, the goddess is not a mere 'machine' dragged in to save those who have made no effort to save themselves. Orestes and Pylades have throughout shown resource and heroism, and if Athena proves their final salvation she may be said to do so only in illustration of the fact that

> ἤν τις πρόθυμος ᾖ,
> σθένειν τὸ θεῖον μᾶλλον εἰκότως ἔχει.

THE TEXT

THE text of the *IT.* depends entirely on two fourteenth-century MSS.: the Laurentian (cod. Laurentianus xxxii, 2, known as L) and the Palatine (cod. Palatinus 287, known as P). The relationship between these two MSS. is a matter of some dispute: Wecklein regarded P as copied from L—as regards, that is to say, the plays that have no scholia—Wilamowitz (in his *Analecta Euripidea*) held that both MSS. came from one source. This source was possibly an edition of the nineteen plays of Euripides we possess compiled by the Alexandrine scholar Aristophanes of Byzantium (*circ.* 200 B.C.), an edition which contained arguments to the different plays but no marginal scholia.

Not long after L was written it was corrected by a first and second hand (L^2), and at the beginning of the fifteenth century by a grammarian (*l*) whose enthusiasm for emendation often caused him to alter much that a calmer judgement would have left as it was. P was similarly corrected by some unknown scholar or scholars. Corrections so made appear in the *apparatus criticus* with the sign '*p*'.

Besides these MSS. we possess a papyrus fragment of the *IT.*, the Hibeh papyrus no. 24. This contains ll. 174–91 (in a hopelessly mangled state), 245–55, 272–86, 581–95, and 600–29. The papyrus dates from the middle of the third century B.C. and contains little of value except for the confirmation of Reiske's κἀντυχόντες in l. 252, Bothe's τήνδε in l. 618 (see notes on these lines; also that on 621) and (possibly) Markland's σφαχθεῖσ' ἃ in l. 177.

SIGLA

L = cod. Laurentianus xxxii, 2 saec. xiv ineuntis.

P = cod. Palatinus 287 et Laurentianus 172 saec. xiv.

L^1P^1 designatur cuiusque codicis prima manus se ipsa corrigens vel scholia scribens; L^2P^2 secunda manus; litteris minusculis (*l*, *p*) manus recentiores correctrices.

Π = Hib. Pap. i. 24.

ΙΦΙΓΕΝΕΙΑ Η ΕΝ ΤΑΥΡΟΙΣ

ΥΠΟΘΕΣΙΣ ΙΦΙΓΕΝΕΙΑΣ ΤΗΣ ΕΝ ΤΑΥΡΟΙΣ

Ὀρέστης κατὰ χρησμὸν ἐλθὼν εἰς Ταύρους τῆς Σκυθίας μετὰ Πυλάδου παραγενηθεὶς τὸ παρ' αὐτοῖς τιμώμενον τῆς Ἀρτέμιδος ξόανον ὑφελέσθαι προῃρεῖτο. προελθὼν δ' ἀπὸ τῆς νεὼς καὶ μανείς, ὑπὸ τῶν ἐντοπίων ἅμα τῷ φίλῳ συλληφθεὶς ἀνήχθη κατὰ τὸν παρ' αὐτοῖς ἐθισμόν, ὅπως τοῦ τῆς Ἀρτέμιδος ἱεροῦ σφάγιον γένωνται. τοὺς γὰρ καταπλεύσαντας ξένους ἀπέσφαττον . . .

ἡ μὲν σκηνὴ τοῦ δράματος ὑπόκειται ἐν Ταύροις τῆς Σκυθίας· ὁ δὲ χορὸς συνέστηκεν ἐξ Ἑλληνίδων γυναικῶν, θεραπαινίδων τῆς Ἰφιγενείας. προλογίζει δὲ Ἰφιγένεια.

Argumentum et personarum indicem habent P et L (vel L²: vide infra) 2 παραγεν***** (h. e. παραγενηθεὶς) L: παραγενόμενος *l*: παρακινηθεὶς P: vide infra 3 μανείς Wilamowitz: φανείς L P, fortasse ex v. 340: παρακινηθείς huc traiecit Wecklein ἐντοπίων P et fortasse L: ἐγχωρίων *l* 6 post ἀπέσφαττον spatium vacuum relictum 5 vel 6 litterarum in L, dimidium lineae in P 7–9 fragmentum argumenti Aristophanei

ΤΑ ΤΟΥ ΔΡΑΜΑΤΟΣ ΠΡΟΣΩΠΑ

Ἰφιγένεια	Βουκόλος
Ὀρέστης	Θόας
Πυλάδης	Ἄγγελος
Χορός	Ἀθηνᾶ

Acta circa annos A.C. 414–412; ut videtur, ante Helenam: cf. Bruhn, praef. editionis pp. 11 sqq.: itaque fortasse ante Electram. Cf. Ar. Ran. 1232. Codices L P, nisi ille potius L^2 nominandus est. Vide Ion. praef. Nulla scholia.

Accedit Π (Hib. Pap. I. 24) fragmenta minutissima continens complurium vv. inde a v. 174 ad v. 629, saec. A.C. iii.

ΙΦΙΓΕΝΕΙΑ Η ΕΝ ΤΑΥΡΟΙΣ

ΙΦΙΓΕΝΕΙΑ

Πέλοψ ὁ Ταντάλειος ἐς Πῖσαν μολὼν
θοαῖσιν ἵπποις Οἰνομάου γαμεῖ κόρην,
ἐξ ἧς Ἀτρεὺς ἔβλαστεν· Ἀτρέως δὲ παῖς
Μενέλαος Ἀγαμέμνων τε· τοῦ δ' ἔφυν ἐγώ
τῆς Τυνδαρείας θυγατρὸς Ἰφιγένεια παῖς,
ἣν ἀμφὶ δίναις ἃς θάμ' Εὔριπος πυκναῖς
αὔραις ἑλίσσων κυανέαν ἅλα στρέφει,
ἔσφαξεν Ἑλένης οὕνεχ', ὡς δοκεῖ, πατὴρ
Ἀρτέμιδι κλειναῖς ἐν πτυχαῖσιν Αὐλίδος.
ἐνταῦθα γὰρ δὴ χιλίων ναῶν στόλον
Ἑλληνικὸν συνήγαγ' Ἀγαμέμνων ἄναξ,
τὸν καλλίνικον στέφανον Ἰλίου θέλων
λαβεῖν Ἀχαιοῖς τούς θ' ὑβρισθέντας γάμους
Ἑλένης μετελθεῖν, Μενέλεῳ χάριν φέρων.
δεινῆς δ' ἀπλοίας πνευμάτων τε τυγχάνων,
ἐς ἔμπυρ' ἦλθε, καὶ λέγει Κάλχας τάδε·
Ὦ τῆσδ' ἀνάσσων Ἑλλάδος στρατηγίας,
Ἀγάμεμνον, οὐ μὴ ναῦς ἀφορμίσῃ χθονός,
πρὶν ἂν κόρην σὴν Ἰφιγένειαν Ἄρτεμις
λάβῃ σφαγεῖσαν· ὅ τι γὰρ ἐνιαυτὸς τέκοι
κάλλιστον, ηὔξω φωσφόρῳ θύσειν θεᾷ.

1 πίσσαν L P 3 δὲ παῖς] δ' ἄπο Badham 8 ἔσφαξ' L P 10 νεῶν Nauck 11 ἑλληνικὸν per compendium L : ἑλληνικὴν P (-ων *p*) 13 Ἀχαιοῖς Lenting, cl. Suppl. 315 : ἀχαιοὺς L P 14 ἑλένης *p* : ἑλένη L P 15 δεινῆς sed ης in rasura alte supra textum exstante, sc. duplicis lectionis, L δ' Barnes : τ' L P τε Witzschel : τ' οὐ L P: cf. Thuc. ii. 85, 6 18 ἀφορμίσῃς Kirchhoff 20 λάβοι L P : corr. Schaefer

παῖδ' οὖν ἐν οἴκοις σὴ Κλυταιμήστρα δάμαρ
τίκτει—τὸ καλλιστεῖον εἰς ἔμ' ἀναφέρων—
ἣν χρή σε θῦσαι.
                καί μ' Ὀδυσσέως τέχναις
μητρὸς παρείλοντ' ἐπὶ γάμοις Ἀχιλλέως.
ἐλθοῦσα δ' Αὐλίδ' ἡ τάλαιν' ὑπὲρ πυρᾶς
μεταρσία ληφθεῖσ' ἐκαινόμην ξίφει·
ἀλλ' ἐξέκλεψεν ἔλαφον ἀντιδοῦσά μου
Ἄρτεμις Ἀχαιοῖς, διὰ δὲ λαμπρὸν αἰθέρα
πέμψασά μ' ἐς τήνδ' ᾤκισεν Ταύρων χθόνα,
οὗ γῆς ἀνάσσει βαρβάροισι βάρβαρος
Θόας, ὃς ὠκὺν πόδα τιθεὶς ἴσον πτεροῖς
ἐς τοὔνομ' ἦλθε τόδε ποδωκείας χάριν.
ναοῖσι δ' ἐν τοῖσδ' ἱερέαν τίθησί με·
ὅθεν νόμοισι τοῖσιν ἥδεται θεὰ
Ἄρτεμις, ἑορτῆς, τοὔνομ' ἧς καλὸν μόνον—
τὰ δ' ἄλλα σιγῶ, τὴν θεὸν φοβουμένη—
[θύω γὰρ ὄντος τοῦ νόμου καὶ πρὶν πόλει,
ὃς ἂν κατέλθῃ τήνδε γῆν Ἕλλην ἀνήρ.]
κατάρχομαι μέν, σφάγια δ' ἄλλοισιν μέλει
ἄρρητ' ἔσωθεν τῶνδ' ἀνακτόρων θεᾶς.
  ἃ καινὰ δ' ἥκει νὺξ φέρουσα φάσματα,
λέξω πρὸς αἰθέρ', εἴ τι δὴ τόδ' ἔστ' ἄκος.
ἔδοξ' ἐν ὕπνῳ τῆσδ' ἀπαλλαχθεῖσα γῆς
οἰκεῖν ἐν Ἄργει, παρθένοισι δ' ἐν μέσαις
εὕδειν, χθονὸς δὲ νῶτα σεισθῆναι σάλῳ,
φεύγειν δὲ κἄξω στᾶσα θριγκὸν εἰσιδεῖν
δόμων πίτνοντα, πᾶν δ' ἐρείψιμον στέγος
βεβλημένον πρὸς οὖδας ἐξ ἄκρων σταθμῶν.

22 κλυταιμνήστρα L P, cf. ad El. 9: vide sub v. 208   24 τέχναι Lenting   34 ἱέρειαν L P: sed �ερει in rasura *l*: ἐν τοῖσδ' ἱέρει in rasura *p*: tum ἱερίαν *l*   35 τοῖσιν P² et nunc L: τοῖσιδ' P et primitus L   38 θύω L: θυ P: θείου *p*: θύειν Kvičala, sed tum displicet τοῦ   38, 39 seclusi: 38-41 del. Usener, ut supplementa duo diversa eius quod v. 37 siletur   44 ἔδοξεν ὕπνῳ primitus L P   45 παρθενῶσι δ' ἐν μέσοις Musgrave

μόνος λελεῖφθαι στῦλος εἷς ἔδοξέ μοι
δόμων πατρῴων, ἐκ δ' ἐπικράνων κόμας
ξανθὰς καθεῖναι, φθέγμα δ' ἀνθρώπου λαβεῖν,
κἀγὼ τέχνην τήνδ' ἣν ἔχω ξενοκτόνον
τιμῶσ' ὑδραίνειν αὐτὸν ὡς θανούμενον,
κλαίουσα. τοὔναρ δ' ὧδε συμβάλλω τόδε·
τέθνηκ' Ὀρέστης, οὗ κατηρξάμην ἐγώ.
στῦλοι γὰρ οἴκων παῖδές εἰσιν ἄρσενες·
θνῄσκουσι δ' οὓς ἂν χέρνιβες βάλωσ' ἐμαί.
[οὐδ' αὖ συνάψαι τοὔναρ ἐς φίλους ἔχω·
Στροφίῳ γὰρ οὐκ ἦν παῖς, ὅτ' ὠλλύμην ἐγώ.]
νῦν οὖν ἀδελφῷ βούλομαι δοῦναι χοὰς
παροῦσ' ἀπόντι—ταῦτα γὰρ δυναίμεθ' ἄν—
σὺν προσπόλοισιν, ἃς ἔδωχ' ἡμῖν ἄναξ
Ἑλληνίδας γυναῖκας. ἀλλ' ἐξ αἰτίας
οὔπω τίνος πάρεισιν; εἶμ' ἔσω δόμων
ἐν οἷσι ναίω τῶνδ' ἀνακτόρων θεᾶς.

ΟΡΕΣΤΗΣ

ὅρα, φυλάσσου μή τις ἐν στίβῳ βροτῶν.

ΠΥΛΑΔΗΣ

ὁρῶ, σκοποῦμαι δ' ὄμμα πανταχῇ στρέφων.

Ορ. *Πυλάδη, δοκεῖ σοι μέλαθρα ταῦτ' εἶναι θεᾶς*
ἔνθ' Ἀργόθεν ναῦν ποντίαν ἐστείλαμεν;
Πυ. *ἔμοιγ', Ὀρέστα· σοὶ δὲ συνδοκεῖν χρεών.*
Ορ. *καὶ βωμός, Ἕλλην οὗ καταστάζει φόνος;*
Πυ. *ἐξ αἱμάτων γοῦν ξάνθ' ἔχει τριχώματα.*
Ορ. *θριγκοῖς δ' ὑπ' αὐτοῖς σκῦλ' ὁρᾷς ἠρτημένα;*

50 δ' *ἐλήφθη στῦλος ὡς* L P (*ἐλείφθη* Victorius): corr. Porson 52 *καθεῖμαι* L P: corr. Brodaeus 54 *ὑδραίνειν* Musgrave: *ὕδραινον* L P[2] (*ὕδραιον* P) 57 *παῖδές εἰσιν* Artemid. ii. 10, Stob. fl. 77. 3, Menand. Mon. 713: *εἰσὶ παῖδες* L P 58 *ὡς ἂν χέρνιβες βάλωσί με* L P: corr. Scaliger 59, 60 delevit Monk: cf. 249, 920 60 *ὠλόμην* ut videtur primitus P 62 *παροῦσα παντὶ* L P: corr. Canter 65 *τινὸς* L P *εἶμ'* Hermann: *εἰς μ'* L P: *εἰς ἔμ'* ut vid. P[2]: *ἐς ἔμ' l* vv. 67, 68 *ἔσωθεν* dicti videntur: cum v. 69 intrant viri 68 *πανταχοῦ* L P: corr. Monk 73 *θριγκώματα* Ruhnken, sed cf. 51, 52

Πυ. τῶν κατθανόντων γ' ἀκροθίνια ξένων.
ἀλλ' ἐγκυκλοῦντ' ὀφθαλμὸν εὖ σκοπεῖν χρεών.
Ορ. ὦ Φοῖβε, ποῖ μ' αὖ τήνδ' ἐς ἄρκυν ἤγαγες
χρήσας, ἐπειδὴ πατρὸς αἷμ' ἐτεισάμην,
μητέρα κατακτάς, διαδοχαῖς δ' Ἐρινύων
ἠλαυνόμεσθα φυγάδες ἔξεδροι χθονὸς
δρόμους τε πολλοὺς ἐξέπλησα καμπίμους,
ἐλθὼν δέ σ' ἠρώτησα πῶς τροχηλάτου
μανίας ἂν ἔλθοιμ' ἐς τέλος πόνων τ' ἐμῶν,
οὓς ἐξεμόχθουν περιπολῶν καθ' Ἑλλάδα. . . .
σὺ δ' εἶπας ἐλθεῖν Ταυρικῆς μ' ὅρους χθονός,
ἔνθ' Ἄρτεμίς σοι σύγγονος βωμοὺς ἔχοι,
λαβεῖν τ' ἄγαλμα θεᾶς, ὅ φασιν ἐνθάδε
ἐς τούσδε ναοὺς οὐρανοῦ πεσεῖν ἄπο·
λαβόντα δ' ἢ τέχναισιν ἢ τύχῃ τινί,
κίνδυνον ἐκπλήσαντ', Ἀθηναίων χθονὶ
δοῦναι—τὸ δ' ἐνθένδ' οὐδὲν ἐρρήθη πέρα—
καὶ ταῦτα δράσαντ' ἀμπνοὰς ἕξειν πόνων.
ἥκω δὲ πεισθεὶς σοῖς λόγοισιν ἐνθάδε
ἄγνωστον ἐς γῆν, ἄξενον. σὲ δ' ἱστορῶ,
Πυλάδη—σὺ γάρ μοι τοῦδε συλλήπτωρ πόνου—
τί δρῶμεν; ἀμφίβληστρα γὰρ τοίχων ὁρᾷς
ὑψηλά· πότερα δωμάτων προσαμβάσεις
ἐκβησόμεσθα; πῶς ἂν οὖν λάθοιμεν ἄν;
ἢ χαλκότευκτα κλῇθρα λύσαντες μοχλοῖς—
ὧν οὐδὲν ἴσμεν; ἢν δ' ἀνοίγοντες πύλας
ληφθῶμεν ἐσβάσεις τε μηχανώμενοι,

75 γ' ἀκροθίνια Hermann : τἀκροθίνια L P 76 Ορ. praef. L P : corr. Reiske 78 ἐτισάμην L *p* : αἰτησάμην P 84 cf. 1455 86 σοι Kirchhoff : σὺ L P: σὴ P² vel *p* ἔχει L P 91 πέρα Brodaeus: πέραν L : πέρας P, fortasse recte 94 ἄξεινον L P : corr. Musurus 97 πρὸς ἀμβάσεις L P: corr. Barnes 98 ἐκβησόμεσθα L, sed in syllabis ἐκ et σο rasurae ἂν] om. L P: add. supra lineam ἂν L (aut certe vetusta manus) : ἂν supra lineam P² vel *p* λάθοιμεν Sallier : μάθοιμεν L P : quo servato lacunam post h. v. statuit Reiske : hoc dicit : 'num simpliciter aditus exscendemus ? Sed omnes videbunt. An seras aliquas clam solvere conemur ? Sed nescimus quales hic sint serae.'

θανούμεθ'. ἀλλὰ πρὶν θανεῖν, νεὼς ἔπι
φεύγωμεν, ᾗπερ δεῦρ' ἐναυστολήσαμεν.
Πυ. φεύγειν μὲν οὐκ ἀνεκτὸν οὐδ' εἰώθαμεν,
τὸν τοῦ θεοῦ δὲ χρησμὸν οὐ κακιστέον·
ναοῦ δ' ἀπαλλαχθέντε κρύψωμεν δέμας
κατ' ἄντρ' ἃ πόντος νοτίδι διακλύζει μέλας—
νεὼς ἄπωθεν, μή τις εἰσιδὼν σκάφος
βασιλεῦσιν εἴπῃ κᾆτα ληφθῶμεν βίᾳ.
ὅταν δὲ νυκτὸς ὄμμα λυγαίας μόλῃ,
τολμητέον τοι ξεστὸν ἐκ ναοῦ λαβεῖν
ἄγαλμα πάσας προσφέροντε μηχανάς.
ὅρα δέ γ' εἴσω τριγλύφων ὅποι κενὸν
δέμας καθεῖναι· τοὺς πόνους γὰρ ἁγαθοὶ
τολμῶσι, δειλοὶ δ' εἰσὶν οὐδὲν οὐδαμοῦ.
Ορ. οὔ τοι μακρὸν μὲν ἤλθομεν κώπῃ πόρον,
ἐκ τερμάτων δὲ νόστον ἀροῦμεν πάλιν.
ἀλλ' εὖ γὰρ εἶπας, πειστέον· χωρεῖν χρεὼν
ὅποι χθονὸς κρύψαντε λήσομεν δέμας.
οὐ γὰρ τὸ τοῦ θεοῦ γ' αἴτιον γενήσεται
πεσεῖν ἄχρηστον θέσφατον· τολμητέον·
μόχθος γὰρ οὐδεὶς τοῖς νέοις σκῆψιν φέρει.

ΧΟΡΟΣ

— εὐφαμεῖτ', ὦ
πόντου δισσὰς συγχωρούσας
πέτρας Ἀξείνου ναίοντες.

— ὦ παῖ τᾶς Λατοῦς,
Δίκτυνν' οὐρεία,
πρὸς σὰν αὐλάν, εὐστύλων

105 δὲ] τε Kirchhoff 106 ἀπαλλαχθέντες P et primitus L δέμας L P[2]: δόμους P 111 τοι in τὸ mutavit *l* 112 προσφέροντα P 113 δὲ γεῖσα Blomfield ὅπῃ Kirchhoff 114 ἀγαθοὶ L P: corr. *p* 115 οὐθὲν L P: corr. *l* 118 χώρει νεκρῶν L P: corr. Scaliger 123 sqq. Choro tribuit Tyrwhitt, Iphigeniae L P 125 Ἀξείνου Markland: εὐξείνου L P: cf. 395, 438, 1388: etiam 218, 253, 341, 94 127 δίκτυν' L: δείκτυν' P: cf. Hip. 1130 et 146

ναῶν χρυσήρεις θριγκούς,
πόδα παρθένιον ὅσιον ὁσίας
κλῃδούχου δούλα πέμπω,
Ἑλλάδος εὐίππου πύργους
καὶ τείχη χόρτων τ' εὐδένδρων
ἐξαλλάξασ' Εὐρώπαν,
πατρῴων οἴκων ἕδρας.

— ἔμολον· τί νέον; τίνα φροντίδ' ἔχεις;
τί με πρὸς ναοὺς ἄγαγες ἄγαγες,
ὦ παῖ τοῦ τᾶς Τροίας πύργους
ἐλθόντος κλεινᾷ σὺν κώπᾳ
χιλιοναύτα
μυριοτευχοῦς Ἀτρείδα; [τῶν κλεινῶν;]

Ιφ. ἰὼ δμωαί,
δυσθρηνήτοις ὡς θρήνοις
ἔγκειμαι, τᾶς οὐκ εὐμούσου
μολπᾶς [βοὰν] ἀλύροις ἐλέγοις, αἰαῖ,
αἰαῖ, κηδείοις οἴκτοισιν·
αἵ μοι συμβαίνουσ' ἆται,
σύγγονον ἁμὸν κατακλαιομένα
ζωᾶς, οἵαν ⟨οἵαν⟩ ἰδόμαν
ὄψιν ὀνείρων
νυκτός, τᾶς ἐξῆλθ' ὄρφνα.
ὀλόμαν ὀλόμαν·
οὐκ εἴσ' οἶκοι πατρῷοι·

132 τῆς ante εὐίππου habent L P (τᾶς L): del. *p* 134, 135 vix sani 137 Χο. praef. L P: paragraphum nos 138 ἄγαγες ἄγαγες suprascr. L P: ἆγες ἆγες in textu L P 141 χιλιοναύτᾳ Musurus μυριοτευχοῦς Seidler: μυριοτεύχοις L P 142 Ἀτρείδα Altenburg: ἀτρειδᾶν L P τῶν κλεινῶν post Rauchensteinium seclusi: μυριοτευχεῖ γένος Ἀτρεϊδᾶν τῶν κλεινῶν post Barnesium Dindorf 143 ἰὼ Hermann: ὦ L P 146 βοᾶν L: seclusit Elmsley: ἰεῖσα vel ἱστᾶσα vel μέλπουσα addunt ante βοὰν alii 146, 147 αἰαῖ αἰαῖ scripsi: ἒε ἐν L P: cf. Alc. 215 148 οἷαι Badham 150 οἵαν duplicavit Hermann: mavult ὀνείρων delere Bothe εἰδόμαν L P: corr. *l* 152 ὠλόμαν ὠλόμαν L P

οἴμοι ⟨μοι⟩ φροῦδος γέννα.
φεῦ φεῦ τῶν Ἄργει μόχθων.
ἰὼ δαῖμον,
μόνον ὅς με κασίγνητον συλᾷς
Ἀίδᾳ πέμψας, ᾧ τάσδε χοὰς
μέλλω κρατῆρά τε τὸν φθιμένων
ὑδραίνειν γαίας ἐν νώτοις
πηγάς τ' οὐρείων ἐκ μόσχων
Βάκχου τ' οἰνηρὰς λοιβὰς
ξουθᾶν τε πόνημα μελισσᾶν,
ἃ νεκροῖς θελκτήρια κεῖται.

ἀλλ' ἔνδος μοι πάγχρυσον
τεῦχος καὶ λοιβὰν Ἅιδα.

ὦ κατὰ γαίας Ἀγαμεμνόνιον
θάλος, ὡς φθιμένῳ τάδε σοι πέμπω·
δέξαι δ'· οὐ γὰρ πρὸς τύμβον σοι
ξανθὰν χαίταν, οὐ δάκρυ' οἴσω.
τηλόσε γὰρ δὴ σᾶς ἀπενάσθην
πατρίδος καὶ ἐμᾶς, ἔνθα δοκήμασι
κεῖμαι σφαχθεῖσ' ἁ τλάμων.

Χο. ἀντιψάλμους ᾠδὰς ὕμνων τ'
Ἀσιητᾶν σοι βάρβαρον ἀχὰν
δεσποίνᾳ γ' ἐξαυδάσω,
τὰν ἐν θρήνοισιν μοῦσαν
νέκυσι μελομέναν, τὰν ἐν μολπαῖς

154 *μοι* add. Hermann 156, 157 *ἰὼ δαῖμον ὃς τὸν μόνον με* L P: correxi: *ἰὼ ἰὼ δαίμων ὃς τὸν μοῦνόν με* Heath 159 *ὦ τάσδε* L P 164 *οἰγηρὰς*, ut videtur, P 166 *κεῖται* Seidler, et sine dubio L: *κεῖτ'* L correctus et P: *χεῖται* Nauck 169 *ἀΐδα* L P 170 *ἀγαμεμνόνειον* L P 172 *πρὸς τύμβον* Heath: *πάρος τύμβου* L P: *παρὰ τύμβῳ* Seidler 175 *τηλοθι* dubie Π 176 *κἐμᾶς* L P *δοκήμασι* Porson, cl. Tro. 411: *δοκίμα* L P: possis etiam *δόκημα σφαχθεῖσ'* . . . *κεῖμαι* 177 *σφαχθεῖσ' ἁ* Markland et dubie Π: *σφαχθεῖσα* L: *σφαγχθεῖσα* P 179 *ὕμνον τ' ἀσιήταν* L P Π: corr. Bothe 180 *ἰαχὰν* L P: corr. Nauck 181 *δέσποινά γ'* (sic) L: *δέσποινα τ'* P 184 *νέκυσι* primitus L: *νέκυσιν* L P *μελομέναν* Markland: *μέλεον* L P: *μεδέων* Kviçala

῞Αιδας ὑμνεῖ δίχα παιάνων.
οἴμοι, τῶν Ἀτρειδᾶν οἴκων·
ἔρρει φῶς σκήπτρων, οἴμοι,
πατρῴων οἴκων.
ἦν ἐκ τῶν εὐόλβων Ἄργει
βασιλέων ἀρχά,
μόχθος δ' ἐκ μόχθων ᾄσσει·
δινευούσαις ἵπποισι ⟨ῥιφαὶ
Πέλοπος⟩ πταναῖς· ἀλλάξας δ' ἐξ
ἕδρας ἱερὸν ⟨ἱερὸν⟩ ὄμμ' αὐγᾶς
ἅλιος. ἄλλαις δ' ἄλλα προσέβα
χρυσέας ἀρνὸς μελάθροις ὀδύνα,
†φόνος ἐπὶ φόνῳ, ἄχεα ἄχεσιν†
ἔνθεν τῶν πρόσθεν δμαθέντων
Ταυταλιδᾶν ἐκβαίνει ποινά γ'
εἰς οἴκους, σπεύδει δ' ἀσπούδαστ'
ἐπὶ σοὶ δαίμων.

Ιφ. ἐξ ἀρχᾶς μοι δυσδαίμων
δαίμων τᾶς ματρὸς ζώνας
καὶ νυκτὸς κείνας· ἐξ ἀρχᾶς
λόχιαι στερρὰν παιδείαν
Μοῖραι ξυντείνουσιν θεαί,
τᾷ μναστευθείσᾳ 'ξ Ἑλλάνων,

186–188 lectio incerta: 188 del. Hartung 186 Ιφ. praef. L P: delevit Hermann 187 φῶς] φόως L P: h. e. nisi fallor φώως: cf. ὤως in Π Orestis 341: vide Bull. Corr. Hell. xvii. p. 569 et xviii. p. 345 189 ἦν scripsi: τίν' L P 191 μοχθω]ν δ' εγ μ[Π ἀΐσσει L P 192–197 nondum expediti: mutilus fuisse videtur archetypus hinc usque ad 232: verba uncis inclusa supplevi exempli causa: cf. Or. 988, El. 727 192 ἵπποισιν P et correctus L 193 πτανοῖς P ἐξέδρασ' L P 195 ἄλλαις Seidler: ἄλλοις P: ***ἄλλοις (deleto fortasse ἐπὶ) L 196 lectio incerta: ἄχεα τ' ἄχεσιν Barnes 200 ἐκβαίνει ποινὰ Ταυταλιδᾶν Monk 203 Ιφ. om. L P: add. Bothe: vide sub v. 186 ἐξορχᾶς L P: correctum in L, dubium qua manu: ἐξ ἆς Elmsley ante 204 personae nota videtur erasa esse in L 206 λόχιαι Hermann: λοχείαν L P 207 συντείνουσι L P 208 τᾷ μναστευθείσᾳ 'ξ Elmsley: ἁ μναστευθεῖσ' ἐξ L P: sed in nomen Κλυταιμνήστρας ludi ratus vv. 209, 208 invicem traiecit Badham 208 post 220 trai. Scaliger

ἂν πρωτόγονον θάλος ἐν θαλάμοις
Λήδας ἁ τλάμων κούρα
σφάγιον πατρῴᾳ λώβᾳ
καὶ θῦμ᾽ οὐκ εὐγάθητον
ἔτεκεν, ἔτρεφεν εὐκταίαν·
ἱππείοις δ᾽ ἐν δίφροισι
ψαμάθων Αὐλίδος ἐπέβασαν
νύμφαιον, οἴμοι, δύσνυμφον
τῷ τᾶς Νηρέως κούρας, αἰαῖ.
νῦν δ᾽ ἀξείνου πόντου ξείνα
δυσχόρτους οἴκους ναίω,
ἄγαμος ἄτεκνος ἄπολις ἄφιλος,
οὐ τὰν Ἄργει μέλπουσ᾽ Ἥραν
οὐδ᾽ ἱστοῖς ἐν καλλιφθόγγοις
κερκίδι Παλλάδος Ἀτθίδος εἰκὼ
⟨καὶ⟩ Τιτάνων ποικίλλουσ᾽, ἀλλ᾽
αἱμόρραντον δυσφόρμιγγα
ξείνων †αἱμάσσουσ᾽ ἄταν βωμούς,†
οἰκτράν τ᾽ αἰαζόντων αὐδὰν
οἰκτρόν τ᾽ ἐκβαλλόντων δάκρυον.
καὶ νῦν κείνων μέν μοι λάθα,
τὸν δ᾽ Ἄργει δμαθέντα κλαίω
σύγγονον, ὃν ἔλιπον ἐπιμαστίδιον,
ἔτι βρέφος, ἔτι νέον, ἔτι θάλος
ἐν χερσὶν ματρὸς πρὸς στέρνοις τ᾽
Ἄργει σκηπτοῦχον Ὀρέσταν.

209 *θάλος* P: *θάλλος* vel *θαλλο** L 213 Fortasse ⟨*θεοῖς*⟩ *ἔτεκεν*, et metri et synapheae causa: cf. 220, 232 *εὐκταίαν ἂν* Kirchhoff 214 *ἱππείοις δ᾽* Monk: *ἱππείοισιν* L P 216 *νύμφαν* Scaliger: sed cf. *παλαιὸν* El. 497 217 post *κούρας* quattuor litterae (fortasse alterum *αἰαῖ*) erasae in L 220 Fortasse ⟨*ἰώ,*⟩ *ἄγαμος*: cf. 213: sed cf. etiam 197, 232, Io. 889 224 *καὶ* add. Tyrwhitt 225 *αἱμορράντων* L P: corr. Monk 226 Fortasse *πάσσουσ᾽*: cf. 40: *βωμούς* del. Matthiae 227, 228 *αὐδὰν οἰκτρόν τ᾽* Tyrwhitt: *οὐδ᾽ ἄνοικτρόν τ᾽* L P 230 *δμαθέντ᾽ ἀγκλαίω* Weil 232 Fortasse ⟨*σύγγονον*⟩ *ἔτι βρέφος*: cf. not. ad 213 *ὅτι θάλος* P 234 *χερσὶ* et *στέρνοισί* L P

Χο. καὶ μὴν ὅδ' ἀκτὰς ἐκλιπὼν θαλασσίους
βουφορβὸς ἥκει σημανῶν τί σοι νέον.

ΒΟΥΚΟΛΟΣ

Ἀγαμέμνονός τε καὶ Κλυταιμήστρας τέκνον,
ἄκουε καινῶν ἐξ ἐμοῦ κηρυγμάτων.
Ιφ. τί δ' ἔστι τοῦ παρόντος ἐκπλῆσσον λόγου;
Βο. ἥκουσιν ἐς γῆν, κυανέαν Συμπληγάδα
πλάτῃ φυγόντες, δίπτυχοι νεανίαι,
θεᾷ φίλον πρόσφαγμα καὶ θυτήριον
Ἀρτέμιδι. χέρνιβας δὲ καὶ κατάργματα
οὐκ ἂν φθάνοις ἂν εὐτρεπῆ ποιουμένη.
Ιφ. ποδαποί; τίνος γῆς σχῆμ' ἔχουσιν οἱ ξένοι;
Βο. Ἕλληνες· ἓν τοῦτ' οἶδα κοὐ περαιτέρω.
Ιφ. οὐδ' ὄνομ' ἀκούσας οἶσθα τῶν ξένων φράσαι;
Βο. Πυλάδης ἐκλῄζεθ' ἅτερος πρὸς θατέρου.
Ιφ. τοῦ ξυζύγου δὲ τοῦ ξένου τί τοὔνομ' ἦν;
Βο. οὐδεὶς τόδ' οἶδεν· οὐ γὰρ εἰσηκούσαμεν.
Ιφ. πῶς δ' εἴδετ' αὐτοὺς κἀντυχόντες εἵλετε;
Βο. ἄκραις ἐπὶ ῥηγμῖσιν ἀξένου πόρου . . .
Ιφ. καὶ τίς θαλάσσης βουκόλοις κοινωνία;
Βο. βοῦς ἤλθομεν νίψοντες ἐναλίᾳ δρόσῳ.
Ιφ. ἐκεῖσε δὴ 'πάνελθε, πῶς νιν εἵλετε
τρόπῳ θ' ὁποίῳ· τοῦτο γὰρ μαθεῖν θέλω.
χρόνιοι γὰρ ἥκουσ'· οὐδέ πω βωμὸς θεᾶς
Ἑλληνικαῖσιν ἐξεφοινίχθη ῥοαῖς.

237 σημαίνων L P: corr. Musurus 238 τε Reiske: παῖ L P 241 κυανέας Συμπληγάδας Bentley 246 σχῆμ' Monk: cf. 248, 250: ὄνομ' L P Π (τίνος γῆς; ὄνομ' Verrall): si vere, fortasse omen ex nomine petit sacerdos 248–256 lineolae pro personarum notis L 250 vix sanus: τῷ συζύγῳ Elmsley: δὲ λέξον αὖ τί Weil 252 πῶς] ποῦ Musgrave κἀντυχόντες Reiske et Π: καὶ τυχόντες L P 253 ἄκραις (et εὐξείνου πόντου) Plut. de exil. p. 602: ἀκταῖσιν L P: αὐταῖς Dawes ἀξένου L P: ευξεινου Π 254 κοινωνίαν P 256 ποῦ Badham 257 θέλει P, sed ω suprascr. 258, 259 varie tentati: del. Monk: post 245 trai. Wecklein, pastori tributos: versum post ῥοαῖς excidisse iudicat Bruhn: sed cf. vv. 588–590: nunquam diserte dicitur Iphigenia Graecum hominem sacrificasse: vid. 37, 72, 347 (ubi ἡνίκ' idem est atque εἴ ποτ'), 585 258 ἥκουσιν L P

Βο. ἐπεὶ τὸν ἐσρέοντα διὰ Συμπληγάδων
βοῦς ὑλοφορβοὺς πόντον εἰσεβάλλομεν,
ἦν τις διαρρὼξ κυμάτων πολλῷ σάλῳ
κοιλωπὸς ἀγμός, πορφυρευτικαὶ στέγαι.
ἐνταῦθα δισσοὺς εἶδέ τις νεανίας
βουφορβὸς ἡμῶν, κἀπεχώρησεν πάλιν
ἄκροισι δακτύλοισι πορθμεύων ἴχνος.
ἔλεξε δ'· Οὐχ ὁρᾶτε; δαίμονές τινες
θάσσουσιν οἵδε.—θεοσεβὴς δ' ἡμῶν τις ὢν
ἀνέσχε χεῖρα καὶ προσηύξατ' εἰσιδών·
Ὦ ποντίας παῖ Λευκοθέας, νεῶν φύλαξ,
δέσποτα Παλαῖμον, ἵλεως ἡμῖν γενοῦ,
εἴτ' οὖν ἐπ' ἀκταῖς θάσσετον Διοσκόρω,
ἢ Νηρέως ἀγάλμαθ', ὃς τὸν εὐγενῆ
ἔτικτε πεντήκοντα Νηρῄδων χορόν.
ἄλλος δέ τις μάταιος, ἀνομίᾳ θρασύς,
ἐγέλασεν εὐχαῖς, ναυτίλους δ' ἐφθαρμένους
θάσσειν φάραγγ' ἔφασκε τοῦ νόμου φόβῳ,
κλύοντας ὡς θύοιμεν ἐνθάδε ξένους.
ἔδοξε δ' ἡμῶν εὖ λέγειν τοῖς πλείοσι,
θηρᾶν τε τῇ θεῷ σφάγια τἀπιχώρια.
κἀν τῷδε πέτραν ἅτερος λιπὼν ξένοιν
ἔστη κάρα τε διετίναξ' ἄνω κάτω
κἀπεστέναξεν ὠλένας τρέμων ἄκρας,
μανίαις ἀλαίνων, καὶ βοᾷ κυναγὸς ὥς·
Πυλάδη, δέδορκας τήνδε; τήνδε δ' οὐχ ὁρᾷς
Ἅιδου δράκαιναν, ὥς με βούλεται κτανεῖν
δειναῖς ἐχίδναις εἰς ἔμ' ἐστομωμένη;
ἡ δ' ἐκ χιτώνων πῦρ πνέουσα καὶ φόνον

260 *ἐκρέοντα* Elmsley 261 praestat fortasse *ὑλοφόρβους* 263 *ἀγμός* L : *ἁρμός* P 265 *κἀνεχώρησεν* Blomfield 268 *ὢν* P *l*: om. L 271 sequitur hunc versum in L folium Ionis vv. 1424–1582 continens 272 *ἀκτῆς* Wecklein, cl. Hec. 28 281 *πέτροις* P *ξένην* L P: corr. Brodaeus 283 *κἀνεστέναξεν* Monk

πτεροῖς ἐρέσσει, μητέρ' ἀγκάλαις ἐμὴν
ἔχουσα—πέτρινον ὄχθον, ὡς ἐπεμβάλῃ.
οἴμοι, κτενεῖ με· ποῖ φύγω;
παρῆν δ' ὁρᾶν
οὐ ταῦτα μορφῆς σχήματ', ἀλλ' ἠλλάσσετο
φθογγάς τε μόσχων καὶ κυνῶν ὑλάγματα,
†ἃς φᾶσ'† Ἐρινῦς ἱέναι μιμήματα.
ἡμεῖς δὲ συσταλέντες, ὡς θαμβούμενοι,
σιγῇ καθήμεθ'· ὁ δὲ χερὶ σπάσας ξίφος,
μόσχους ὀρούσας ἐς μέσας λέων ὅπως,
παίει σιδήρῳ λαγόνας ἐς πλευράς θ' ἱείς,
δοκῶν Ἐρινῦς θεὰς ἀμύνεσθαι τάδε,
ὡς αἱματηρὸν πέλαγος ἐξανθεῖν ἁλός.
κἀν τῷδε πᾶς τις, ὡς ὁρᾷ βουφόρβια
πίπτοντα καὶ πορθούμεν', ἐξωπλίζετο,
κόχλους τε φυσῶν συλλέγων τ' ἐγχωρίους·
πρὸς εὐτραφεῖς γὰρ καὶ νεανίας ξένους
φαύλους μάχεσθαι βουκόλους ἡγούμεθα.
πολλοὶ δ' ἐπληρώθημεν ἐν μακρῷ χρόνῳ.
πίπτει δὲ μανίας πίτυλον ὁ ξένος μεθείς,
στάζων ἀφρῷ γένειον· ὡς δ' ἐσείδομεν
προύργου πεσόντα, πᾶς ἀνὴρ ἔσχεν πόνον
βάλλων ἀράσσων. ἅτερος δὲ τοῖν ξένοιν
ἀφρόν τ' ἀπέψη σώματός τ' ἐτημέλει
πέπλων τε προυκάλυπτεν εὐπήνους ὑφάς,
καραδοκῶν μὲν τἀπιόντα τραύματα,
φίλον δὲ θεραπείαισιν ἄνδρ' εὐεργετῶν.

291 κτείνει L P : corr. *p* 292 ταυτὰ nisi fallor L P lacunam post 292 statuit Bruhn: post 293 Kirchhoff 294 ἃ ˇφασκ' Badham: fortasse δόξας 295 θανούμενοι L P, sed suprascr. μβ super αν L : θανουμένου Wilamowitz 296 ὁ L *p* : ἡ P χερὶ σπάσας Pierson : περισπάσας L P 298 πλευράς θ' Reiske : πλευρὰς L P 300 ὥσθ' Markland: cf. Cycl. 647 πέλαγος L P: πέλανον *p* 303 συλλέγοντ' P : corr. *p* 306 ἐν παύρῳ Wecklein : οὐ μακρῷ Nauck (ἐν μικρῷ *l*) 311 ἀπέψα L P et libri Luciani Amor. 47: corr. Elmsley 312 πέπλου τε Lucianus εὐπήκτους ὑφάς *p* et codd. aliquot Luciani: εὐπήκτοις ὑφαῖς codd. alii Luciani et Musurus

ἔμφρων δ' ἀνᾴξας ὁ ξένος πεσήματος
ἔγνω κλύδωνα πολεμίων προσκείμενον
καὶ τὴν παροῦσαν συμφορὰν αὐτοῖν πέλας,
ᾤμωξέ θ'· ἡμεῖς δ' οὐκ ἀνίεμεν πέτροις
βάλλοντες, ἄλλος ἄλλοθεν προσκείμενοι.
οὗ δὴ τὸ δεινὸν παρακέλευσμ' ἠκούσαμεν·
Πυλάδη, θανούμεθ', ἀλλ' ὅπως θανούμεθα
κάλλισθ'· ἕπου μοι, φάσγανον σπάσας χερί.—
ὡς δ' εἴδομεν δίπαλτα πολεμίων ξίφη,
φυγῇ λεπαίας ἐξεπίμπλαμεν νάπας.
ἀλλ', εἰ φύγοι τις, ἅτεροι προσκείμενοι
ἔβαλλον αὐτούς· εἰ δὲ τούσδ' ὠσαίατο,
αὖθις τὸ νῦν ὑπεῖκον ἤρασσεν πέτροις.
ἀλλ' ἦν ἄπιστον· μυρίων γὰρ ἐκ χερῶν
οὐδεὶς τὰ τῆς θεοῦ θύματ' εὐτύχει βαλών.
μόλις δέ νιν τόλμῃ μὲν οὐ χειρούμεθα,
κύκλῳ δὲ περιβαλόντες ἐξεκλέψαμεν
πέτροισι χειρῶν φάσγαν', ἐς δὲ γῆν γόνυ
καμάτῳ καθεῖσαν. πρὸς δ' ἄνακτα τῆσδε γῆς
κομίζομέν νιν. ὁ δ' ἐσιδὼν ὅσον τάχος
ἐς χέρνιβάς τε καὶ σφαγεῖ' ἔπεμπέ σοι.
ηὔχου δὲ τοιάδ', ὦ νεᾶνί, σοι ξένων
σφάγια παρεῖναι· κἂν ἀναλίσκῃς ξένους
τοιούσδε, τὸν σὸν Ἑλλὰς ἀποτείσει φόνον
δίκας τίνουσα τῆς ἐν Αὐλίδι σφαγῆς.

Χο. θαυμάστ' ἔλεξας τὸν μανένθ', ὅστις ποτὲ
Ἕλληνος ἐκ γῆς πόντον ἦλθεν ἄξενον.

Ιφ. εἶέν· σὺ μὲν κόμιζε τοὺς ξένους μολών,

316 ἔγνωκε L P: corr. Scaliger 318 πέτροις suprascr. L: πέτρους in textu L P 327 αὖθις] αὖτις *l*: οὗτις P et ut videtur L ἤρασσον P L: corr. Musurus 329 λαβών P 331 περιβάλλοντες L P: corr. Reiske ἐξεκόψαμεν Bothe 332 πέπλοισι Koechly 333 καθεῖσα P: corr. *p* 335 ἐς Valckenaer: τε L P: πρὸς (πρ) Housman σφάγι' L P: corr. Musgrave: cf. Lycophr. 196 336 ηὔχου Mekler, cf. 354 seqq.: εὔχου L P σοι ξένων] σοι θαμὰ Stadtmueller: πολλά σοι Barthold 340 μανένθ' Kaehler: φανένθ' L P

τὰ δ' ἐνθάδ' ἡμεῖς ὅσια φροντιούμεθα. . . .
ὦ καρδία τάλαινα, πρὶν μὲν ἐς ξένους
γαληνὸς ἦσθα καὶ φιλοικτίρμων ἀεί,
ἐς θοὐμόφυλον ἀναμετρουμένη δάκρυ,
Ἕλληνας ἄνδρας ἡνίκ' ἐς χέρας λάβοις.
νῦν δ' ἐξ ὀνείρων οἷσιν ἠγριώμεθα,
δοκοῦσ' Ὀρέστην μηκέθ' ἥλιον βλέπειν,
δύσνουν με λήψεσθ', οἵτινές ποθ' ἥκετε.
καὶ τοῦτ' ἄρ' ἦν ἀληθές, ᾐσθόμην, φίλαι·
οἱ δυστυχεῖς γὰρ τοῖσι δυστυχεστέροις
αὐτοὶ κακῶς πράξαντες οὐ φρονοῦσιν εὖ.
ἀλλ' οὔτε πνεῦμα Διόθεν ἦλθε πώποτε,
οὐ πορθμίς, ἥτις διὰ πέτρας Συμπληγάδας
Ἑλένην ἀπήγαγ' ἐνθάδ', ἥ μ' ἀπώλεσεν,
Μενέλεών θ', ἵν' αὐτοὺς ἀντετιμωρησάμην,
τὴν ἐνθάδ' Αὖλιν ἀντιθεῖσα τῆς ἐκεῖ,
οὗ μ' ὥστε μόσχον Δαναΐδαι χειρούμενοι
ἔσφαζον, ἱερεὺς δ' ἦν ὁ γεννήσας πατήρ.
οἴμοι—κακῶν γὰρ τῶν τότ' οὐκ ἀμνημονῶ—
ὅσας γενείου χεῖρας ἐξηκόντισα
γονάτων τε τοῦ τεκόντος, ἐξαρτωμένη,
λέγουσα τοιάδ'· Ὦ πάτερ, νυμφεύομαι
νυμφεύματ' αἰσχρὰ πρὸς σέθεν· μήτηρ δ' ἐμὲ
σέθεν κατακτείνοντος Ἀργεῖαί τε νῦν
ὑμνοῦσιν ὑμεναίοισιν, αὐλεῖται δὲ πᾶν
μέλαθρον· ἡμεῖς δ' ὀλλύμεσθα πρὸς σέθεν.
Ἅιδης Ἀχιλλεὺς ἦν ἄρ', οὐχ ὁ Πηλέως,
ὅν μοι προσείσας πόσιν, ἐν ἁρμάτων ὄχοις
ἐς αἱματηρὸν γάμον ἐπόρθμευσας δόλῳ.

343 ὅσια Reiske : οἷα L P 346 εἰς τὸ ὁμόφυλον L P 347 vide sub v. 258 351 ᾐσθόμην Ludv. Dindorf : ἠχθόμην L P 352 τοῖσιν εὐτυχεστέροις L P : corr. Wecklein 357 Μενέλαον L P 359 οὗ Pierson : οἷ L P 361 τότ' Musurus : τοῦδ' L P 365 ἐμὲ Reiske : ἐμὴ L P 366 νῦν Heath : νιν L P 370 προσεῖπας L P : corr. Bothe : προειπὼν Hartung μ' ὄχοις Nauck

ἐγὼ δὲ λεπτῶν ὄμμα διὰ καλυμμάτων
ἔχουσ', ἀδελφόν τ' οὐκ ἀνειλόμην χεροῖν,
—ὃς νῦν ὄλωλεν—οὐ κασιγνήτῃ στόμα
συνῆψ' ὑπ' αἰδοῦς, ὡς ἰοῦσ' ἐς Πηλέως
μέλαθρα· πολλὰ δ' ἀπεθέμην ἀσπάσματα
ἐς αὖθις, ὡς ἥξουσ' ἐς Ἄργος αὖ πάλιν.
ὦ τλῆμον, εἰ τέθνηκας, ἐξ οἵων καλῶν
ἔρρεις, Ὀρέστα, καὶ πατρὸς ζηλωμάτων. . . .
τὰ τῆς θεοῦ δὲ μέμφομαι σοφίσματα,
ἥτις βροτῶν μὲν ἤν τις ἅψηται φόνου,
ἢ καὶ λοχείας ἢ νεκροῦ θίγῃ χεροῖν,
βωμῶν ἀπείργει, μυσαρὸν ὡς ἡγουμένη,
αὐτὴ δὲ θυσίαις ἥδεται βροτοκτόνοις.
οὐκ ἔσθ' ὅπως ἔτεκεν ἂν ἡ Διὸς δάμαρ
Λητὼ τοσαύτην ἀμαθίαν. ἐγὼ μὲν οὖν
τὰ Ταντάλου θεοῖσιν ἑστιάματα
ἄπιστα κρίνω, παιδὸς ἡσθῆναι βορᾷ,
τοὺς δ' ἐνθάδ', αὐτοὺς ὄντας ἀνθρωποκτόνους,
ἐς τὴν θεὸν τὸ φαῦλον ἀναφέρειν δοκῶ·
οὐδένα γὰρ οἶμαι δαιμόνων εἶναι κακόν.

Χο. — κυάνεαι κυάνεαι [στρ.
σύνοδοι θαλάσσας, ἵν' οἶ-
στρος ὁ πετόμενος Ἀργόθεν ἄ-
ξενον ἐπ' οἶδμα διεπέρασεν . . .
Ἀσιήτιδα γαῖαν
Εὐρώπας διαμείψας.

373 τ' οὐκ ἀνειλόμην Hermann (οὔτ' ἀνειλόμην Tyrwhitt) : τοῦτον εἱλόμην L P 374 κασιγνήτω suprascr. in L 377 εἰσαῦτις L P 378 καλῶν Reiske : κακῶν L P 384 αὔτη L P 385 ἔτεκεν ἂν] ἔτικτεν Porson : ἂν ἔτεκεν Hartung 387, 389 Ταντάλου τε et τούς τ' Hermann 390 τὴν Markland : τὸν L P τὸ L : τὸν P 393 ἵν' Hermann : ἣν L P 394 πετόμενος L P : ποτώμενος *l* 395 ἄξενον Markland : εὔξενον *l* : εὔξεινον L P post διεπέρασεν add. ποτε *l* : Ἰώ Kirchhoff : Ἰοῦς Erfurdt

τίνες ποτ' ἄρα τὸν εὔυδρον δονακόχλοα
λιπόντες Εὐρώταν ἢ
ῥεύματα σεμνὰ Δίρκας
ἔβασαν ἔβασαν ἄμεικτον αἶαν, ἔνθα κούρᾳ
δίᾳ τέγγει
βωμοὺς καὶ περικίονας
ναοὺς αἷμα βρότειον;

ἦ ῥοθίοις εἰλατίνας [ἀντ.
δικρότοισι κώπας ἔπλευ-
σαν ἐπὶ πόντια κύματα, νά-
ιον ὄχημα λινοπόροις αὔραις,
φιλόπλουτον ἅμιλλαν
αὔξοντες μελάθροισιν;
φίλα γὰρ ἐλπίς γ', ἐπί τε πήμασιν βροτῶν
ἄπληστος ἀνθρώποις, ὄλ-
βου βάρος οἳ φέρονται
πλάνητες ἐπ' οἶδμα πόλεις τε βαρβάρους περῶντες,
κοινᾷ δόξᾳ·
γνώμα δ' οἷς μὲν ἄκαιρος ὄλβου, τοῖς δ' ἐς μέσον ἥκει.

πῶς πέτρας τὰς συνδρομάδας, [στρ.
πῶς Φινεϊδᾶν ἀΰ-
πνους ἀκτὰς ἐπέρασαν
παρ' ἅλιον
αἰγιαλὸν ἐπ' Ἀμφιτρί-

399 δονακόχλοα L^2 P: δονακόχλοον primitus, ut videtur, L 403 sq. κούρα διατέγγει L P: corr. Elmsley 405 sq. περὶ κίονας ναοῦ (ναῶν *l*) L P: corr. Elmsley 407 ἐλατίνοις (εἰλατίνοις *l*) et κώπαις L P: corr. Wecklein 409 ἔκελσαν Stadtmueller νότια Bergk: cf. 394 414 γ' ἐπί τε scripsi: γένετ' ἐπὶ L P, sc. γ' ἔν τε, suprascripto ἐπὶ: ἐγένετ' Musurus: ἔν τ' ἐπιπάμασιν Housman πήμασιν P: πήμασι L 417 τε *l* in rasura: om. P 418 κοιναὶ δόξαι L P: κεναὶ *l* 421 τὰς συνδρομάδας πέτρας L P: trai. Musgrave: cf. v. 439 422 φινηΐδας L P: corr. Rauchenstein 423 ἀΰπνους suspectum: λιγύπνους Wilamowitz 425 παράλιον L P: divisit Seidler: παρ' ἀλίμενον olim Wecklein

τας ῥοθίῳ δραμόντες,
ὅπου πεντήκοντα κορᾶν
Νηρῄδων . . . . χοροὶ
μέλπουσιν ἐγκύκλιοι,
πλησιστίοισι πνοαῖς
συριζόντων κατὰ πρύμναν
εὐναίων πηδαλίων
αὔραις ⟨σὺν⟩ νοτίαις
ἢ πνεύμασι Ζεφύρου,
τὰν πολυόρνιθον ἐπ᾽ αἶ-
αν, λευκὰν ἀκτάν, Ἀχιλῆ-
ος δρόμους καλλισταδίους,
ἄξεινον κατὰ πόντον;

εἴθ᾽ εὐχαῖσιν δεσποσύνοις [ἀντ.
Λήδας Ἑλένα φίλα
παῖς ἐλθοῦσα τύχοι τὰν
Τρῳάδα λι-
ποῦσα πόλιν, ἵν᾽ ἀμφὶ χαί-
τᾳ δρόσον αἱματηρὰν
ἑλιχθεῖσα λαιμοτόμῳ
δεσποίνας χειρὶ θάνοι
ποινὰς δοῦσ᾽ ἀντιπάλους.
ἅδισταν δ᾽ ἀγγελίαν
δεξαίμεσθ᾽, Ἑλλάδος ἐκ γᾶς
πλωτήρων εἴ τις ἔβα,
δουλείας ἐμέθεν

428 *νηρηίδων* L P Νηρῄδων ⟨ποσὶ⟩ χοροί, miro metro, Hermann: cf. 445: fortasse δῆλα χοροί vel Νηρέως ἔκδηλα χοροί: nam ubique saltant, hic conspiciuntur: cf. Catull. 64, 15 sq., Mosch. 2, 118 429 *ἐγκυκλίοις* L P: corr. Heath 430 *καὶ* ante *πλησιστίοισι* add. incertum mihi utrum L an *l* 432 *εὐνάων* Bothe 433 *σὺν* add. Wecklein: *ἐν* add. *l* 435 *πολιόρνιθον* L P 436 *ἀχιλλῆος* L P 438 *ἄξεινον* P: *ξεινον L: *εὔ* versui antecedenti add. *l* 439 *δεσποσύνας* L P: corr. Markland 442 *τρωϊάδα* L P 444 *εἱλιχθεῖσα* L P: corr. *l* 445 *χερὶ* L P *θάνῃ* L P: corr. Seidler 447 *ἥδιστ᾽ ἂν τήνδ᾽* L P: post multos correxi 448 *δεξαίμεθ᾽* L P: corr. *l*

δειλαίας παυσίπονος·
κἂν γὰρ ὀνείροισι συνεί-
ην δόμοις πόλει τε πατρῴ-
ᾳ, τερπνῶν ὕπνων ἀπόλαυ-
σιν, κοινὰν χάριν ὄλβου.

— ἀλλ' οἵδε χέρας δεσμοῖς δίδυμοι
συνερεισθέντες χωροῦσι, νέον
πρόσφαγμα θεᾶς· σιγᾶτε, φίλαι.
τὰ γὰρ Ἑλλήνων ἀκροθίνια δὴ
ναοῖσι πέλας τάδε βαίνει·
οὐδ' ἀγγελίας ψευδεῖς ἔλακεν
βουφορβὸς ἀνήρ.
— ὦ πότνι', εἴ σοι τάδ' ἀρεσκόντως
πόλις ἥδε τελεῖ, δέξαι θυσίας,
ἃς ὁ παρ' ἡμῖν νόμος οὐχ ὁσίας
[Ἕλλησι διδοὺς] ἀναφαίνει.

Ιφ. εἶέν·
τὰ τῆς θεοῦ μὲν πρῶτον ὡς καλῶς ἔχῃ
φροντιστέον μοι. μέθετε τῶν ξένων χέρας,
ὡς ὄντες ἱεροὶ μηκέτ' ὦσι δέσμιοι.
ναοῦ δ' ἔσω στείχοντες εὐτρεπίζετε
ἃ χρὴ 'πὶ τοῖς παροῦσι καὶ νομίζεται.
φεῦ·
τίς ἆρα μήτηρ ἡ τεκοῦσ' ὑμᾶς ποτε
πατήρ τ'; ἀδελφή τ', εἰ γεγῶσα τυγχάνει . . .
οἵων στερεῖσα διπτύχων νεανιῶν

452 κἂν γὰρ Herwerden: καὶ γὰρ *l*: γὰρ L P: ὡς γὰρ Wecklein ὀνείροισι συνείην Fritzsche: ὀνείρασι συμβαίην L P: lectio incerta 454 ὕπνων Hermann: ὕμνων L P ἀπολαύειν *l* 455 ὄλβα L P: corr. Köchly: ὄλβῳ *l* 456 Iphigeniae 463 Chori notas praef. L P: delevit Seidler: paragraphos nos posuimus δίδυμοι Markland: διδύμοις L P 466 Ἕλλησι διδοὺς seclusit Bergk: lectio dubia 470 ναοὺς L P: corr. Valckenaer 474 στερηθεῖσα L P: corr. Scaliger

ἀνάδελφος ἔσται.—τὰς τύχας τίς οἶδ' ὅτῳ
τοιαίδ' ἔσονται; πάντα γὰρ τὰ τῶν θεῶν
ἐς ἀφανὲς ἕρπει, κοὐδὲν οἶδ' οὐδεὶς κακὸν
. . . .
ἡ γὰρ τύχη παρήγαγ' ἐς τὸ δυσμαθές.
  πόθεν ποθ' ἥκετ', ὦ ταλαίπωροι ξένοι;
ὡς διὰ μακροῦ μὲν τήνδ' ἐπλεύσατε χθόνα,
μακρὸν δ' ἀπ' οἴκων χρόνον ἔσεσθ' ἀεὶ κάτω.
Ορ. τί ταῦτ' ὀδύρῃ, κἀπὶ τοῖς μέλλουσι νῷν
κακοῖσι λυπεῖς, ἥτις εἶ ποτ', ὦ γύναι;
οὔτοι νομίζω σοφόν, ὃς ἂν μέλλων κτενεῖν
οἴκτῳ τὸ δεῖμα τοὐλέθρου νικᾶν θέλῃ,
οὐχ ὅστις Ἅιδην ἐγγὺς ὄντ' οἰκτίζεται
σωτηρίας ἄνελπις· ὡς δύ' ἐξ ἑνὸς
κακὼ συνάπτει, μωρίαν τ' ὀφλισκάνει
θνῄσκει θ' ὁμοίως· τὴν τύχην δ' ἐᾶν χρεών.
ἡμᾶς δὲ μὴ θρήνει σύ· τὰς γὰρ ἐνθάδε
θυσίας ἐπιστάμεσθα καὶ γιγνώσκομεν.
Ιφ. πότερος ἄρ' ὑμῶν ἐνθάδ' ὠνομασμένος
Πυλάδης κέκληται; τόδε μαθεῖν πρῶτον θέλω.
Ορ. ὅδ', εἴ τι δή σοι τοῦτ' ἐν ἡδονῇ μαθεῖν.
Ιφ. ποίας πολίτης πατρίδος Ἕλληνος γεγώς;
Ορ. τί δ' ἂν μαθοῦσα τόδε πλέον λάβοις, γύναι;
Ιφ. πότερον ἀδελφὼ μητρός ἐστον ἐκ μιᾶς;
Ορ. φιλότητί γ'· ἐσμὲν δ' οὐ κασιγνήτω, γύναι.
Ιφ. σοὶ δ' ὄνομα ποῖον ἔθεθ' ὁ γεννήσας πατήρ;
Ορ. τὸ μὲν δίκαιον Δυστυχὴς καλοίμεθ' ἄν.
Ιφ. οὐ τοῦτ' ἐρωτῶ· τοῦτο μὲν δὸς τῇ τύχῃ.
Ορ. ἀνώνυμοι θανόντες οὐ γελῴμεθ' ἄν.

477 lacunam indicavit Bruhn: σαφῶς pro κακὸν Wecklein 481 μακρὰν δ' ἀπ' οἴκων χθονὸς Hirzel 482 sqq. Oresti L P: Pyladae tribuit Monk: cf. 494 482 νῷν L *p*: rasura in P: νὼ Porson 484 κτενεῖν Seidler: θανεῖν L P 486 οὐχ] οὐδ' Hermann 487 ἂν ἐλπίς L P 494 Oresti L P, Pyladi tribuit Blomfield ὅδ' ἔστι δή L P: corr. *l* 496–569 lineolae pro personarum notis in L 500 δυστυχεῖς L P: corr. Barthold 502 γελώμεθ' L P

Ιφ. τί δὲ φθονεῖς τοῦτο; ἢ φρονεῖς οὕτω μέγα;
Ορ. τὸ σῶμα θύσεις τοὐμόν, οὐχὶ τοὔνομα.
Ιφ. οὐδ' ἂν πόλιν φράσειας ἥτις ἐστί σοι;
Ορ. ζητεῖς γὰρ οὐδὲν κέρδος, ὡς θανουμένῳ.
Ιφ. χάριν δὲ δοῦναι τήνδε κωλύει τί σε;
Ορ. τὸ κλεινὸν Ἄργος πατρίδ' ἐμὴν ἐπεύχομαι.
Ιφ. πρὸς θεῶν, ἀληθῶς, ὦ ξέν', εἶ κεῖθεν γεγώς;
Ορ. ἐκ τῶν Μυκηνῶν ⟨γ'⟩, αἵ ποτ' ἦσαν ὄλβιαι.
Ιφ. φυγὰς ⟨δ'⟩ ἀπῆρας πατρίδος, ἢ ποίᾳ τύχῃ;
Ορ. φεύγω τρόπον γε δή τιν' οὐχ ἑκὼν ἑκών.
Ιφ. ἆρ' ἄν τί μοι φράσειας ὧν ἐγὼ θέλω;
Ορ. ὡς ἐν παρέργῳ τῆς ἐμῆς δυσπραξίας.
Ιφ. καὶ μὴν ποθεινός γ' ἦλθες ἐξ Ἄργους μολών.
Ορ. οὔκουν ἐμαυτῷ γ'· εἰ δὲ σοί, σὺ τοῦτ' ἔρα.
Ιφ. Τροίαν ἴσως οἶσθ', ἧς ἁπανταχοῦ λόγος.
Ορ. ὡς μήποτ' ὤφελόν γε μηδ' ἰδὼν ὄναρ.
Ιφ. φασίν νιν οὐκέτ' οὖσαν οἴχεσθαι δορί.
Ορ. ἔστιν γὰρ οὕτως οὐδ' ἄκραντ' ἠκούσατε.
Ιφ. Ἑλένη δ' ἀφῖκται δῶμα Μενέλεω πάλιν;
Ορ. ἥκει, κακῶς γ' ἐλθοῦσα τῶν ἐμῶν τινι.
Ιφ. καὶ ποῦ 'στι; κἀμοὶ γάρ τι προυφείλει κακόν.
Ορ. Σπάρτῃ ξυνοικεῖ τῷ πάρος ξυνευνέτῃ.
Ιφ. ὦ μῖσος εἰς Ἕλληνας, οὐκ ἐμοὶ μόνῃ.
Ορ. ἀπέλαυσα κἀγὼ δή τι τῶν κείνης γάμων.
Ιφ. νόστος δ' Ἀχαιῶν ἐγένεθ', ὡς κηρύσσεται;
Ορ. ὡς πάνθ' ἅπαξ με συλλαβοῦσ' ἀνιστορεῖς.
Ιφ. πρὶν γὰρ θανεῖν σε, τοῦδ' ἐπαυρέσθαι θέλω.
Ορ. ἔλεγχ', ἐπειδὴ τοῦδ' ἐρᾷς· λέξω δ' ἐγώ.
Ιφ. Κάλχας τις ἦλθε μάντις ἐκ Τροίας πάλιν;
Ορ. ὄλωλεν, ὡς ἦν ἐν Μυκηναίοις λόγος.

503 *φθονεῖς* L: *φρονεῖς* P *ἢ* L P 507 *σὲ τί;* Monk, sed *τι* indefinitum esse videtur 510 *γ'* add. Monk 511 *δ'* add. Scaliger 513 sq. post 516 trai. Badham 521 *λεκτρὰ Μενέλεω* Weil: , *λῦμα Μενέλεω,* Bruhn 529 *τοῦδ'*] *τοῦτ'* Paley 532 *ὥς γ' ἦν* Lenting

Ιφ. ὦ πότνι', ὡς εὖ.—τί γὰρ ὁ Λαέρτου γόνος;
Ορ. οὔπω νενόστηκ' οἶκον, ἔστι δ', ὡς λόγος.
Ιφ. ὄλοιτο, νόστου μήποτ' ἐς πάτραν τυχών.
Ορ. μηδὲν κατεύχου· πάντα τἀκείνου νοσεῖ.
Ιφ. Θέτιδος δ' ὁ τῆς Νηρῇδος ἔστι παῖς ἔτι;
Ορ. οὐκ ἔστιν· ἄλλως λέκτρ' ἔγημ' ἐν Αὐλίδι.
Ιφ. δόλια γάρ, ὡς ἴσασιν οἱ πεπονθότες.
Ορ. τίς εἶ ποθ'; ὡς εὖ πυνθάνῃ τἀφ' Ἑλλάδος.
Ιφ. ἐκεῖθέν εἰμι· παῖς ἔτ' οὖσ' ἀπωλόμην.
Ορ. ὀρθῶς ποθεῖς ἄρ' εἰδέναι τἀκεῖ, γύναι.
Ιφ. τί δ' ὁ στρατηγός, ὃν λέγουσ' εὐδαιμονεῖν;
Ορ. τίς; οὐ γὰρ ὅν γ' ἐγᾦδα τῶν εὐδαιμόνων.
Ιφ. Ἀτρέως ἐλέγετο δή τις Ἀγαμέμνων ἄναξ.
Ορ. οὐκ οἶδ'· ἄπελθε τοῦ λόγου τούτου, γύναι.
Ιφ. μὴ πρὸς θεῶν, ἀλλ' εἴφ', ἵν' εὐφρανθῶ, ξένε.
Ορ. τέθνηχ' ὁ τλήμων, πρὸς δ' ἀπώλεσέν τινα.
Ιφ. τέθνηκε; ποίᾳ συμφορᾷ; τάλαιν' ἐγώ.
Ορ. τί δ' ἐστέναξας τοῦτο; μῶν προσῆκέ σοι;
Ιφ. τὸν ὄλβον αὐτοῦ τὸν πάροιθ' ἀναστένω.
Ορ. δεινῶς γὰρ ἐκ γυναικὸς οἴχεται σφαγείς.
Ιφ. ὦ πανδάκρυτος ἡ κτανοῦσα . . . χὡ κτανών.
Ορ. παῦσαί νυν ἤδη μηδ' ἐρωτήσῃς πέρα.
Ιφ. τοσόνδε γ', εἰ ζῇ τοῦ ταλαιπώρου δάμαρ.
Ορ. οὐκ ἔστι· παῖς νιν ὃν ἔτεχ', οὗτος ὤλεσεν.
Ιφ. ὦ συνταραχθεὶς οἶκος. ὡς τί δὴ θέλων;
Ορ. πατρὸς θανόντος τήνδε τιμωρούμενος.
Ιφ. φεῦ·
ὡς εὖ κακὸν δίκαιον εἰσεπράξατο.

533 εὖ· τί Musgrave : ἔστι L P 537 δ' ὁ L P : δὲ Elmsley 538 ἄλλως *l* : ἄλλως δὲ P et fortasse L ἔγημ' ἐν Markland : ἔγημεν L P 539 ἴσασιν Nauck : φασιν L P : γε φασιν *l* 541 ἀπῳχόμην Badham 552 δεινὸς P 553 θανών *l* (*ανών L) : de Aulide cogitat 554 ἐρωτήσεις L P 556 παῖς L : πῶς P 558 τήνδε suspectum : fortasse etiam nunc illam aspicere videtur : τήνδε τιμωρῶν δίκην Weil

Ορ. ἀλλ' οὐ τὰ πρὸς θεῶν εὐτυχεῖ δίκαιος ὤν.
Ιφ. λείπει δ' ἐν οἴκοις ἄλλον Ἀγαμέμνων γόνον;
Ορ. λέλοιπεν Ἠλέκτραν γε παρθένον μίαν.
Ιφ. τί δέ; σφαγείσης θυγατρὸς ἔστι τις λόγος;
Ορ. οὐδείς γε, πλὴν θανοῦσαν οὐχ ὁρᾶν φάος.
Ιφ. τάλαιν' ἐκείνη χὠ κτανὼν αὐτὴν πατήρ.
Ορ. κακῆς γυναικὸς χάριν ἄχαριν ἀπώλετο.
Ιφ. ὁ τοῦ θανόντος δ' ἔστι παῖς Ἄργει πατρός;
Ορ. ἔστ', ἄθλιός γε, κοὐδαμοῦ καὶ πανταχοῦ.
Ιφ. ψευδεῖς ὄνειροι, χαίρετ'· οὐδὲν ἦτ' ἄρα.
Ορ. οὐδ' οἱ σοφοί γε δαίμονες κεκλημένοι
πτηνῶν ὀνείρων εἰσὶν ἀψευδέστεροι.
πολὺς ταραγμὸς ἔν τε τοῖς θείοις ἔνι
κἀν τοῖς βροτείοις· ἓν δὲ λυπεῖται μόνον,
ὃς οὐκ ἄφρων ὢν μάντεων πεισθεὶς λόγοις
ὄλωλεν—ὡς ὄλωλε τοῖσιν εἰδόσιν.
Χο. φεῦ φεῦ· τί δ' ἡμεῖς οἵ τ' ἐμοὶ γεννήτορες;
ἆρ' εἰσίν; ἆρ' οὐκ εἰσί; τίς φράσειεν ἄν;
Ιφ. ἀκούσατ'· ἐς γὰρ δή τιν' ἥκομεν λόγον,
ὑμῖν τ' ὄνησιν, ὦ ξένοι, σπ̣ουδῆς ἅμα
κἀμοί. τὸ δ' εὖ μάλιστά γ' οὕτω γίγνεται,
εἰ πᾶσι ταὐτὸν πρᾶγμ' ἀρεσκόντως ἔχει.
θέλοις ἄν, εἰ σῴσαιμί σ', ἀγγεῖλαί τί μοι
πρὸς Ἄργος ἐλθὼν τοῖς ἐμοῖς ἐκεῖ φίλοις,
δέλτον τ' ἐνεγκεῖν, ἥν τις οἰκτίρας ἐμὲ
ἔγραψεν αἰχμάλωτος, οὐχὶ τὴν ἐμὴν
φονέα νομίζων χεῖρα, τοῦ νόμου δ' ὕπο
θνῄσκειν τὰ τῆς θεοῦ, τάδε δίκαι' ἡγουμένης;

570 Ορ. add. Heath: om. L P: vide sub v. 572 οὐδ' Hermann: οὔθ' L P 572 lineolam praef. (sc. Oresti tribuit) *l*, ut videtur θεοῖς L P: corr. Barnes 573 λυπεῖται L P[2]: ****ται P: λείπεται *l* 574 ὃς olim Wecklein, cf. 487, 488: ὅτ' L P 576 τ' ἐμοὶ om. P sed ipse, ut videtur, supplevit 579 σπεύδουσ' Musgrave (et ἱκόμην λόγον supra) 580 τόδ' εὖ L P γ' οὕτω] τοῦτο Nauck: γ' ὧδε Porson 582 θέλεις ἂν L P 587 τὰ τῆς scripsi: τα του Π: γε τῆς L P: σφε, τῆς Markland τάδε Pierson: ταῦτα L P , ἡγουμένου (sc. νόμου) Grenfell et Hunt

οὐδένα γὰρ εἶχον ὅστις ἀγγεῖλαι μολὼν
ἐς Ἄργος αὖθις, τάς ⟨τ'⟩ ἐμὰς ἐπιστολὰς
πέμψειε σωθεὶς τῶν ἐμῶν φίλων τινί.
σὺ δ'—εἶ γάρ, ὡς ἔοικας, οὔτε δυσμενὴς
καὶ τὰς Μυκήνας οἶσθα χοὓς κἀγὼ θέλω—
σώθητι, καὶ σὺ μισθὸν οὐκ αἰσχρὸν λαβών,
κούφων ἕκατι γραμμάτων σωτηρίαν.
  οὗτος δ', ἐπείπερ πόλις ἀναγκάζει τάδε,
θεᾷ γενέσθω θῦμα χωρισθεὶς σέθεν.
Ορ. καλῶς ἔλεξας τἄλλα πλὴν ἕν, ὦ ξένη·
τὸ γὰρ σφαγῆναι τόνδε μοι βάρος μέγα.
ὁ ναυστολῶν γάρ εἰμ' ἐγὼ τὰς συμφοράς,
οὗτος δὲ συμπλεῖ τῶν ἐμῶν μόχθων χάριν.
οὔκουν δίκαιον ἐπ' ὀλέθρῳ τῷ τοῦδ' ἐμὲ
χάριν τίθεσθαι καὐτὸν ἐκδῦναι κακῶν.
ἀλλ' ὡς γενέσθω· τῷδε μὲν δέλτον δίδου·
πέμψει γὰρ Ἄργος, ὥστε σοι καλῶς ἔχειν·
ἡμᾶς δ' ὁ χρῄζων κτεινέτω. τὰ τῶν φίλων
αἴσχιστον ὅστις καταβαλὼν ἐς ξυμφορὰς
αὐτὸς σέσῳσται. τυγχάνει δ' ὅδ' ὢν φίλος,
ὃν οὐδὲν ἧσσον ἢ 'μὲ φῶς ὁρᾶν θέλω.
Ιφ. ὦ λῆμ' ἄριστον, ὡς ἀπ' εὐγενοῦς τινος
ῥίζης πέφυκας τοῖς φίλοις τ' ὀρθῶς φίλος.
τοιοῦτος εἴη τῶν ἐμῶν ὁμοσπόρων
ὅσπερ λέλειπται. καὶ γὰρ οὐδ' ἐγώ, ξένοι,
ἀνάδελφός εἰμι, πλὴν ὅσ' οὐχ ὁρῶσά νιν.

588-590 delevit Monk: sed ideo videtur neminem habuisse quem mitteret, quod primo lex id vetabat, deinde nemo Graecus advenerat (v. 258) cuius causa contra legem facere vellet 588 ἀγγείλαι L: ἀγγεῖλαι P *l* 589 αὖθις L: αὖτις P: οὐδ' ὃς Nauck τάς τ' Elmsley: τὰς L P Π 590 τινί suprascr. L P: τινός in textu L P 591 δυσμενὴς P: δυσγενὴς L 592 φιλῶ Musgrave: δοὺς ἁγὼ θέλω Badham 598 τόνδ' ἐμοὶ Luc. Amor. c. 47 599 εἶμ' L P: corr. L aut *l* 601 ἐμοὶ suprascr. P 604 πέμψω Lucianus 606 εις συμ[Π 607 σέσωσται L: σώσεται in rasura P 608 ὃν L *p*: ὧν P ἤ με L P 610 ὀρθῶς suprascr. L vel *l*: ὀρθὸς L P

ἐπεὶ δὲ βούλῃ ταῦτα, τόνδε πέμψομεν
δέλτον φέροντα, σὺ δὲ θανῇ· πολλὴ δέ τις
προθυμία σε τοῦδ᾽ ἔχουσα τυγχάνει.
Ορ. θύσει δὲ τίς με καὶ τὰ δεινὰ τλήσεται;
Ιφ. ἐγώ· θεᾶς γὰρ τῆσδε προστροπὴν ἔχω.
Ορ. ἄζηλά γ᾽, ὦ νεᾶνι, κοὐκ εὐδαίμονα.
Ιφ. ἀλλ᾽ εἰς ἀνάγκην κείμεθ᾽, ἣν φυλακτέον.
Ορ. αὐτὴ ξίφει θύουσα θῆλυς ἄρσενας;
Ιφ. οὔκ, ἀλλὰ χαίτην ἀμφὶ σὴν χερνίψομαι.
Ορ. ὁ δὲ σφαγεὺς τίς; εἰ τάδ᾽ ἱστορεῖν με χρή.
Ιφ. ἔσω δόμων τῶνδ᾽ εἰσὶν οἷς μέλει τάδε.
Ορ. τάφος δὲ ποῖος δέξεταί μ᾽, ὅταν θάνω;
Ιφ. πῦρ ἱερὸν ἔνδον χάσμα τ᾽ εὐρωπὸν πέτρας.
Ορ. φεῦ·
πῶς ἄν μ᾽ ἀδελφῆς χεὶρ περιστείλειεν ἄν;
Ιφ. μάταιον εὐχήν, ὦ τάλας, ὅστις ποτ᾽ εἶ,
ηὔξω· μακρὰν γὰρ βαρβάρου ναίει χθονός.
οὐ μήν, ἐπειδὴ τυγχάνεις Ἀργεῖος ὤν,
ἀλλ᾽ ὧν γε δυνατὸν οὐδ᾽ ἐγὼ λείψω χάριν.
πολύν τε γάρ σοι κόσμον ἐνθήσω τάφῳ,
ξανθῷ τ᾽ ἐλαίῳ σῶμα σὸν κατασβέσω,
καὶ τῆς ὀρείας ἀνθεμόρρυτον γάνος
ξουθῆς μελίσσης ἐς πυρὰν βαλῶ σέθεν.
ἀλλ᾽ εἶμι δέλτον τ᾽ ἐκ θεᾶς ἀνακτόρων
οἴσω· τὸ μέντοι δυσμενὲς μὴ ᾽μοὶ λάβῃς.
φυλάσσετ᾽ αὐτούς, πρόσπολοι, δεσμῶν ἄτερ. . . .
ἴσως ἄελπτα τῶν ἐμῶν φίλων τινὶ
πέμψω πρὸς Ἄργος, ὃν μάλιστ᾽ ἐγὼ φιλῶ,
καὶ δέλτος αὐτῷ ζῶντας οὓς δοκεῖ θανεῖν

618 τήνδε Bothe et Π   συμ**ραν ε[χω Π   619 ἄζηλον Bothe   621 κτεινουσα Π   622 οὐκ Π *l* : οὔκουν L P   χερνίψομαι suprascr. L P : χερνίσομαι L P in textu   626 χασματα ευρω[Π   πέτρας] χθονός Diod. 20. 14   628 om. Π   631 ᾽λλείψω Markland   633 versum om. Musurus : κατασκεδῶ Geel   635 εἰς πῦρ ἐμβαλὼν L P : corr. Canter   636 τ᾽ ἐκ *l* : τε L P   637 εἴσω P   μή μου L P : corr. Reiske   βάλῃς P

λέγουσα πιστὰς ἡδονὰς ἀπαγγελεῖ.

Χο. — κατολοφύρομαι σὲ τὸν χερνίβων
ῥανίσι μελόμενον αἱμακταῖς.
Ορ. οἶκτος γὰρ οὐ ταῦτ᾽, ἀλλὰ χαίρετ᾽, ὦ ξέναι.
Χο. — σὲ δὲ τύχας μάκαρος, ὦ
νεανία, σεβόμεθ᾽, ἐς
πάτραν ὅτι ποτ᾽ ἐπεμβάσῃ.
Πυ. ἄζηλά τοι φίλοισι, θνῃσκόντων φίλων.
Χο. — ὦ σχέτλιοι πομπαί.
— φεῦ φεῦ, διόλλυσαι.
— αἰαῖ αἰαῖ. πότερος ὁ μᾶλλον;
— ἔτι γὰρ ἀμφίλογα δίδυμα μέμονε φρήν,
σὲ πάρος ἢ σὲ ἀναστενάξω γόοις.

Ορ. Πυλάδη, πέπονθας ταὐτὸ πρὸς θεῶν ἐμοί;
Πυ. οὐκ οἶδ᾽· ἐρωτᾷς οὐ λέγειν ἔχοντά με.
Ορ. τίς ἐστιν ἡ νεᾶνις; ὡς Ἑλληνικῶς
ἀνήρεθ᾽ ἡμᾶς τούς τ᾽ ἐν Ἰλίῳ πόνους
νόστον τ᾽ Ἀχαιῶν τόν τ᾽ ἐν οἰωνοῖς σοφὸν
Κάλχαντ᾽ Ἀχιλλέως τ᾽ ὄνομα, καὶ τὸν ἄθλιον
Ἀγαμέμνον᾽ ὡς ᾤκτιρ᾽ ἀνηρώτα τέ με
γυναῖκα παῖδάς τε. ἔστιν ἡ ξένη γένος
ἐκεῖθεν Ἀργεία τις· οὐ γὰρ ἄν ποτε
δέλτον τ᾽ ἔπεμπε καὶ τάδ᾽ ἐξεμάνθανεν,
ὡς κοινὰ πράσσουσ᾽, Ἄργος εἰ πράσσει καλῶς.
Πυ. ἔφθης με μικρόν· ταὐτὰ δὲ φθάσας λέγεις,
πλὴν ἕν· τὰ γὰρ τῶν βασιλέων παθήματα

642 λέγουσ᾽ ἀπίστους Portus inter 643–5 et 647–9 responsionem fecit Hermann 649 ὅτι] ὃς Seidler ποτ᾽] πόδ᾽ Elmsley 650 τοι Hermann: τοῖς L P 651–655 paragraphos post Kirchhoffium addidi: notam Χο. ante 651 L², ante 653 L P 654 μᾶλλον Musgrave: μέλλων L P 655 ἀμφίλογα editio Brubachiana: ἀμφίφλογα L: ἀμφίβλογα P ut videtur: ἀμφίβολα p μέμονε suprascr. L: μέμηνε L P 656 ἢ σ᾽ L P 664 ᾤκτειρεν L P 668 πράσσοι Hermann 669 φθάσας L: φράσας P 670 τὰ γάρ τοι Hermann

ἴσασι πάντες, ὧν ἐπιστροφή τις ἦν.
ἀτὰρ διῆλθον χἄτερον λόγον τινά.
Ορ. τίν'; ἐς τὸ κοινὸν δοὺς ἄμεινον ἂν μάθοις.
Πυ. αἰσχρὸν θανόντος σοῦ βλέπειν ἡμᾶς φάος·
κοινῇ τ' ἔπλευσα . . . δεῖ με καὶ κοινῇ θανεῖν.
καὶ δειλίαν γὰρ καὶ κάκην κεκτήσομαι
Ἄργει τε Φωκέων τ' ἐν πολυπτύχῳ χθονί,
δόξω δὲ τοῖς πολλοῖσι—πολλοὶ γὰρ κακοί—
προδοὺς σεσῷσθαί σ' αὐτὸς εἰς οἴκους μόνος
ἢ καὶ φονεύσας ἐπὶ νοσοῦσι δώμασι
ῥάψαι μόρον σοι σῆς τυραννίδος χάριν,
ἔγκληρον ὡς δὴ σὴν κασιγνήτην γαμῶν.
ταῦτ' οὖν φοβοῦμαι καὶ δι' αἰσχύνης ἔχω,
κοὐκ ἔσθ' ὅπως οὐ χρὴ συνεκπνεῦσαί μέ σοι
καὶ σὺν σφαγῆναι καὶ πυρωθῆναι δέμας,
φίλον γεγῶτα καὶ φοβούμενον ψόγον.
Ορ. εὔφημα φώνει· τἀμὰ δεῖ φέρειν κακά,
ἁπλᾶς δὲ λύπας ἐξόν, οὐκ οἴσω διπλᾶς.
ὃ γὰρ σὺ λυπρὸν κἀπονείδιστον λέγεις,
ταὔτ' ἔστιν ἡμῖν, εἴ σε συμμοχθοῦντ' ἐμοὶ
κτενῶ· τὸ μὲν γὰρ εἰς ἔμ' οὐ κακῶς ἔχει,
πράσσονθ' ἃ πράσσω πρὸς θεῶν, λῦσαι βίον.
σὺ δ' ὄλβιός τ' εἶ, καθαρά τ', οὐ νοσοῦντ', ἔχεις
μέλαθρ', ἐγὼ δὲ δυσσεβῆ καὶ δυστυχῆ.
σωθεὶς δέ, παῖδας ἐξ ἐμῆς ὁμοσπόρου
κτησάμενος, ἣν ἔδωκά σοι δάμαρτ' ἔχειν—
ὄνομά τ' ἐμοῦ γένοιτ' ἄν, οὐδ' ἄπαις δόμος
πατρῷος οὑμὸς ἐξαλειφθείη ποτ' ἄν.

671 ἧ Hartung 672 διῆλθε L P: corr. Porson 673 μάθης L P, sed suprascr. οις 675 κοινῇ δὲ πλεύσας Elmsley 679 σεσῶσθαί σ' (vel σε σωθείς τ') Elmsley: σε σώζεσθ' L P 680 ἢ κἀφεδρεύσας Lobeck 685 συσφαγῆναι L P: divisi 690 ταῦτ' L P 692 λῦσαι Schenkl: λύσειν P: λήσειν, suprascripto λήγειν, L: λιπεῖν Badham, sed ex duplice lectione λῦσαι et λύειν ortae videntur vv. ll. 697 γένοι' ἂν Ellis

ἀλλ' ἕρπε καὶ ζῆ καὶ δόμους οἴκει πατρός.
ὅταν δ' ἐς Ἑλλάδ' ἵππιόν τ' Ἄργος μόλῃς,
πρὸς δεξιᾶς σε τῆσδ' ἐπισκήπτω τάδε·
τύμβον τε χῶσον κἀπίθες μνημεῖά μοι,
καὶ δάκρυ' ἀδελφὴ καὶ κόμας δότω τάφῳ.
ἄγγελλε δ' ὡς ὄλωλ' ὑπ' Ἀργείας τινὸς
γυναικός, ἀμφὶ βωμὸν ἁγνισθεὶς φόνῳ.
καὶ μὴ προδῷς μου τὴν κασιγνήτην ποτέ,
ἔρημα κήδη καὶ δόμους ὁρῶν πατρός.
καὶ χαῖρ'· ἐμῶν γὰρ φίλτατόν σ' ηὗρον φίλων,
ὦ συγκυναγὲ καὶ συνεκτραφεὶς ἐμοί,
ὦ πόλλ' ἐνεγκὼν τῶν ἐμῶν ἄχθη κακῶν.
   ἡμᾶς δ' ὁ Φοῖβος μάντις ὢν ἐψεύσατο·
τέχνην δὲ θέμενος ὡς προσώταθ' Ἑλλάδος
ἀπήλασ', αἰδοῖ τῶν πάρος μαντευμάτων.
ᾧ πάντ' ἐγὼ δοὺς τἀμὰ καὶ πεισθεὶς λόγοις,
μητέρα κατακτὰς αὐτὸς ἀνταπόλλυμαι.

Πυ. ἔσται τάφος σοι, καὶ κασιγνήτης λέχος
οὐκ ἂν προδοίην, ὦ τάλας, ἐπεί σ' ἐγὼ
θανόντα μᾶλλον ἢ βλέπονθ' ἕξω φίλον.
ἀτὰρ τὸ τοῦ θεοῦ σ' οὐ διέφθορέν γέ πω
μάντευμα· καίτοι γ' ἐγγὺς ἕστηκας φόνου.
ἀλλ' ἔστιν, ἔστιν, ἡ λίαν δυσπραξία
λίαν διδοῦσα μεταβολάς, ὅταν τύχῃ.

Ορ. σίγα· τὰ Φοίβου δ' οὐδὲν ὠφελεῖ μ' ἔπη·
γυνὴ γὰρ ἥδε δωμάτων ἔξω περᾷ.

Ιφ. ἀπέλθεθ' ὑμεῖς καὶ παρευτρεπίζετε
τἄνδον μολόντες τοῖς ἐφεστῶσι σφαγῇ.
   δέλτου μὲν αἵδε πολύθυροι διαπτυχαί,
ξένοι, πάρεισιν· ἃ δ' ἐπὶ τοῖσδε βούλομαι,

702 *μοι*] *μου* Monk   714 *ὦ* *l*: *ὧ* L P   719 *σ' οὐ . . . γέ* Nauck : *γ' οὐ . . . μέ* L P : *γ' οὐ . . . σ'* apogr. Paris.   *διέφθορέν* L : *διέφθειρέν* P   720 delet Herwerden   727 *πολύθυροι* Ar. Rhet. 1407 B 34 : *πολύθρηνοι* L P   728 *ξένοι* Pierson (et codd. recc. quidam) : *ξένοις* L P

ἀκούσατ᾽. οὐδεὶς αὑτὸς ἐν πόνοις ⟨τ᾽⟩ ἀνὴρ
ὅταν τε πρὸς τὸ θάρσος ἐκ φόβου πέσῃ.
ἐγὼ δὲ ταρβῶ μὴ ἀπονοστήσας χθονὸς
θῆται παρ᾽ οὐδὲν τὰς ἐμὰς ἐπιστολὰς
ὁ τήνδε μέλλων δέλτον εἰς Ἄργος φέρειν.
Ορ. τί δῆτα βούλῃ; τίνος ἀμηχανεῖς πέρι;
Ιφ. ὅρκον δότω μοι τάσδε πορθμεύσειν γραφὰς
πρὸς Ἄργος, οἷσι βούλομαι πέμψαι φίλων.
Ορ. ἦ κἀντιδώσεις τῷδε τοὺς αὐτοὺς λόγους;
Ιφ. τί χρῆμα δράσειν ἢ τί μὴ δράσειν; λέγε.
Ορ. ἐκ γῆς ἀφήσειν μὴ θανόντα βαρβάρου.
Ιφ. δίκαιον εἶπας· πῶς γὰρ ἀγγείλειεν ἄν;
Ορ. ἦ καὶ τύραννος ταῦτα συγχωρήσεται;
Ιφ. ναί.
πείσω σφε, καὐτὴ ναὸς εἰσβήσω σκάφος.
Ορ. ὄμνυ· σὺ δ᾽ ἔξαρχ᾽ ὅρκον ὅστις εὐσεβής.
Ιφ. δώσω, λέγειν χρή, τήνδε τοῖσι σοῖς φίλοις.
Πυ. τοῖς σοῖς φίλοισι γράμματ᾽ ἀποδώσω τάδε.
Ιφ. κἀγὼ σὲ σώσω κυανέας ἔξω πέτρας.
Πυ. τίν᾽ οὖν ἐπόμνυς τοισίδ᾽ ὅρκιον θεῶν;
Ιφ. Ἄρτεμιν, ἐν ἧσπερ δώμασιν τιμὰς ἔχω.
Πυ. ἐγὼ δ᾽ ἄνακτά γ᾽ οὐρανοῦ, σεμνὸν Δία.
Ιφ. εἰ δ᾽ ἐκλιπὼν τὸν ὅρκον ἀδικοίης ἐμέ;
Πυ. ἄνοστος εἴην· τί δὲ σύ, μὴ σῴσασά με;
Ιφ. μήποτε κατ᾽ Ἄργος ζῶσ᾽ ἴχνος θείην ποδός.
Πυ. ἄκουε δή νυν ὃν παρήλθομεν λόγον.
Ιφ. ἀλλ᾽ αὖθις ἔσται καινός, ἢν καλῶς ἔχῃ.
Πυ. ἐξαίρετόν μοι δὸς τόδ᾽, ἤν τι ναῦς πάθῃ,
χἠ δέλτος ἐν κλύδωνι χρημάτων μέτα

729 *αὐτὸς* L P *τ᾽* add. Koechly 733 *ὅταν δὲ* P 742 *ναί* in versu P et sine dubio L: delevit et supra versum addidit *l*: recte haesitat Iphigenia *εἰσβήσω* L P[2]: *εἰσθήσω* vel *εἰσφρήσω*, ut videtur, P 744 *τοῖς ἐμοῖς* L P: corr. Bothe (qui etiam *δώσειν* coniecit, *τοῖς ἐμοῖς* servato) 745–755 Πυ. L: Ορ. P 747 *τοισίδ᾽* Markland: *τοῖσιν* L P 752 *ποδός*] *ποτε* primitus L 754 *αὖτις* L P, ut solent (*ἀλλ᾽ οὔτις ἔστ᾽ ἄκαιρος* Bothe) *κακῶς* Kirchhoff

ἀφανὴς γένηται, σῶμα δ' ἐκσῴσω μόνον,
τὸν ὅρκον εἶναι τόνδε μηκέτ' ἔμπεδον.
Ιφ. ἀλλ' οἶσθ' ὃ δράσω; πολλὰ γὰρ πολλῶν κυρεῖ·
τἀνόντα κἀγγεγραμμέν' ἐν δέλτου πτυχαῖς
λόγῳ φράσω σοι πάντ' ἀναγγεῖλαι φίλοις.
ἐν ἀσφαλεῖ γάρ· ἢν μὲν ἐκσῴσῃς γραφήν,
αὐτὴ φράσει σιγῶσα τἀγγεγραμμένα·
ἢν δ' ἐν θαλάσσῃ γράμματ' ἀφανισθῇ τάδε,
τὸ σῶμα σῴσας τοὺς λόγους σῴσεις ἐμοί.
Πυ. καλῶς ἔλεξας τῶν θεῶν ἐμοῦ θ' ὕπερ.
σήμαινε δ' ᾧ χρὴ τάσδ' ἐπιστολὰς φέρειν
πρὸς Ἄργος ὅ τι τε χρὴ κλύοντα σοῦ λέγειν.
Ιφ. ἄγγελλ' Ὀρέστῃ, παιδὶ τῷ Ἀγαμέμνονος·
Ἡ 'ν Αὐλίδι σφαγεῖσ' ἐπιστέλλει τάδε
ζῶσ' Ἰφιγένεια, τοῖς ἐκεῖ δ' οὐ ζῶσ' ἔτι . . .
Ορ. ποῦ δ' ἔστ' ἐκείνη; κατθανοῦσ' ἥκει πάλιν;
Ιφ. ἥδ' ἣν ὁρᾷς σύ· μὴ λόγοις ἔκπλησσέ με.
Κόμισαί μ' ἐς Ἄργος, ὦ σύναιμε, πρὶν θανεῖν,
ἐκ βαρβάρου γῆς καὶ μετάστησον θεᾶς
σφαγίων, ἐφ' οἷσι ξενοφόνους τιμὰς ἔχω.
Ορ. Πυλάδη, τί λέξω; ποῦ ποτ' ὄνθ' ηὑρήμεθα;
Ιφ. ἢ σοῖς ἀραία δώμασιν γενήσομαι.
Πυ. Ὀρέστα . . .; Ιφ. ἵν' αὖθις ὄνομα δὶς κλύων μάθῃς.
Πυ. ὦ θεοί. Ιφ. τί τοὺς θεοὺς ἀνακαλεῖς ἐν τοῖς ἐμοῖς;
Πυ. οὐδέν· πέραινε δ'· ἐξέβην γὰρ ἄλλοσε.
τάχ' οὐκ ἐρωτῶν σ' εἰς ἄπιστ' ἀφίξομαι.
Ιφ. λέγ' οὕνεκ' ἔλαφον ἀντιδοῦσά μου θεὰ
Ἄρτεμις ἔσῳσέ μ', ἣν ἔθυσ' ἐμὸς πατήρ,

758 *μηκέτ' ἐμπόδων* Housman 762 *εἰ μὲν ἐκσώσεις* primitus P 763 *αὔτη* L P (sic) 765 *ἐμοί*] *δμοῦ* Badham 766 *τῶν τε σῶν* Haupt (*τῶν θ' ἑῶν*, cl. El. 1206, Bothe) 773 *λόγων* Seidler 776 *ξενοκτόνους* P 779 Ὀρέστα L : Ὀρέστ' *l* P Ιφ. notam ab L P omissam addidi : verba Ὀρέστ' . . . *θεοί* Pyladi tribuuntur in L P : notam Πυλ ante 779 erasit et ante 780 posuit *l* 782 *ἐρωτῶσ'* P, corr. *p* *οὐκ* post Musgravium (*οὐδ'*) scripsi : *οὖν* L P versum del. Dindorf : sed videtur sibi seorsum loqui Pylades

δοκῶν ἐς ἡμᾶς ὀξὺ φάσγανον βαλεῖν,
ἐς τήνδε δ' ᾤκισ' αἶαν. αἵδ' ἐπιστολαί,
τάδ' ἐστὶ τἀν δέλτοισιν ἐγγεγραμμένα.
Πυ. ὦ ῥᾳδίοις ὅρκοισι περιβαλοῦσά με,
κάλλιστα δ' ὀμόσασ', οὐ πολὺν σχήσω χρόνον,
τὸν δ' ὅρκον ὃν κατώμοσ' ἐμπεδώσομεν.
ἰδού, φέρω σοι δέλτον ἀποδίδωμί τε,
Ὀρέστα, τῆσδε σῆς κασιγνήτης πάρα.
Ορ. δέχομαι· παρεὶς δὲ γραμμάτων διαπτυχὰς
τὴν ἡδονὴν πρῶτ' οὐ λόγοις αἱρήσομαι.
ὦ φιλτάτη μοι σύγγον', ἐκπεπληγμένος
ὅμως σ' ἀπίστῳ περιβαλὼν βραχίονι
ἐς τέρψιν εἶμι, πυθόμενος θαυμάστ' ἐμοί.
Χο. ξέν', οὐ δικαίως τῆς θεοῦ τὴν πρόσπολον
χραίνεις ἀθίκτοις περιβαλὼν πέπλοις χέρα.
Ορ. ὦ συγκασιγνήτη τε κἀκ ταὐτοῦ πατρὸς
Ἀγαμέμνονος γεγῶσα, μή μ' ἀποστρέφου,
ἔχουσ' ἀδελφόν, οὐ δοκοῦσ' ἕξειν ποτέ.
Ιφ. ἐγώ σ' ἀδελφὸν τὸν ἐμόν; οὐ παύσῃ λέγων;
τὸ δ' Ἄργος αὐτοῦ μεστὸν ἥ τε Ναυπλία.
Ορ. οὐκ ἔστ' ἐκεῖ σός, ὦ τάλαινα, σύγγονος.
Ιφ. ἀλλ' ἡ Λάκαινα Τυνδαρίς σ' ἐγείνατο;
Ορ. Πέλοπός γε παιδὶ παιδός, οὗ 'κπέφυκ' ἐγώ.
Ιφ. τί φῄς; ἔχεις τι τῶνδέ μοι τεκμήριον;
Ορ. ἔχω· πατρῴων ἐκ δόμων τι πυνθάνου.
Ιφ. οὐκοῦν λέγειν μὲν χρὴ σέ, μανθάνειν δ' ἐμέ.
Ορ. λέγοιμ' ἄν, ἀκοῇ πρῶτον Ἠλέκτρας τάδε·
Ἀτρέως Θυέστου τ' οἶσθα γενομένην ἔριν;

786 ὤκησ' L P : corr. *p* 787 ταῦτ' ἐστὶ τἄν Plut. Apophth. Reg. p. 182 E : τάδ' ἐστιν ἐν L P 796 σ' ἀπίστῳ Markland : ἀπιστῶ L P : ἀπίστω ... βραχίονε Doederlein 798 ξεῖν' L P 806 ἡ] ἦ Monk 807 γε Seidler : τε L P οὗ 'κπέφυκ' Elmsley : ἐκπέφυκ' L P 808 τῶνδ' ἐμοὶ L P 811 suspectus Monkio, sed cf. 822 ἀκοῇ Reiske : ἄκουε L P Ἠλέκτρας suprascr. L vel *l*: ἠλέκτρᾳ L : ἠλέκτρα P λεγόμεν' ἄκουε πρῶτον Ἠλέκτρᾳ Mekler 812 οἶσθα editio Brubachiana : οἶδα L P

Ιφ. ἤκουσα· χρυσῆς ἀρνὸς ἦν νείκη πέρι.
Ορ. ταῦτ' οὖν ὑφήνασ' οἶσθ' ἐν εὐπήνοις ὑφαῖς;
Ιφ. ὦ φίλτατ', ἐγγὺς τῶν ἐμῶν κάμπτεις φρενῶν.
Ορ. εἰκώ τ' ἐν ἱστοῖς ἡλίου μετάστασιν;
Ιφ. ὕφηνα καὶ τόδ' εἶδος εὐμίτοις πλοκαῖς.
Ορ. καὶ λούτρ' ἐς Αὖλιν μητρὸς ἀνεδέξω πάρα;
Ιφ. οἶδ'· οὐ γὰρ ὁ γάμος ἐσθλὸς ὤν μ' ἀφείλετο.
Ορ. τί γάρ; κόμας σὰς μητρὶ δοῦσα σῇ φέρειν;
Ιφ. μνημεῖά γ' ἀντὶ σώματος τοὐμοῦ τάφῳ.
Ορ. ἃ δ' εἶδον αὐτός, τάδε φράσω τεκμήρια·
Πέλοπος παλαιὰν ἐν δόμοις λόγχην πατρός,
ἣν χερσὶ πάλλων παρθένον Πισάτιδα
ἐκτήσαθ' Ἱπποδάμειαν, Οἰνόμαον κτανών,
ἐν παρθενῶσι τοῖσι σοῖς κεκρυμμένην.

Ιφ. ὦ φίλτατ', οὐδὲν ἄλλο, φίλτατος γὰρ εἶ,
ἔχω σ', Ὀρέστα, τηλύγετον [χθονὸς] ἀπὸ πατρίδος
Ἀργόθεν, ὦ φίλος.
Ορ. κἀγώ σε τὴν θανοῦσαν, ὡς δοξάζεται.
κατὰ δὲ δάκρυ, κατὰ δὲ γόος ἅμα χαρᾷ
τὸ σὸν νοτίζει βλέφαρον, ὡσαύτως δ' ἐμόν.
Ιφ. τόδ' ἔτι βρέφος
ἔλιπον ἀγκάλαισι νεαρὸν τροφοῦ
νεαρὸν ἐν δόμοις.
ὦ κρεῖσσον ἢ λόγοισιν εὐτυχοῦσά μου
ψυχά, τί φῶ; θαυμάτων
πέρα καὶ λόγου πρόσω τάδ' ἐπέβα.
Ορ. τὸ λοιπὸν εὐτυχοῖμεν ἀλλήλων μέτα.

813 ἤκουσ' ἃ Mekler ἦν νείκη Mekler: ἡνίκ' ἦν L P: ἡνίκ' ἦν τέρας olim Wecklein 815 κάμπτεις Blomfield: κάμπτῃ L P: χρίμπτῃ Wecklein 819 εἰ γὰρ Bruhn ad finem v. adscr. τοῦτο, τὸ μὴ εἰδέναι *l* 824 πισσάτιδα L P 829 χθονὸς seclusi 832 δάκρυ] δάκρυα δάκρυα Musurus 834 τὸ δέ τι L P: divisit Barnes: τὸν ἔτι Bergk ἔλιπον ἔλιπον Fix 837 εὐτυχῶν ἐμοῦ L P: corr. Markland Wecklein: εὐτυχῶν ἐμοῖς· ὦ Monk 839 verba τί φῶ Oresti tribuit P

Ιφ. ἄτοπον ἁδονὰν ἔλαβον, ὦ φίλαι·
δέδοικα δ' ἐκ χερῶν με μὴ πρὸς αἰθέρα
ἀμπτάμενος φύγῃ·
ἰὼ Κυκλωπὶς ἑστία· ἰὼ πατρίς,
Μυκήνα φίλα,
χάριν ἔχω ζόας, χάριν ἔχω τροφᾶς,
ὅτι μοι συνομαίμονα τόνδε δόμοις
ἐξεθρέψω φάος.

Ορ. γένει μὲν εὐτυχοῦμεν, ἐς δὲ συμφοράς,
ὦ σύγγον', ἡμῶν δυστυχὴς ἔφυ βίος.
Ιφ. ἐγᾦδ' ἁ μέλεος, οἶδ', ὅτε φάσγανον
δέρᾳ θῆκέ μοι μελεόφρων πατήρ.
Ορ. οἴμοι. δοκῶ γὰρ οὐ παρών σ' ὁρᾶν ἐκεῖ.
Ιφ. ἀνυμέναιος, ⟨ὦ⟩ σύγγον', Ἀχιλλέως
ἐς κλισίαν λέκτρων
δολίαν ὅτ' ἀγόμαν·
παρὰ δὲ βωμὸν ἦν δάκρυα καὶ γόοι.
φεῦ φεῦ χερνίβων ⟨τῶν⟩ ἐκεῖ.
Ορ. ᾤμωξα κἀγὼ τόλμαν ἣν ἔτλη πατήρ.
Ιφ. ἀπάτορ' ἀπάτορα πότμον ἔλαχον.
ἄλλα δ' ἐξ ἄλλων κυρεῖ 865
δαίμονος τύχᾳ τινός. 867
Ορ. εἰ σόν γ' ἀδελφόν, ὦ τάλαιν', ἀπώλεσας. 866
Ιφ. ὦ μελέα δεινᾶς τόλμας. δείν' ἔτλαν
δείν' ἔτλαν, ὤμοι σύγγονε. παρὰ δ' ὀλίγον
ἀπέφυγες ὄλεθρον ἀνόσιον ἐξ ἐμᾶν 871
δαϊχθεὶς χερῶν.

842 ἡδονὰν L : ἡδονῆς P 845 ἰὼ . . . ἰὼ primitus L : ὦ . . . ὦ P et post rasuram L κυκλωπὶς ἑστία Hermann : κυκλωπίδες ἑστίαι L P 847 ζωᾶς L P 852 ἐγᾦδ' ἁ Bruhn : ἐγὼ L P 854 'φῆκέ Elmsley 856 ὦ add. Seidler 857 λέκων L P : corr. *l* : λύκων *p* 859 δόλι' ὅτ' Hermann : fortasse ἐς δολίαν λέκτρων κλίσιν ὅτ' : cf. Tro. 113 861-869 Ορ. φεῦ φεῦ . . . Ιφ. ᾤμωξα . . . Ορ. ἄλλα δ' . . . Ιφ. δείν' ἔτλαν L P : corr. Tyrwhitt, Monk 861 τῶν add. Seidler 864 ἀπάτορα πατέρα πότμον ἄποτμον ἔλαχον Hartung 867 ante 866 trai. Monk 871 ἀμφέφυγες L P : corr. editio Brubachiana

ἁ δ' ἐπ' αὐτοῖσι τίς τελευτά;
τίς τύχα μοι συγχωρήσει;
τίνα σοι πόρον εὑρομένα . . .
πάλιν ἀπὸ πόλεως, ἀπὸ φόνου πέμψω
πατρίδ' ἐς Ἀργείαν,
πρὶν ἐπὶ ξίφος αἵματι σῷ πελάσαι;
τόδε τόδε σόν, ὦ μελέα ψυχά,
χρέος ἀνευρίσκειν.
πότερον κατὰ χέρσον, οὐχὶ ναΐ . . ;
ἀλλὰ ποδῶν ῥιπᾷ
θανάτῳ πελάσεις ἄρα βάρβαρα φῦλα
καὶ δι' ὁδοὺς ἀνόδους στείχων· διὰ κυανέας μὴν
στενοπόρου πέτρας μακρὰ κέλευθα να-
ΐοισιν δρασμοῖς.
τάλαινα, τάλαινα.
τίς ἂν οὖν τάδ' ἂν ἢ θεὸς ἢ βροτὸς ἢ
τί τῶν ἀδοκήτων,
πόρον ἄπορον ἐξανύσας, δυοῖν
τοῖν μόνοιν Ἀτρείδαιν ⟨φαίνοι⟩
κακῶν ἔκλυσιν;

Χο. ἐν τοῖσι θαυμαστοῖσι καὶ μύθων πέρα
τάδ' εἶδον αὐτὴ κοὐ κλύουσ' ἀπαγγελῶ.

Πυ. τὸ μὲν φίλους ἐλθόντας εἰς ὄψιν φίλων,
Ὀρέστα, χειρῶν περιβολὰς εἰκὸς λαβεῖν·
λήξαντα δ' οἴκτων κἀπ' ἐκεῖν' ἐλθεῖν χρεών,

874–876 συγχωρήσει τινά . . . εὑρομένᾳ . . . πέμψαι Markland 875 deest aliquid: fortasse ⟨τᾶς ἀξείνου⟩: πάλιν ⟨αὖ ξένας σ'⟩ ἀπὸ πόλεως supplet Bruhn 881 παλαῖσαι P 884 ναΐῳ στόλῳ Wilamowitz: νάϊος Badham: χέρσον; οὐχί. ναί. Verrall 887 διόδους L P: divisit Reiske 895–899 lectio incerta: τίς ἄρ' οὖν τάλαν post Marklandium Badham, ut φανεῖ v. 898 servaret: lacunam statuunt ἢ τί ⟨τρίτον⟩ τῶν ἀδοκήτων Weil: τί ⟨μέσον τῶνδ' ὂν⟩ τῶν Bruhn 897 Fortasse ἕν' ἀνύσας δυοῖν 898 φαίνοι scripsi: πόροι Bergk: **** L, ut videtur, in fine huius versus: φανεῖ initio sequentis supplet *l*: om. P 901 κοὐ Hermann (et ἀπ' ἀγγέλων): καὶ L P 902 Πυ. notam om. L P: add. Heath

ὅπως τὸ κλεινὸν ὄνομα τῆς σωτηρίας
λαβόντες ἐκ γῆς βησόμεσθα βαρβάρου.
σοφῶν γὰρ ἀνδρῶν ταῦτα, μὴ 'κβάντας τύχης,
καιρὸν λαβόντας, ἡδονὰς ἄλλας λαβεῖν.
Ορ. καλῶς ἔλεξας· τῇ τύχῃ δ' οἶμαι μέλειν
τοῦδε ξὺν ἡμῖν· ἢν δέ τις πρόθυμος ᾖ,
σθένειν τὸ θεῖον μᾶλλον εἰκότως ἔχει.
Ιφ. μηδέν μ' ἐπίσχῃ γ'· οὐδ' ἀποστήσει λόγου,
πρῶτον πυθέσθαι τίνα ποτ' Ἠλέκτρα πότμον
εἴληχε βιότου· φίλα γὰρ ἔστε πάντ' ἐμοί.
Ορ. τῷδε ξυνοικεῖ βίον ἔχουσ' εὐδαίμονα.
Ιφ. οὗτος δὲ ποδαπὸς καὶ τίνος πέφυκε παῖς;
Ορ. Στρόφιος ὁ Φωκεὺς τοῦδε κλῄζεται πατήρ.
Ιφ. ὁ δ' ἐστί γ' Ἀτρέως θυγατρός, ὁμογενὴς ἐμός;
Ορ. ἀνεψιός γε, μόνος ἐμοὶ σαφὴς φίλος.
Ιφ. οὐκ ἦν τόθ' οὗτος ὅτε πατὴρ ἔκτεινέ με.
Ορ. οὐκ ἦν· χρόνον γὰρ Στρόφιος ἦν ἄπαις τινά.
Ιφ. χαῖρ' ὦ πόσις μοι τῆς ἐμῆς ὁμοσπόρου.
Ορ. κἀμός γε σωτήρ, οὐχὶ συγγενὴς μόνον.
Ιφ. τὰ δεινὰ δ' ἔργα πῶς ἔτλης μητρὸς πέρι;
Ορ. σιγῶμεν αὐτά· πατρὶ τιμωρῶν ἐμῷ.
Ιφ. ἡ δ' αἰτία τίς ἀνθ' ὅτου κτείνει πόσιν;
Ορ. ἔα τὰ μητρός· οὐδὲ σοὶ κλύειν καλόν.
Ιφ. σιγῶ· τὸ δ' Ἄργος πρὸς σὲ νῦν ἀποβλέπει;
Ορ. Μενέλαος ἄρχει· φυγάδες ἐσμὲν ἐκ πάτρας.
Ιφ. οὔ που νοσοῦντας θεῖος ὕβρισεν δόμους;
Ορ. οὔκ, ἀλλ' Ἐρινύων δεῖμά μ' ἐκβάλλει χθονός.
Ιφ. ταῦτ' ἆρ' ἐπ' ἀκταῖς κἀνθάδ' ἠγγέλης μανείς;

905, 906 suspecti: ὄμμα apogr. Paris.: sed τῆς vix sanum 908 καιρὸν λιπόντας Heimsoeth 909 μέλλειν primitus L P 912 μηδέν scripsi (‘*Ne ille me prohibeat! Nec avertet &c.*’) : οὐδέν L P : οὐδέν μ'· ἐπίσχες· τοῦδ' Enger : οὐ μή μ' ἐπίσχῃς οὐδ' ἀποστήσεις Monk ἀποστήσει P : ἀποστήσῃ L 913 πυθέσθαι L : τι θέσθαι P 914 ἔστε Vitelli : ἔσται L P 918 ὅδ' L P 918–939 lineolae praefixae in P 930 οὔ που L P : ἦπου *l p* : etiam οὔ πω *l* : cf. I. A. 670, Med. 695, El. 235 932 ἠγγέλθης Porson

Ορ. ὤφθημεν οὐ νῦν πρῶτον ὄντες ἄθλιοι.
Ιφ. ἔγνωκα· μητρός σ' οὕνεκ' ἠλάστρουν θεαί.
Ορ. ὥσθ' αἱματηρὰ στόμι' ἐπεμβαλεῖν ἐμοί.
Ιφ. τί γάρ ποτ' ἐς γῆν τήνδ' ἐπόρθμευσας πόδα;
Ορ. Φοίβου κελευσθεὶς θεσφάτοις ἀφικόμην.
Ιφ. τί χρῆμα δράσειν; ῥητὸν ἢ σιγώμενον;
Ορ. λέγοιμ' ἄν· ἀρχαὶ δ' αἵδε μοι πολλῶν πόνων.
ἐπεὶ τὰ μητρὸς ταῦθ' ἃ σιγῶμεν κακὰ
ἐς χεῖρας ἦλθε, μεταδρομαῖς Ἐρινύων
ἠλαυνόμεσθα φυγάδες, ἔνθεν μοι πόδα
ἐς τὰς Ἀθήνας δῆτ' ἔπεμψε Λοξίας,
δίκην παρασχεῖν ταῖς ἀνωνύμοις θεαῖς.
ἔστιν γὰρ ὁσία ψῆφος, ἣν Ἄρει ποτὲ
Ζεὺς εἵσατ' ἔκ του δὴ χερῶν μιάσματος.
ἐλθὼν δ' ἐκεῖσε . . . πρῶτα μέν μ' οὐδεὶς ξένων
ἑκὼν ἐδέξαθ', ὡς θεοῖς στυγούμενον·
οἳ δ' ἔσχον αἰδῶ, ξένια μονοτράπεζά μοι
παρέσχον, οἴκων ὄντες ἐν ταὐτῷ στέγει,
σιγῇ δ' ἐτεκτήναντ' ἀπόφθεγκτόν μ', ὅπως
δαιτὸς γενοίμην πώματός τ' αὐτοῖς δίχα,
ἐς δ' ἄγγος ἴδιον ἴσον ἅπασι βακχίου
μέτρημα πληρώσαντες εἶχον ἡδονήν.
κἀγὼ 'ξελέγξαι μὲν ξένους οὐκ ἠξίουν,
ἤλγουν δὲ σιγῇ κἀδόκουν οὐκ εἰδέναι,
μέγα στενάζων οὕνεκ' ἦ μητρὸς φονεύς.
κλύω δ' Ἀθηναίοισι τἀμὰ δυστυχῆ
τελετὴν γενέσθαι, κἄτι τὸν νόμον μένειν,

934 σ' add. Markland 935 στόμιά γ' ἐμβαλεῖν Elmsley 938 aut δρᾶσαι aut δράσων Elmsley 942 ἔστε μοι πόδα Badham: ἐμμανῆ (malim ἔνθεον) πόδα, ἔστ' εἰς Ἀθήνας δή μ' Weil: sed cf. 1087, Hclid. 839, 806, 829 943 δῆτ' Scaliger: δή γ' L P 947 μ' om. L P: add. Barnes 950 στέγει Musurus et fortasse primitus P: τέγει L et in ras. P[1] 951 ἐτεκτήνατ' P ἀπρόσφθεγκτόν Hermann: ἐτεκτήναντο προσφθεγκτόν Wilamowitz 952 αὐτοῖς Seidler: αὐτοῦ L P: αὐτῶν Hermann 955 κἀγώγ' ἐξελέγξαι L P: corr. Markland 957 ἦν L P

χοῆρες ἄγγος Παλλάδος τιμᾶν λεών.
ὡς δ' εἰς Ἄρειον ὄχθον ἧκον, ἐς δίκην
ἔστην, ἐγὼ μὲν θάτερον λαβὼν βάθρον,
τὸ δ' ἄλλο πρέσβειρ' ἥπερ ἦν Ἐρινύων.
εἰπὼν ⟨δ'⟩ ἀκούσας θ' αἵματος μητρὸς πέρι,
Φοῖβός μ' ἔσῳσε μαρτυρῶν, ἴσας δέ μοι
ψήφους διηρίθμησε Παλλὰς ὠλένῃ·
νικῶν δ' ἀπῆρα φόνια πειρατήρια.
ὅσαι μὲν οὖν ἕζοντο πεισθεῖσαι δίκῃ,
ψῆφον παρ' αὐτὴν ἱερὸν ὡρίσαντ' ἔχειν·
ὅσαι δ' Ἐρινύων οὐκ ἐπείσθησαν νόμῳ,
δρόμοις ἀνιδρύτοισιν ἠλάστρουν μ' ἀεί,
ἕως ἐς ἁγνὸν ἦλθον αὖ Φοίβου πέδον,
καὶ πρόσθεν ἀδύτων ἐκταθείς, νῆστις βορᾶς,
ἐπώμοσ' αὐτοῦ βίον ἀπορρήξειν θανών,
εἰ μή με σώσει Φοῖβος, ὅς μ' ἀπώλεσεν.
ἐντεῦθεν αὐδὴν τρίποδος ἐκ χρυσοῦ λακὼν
Φοῖβός μ' ἔπεμψε δεῦρο, διοπετὲς λαβεῖν
ἄγαλμ' Ἀθηνῶν τ' ἐγκαθιδρῦσαι χθονί.
ἀλλ' ἥνπερ ἡμῖν ὥρισεν σωτηρίαν,
σύμπραξον· ἢν γὰρ θεᾶς κατάσχωμεν βρέτας,
μανιῶν τε λήξω καὶ σὲ πολυκώπῳ σκάφει
στείλας Μυκήναις ἐγκαταστήσω πάλιν.
ἀλλ', ὦ φιληθεῖσ', ὦ κασίγνητον κάρα,
σῷσον πατρῷον οἶκον, ἔκσῳσον δ' ἐμέ·
ὡς τἄμ' ὄλωλε πάντα καὶ τὰ Πελοπιδῶν,
οὐράνιον εἰ μὴ ληψόμεσθα θεᾶς βρέτας.

Χο. δεινή τις ὀργὴ δαιμόνων ἐπέζεσε

962 ἔστην Elmsley: τ' ἔστην L P 964 δ' add. Elmsley 966 διηρίθμησε L: διηρίθμιζε P: unde διερρύθμιζε Seidler ὠλένῃ suspectum (sed cf. Bac. 1125, Lycophr. 205): ὧδε δὴ (omisso δ' v. sequenti) Kviçala 974 ἐπώμωσ' P: et certe etiam quod L habet ἐπώμωσ' potest esse 976 λακὼν Scaliger: λαβὼν L P 980 ἢν Seidler: ἂν L P 983 φιληθεῖσ' L: φίλεῖσ' (ει ex η facto) P 984 δέ με L P 986 ληψόμεθα L P: corr. *p* 987 ἐπιζαρεῖ Herwerden, cl. Rhes. 441

τὸ Ταντάλειον σπέρμα διὰ πόνων τ' ἄγει.
Ιφ. τὸ μὲν πρόθυμον, πρίν σε δεῦρ' ἐλθεῖν, ἔχω
Ἄργει γενέσθαι καὶ σέ, σύγγον', εἰσιδεῖν.
θέλω δ' ἅπερ σύ, σέ τε μεταστῆσαι πόνων
νοσοῦντά τ' οἶκον, οὐχὶ τῷ κτανόντι με
θυμουμένη, πατρῷον ὀρθῶσαι· θέλω·
σφαγῆς τε γὰρ σῆς χεῖρ' ἀπαλλάξαιμεν ἂν
σῷσαιμί τ' οἴκους. τὴν θεὸν δ' ὅπως λάθω
δέδοικα καὶ τύραννον, ἡνίκ' ἂν κενὰς
κρηπῖδας εὕρῃ λαΐνας ἀγάλματος.
πῶς δ' οὐ θανοῦμαι; τίς δ' ἔνεστί μοι λόγος;
ἀλλ', εἰ μὲν—ἕν τι—τοῦθ' ὁμοῦ γενήσεται,
ἄγαλμά τ' οἴσεις κἄμ' ἐπ' εὐπρύμνου νεὼς
ἄξεις, τὸ κινδύνευμα γίγνεται καλόν·
τούτου δὲ χωρισθεῖσ' . . . . ἐγὼ μὲν ὄλλυμαι,
σὺ δ' ἂν τὸ σαυτοῦ θέμενος εὖ νόστου τύχοις.
οὐ μήν τι φεύγω γ', οὐδέ σ' εἰ θανεῖν χρεὼν
σῴσασαν· οὐ γὰρ ἀλλ' ἀνὴρ μὲν ἐκ δόμων
θανὼν ποθεινός, τὰ δὲ γυναικὸς ἀσθενῆ.
Ορ. οὐκ ἂν γενοίμην σοῦ τε καὶ μητρὸς φονεύς·
ἅλις τὸ κείνης αἷμα· κοινόφρων δὲ σοὶ
καὶ ζῆν θέλοιμ' ἂν καὶ θανὼν λαχεῖν ἴσον.
ἄξω δέ γ', ἤνπερ καὐτὸς ἐνταυθοῖ περῶ,
πρὸς οἶκον, ἢ σοῦ κατθανὼν μενῶ μέτα.
γνώμης δ' ἄκουσον· εἰ πρόσαντες ἦν τόδε
Ἀρτέμιδι, πῶς ἂν Λοξίας ἐθέσπισε

988 ἄγει Canter: ἀεὶ L P 991 σέ . . . πόνων Canter: σοί . . . πόνον L P: πόνων apogr. Paris. 992 τῷ κτανοῦντι L P: corr. Heath: τοῖς κτανοῦσί Hermann 993 ὀρθῶσαι πάλιν Markland: punctum post ὀρθῶσαι addidi 995 τ' οἴκους Markland: δ' οἴκους L P 999 εἰ μὲν ἔσθ' ᾗ ταῦθ' Wecklein: εἰ μὲν ἡμῖν τοῦθ' (sc. τό ἄγαλμα, cf. 1002) Sitzler. εἰς ἓν ταῦθ' et mox τούτω δὲ χωρισθέντ' . . . post Paleium Weilium Bruhn 1004, 1005 σ' . . . σώσασαν Kirchhoff (μ' . . . σῶσαι τὰ σ' idem): μ' . . . σώσασά σ' L P 1006 γυναικὸς P: γυναικῶν L 1010 ἄξω Canter (etiam σ' pro γ'): ἥξω L P ἐνταυθοῖ forma suspecta περῶ Hermann: πέσω L P 1011 ἢ σοῦ suprascr. L: εἰ σοῦ L P

κομίσαι μ' ἄγαλμα θεᾶς πόλισμ' ἐς Παλλάδος
. . . .
καὶ σὸν πρόσωπον εἰσιδεῖν; ἅπαντα γὰρ
συνθεὶς τάδ' εἰς ἓν νόστον ἐλπίζω λαβεῖν.
Ιφ. πῶς οὖν γένοιτ' ἂν ὥστε μήθ' ἡμᾶς θανεῖν,
λαβεῖν θ' ἃ βουλόμεσθα; τῇδε γὰρ νοσεῖ
νόστος πρὸς οἴκους· ἡ δὲ βούλησις πάρα.
Ορ. ἆρ' ἂν τύραννον διολέσαι δυναίμεθ' ἄν;
Ιφ. δεινὸν τόδ' εἶπας, ξενοφονεῖν ἐπήλυδας.
Ορ. ἀλλ', εἰ σὲ σώσει κἀμέ, κινδυνευτέον.
Ιφ. οὐκ ἂν δυναίμην· τὸ δὲ πρόθυμον ᾕνεσα.
Ορ. τί δ', εἴ με ναῷ τῷδε κρύψειας λάθρα;
Ιφ. ὡς δὴ σκότον λαβόντες ἐκσωθεῖμεν ἄν;
Ορ. κλεπτῶν γὰρ ἡ νύξ, τῆς δ' ἀληθείας τὸ φῶς.
Ιφ. εἴσ' ἔνδον ἱεροὶ φύλακες, οὓς οὐ λήσομεν.
Ορ. οἴμοι, διεφθάρμεσθα· πῶς σωθεῖμεν ἄν;
Ιφ. ἔχειν δοκῶ μοι καινὸν ἐξεύρημά τι.
Ορ. ποῖόν τι; δόξης μετάδος, ὡς κἀγὼ μάθω.
Ιφ. ταῖς σαῖς ἀνίαις χρήσομαι σοφίσμασι.
Ορ. δειναὶ γὰρ αἱ γυναῖκες εὑρίσκειν τέχνας.
Ιφ. φονέα σε φήσω μητρὸς ἐξ Ἄργους μολεῖν.
Ορ. χρῆσαι κακοῖσι τοῖς ἐμοῖς, εἰ κερδανεῖς.
Ιφ. ὡς οὐ θέμις γε λέξομεν θύειν θεᾷ,
Ορ. τίν' αἰτίαν ἔχουσ'; ὑποπτεύω τι γάρ.
Ιφ. οὐ καθαρὸν ὄντα· τὸ δ' ὅσιον δώσω φόβῳ.
Ορ. τί δῆτα μᾶλλον θεᾶς ἄγαλμ' ἁλίσκεται;
Ιφ. πόντου σε πηγαῖς ἁγνίσαι βουλήσομαι,

1014 πόλισμ' εἰς L P : πόλισμα Elmsley post 1014 lacunam statuit Kirchhoff 1017 θανεῖν L : κτανεῖν P 1018 λαβεῖν L : λαθεῖν P νοσεῖ Markland : νόει L P (quo servato νόστον v. sequenti Musurus) 1022–1051 lineolae praefixae in P 1022 εἴ με L : εἴ σε P 1025, 1026 delevit Markland 1025 σκότος L P ἔξω θεῖμεν L P : corr. Brodaeus 1028 διεφάρμεσθα P 1031 σαῖσι μανίαις Kirchhoff 1032 γὰρ L P : μὲν Stob. fl. 73. 26 1035 γε] σε Reiske 1036 ἔχονθ' Reiske 1037 τόδ' P

Ορ. ἔτ' ἐν δόμοισι βρέτας, ἐφ' ᾧ πεπλεύκαμεν·
Ιφ. κἀκεῖνο νίψαι, σοῦ θιγόντος ὥς, ἐρῶ.
Ορ. ποῖ δῆτα; πόντου νοτερὸν εἶπας ἔκβολον;
Ιφ. οὗ ναῦς χαλινοῖς λινοδέτοις ὁρμεῖ σέθεν.
Ορ. σὺ δ' ἤ τις ἄλλος ἐν χεροῖν οἴσει βρέτας;
Ιφ. ἐγώ· θιγεῖν γὰρ ὅσιόν ἐστ' ἐμοὶ μόνῃ.
Ορ. Πυλάδης δ' ὅδ' ἡμῖν ποῦ τετάξεται πόνου;
Ιφ. ταὐτὸν χεροῖν σοὶ λέξεται μίασμ' ἔχων.
Ορ. λάθρα δ' ἄνακτος ἢ εἰδότος δράσεις τάδε;
Ιφ. πείσασα μύθοις· οὐ γὰρ ἂν λάθοιμί γε.
Ορ. καὶ μὴν νεώς γε πίτυλος εὐήρης πάρα.
Ιφ. σοὶ δὴ μέλειν χρὴ τἄλλ' ὅπως ἕξει καλῶς.
Ορ. ἑνὸς μόνου δεῖ, τάσδε συγκρύψαι τάδε.
ἀλλ' ἀντίαζε καὶ λόγους πειστηρίους
εὕρισκ'· ἔχει τοι δύναμιν εἰς οἶκτον γυνή.
τὰ δ' ἄλλ' ἴσως—. ἅπαντα συμβαίη καλῶς.

Ιφ. ὦ φίλταται γυναῖκες, εἰς ὑμᾶς βλέπω,
καὶ τἄμ' ἐν ὑμῖν ἐστιν ἢ καλῶς ἔχειν
ἢ μηδὲν εἶναι καὶ στερηθῆναι πάτρας
φίλου τ' ἀδελφοῦ φιλτάτης τε συγγόνου.
καὶ πρῶτα μέν μοι τοῦ λόγου τάδ' ἀρχέτω·
γυναῖκές ἐσμεν, φιλόφρον ἀλλήλαις γένος
σῴζειν τε κοινὰ πράγματ' ἀσφαλέσταται.
σιγήσαθ' ἡμῖν καὶ συνεκπονήσατε
φυγάς. καλόν τοι γλῶσσ' ὅτῳ πιστὴ παρῇ.
ὁρᾶτε δ' ὡς τρεῖς μία τύχη τοὺς φιλτάτους,
ἢ γῆς πατρῴας νόστον ἢ θανεῖν ἔχει.

1040 ἔτ' L: ἔστ' P 1042 Cf. 1196: εἶπας] εἶ παρ' Reiske 1044 σὺ δ' ἤ τις Jacobs: σοὶ δή τις L P (τίς P) 1046 πόνου Brodaeus: φόνου L P: χοροῦ Winckelmann 1047 ἔχειν Kirchhoff 1051 μέλλειν primitus L P 1055 distinxit Verrall: ἴσως ἂν πάντα Markland 1056 εἰς Hermann: ὡς L P 1059 φιλτάτης Bothe: φιλτάτου L P: v. delet Paley 1061 ἀλλήλων P 1064 τοι L: τι P πιστὴ Bothe: πιστις L P 1066 νόστος Heath: tum μένει pro ἔχει Polle sed fortasse νόστον quasi ὥστε νοστεῖν dicitur

σωθεῖσα δ', ὡς ἂν καὶ σὺ κοινωνῇς τύχης,
σώσω σ' ἐς Ἑλλάδ'. ἀλλὰ πρός σε δεξιᾶς
σὲ καὶ σὲ ἱκνοῦμαι, σὲ δὲ φίλης παρηΐδος,
γονάτων τε καὶ τῶν ἐν δόμοισι φιλτάτων
μητρὸς πατρός τε καὶ τέκνων ὅτῳ κυρεῖ.
τί φατέ; τίς ὑμῶν φησιν ἢ τίς οὐ θέλειν—
φθέγξασθε—ταῦτα; μὴ γὰρ αἰνουσῶν λόγους
ὄλωλα κἀγὼ καὶ κασίγνητος τάλας.

Χο. θάρσει, φίλη δέσποινα, καὶ σῴζου μόνον·
ὡς ἔκ γ' ἐμοῦ σοι πάντα σιγηθήσεται—
ἴστω μέγας Ζεύς—ὧν ἐπισκήπτεις πέρι.

Ιφ. ὄναισθε μύθων καὶ γένοισθ' εὐδαίμονες.
σὸν ἔργον ἤδη καὶ σὸν ἐσβαίνειν δόμους·
ὡς αὐτίχ' ἥξει τῆσδε κοίρανος χθονός,
θυσίαν ἐλέγχων εἰ κατείργασται ξένων.
ὦ πότνι', ἥπερ μ' Αὐλίδος κατὰ πτυχὰς
δεινῆς ἔσωσας ἐκ πατροκτόνου χερός,
σῶσόν με καὶ νῦν τούσδε τ'· ἢ τὸ Λοξίου
οὐκέτι βροτοῖσι διὰ σὲ ἐτήτυμον στόμα.
ἀλλ' εὐμενὴς ἔκβηθι βαρβάρου χθονὸς
ἐς τὰς Ἀθήνας· καὶ γὰρ ἐνθάδ' οὐ πρέπει
ναίειν, παρόν σοι πόλιν ἔχειν εὐδαίμονα.

Χο. — ὄρνις, ἃ παρὰ πετρίνας [στρ.
πόντου δειράδας, ἀλκυών,
ἔλεγον οἶτον ἀείδεις,
εὐξύνετον ξυνετοῖς βοάν,
ὅτι πόσιν κελαδεῖς ἀεὶ μολπαῖς,
ἐγώ σοι παραβάλλομαι

1069 *σὲ καὶ σ'* L P: sed cf. 1085 1071 *τε* P et postmodo additum L 1072 *θέλειν* Musgrave: *θέλει* L P 1078 Ιφ. praef. L: om. P, et v. sequenti praef. *p* *ὄναισθε* L *p*: *ὄν**θ** P 1080 *κοίρανος* L: *τύραννος* P 1081 *ἐλέγξων* Markland 1085 *σὲ* L P (*σ'* *p*) 1090 *ἀλκυών* L P: *ἁλκυών* vulgo post Musurum 1091 *οἰκτρὸν* Barnes 1092 *εὐξύνετον* P et suprascr. L: *ἀξύνετον* L *ξυνετοῖσι* *l*· cf. v. 1109

θρήνους, ἄπτερος ὄρνις,
ποθοῦσ᾽ Ἑλλάνων ἀγόρους,
ποθοῦσ᾽ Ἄρτεμιν λοχίαν,
ἃ παρὰ Κύνθιον ὄχθον οἰ-
κεῖ φοίνικά θ᾽ ἁβροκόμαν
δάφναν τ᾽ εὐερνέα καὶ
γλαυκᾶς θαλλὸν ἱερὸν ἐλαίας, Λατοῦς ὠδῖνα φίλαν,
λίμναν θ᾽ εἱλίσσουσαν ὕδωρ
κύκλιον, ἔνθα κύκνος μελῳ-
δὸς Μούσας θεραπεύει.

— ὦ πολλαὶ δακρύων λιβάδες, [ἀντ.
αἳ παρηίδας εἰς ἐμὰς
ἔπεσον, ἁνίκα πύργων
ὀλομένων ἐν ναυσὶν ἔβαν
πολεμίων ἐρετμοῖσι καὶ λόγχαις.
ζαχρύσου δὲ δι᾽ ἐμπολᾶς
νόστον βάρβαρον ἦλθον,
ἔνθα τᾶς ἐλαφοκτόνου
θεᾶς ἀμφίπολον κόραν
παῖδ᾽ Ἀγαμεμνονίαν λατρεύ-
ω βωμούς τ᾽ οὐ μηλοθύτας,
ζηλοῦσ᾽ ἄταν διὰ παν-
τὸς δυσδαίμον᾽· ἐν γὰρ ἀνάγκαις οὐ κάμνεις σύντροφος ὤν.
μεταβάλλει δυσδαιμονία·

1096, 1097 ποθοῦσ᾽ ad finem utriusque trai. Weil: cf. 1113, 1114 1097 λοχείαν L P, sed λοχίαν primitus fortasse L 1101 θάλλον (sic) ed. Brubachiana: θάλλος L: θάλος P ἱρὸν *l* 1102 ὠδῖνι Portus 1104 κύκλιον Seidler, cl. Call. Hymn. Apoll. 59, Del. 260: κύκνειον L P 1105 μοῦσα P 1107 ἐσ ᾽μὰς L P[2] (ἐσμᾶς P): corr. *l* 1109 οὐλομένων *l*: ὀλλυμένων Erfurdt: cf. v. 1092. Fortasse ἐπὶ ναῦς 1112 νόστον] νᾶσον Bothe: νόμον Musgrave 1116 τ᾽ οὐ Musgrave: τοὺς L P 1117-1120 lectio dubia 1117 ζηλοῦσ᾽ ἄταν L: ζητοῦσ᾽ ἄταν P: ζηλοῦσα τὸν Greverus (τὰν Bothe) 1119 κάμνει codd. recc. quidam 1120 μεταβάλλειν Bergk

τὸ δὲ μετ' εὐτυχίας κακοῦ-
σθαι θνατοῖς βαρὺς αἰών.

— καὶ σὲ μέν, πότνι', Ἀργεία [στρ.
πεντηκόντορος οἶκον ἄξει·
συρίζων θ' ὁ κηροδέτας
κάλαμος οὐρείου Πανὸς
κώπαις ἐπιθωΰξει,
ὁ Φοῖβός θ' ὁ μάντις ἔχων
κέλαδον ἑπτατόνου λύρας
ἀείδων ἄξει λιπαρὰν
εὖ σ' Ἀθηναίων ἐπὶ γᾶν.
ἐμὲ δ' αὐτοῦ λιποῦσα
βήσῃ ῥοθίοισι πλάταις·
ἀέρι δὲ [ἱστία] πρότονοι κατὰ πρῷραν ὑ-
πὲρ στόλον ἐκπετάσουσι πόδα
ναὸς ὠκυπόμπου.

— λαμπροὺς ἱπποδρόμους βαίην, [ἀντ.
ἔνθ' εὐάλιον ἔρχεται πῦρ·
οἰκείων δ' ὑπὲρ θαλάμων
πτέρυγας ἐν νώτοις ἁμοῖς
λήξαιμι θοάζουσα·
χοροῖς δ' ἑσταίην, ὅθι καὶ
παρθένος, εὐδοκίμων γάμων,
παρὰ πόδ' εἱλίσσουσα φίλας
ματρὸς ἡλίκων θιάσους,
χαρίτων εἰς ἁμίλλας,

1121 δὲ P: ** L: γὰρ *l* εὐτυχίαν Scaliger 1125 θ' Elmsley: δ' L P 1126 οὐρείου Πανὸς κάλαμος Hartung: cf. 1141 1130 ἄξει] πέμψει Paley, cl. v. 1124 1131 εὖ σ' Bothe: ἐς L P 1133 ῥοθίοις L P 1134–1136 lectio incerta: πρότονος et στόλων ἐκπετάσουσιν P δ' ἱστία L P: ἱστία seclusit Bothe 1135 πόδα] πόδες Seidler: πνοαὶ Bruhn 1138 λαμπρὸν ἱππόδρομον *l* vel fortasse L 1141 ἐν νώτοις ἁμοῖς πτέρυγας Fritzsche: cf. 1126 1143–1151 lectio incerta 1143 δὲ σταίην L P: corr. Bruhn 1144 παρθένος] πάροιθ' Kirchhoff: πάροχος Nauck 1146 ματρὸς *l*: ματέρος L P θιάσοις Fritzsche 1147 ἐς ἁμίλλας χαρίτων L P: traieci

χαίτας ἁβρόπλουτον ἔριν,
ὀρνυμένα, πολυποίκιλα φάρεα
καὶ πλοκάμους περιβαλλομένα
γένυσιν ἐσκίαζον.

ΘΟΑΣ

ποῦ 'σθ' ἡ πυλωρὸς τῶνδε δωμάτων γυνὴ
Ἑλληνίς; ἤδη τῶν ξένων κατήρξατο;
ἀδύτοις ἐν ἁγνοῖς σῶμα λάμπονται πυρί;
Χο. ἥδ' ἐστίν, ἥ σοι πάντ', ἄναξ, ἐρεῖ σαφῶς.
Θο. ἔα·
τί τόδε μεταίρεις ἐξ ἀκινήτων βάθρων,
'Αγαμέμνονος παῖ, θεᾶς ἄγαλμ' ἐν ὠλέναις;
Ιφ. ἄναξ, ἔχ' αὐτοῦ πόδα σὸν ἐν παραστάσιν.
Θο. τί δ' ἔστιν, 'Ιφιγένεια, καινὸν ἐν δόμοις;
Ιφ. ἀπέπτυσ'· Ὁσίᾳ γὰρ δίδωμ' ἔπος τόδε.
Θο. τί φροιμιάζῃ νεοχμόν; ἐξαύδα σαφῶς.
Ιφ. οὐ καθαρά μοι τὰ θύματ' ἠγρεύσασθ', ἄναξ.
Θο. τί τοὐκδιδάξαν τοῦτό σ'; ἢ δόξαν λέγεις;
Ιφ. βρέτας τὸ τῆς θεοῦ πάλιν ἕδρας ἀπεστράφη.
Θο. αὐτόματον, ἤ νιν σεισμὸς ἔστρεψε χθονός;
Ιφ. αὐτόματον· ὄψιν δ' ὀμμάτων ξυνήρμοσεν.
Θο. ἡ δ' αἰτία τίς; ἦ τὸ τῶν ξένων μύσος;
Ιφ. ἥδ', οὐδὲν ἄλλο· δεινὰ γὰρ δεδράκατον.
Θο. ἀλλ' ἦ τιν' ἔκανον βαρβάρων ἀκτῆς ἔπι;
Ιφ. οἰκεῖον ἦλθον τὸν φόνον κεκτημένοι.
Θο. τίν'; εἰς ἔρον γὰρ τοῦ μαθεῖν πεπτώκαμεν.
Ιφ. μητέρα κατειργάσαντο κοινωνῷ ξίφει.
Θο. Ἄπολλον, οὐδ' ἐν βαρβάροις ἔτλη τις ἄν.

1148 χαίτας ἁβρόπλουτον ἔριν post Bothium scripsi : χαίτας ἁβροπλούτοιο εἰς ἔριν L P (ἁβροπλούτοιο χαίτας *l*) 1149 in rasura litteras μένα vocabuli ὀρνυμένα et φάρεα καὶ πλοκά scripsit *l* 1154 ἡ δὴ L P : corr. Reiske τοῖν ξένοιν Elmsley : cf. 1168 1155 ἀδύτοις] ις in rasura *p* : ἀδύτοις τ' Bothe σώμαθ' ἅπτονται Heimsoeth 1159 παραστάσει P 1162–1221 lineolas pro personarum notis L 1168 τοῖν ξένοιν Wecklein : cf. 1154 1170 ἦ] ἢ L P[2] : εἰ P 1173 κατειργάσατο L P : corr. *l* κοινουργῷ Bruhn 1174 ἔτλη Gaisford : τόδ' ἔτλη L P

Ιφ. πάσης διωγμοῖς ἠλάθησαν Ἑλλάδος.
Θο. ἦ τῶνδ' ἕκατι δῆτ' ἄγαλμ' ἔξω φέρεις;
Ιφ. σεμνόν γ' ὑπ' αἰθέρ', ὡς μεταστήσω φόνου.
Θο. μίασμα δ' ἔγνως τοῖν ξένοιν ποίῳ τρόπῳ;
Ιφ. ἤλεγχον, ὡς θεᾶς βρέτας ἀπεστράφη πάλιν.
Θο. σοφήν σ' ἔθρεψεν Ἑλλάς, ὡς ᾔσθου καλῶς.
Ιφ. καὶ μὴν καθεῖσαν δέλεαρ ἡδύ μοι φρενῶν.
Θο. τῶν Ἀργόθεν τι φίλτρον ἀγγέλλοντέ σοι;
Ιφ. τὸν μόνον Ὀρέστην ἐμὸν ἀδελφὸν εὐτυχεῖν.
Θο. ὡς δή σφε σῴσαις ἡδοναῖς ἀγγελμάτων.
Ιφ. καὶ πατέρα γε ζῆν καὶ καλῶς πράσσειν ἐμόν.
Θο. σὺ δ' ἐς τὸ τῆς θεοῦ γ' ἐξένευσας εἰκότως.
Ιφ. πᾶσάν γε μισοῦσ' Ἑλλάδ', ἥ μ' ἀπώλεσεν.
Θο. τί δῆτα δρῶμεν, φράζε, τοῖν ξένοιν πέρι;
Ιφ. τὸν νόμον ἀνάγκη τὸν προκείμενον σέβειν.
Θο. οὔκουν ἐν ἔργῳ χέρνιβες ξίφος τε σόν;
Ιφ. ἁγνοῖς καθαρμοῖς πρῶτά νιν νίψαι θέλω.
Θο. πηγαῖσιν ὑδάτων ἢ θαλασσίᾳ δρόσῳ;
Ιφ. θάλασσα κλύζει πάντα τἀνθρώπων κακά.
Θο. ὁσιώτερον γοῦν τῇ θεῷ πέσοιεν ἄν.
Ιφ. καὶ τἀμά γ' οὕτω μᾶλλον ἂν καλῶς ἔχοι.
Θο. οὔκουν πρὸς αὐτὸν ναὸν ἐκπίπτει κλύδων;
Ιφ. ἐρημίας δεῖ· καὶ γὰρ ἄλλα δράσομεν.
Θο. ἄγ' ἔνθα χρῄζεις· οὐ φιλῶ τἄρρηθ' ὁρᾶν.
Ιφ. ἁγνιστέον μοι καὶ τὸ τῆς θεοῦ βρέτας.
Θο. εἴπερ γε κηλὶς ἔβαλέ νιν μητροκτόνος.
Ιφ. οὐ γάρ ποτ' ἄν νιν ἠράμην βάθρων ἄπο.
Θο. δίκαιος ηὑσέβεια καὶ προμηθία.
Ιφ. οἶσθά νυν ἅ μοι γενέσθω; Θο. σὸν τὸ σημαίνειν τόδε.
Ιφ. δεσμὰ τοῖς ξένοισι πρόσθες. Θο. ποῖ δέ σ' ἐκφύγοιεν ἄν;

1181 μὴν Monk : νῦν L P καθῆσαν L P : corr. *l p* 1184 Cf. Med. 325 : σώσῃς Markland 1185 ζῆν καὶ L : ζῆν P 1194 ὁσιώτεροι Tournier 1201 ἠράμην Musgrave : ἀνηράμην P : ἀνῃράμην L 1203 οἶσθα νῦν L P

Ιφ. πιστὸν Ἑλλὰς οἶδεν οὐδέν. Θο. ἴτ' ἐπὶ δεσμά, πρόσπολοι.
Ιφ. κἀκκομιζόντων δὲ δεῦρο τοὺς ξένους . . . Θο. ἔσται τάδε.
Ιφ. κρᾶτα κρύψαντες πέπλοισιν. Θο. ἡλίου πρόσθεν φλογός.
Ιφ. σῶν τέ μοι σύμπεμπ' ὀπαδῶν. Θο. οἵδ' ὁμαρτήσουσί σοι.
Ιφ. καὶ πόλει πέμψον τιν' ὅστις σημανεῖ . . . Θο. ποίας τύχας;
Ιφ. ἐν δόμοις μίμνειν ἅπαντας. Θο. μὴ συναντῷεν φόνῳ;
Ιφ. μυσαρὰ γὰρ τὰ τοιάδ' ἐστί. Θο. στεῖχε καὶ σήμαινε σύ . . .
Ιφ. μηδέν' εἰς ὄψιν πελάζειν. Θο. εὖ γε κηδεύεις πόλιν.
Ιφ. καὶ φίλων γ' οὓς δεῖ μάλιστα. Θο. τοῦτ' ἔλεξας εἰς ἐμέ.
Ιφ. . . . Θο. ὡς εἰκότως σε πᾶσα θαυμάζει πόλις.
Ιφ. σὺ δὲ μένων αὐτοῦ πρὸ ναῶν τῇ θεῷ . . . Θο. τί χρῆμα δρῶ;
Ιφ. ἅγνισον πυρσῷ μέλαθρον. Θο. καθαρὸν ὡς μόλῃς πάλιν.
Ιφ. ἡνίκ' ἂν δ' ἔξω περῶσιν οἱ ξένοι . . . Θο. τί χρή με δρᾶν;
Ιφ. πέπλον ὀμμάτων προθέσθαι. Θο. μὴ παλαμναῖον λάβω.
Ιφ. ἢν δ' ἄγαν δοκῶ χρονίζειν . . . Θο. τοῦδ' ὅρος τίς ἐστι μοι;

1207 κρᾶτα κρύψαντες Musgrave: κατακρύψαντες L P 1207–1213 lineolas 1207 ante ἡλίου, 1208 ante σῶν, 1212 ante μηδέν', om. L (cf. ad 1162): notam Θο. ante ἡλίου om. P, ideoque pro Iphigenia Thoantem, pro Thoante Iphigeniam usque ad 1213 posuit: corr. apogr. Paris, et 1214 Thoanti sine nota continuat 1213 οὓς δεῖ Badham: οὐδεὶς L P 1214 verba Iphigeniae initio desiderari perspexit Hermann: versum post v. 1202 trai. Markland, Thoanti tributum: delevit Dindorf 1215 'πι ναῷ Wecklein 1216 πυρσῷ Reiske: χρυσῷ L P 1219 lineolas et litteras ζειν in rasura add. *l*

Ιφ. θαυμάσῃς μηδέν. Θο. τὰ τῆς θεοῦ πρᾶσσ'—ἐπεὶ
σχολή—καλῶς.
Ιφ. εἰ γὰρ ὡς θέλω καθαρμὸς ὅδε πέσοι. Θο. συνεύχομαι.
Ιφ. τούσδ' ἄρ' ἐκβαίνοντας ἤδη δωμάτων ὁρῶ ξένους
καὶ θεᾶς κόσμους νεογνούς τ' ἄρνας, ὡς φόνῳ φόνον
μυσαρὸν ἐκνίψω, σέλας τε λαμπάδων τά τ' ἄλλ' ὅσα
προυθέμην ἐγὼ ξένοισι καὶ θεᾷ καθάρσια.
ἐκποδὼν δ' αὐδῶ πολίταις τοῦδ' ἔχειν μιάσματος,
εἴ τις ἢ ναῶν πυλωρὸς χεῖρας ἁγνεύει θεοῖς
ἢ γάμον στείχει συνάψων ἢ τόκοις βαρύνεται,
φεύγετ', ἐξίστασθε, μή τῳ προσπέσῃ μύσος τόδε.
ὦ Διὸς Λητοῦς τ' ἄνασσα παρθέν', ἢν νίψω φόνον
τῶνδε καὶ θύσωμεν οὗ χρή, καθαρὸν οἰκήσεις δόμον,
εὐτυχεῖς δ' ἡμεῖς ἐσόμεθα. τἄλλα δ' οὐ λέγουσ', ὅμως
τοῖς τὰ πλείον' εἰδόσιν θεοῖς σοί τε σημαίνω, θεά.

Χο. — εὔπαις ὁ Λατοῦς γόνος, [στρ.
τόν ποτε Δηλιὰς ἐν καρποφόροις γυάλοις
⟨ἔτικτε,⟩ χρυσοκόμαν
ἐν κιθάρᾳ σοφόν, ἅ τ' ἐπὶ τόξων
εὐστοχίᾳ γάνυται· φέρε ⟨δ' αὐτά⟩
νιν ἀπὸ δειράδος εἰναλίας,
λοχεῖα κλεινὰ λιποῦσα μά-
τηρ, τὰν ἀστάκτων ὑδάτων
βακχεύουσαν Διονύ-

1220 ἐπεὶ σχολῆ P et, me iudice, L: ἐπὶ σχολῆ teste Prinzio 1222 δομάτων P et fortasse ante correct. L 1223 ἄρνας Pierson: ἄρσενας L P 1233 θεᾶ L P: corr. *l* 1235 τόν Hermann: ὅν L P Δηλιάσιν καρποφόρει post Seidlerum Wilamowitz 1236–1263 bis pertusa fuisse videtur membrana archetypi, itaque lacunae factae vv. 1236, 1239 iterumque post vv. viginti quattuor, 1260, 1263: idem accidit infra vv. 1380, 1404: lacunas ex. gr. explevimus 1236 ἔτικτε suppl. Kirchhoff χρυσοκόμαν φοῖβον L P: φοῖβον delevit Musgrave 1238 fortasse ἃ δ' 1239 γάννυται L P: corr. Barnes δ' αὐτά supplevi: vide ad 1236–1263: φέρει νιν L P: φέρε δ' ἶνιν Kirchhoff 1240 εἰναλίας *l*: ἐναλίας L P 1241, 1242 λιποῦσα (λιποῦσ' *l* P) ἀστά-κτων μάτηρ ὑδάτων τὰν L P: traieci: λιποῦσ', ἀστάκτων ματέρα παγᾶν Wilamowitz: cf. 1267: μάστειρ' ὑδάτων Wecklein 1243 βαχεύ*ουσαν P

σῳ Παρνάσιον κορυφάν·
ὅθι ποικιλόνωτος οἰ-
νωπὸς δράκων,
σκιερᾷ κατάχαλκος εὐ-
φύλλῳ δάφνᾳ,
γᾶς πελώριον τέρας, ἄμφεπε μαντεῖον Χθόνιον.
ἔτι μιν ἔτι βρέφος, ἔτι φίλας
ἐπὶ ματέρος ἀγκάλαισι θρῴσκων
ἔκανες, ὦ Φοῖβε, μαντείων δ' ἐπέβας ζαθέων,
τρίποδί τ' ἐν χρυσέῳ θάσσεις, ἐν ἀψευδεῖ θρόνῳ
μαντείας βροτοῖς θεσφάτων νέμων
ἀδύτων ὕπο, Κασταλίας ῥεέθρων γείτων, μέσον
γᾶς ἔχων μέλαθρον.

— Θέμιν δ' ἐπεὶ γᾶς ἰὼν [ἀντ.
παῖδ' ἀπενάσσατο ⟨Πυθῶνος⟩ ἀπὸ ζαθέων
χρηστηρίων, νύχια
Χθὼν ἐτεκνώσατο φάσματ' ὀ⟨νείρων⟩,
οἳ πολέσιν μερόπων τά τε πρῶτα, τά τ'
ἔπειθ', ὅσσα τ' ἔμελλε τυχεῖν,
ὕπνου κατὰ δνοφερὰς γᾶς εὐνὰς ἔφραζον· Γαῖα δὲ τὰν
μαντεῖον ἀφείλετο τι-
μὰν Φοῖβον, φθόνῳ θυγατρός.
ταχύπους δ' ἐς Ὄλυμπον ὁρ-

1246 κατάκαλχος (h. e. ἕλικτος) Verrall εὐφύλλω L : εὐφύλλων P 1247 ἀμφέπει L P: corr. Seidler 1249 νιν Seidler 1254 θρόνῳ L: χρόνῳ P 1255 post βροτοῖς habent ἀναφαίνων L P: delevit Seidler 1256 νέμων Musgrave : ἐμῶν L P 1257 ὕπο Seidler : ὕπερ L : ὑπὲρ P 1259 ἐπεὶ Scaliger : ἐπὶ L P γᾶς ἰὼν] Γαΐαν Bruhn (γάϊον Nauck) 1260, 1261 ἀπενάσατο ἀπὸ ζαθέων L P : supplevit Hermann : παῖς ἀπένασσεν ὁ Λατῷος Nauck 1263 φάσματ' ὀ L P: supplevit *l* 1264 πόλεσι P 1265 ὅσσα τ' (cf. 1240) Musgrave : ὅσα τ' L P : ὅσ' Burges 1266 ὕπνῳ Markland δνοφερᾶς L P 1267 τὰν Seidler : τὴν supra μαντεῖον suprascr. L, et videtur in fine versus (post γαῖα δὲ) scriptum habuisse (nunc erasum): om. P γᾶς εὐνὰς φράζε, πάλιν δὲ (et οἷς πολέσιν v. 1264) Wilamowitz : cf. 1242

μαθεὶς ἄναξ
χέρα παιδνὸν ἕλιξεν ἐκ
Διὸς θρόνων
Πυθίων δόμων χθονίαν ἀφελεῖν μῆνιν θεᾶς. [νυχίους τ' ἐνοπάς.]
γέλασε δ', ὅτι τέκος ἄφαρ ἔβα
πολύχρυσα θέλων λατρεύματα σχεῖν·
ἐπὶ δ' ἔσεισεν κόμαν, παῦσαι νυχίους ἐνοπάς,
ἀπὸ δ' ἀλαθοσύναν νυκτωπὸν ἐξεῖλεν βροτῶν,
καὶ τιμὰς πάλιν θῆκε Λοξίᾳ,
πολυάνορι δ' ἐν ξενόεντι θρόνῳ θάρση βροτοῖς
θεσφάτων ἀοιδαῖς.

ΑΓΓΕΛΟΣ

ὦ ναοφύλακες βώμιοί τ' ἐπιστάται,
Θόας ἄναξ γῆς τῆσδε ποῦ κυρεῖ βεβώς;
καλεῖτ' ἀναπτύξαντες εὐγόμφους πύλας
ἔξω μελάθρων τῶνδε κοίρανον χθονός.
Χο. τί δ' ἔστιν, εἰ χρὴ μὴ κελευσθεῖσαν λέγειν;
Αγ. βεβᾶσι φροῦδοι δίπτυχοι νεανίαι
'Αγαμεμνονείας παιδὸς ἐκ βουλευμάτων
φεύγοντες ἐκ γῆς τῆσδε καὶ σεμνὸν βρέτας
λαβόντες ἐν κόλποισιν Ἑλλάδος νεώς.
Χο. ἄπιστον εἶπας μῦθον· ὃν δ' ἰδεῖν θέλεις
ἄνακτα χώρας, φροῦδος ἐκ ναοῦ συθείς.
Αγ. ποῖ; δεῖ γὰρ αὐτὸν εἰδέναι τὰ δρώμενα.
Χο. οὐκ ἴσμεν· ἀλλὰ στεῖχε καὶ δίωκέ νιν
ὅπου κυρήσας τούσδ' ἀπαγγελεῖς λόγους.

1271 ἕλιξεν fortasse primitus L : ἕλιξ' P et nunc L vel *l* Διὸς] Ζηνὸς Seidler : ἐς Δῖον θρόνον post Iacobsium Badham 1273 θεᾶς μῆνιν L P : trai. Wilamowitz νυχίους τ' ἐνοπάς seclusit Seidler : cf. 1277 1276 ἐπεὶ δ' ἔσεισε κόμαν παῦσε L P : corr. Badham : ἐπὶ δὲ σείσας κόμαν παῦσεν Musgrave 1277 ἐνοπάς ex v. 1273 Burges : ὀνείρους L P, glossema : νυχίους ἐνέρους Badham 1278 δὲ λαθοσύναν L P : corr. Nauck (sc. *tunc veridica, nunc fallacia sunt somnia*) 1279 ἐξεῖλε L P 1283 θάρση L P, sed θάρσει primitus L 1284 Ἄγγελος] Θεράπων Wecklein, cl. 1205 et 1329 1285 τῆσδε γῆς L P : trai. *l*

Αγ. ὁρᾶτ', ἄπιστον ὡς γυναικεῖον γένος·
μέτεστι χὑμῖν τῶν πεπραγμένων μέρος.
Χο. μαίνῃ· τί δ' ἡμῖν τῶν ξένων δρασμοῦ μέτα;
οὐκ εἶ κρατούντων πρὸς πύλας ὅσον τάχος;
Αγ. οὔ, πρίν γ' ἂν εἴπῃ τοὔπος ἑρμηνεὺς ὅδε,
εἴτ' ἔνδον εἴτ' οὐκ ἔνδον ἀρχηγὸς χθονός.
ὠή, χαλᾶτε κλῇθρα, τοῖς ἔνδον λέγω,
καὶ δεσπότῃ σημήναθ' οὕνεκ' ἐν πύλαις
πάρειμι, καινῶν φόρτον ἀγγέλλων κακῶν.
Θο. τίς ἀμφὶ δῶμα θεᾶς τόδ' ἵστησιν βοήν,
πύλας ἀράξας καὶ ψόφον πέμψας ἔσω;
Αγ. φεῦ·
πῶς ἔλεγον αἵδε, καί μ' ἀπήλαυνον δόμων,
ὡς ἐκτὸς εἴης· σὺ δὲ κατ' οἶκον ἦσθ' ἄρα.
Θο. τί προσδοκῶσαι κέρδος ἢ θηρώμεναι;
Αγ. αὖθις τὰ τῶνδε σημανῶ· τὰ δ' ἐν ποσὶ
παρόντ' ἄκουσον. ἡ νεᾶνις ἣ 'νθάδε
βωμοῖς παρίστατ', Ἰφιγένει', ἔξω χθονὸς
σὺν τοῖς ξένοισιν οἴχεται, σεμνὸν θεᾶς
ἄγαλμ' ἔχουσα· δόλια δ' ἦν καθάρματα.
Θο. πῶς φῄς; τί πνεῦμα συμφορᾶς κεκτημένη;
Αγ. σῴζουσ' Ὀρέστην· τοῦτο γὰρ σὺ θαυμάσῃ.
Θο. τὸν ποῖον; ἆρ' ὃν Τυνδαρὶς τίκτει κόρη;
Αγ. ὃν τοῖσδε βωμοῖς θεὰ καθωσιώσατο.
Θο. ὢ θαῦμα—πῶς σε μεῖζον ὀνομάσας τύχω;
Αγ. μὴ 'νταῦθα τρέψῃς σὴν φρέν', ἀλλ' ἄκουέ μου·
σαφῶς δ' ἀθρήσας καὶ κλύων ἐκφρόντισον
διωγμὸς ὅστις τοὺς ξένους θηράσεται.
Θο. λέγ'· εὖ γὰρ εἶπας· οὐ γὰρ ἀγχίπλουν πόρον

1299 χὑμῖν Markland: θ' ὑμῖν L P 1301 Nuntio, 1302 Choro tribuunt L P: corr. Heath 1302 εἴπῃ fortasse primitus L: εἴποι L P ὅδε scripsi: '*hic interpres*': cornu sonat, ni fallor, vel ῥόπτρῳ (cf. Io. 1612) pulsat: cf. 1307: τόδε L P 1307 τόδ'] ὅδ' Tournier 1309 φεῦ· | πῶς Wilamowitz (φεῦ· ὡς Kvičala): ψευδῶς L P 1310 εἴης Scaliger: ἦς L P 1312 αὖτις L P 1319 τὸ ποῖον P

φεύγουσιν, ὥστε διαφυγεῖν τοὐμὸν δόρυ.
Αγ. ἐπεὶ πρὸς ἀκτὰς ἤλθομεν θαλασσίας,
οὗ ναῦς Ὀρέστου κρύφιος ἦν ὡρμισμένη,
ἡμᾶς μέν, οὓς σὺ δεσμὰ συμπέμπεις ξένων
ἔχοντας, ἐξένευσ' ἀποστῆναι πρόσω
Ἀγαμέμνονος παῖς, ὡς ἀπόρρητον φλόγα
θύουσα καὶ καθαρμὸν ὃν μετῴχετο,
αὐτὴ δ' ὄπισθε δέσμ' ἔχουσα τοῖν ξένοιν
ἔστειχε χερσί. καὶ τάδ' ἦν ὕποπτα μέν,
ἤρεσκε μέντοι σοῖσι προσπόλοις, ἄναξ.
χρόνῳ δ', ἵν' ἡμῖν δρᾶν τι δὴ δοκοῖ πλέον,
ἀνωλόλυξε καὶ κατῇδε βάρβαρα
μέλη μαγεύουσ', ὡς φόνον νίζουσα δή.
ἐπεὶ δὲ δαρὸν ἦμεν ἥμενοι χρόνον,
ἐσῆλθεν ἡμᾶς μὴ λυθέντες οἱ ξένοι
κτάνοιεν αὐτὴν δραπέται τ' οἰχοίατο.
φόβῳ δ' ἃ μὴ χρῆν εἰσορᾶν καθήμεθα
σιγῇ· τέλος δὲ πᾶσιν ἦν αὑτὸς λόγος
στείχειν ἵν' ἦσαν, καίπερ οὐκ ἐωμένοις.
κἀνταῦθ' ὁρῶμεν Ἑλλάδος νεὼς σκάφος
ταρσῷ κατήρει πίτυλον ἐπτερωμένον,
ναύτας τε πεντήκοντ' ἐπὶ σκαλμῶν πλάτας
ἔχοντας, ἐκ δεσμῶν δὲ τοὺς νεανίας
ἐλευθέρους πρύμνηθεν ἑστῶτας νεώς.
κοντοῖς δὲ πρῷραν εἶχον, οἱ δ' ἐπωτίδων
ἄγκυραν ἐξανῆπτον· οἱ δέ, κλίμακας
σπεύδοντες, ἦγον διὰ χερῶν πρυμνήσια,

1327 *θαλασσίους* Hermann 1329 *οὗ* in *οὓς* mutavit L *ξένοιν* Wecklein 1334 *χερσί lp* : *χεροῖν* L P *αὐτὴ δὲ χερσὶ . . . ἔστειχ' ὄπισθε* Nauck 1336 *δοκοῖ*] *δοκῇ* L P, sed *δοκ*** primitus L 1337 *ἀνωλόλυζε* Herwerden 1338 *ματεύουσ'* L P : corr. Reiske 1340 *ἐσῆλθεν* hic L P 1343 *αὐτὸς* L P 1346 *κατῆρες*, Barnes 1349 *νεώς* Musurus : *νεῶν* L P 1350 *πρῷραν* L : *πρώροις* P (unde *κοντοὺς δὲ πρωρεῖς* Reiske) 1351 *ἀγκύρας* L P : corr. Scaliger *κλίμακα* Kirchhoff 1352 eiecit Bergk 1351–1353 *ἢ πρυμνήσια σπεύδοντες ἦγον διὰ χερῶν καὶ κλίμακα πόντῳ διδόντες* Kirchhoff

πόντῳ δὲ δόντες τοῖν ξένοιν καθίεσαν.
ἡμεῖς δ' ἀφειδήσαντες, ὡς ἐσείδομεν
δόλια τεχνήματ', εἰχόμεσθα τῆς ξένης
πρυμνησίων τε, καὶ δι' εὐθυντηρίας
οἴακας ἐξῃροῦμεν εὐπρύμνου νεώς.
λόγοι δ' ἐχώρουν· Τίνι λόγῳ πορθμεύετε
κλέπτοντες ἐκ γῆς ξόανα καὶ θυηπόλους;
τίνος τίς ὢν σὺ τήνδ' ἀπεμπολᾷς χθονός;
ὁ δ' εἶπ'· Ὀρέστης, τῆσδ' ὅμαιμος, ὡς μάθῃς,
Ἀγαμέμνονος παῖς, τήνδ' ἐμὴν κομίζομαι
λαβὼν ἀδελφήν, ἣν ἀπώλεσ' ἐκ δόμων.
ἀλλ' οὐδὲν ἧσσον εἰχόμεσθα τῆς ξένης
καὶ πρὸς σὲ ἕπεσθαι διεβιαζόμεσθά νιν·
ὅθεν τὰ δεινὰ πλήγματ' ἦν γενειάδων.
κεῖνοί τε γὰρ σίδηρον οὐκ εἶχον χεροῖν
ἡμεῖς τε· πυγμαί τ' ἦσαν ἐγκροτούμεναι,
καὶ κῶλ' ἀπ' ἀμφοῖν τοῖν νεανίαιν ἅμα
ἐς πλευρὰ καὶ πρὸς ἧπαρ ἠκοντίζετο,
ὡς τῷ ξυνάπτειν καὶ συναποκαμεῖν μέλη.
δεινοῖς δὲ σημάντροισιν ἐσφραγισμένοι
ἐφεύγομεν πρὸς κρημνόν, οἱ μὲν ἐν κάρᾳ
κάθαιμ' ἔχοντες τραύμαθ', οἱ δ' ἐν ὄμμασιν·
ὄχθοις δ' ἐπισταθέντες εὐλαβεστέρως
ἐμαρνάμεσθα καὶ πέτρους ἐβάλλομεν.
ἀλλ' εἶργον ἡμᾶς τοξόται πρύμνης ἔπι
σταθέντες ἰοῖς, ὥστ' ἀναστεῖλαι πρόσω.
κἀν τῷδε—δεινὸς γὰρ κλύδων ὤκειλε ναῦν
πρὸς γῆν, φόβος δ' ἦν ⟨παρθένῳ⟩ τέγξαι πόδα—

1353 τὴν ξένοιν P: τὴν ξένην L: corr. Seidler: τῇ ξένῃ cl. 1355 Musgrave 1358 τίνι νόμῳ Nauck πορθεύετε L et sine dubio P: corr. *p* 1359 ξόανον καὶ θυηπόλον L P: corr. Musgrave 1360 σὺ add. Markland 1368 πυγμαὶ δ' Musurus ἧσσον Badham, cl. 1370 1371 ὡς τῷ Hermann: ὥστε L P: versum delet Paley 1376 πέτροις Paley 1377 εἶργον L P 1380 παρθένῳ supplevit Wilamowitz: spatium vacuum in L P: tum coni. ὥστε μὴ *l*, ναυάταις *p*: cf. v. 1404: nempe pertusa fuit hoc loco membrana archetypi

λαβὼν Ὀρέστης ὦμον εἰς ἀριστερόν,
βὰς ἐς θάλασσαν κἀπὶ κλίμακος θορών,
ἔθηκ' ἀδελφὴν ἐντὸς εὐσήμου νεώς,
τό τ' οὐρανοῦ πέσημα, τῆς Διὸς κόρης
ἄγαλμα. ναὸς ⟨δ'⟩ ἐκ μέσης ἐφθέγξατο
βοή τις· Ὦ γῆς Ἑλλάδος ναῦται, νεὼς
λάβεσθε κώπαις ῥόθιά τ' ἐκλευκαίνετε·
ἔχομεν γὰρ ὧνπερ οὕνεκ' ἄξενον πόρον
Συμπληγάδων ἔσωθεν εἰσεπλεύσαμεν.
οἳ δὲ στεναγμὸν ἡδὺν ἐκβρυχώμενοι
ἔπαισαν ἅλμην. ναῦς δ', ἕως μὲν ἐντὸς ἦν
λιμένος, ἐχώρει στόμια, διαπερῶσα δὲ
λάβρῳ κλύδωνι συμπεσοῦσ' ἠπείγετο·
δεινὸς γὰρ ἐλθὼν ἄνεμος ἐξαίφνης νεὼς
ὠθεῖ παλίμπρυμν' ἱστί'· οἳ δ' ἐκαρτέρουν
πρὸς κῦμα λακτίζοντες· ἐς δὲ γῆν πάλιν
κλύδων παλίρρους ἦγε ναῦν. σταθεῖσα δὲ
Ἀγαμέμνονος παῖς ηὔξατ'· Ὦ Λητοῦς κόρη
σῷσόν με τὴν σὴν ἱερέαν πρὸς Ἑλλάδα
ἐκ βαρβάρου γῆς καὶ κλοπαῖς σύγγνωθ' ἐμαῖς.
φιλεῖς δὲ καὶ σὺ σὸν κασίγνητον, θεά·
φιλεῖν δὲ κἀμὲ τοὺς ὁμαίμονας δόκει.
ναῦται δ' ἐπευφήμησαν εὐχαῖσιν κόρης
παιᾶνα, γυμνὰς ἐκ ⟨πέπλων⟩ ἐπωμίδας
κώπῃ προσαρμόσαντες ἐκ κελεύσματος.

1383 *εὐσήμου* cf. I. A. 255: *εὐσέλμου* Pierson 1384 *τό τ'* Markland: *τὸ δ'* L P 1385 *ναὸς* Nauck: *νηὸς* L P, cf. Hec. 1263, Med. 523 δ' add. Markland 1386, 1387 *ναύτης λεώς, λάβεσθε κώπης* F. G. Schmidt (*κώπης* Reiske) *τε λευκαίνετε* L P: corr. Scaliger 1388 *ἄξενον* Markland: vid. 125: *εὔξεινον* L P 1392 Fortasse *ἐχώρει, διαπερῶσα δὲ στόμα* 1395 *ὠθεῖ* Kirchhoff: *ὤθει* L P *παλίμπρυμν' ἱστί'* Mekler: *πάλιν πρυμνήσι'* L P: *παλιμπρυμνηδόν* Hermann v. 1346 huc post 1394 traiecto 1396 *δὲ γῆν* editio Brubachiana: *γῆν δὲ* L P: *γῆν δὴ* *l* 1397 *παλλίρους* L P: corr. *l* 1399 *ἱέρειαν* L P 1404 *πέπλων* supplevit Markland: spatium vacuum in L P: *βαλόντες* suppl. *l* (vel L): *χερῶν* *p*

μᾶλλον δὲ μᾶλλον πρὸς πέτρας ᾔει σκάφος·
χὠ μέν τις ἐς θάλασσαν ὡρμήθη ποσίν,
ἄλλος δὲ πλεκτὰς ἐξανῆπτεν ἀγκύλας.
κἀγὼ μὲν εὐθὺς πρὸς σὲ δεῦρ' ἀπεστάλην,
σοὶ τὰς ἐκεῖθεν σημανῶν, ἄναξ, τύχας.
ἀλλ' ἕρπε, δεσμὰ καὶ βρόχους λαβὼν χεροῖν·
εἰ μὴ γὰρ οἶδμα νήνεμον γενήσεται,
οὐκ ἔστιν ἐλπὶς τοῖς ξένοις σωτηρίας.
πόντου δ' ἀνάκτωρ Ἴλιόν τ' ἐπισκοπεῖ
σεμνὸς Ποσειδῶν, Πελοπίδαις ἐναντίος,
καὶ νῦν παρέξει τὸν Ἀγαμέμνονος γόνον
σοὶ καὶ πολίταις, ὡς ἔοικεν, ἐν χεροῖν
λαβεῖν, ἀδελφήν θ', ἣ φόνον τὸν Αὐλίδι
ἀμνημόνευτον θεᾷ προδοῦσ' ἁλίσκεται.
Χο. ὦ τλῆμον Ἰφιγένεια, συγγόνου μέτα
θανῇ πάλιν μολοῦσα δεσποτῶν χέρας.
Θο. ὦ πάντες ἀστοὶ τῆσδε βαρβάρου χθονός,
οὐκ εἶα πώλοις ἐμβαλόντες ἡνίας
παράκτιοι δραμεῖσθε κἀκβολὰς νεὼς
Ἑλληνίδος δέξεσθε, σὺν δὲ τῇ θεῷ
σπεύδοντες ἄνδρας δυσσεβεῖς θηράσετε,
οἱ δ' ὠκυπομποὺς ἕλξετ' ἐς πόντον πλάτας;
ὡς ἐκ θαλάσσης ἔκ τε γῆς ἱππεύμασι
λαβόντες αὐτοὺς ἢ κατὰ στύφλου πέτρας
ῥίψωμεν, ἢ σκόλοψι πήξωμεν δέμας.
ὑμᾶς δὲ τὰς τῶνδ' ἵστορας βουλευμάτων,
γυναῖκες, αὖθις, ἡνίκ' ἂν σχολὴν λάβω,
ποινασόμεσθα· νῦν δὲ τὴν προκειμένην
σπουδὴν ἔχοντες οὐ μενοῦμεν ἥσυχοι.

1408 ἄλλος P et ex ἄλλω factum L : ἄλλοι *p*   ἐξανῆπτεν L : ἐξανῆπτον P et fortasse primitus L   1415 δ' post Πελοπίδαις L P : del. Matthiae   1418 ἀδελφήν θ' Musgrave : τ' ἀδελφὴν L P   Fortasse post Marklandum et Badhamum ἥ, φόνων τῶν Αὐλίδι ἀμνημόνευτος, θεὰν προδοῦσ'   1421 πάλιν L : πόλιν P   1430 ἢ 'ν σκόλοψι Wecklein   1432 γυναῖκες Markland : γυναῖκας L P   αὖτις L P

ΑΘΗΝΑ

ποῖ ποῖ διωγμὸν τόνδε πορθμεύεις, ἄναξ
Θόας; ἄκουσον τῆσδ' Ἀθηναίας λόγους.
παῦσαι διώκων ῥεῦμά τ' ἐξορμῶν στρατοῦ·
πεπρωμένος γὰρ θεσφάτοισι Λοξίου
δεῦρ' ἦλθ' Ὀρέστης, τόν τ' Ἐρινύων χόλον
φεύγων ἀδελφῆς τ' Ἄργος ἐσπέμψων δέμας
ἄγαλμά θ' ἱερὸν εἰς ἐμὴν ἄξων χθόνα,
τῶν νῦν παρόντων πημάτων ἀναψυχάς.
πρὸς μὲν σὲ ὅδ' ἡμῖν μῦθος· ὃν δ' ἀποκτενεῖν
δοκεῖς Ὀρέστην ποντίῳ λαβὼν σάλῳ,
ἤδη Ποσειδῶν χάριν ἐμὴν ἀκύμονα
πόντου τίθησι νῶτα πορθμεύειν πλάτῃ.
μαθὼν δ', Ὀρέστα, τὰς ἐμὰς ἐπιστολάς—
κλύεις γὰρ αὐδὴν καίπερ οὐ παρὼν θεᾶς—
χώρει λαβὼν ἄγαλμα σύγγονόν τε σήν.
ὅταν δ' Ἀθήνας τὰς θεοδμήτους μόλῃς,
χῶρός τις ἔστιν Ἀτθίδος πρὸς ἐσχάτοις
ὅροισι, γείτων δειράδος Καρυστίας,
ἱερός, Ἁλάς νιν οὑμὸς ὀνομάζει λεώς·
ἐνταῦθα τεύξας ναὸν ἵδρυσαι βρέτας,
ἐπώνυμον γῆς Ταυρικῆς πόνων τε σῶν,
οὓς ἐξεμόχθεις περιπολῶν καθ' Ἑλλάδα
οἴστροις Ἐρινύων. Ἄρτεμιν δέ νιν βροτοὶ
τὸ λοιπὸν ὑμνήσουσι Ταυροπόλον θεάν.
νόμον τε θὲς τόνδ'· ὅταν ἑορτάζῃ λεώς,
τῆς σῆς σφαγῆς ἄποιν' ἐπισχέτω ξίφος
δέρῃ πρὸς ἀνδρὸς αἷμά τ' ἐξανιέτω,
ὁσίας ἕκατι θεά θ' ὅπως τιμὰς ἔχῃ.

1438 πεπρωμένοις L P: corr. Hermann: πεπρωμένον Monk 1439 τόν τ' L: τῶν τ' P 1441b habet L: om. P (ideoque Musurus et veteres libri impressi) 1442 σὲ L: σ' P *l* 1445 πορθμεύειν Tyrwhitt: πορθμεύων L P 1452 ἅλας L P 1453 τεύξας Pierson: τάξας L P 1454 γῆς Hermann: τῆς L P 1458 θὲς Porson: θέσθε L P 1460 ἐξανυέτω L P: corr. Heath 1461 θεά θ' Markland: θεᾶς L P

σὲ δ' ἀμφὶ σεμνάς, Ἰφιγένεια, κλίμακας
Βραυρωνίας δεῖ τῇδε κληδουχεῖν θεᾷ·
οὗ καὶ τεθάψῃ κατθανοῦσα, καὶ πέπλων
ἄγαλμά σοι θήσουσιν εὐπήνους ὑφάς,
ἃς ἂν γυναῖκες ἐν τόκοις ψυχορραγεῖς
λίπωσ' ἐν οἴκοις. τάσδε δ' ἐκπέμπειν χθονὸς
Ἑλληνίδας γυναῖκας ἐξεφίεμαι
γνώμης δικαίας οὕνεκ'

. . . .

ἐκσῴσασα δὲ
καὶ πρίν σ' Ἀρείοις ἐν πάγοις ψήφους ἴσας
κρίνασ', Ὀρέστα· καὶ νόμισμ' ἔσται τόδε,
νικᾶν ἰσήρεις ὅστις ἂν ψήφους λάβῃ.
ἀλλ' ἐκκομίζου σὴν κασιγνήτην χθονός,
Ἀγαμέμνονος παῖ.—καὶ σὺ μὴ θυμοῦ, Θόας.

Θο. ἄνασσ' Ἀθάνα, τοῖσι τῶν θεῶν λόγοις
ὅστις κλύων ἄπιστος, οὐκ ὀρθῶς φρονεῖ.
ἐγὼ δ' Ὀρέστῃ τ', εἰ φέρων βρέτας θεᾶς
βέβηκ', ἀδελφῇ τ' οὐχὶ θυμοῦμαι· τί γὰρ
πρὸς τοὺς σθένοντας θεοὺς ἁμιλλᾶσθαι καλόν;
ἴτωσαν ἐς σὴν σὺν θεᾶς ἀγάλματι
γαῖαν, καθιδρύσαιντό τ' εὐτυχῶς βρέτας.
πέμψω δὲ καὶ τάσδ' Ἑλλάδ' εἰς εὐδαίμονα
γυναῖκας, ὥσπερ σὸν κέλευσμ' ἐφίεται.
παύσω δὲ λόγχην ἣν ἐπαίρομαι ξένοις
ναῶν τ' ἐρετμά, σοὶ τάδ' ὡς δοκεῖ, θεά.

Αθ. αἰνῶ· τὸ γὰρ χρεὼν σοῦ τε καὶ θεῶν κρατεῖ.

1462 λείμακας Pierson 1463 τῆσδε κληδουχεῖν θεᾶς L P : corr. Markland 1467 λείπωσ' L P 1469 lacunam post οὕνεκ' statuit Reiske (post ἐξεφίεμαι Brodaeus) 1469, 1470 ἐκσώσασά σε καὶ πρίν γ' L P : ἐξέσωσα δὲ καὶ πρίν σ' Schol. Ar. Ran. 685 1471 ἔσται τόδε Markland : εἰς ταὐτό γε L P 1473 κασιγνήτην Elmsley : κασίγνητον L P 1478, 1479 τί γάρ; et ἁμιλλᾶσθαι κενόν Bruhn 1485 ναῶν Radermacher: νηῶν L P θεά Musurus : θεᾷ L P 1486 Αθ. notam om. L P : add. Musurus et recentior manus in L (non *l*) τὸ γὰρ χρῆν Dindorf (χρὴ Wecklein)

ἴτ᾽, ὦ πνοαί, ναυσθλοῦσθε τὸν Ἀγαμέμνονος
παῖδ᾽ εἰς Ἀθήνας· συμπορεύσομαι δ᾽ ἐγὼ
σῴζουσ᾽ ἀδελφῆς τῆς ἐμῆς σεμνὸν βρέτας.

Χο. — ἴτ᾽ ἐπ᾽ εὐτυχίᾳ τῆς σῳζομένης
μοίρας εὐδαίμονες ὄντες.
— ἀλλ᾽, ὦ σεμνὴ παρά τ᾽ ἀθανάτοις
καὶ παρὰ θνητοῖς, Παλλὰς Ἀθάνα,
δράσομεν οὕτως ὡς σὺ κελεύεις.
μάλα γὰρ τερπνὴν κἀνέλπιστον
φήμην ἀκοαῖσι δέδεγμαι.

ὦ μέγα σεμνὴ Νίκη, τὸν ἐμὸν
βίοτον κατέχοις
καὶ μὴ λήγοις στεφανοῦσα.

1487 Apollinis notam praefigunt L P (σώζων v. 1489 codd. recc. quidam): notam delevit Musurus τὼ Ἀγαμέμνονος Markland 1490 Χο. Seidler: Αθ. L P 1491 εὐδαίμονος L P: corr. Musurus ὄντες L P: ὄντος primitus L 1492 Χο. L^2 P: notam om. L 1495 τερπνὴν Ludv. Dindorf: τερπνὸν L P 1497 νίκα L P: corr. *l* 1497–1499 tales versus etiam ad fin. Orestis et Phoenissarum leguntur: cf. Lucian. Piscator. c. 39: seclusit amicus Matthiaei. Subscriptionem εὐριπίδου ἰφιγένεια ἡ ἐν ταύροις habet P et, postmodo additam, L (h. e. is qui in hac fabula L, alias L^2, me iudice, nuncupatur: vide Praef. Ionis)

ο

χαριεεις = χαριεῖ

άς
ι

α + εις =

ΘΕΜΙΝΔΕΠΕΙΤΑCΙωΝ

ΠΑΙΔΑΠΕΝΑCCΑΤΟ —

1 μηλ

Just Remember

PRESBYTERIAN MINISTERS' FUND

HE THAT SOWETH BOUNTIFULLY SHALL REAP BOUNTIFULLY

43,44, 45,46

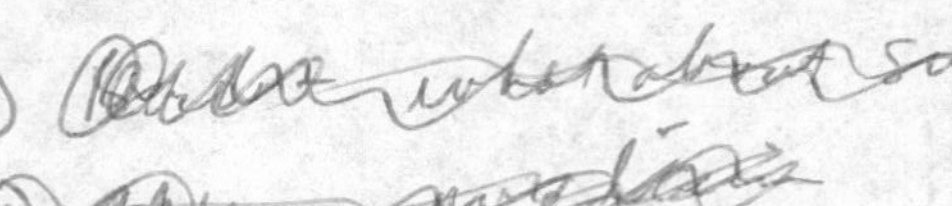

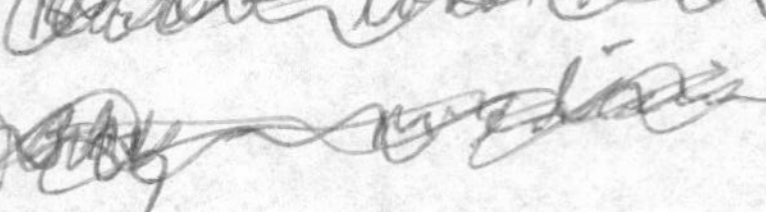

COMMENTARY

Ὑπόθεσις. The hypothesis goes back in content, if not in form, to Aristophanes of Byzantium. Unfortunately it is corrupt and fragmentary and lacks the usual note on the date of production, the concomitant plays, and their order in the competition.

l. 2. L's παραγεν⟨ηθείς⟩ and the grammatical correction παραγενόμενος are redundant with and after ἐλθών. P's παρακινηθείς ('maddened') gives good sense, but it is here out of place. It probably stood, as Wecklein suggests, after τῆς νεὼς καί, whence it was ousted by a marginal gloss μανείς which in its turn was corrupted to φανείς (for a similar corruption see l. 340 below). If we keep παραγενηθείς here, we must at least correct φανείς to μανείς, as our text, following Wilamowitz, does.

Πρόλογος 1–122:

(*a*) Prologue proper spoken by Iph., 1–41.
(*b*) Iph.'s dream, 42–66.
(*c*) Or. and Pyl. stichomythia, 67–76.
(*d*) Or. reproaches Apollo; consents to hide during the day and at night steal the image, 77–122.

1. The typical Euripidean genealogy; cf. Eur.'s own claim in Ar. *Ra.* (946–7) οὐξιὼν πρώτιστα μέν μοι τὸ γένος εἶπ' ἂν εὐθὺς | τοῦ δράματος. The schol. on Ar. *Ach.* 47 tells us that Amphitheos' comic genealogy is a parody of this, but we cannot place the *IT.* before 425 B.C., the date of Ar. *Ach.* In Ar. *Ra.* 1232 the opening of our prologue is subjected to the ληκύθιον joke.

Ταντάλειος, son of Tantalus; cf. Τυνδαρείας (l. 5) = daughter of Tyndareus, and Ἀγαμεμνόνιον (l. 170), etc.

2. **θοαῖσιν ἵπποις:** it is true that *by means of* his horses' speed Pelops won the hand of Hippodamia, daughter of Oenomaus. The story is told in Pi. *O.* 1. So here ἵπποις may be an instrumental dat. going with γαμεῖ. It is, however, easier to take it as either an instrumental or, more likely, a comitative dat. with μολών; i.e. 'arriving by means of' or 'arriving with'; cf. *Il.* 16. 154 ὃς καὶ θνητὸς ἐὼν ἕπεθ' ἵπποις ἀθανάτοισιν (Kühner-Gerth, *Griech. Gram.* II. i, p. 430). **γαμεῖ,** historic pres., common in words expressing relationship, cf. τίκτει (l. 23).

3. The παῖς of the MSS. is difficult with a plural subject. It is better to accept Badham's ἄπο or παῖδε δ' Ἀτρέως, taking παῖς as a copyist's error caused by the παῖς of l. 5.

6. **δίναις . . . πυκναῖς:** the dangerous currents of the Euripus mentioned by Aesch. (*Ag.* 190) παλιρρόχθοις ἐν Αὐλίδος τόποις, and Soph. (*Ant.* 1145) στονόεντα πορθμόν and described by Livy (28. 6. 10).

8. **ὡς δοκεῖ:** explained by l. 28 sqq. Iph. was not really sacrificed. Better translated 'as he thought (lit. thinks)' than 'as is generally believed'. Cf. the δοκῶν of l. 785. The form οὕνεκα for the *preposition* as well as the conjunction is well attested in inscriptions (see Meisterhans, *Gram. der att. Insch.*[3], p. 216).

9. κλειναῖς: explained in the following lines (note γάρ). In *IA.* 1600 Eur. writes Αὐλίδος κοίλους μυχούς and some edd. have for that reason wished to read κοίλαις here. This is quite unnecessary.

10. χιλίων: cf. below, l. 141, E. *IA.* 174 ἐλάταις χιλιόναυσι and *ib.* 355 νεῶν | χιλίων ἄρχων; (also *Andr.* 106; *Or.* 352; *Rh.* 262). So Thuc. gives the round number 1,200 (1. 10. 4). Homer in the Catalogue gives a total of 1,186.

11. P's Ἑλληνικήν may be due to some such gloss on στόλον as παρασκευήν. This view is preferable to that which discards στόλον in favour of στολήν, a word which Eur. does not use = fleet. It is of course possible that στόλον is itself a gloss introduced into the text; hence Weil's suggestion πλάτην Ἑλληνικήν.

12. The compound **καλλίνικον** stands for a descriptive gen.: τὸν καλῆς νίκης στέφανον, to win the fair crown of victory over Ilium; cf. τὰ μεσόμφαλα γᾶς . . . μαντεῖα (Soph. *OT.* 480) = τὰ μέσου ὀμφαλοῦ γᾶς μαντεῖα, and καλλίπαιδα στέφανον (E. *HF.* 839) = στεφ. καλῶν παίδων.

13. If the **Ἀχαιούς** of the MSS. is right we must take it as subj. of λαβεῖν, 'wishing the Achaeans to get'. But with E. *Supp.* 315 before us (πόλει παρόν σοι στέφανον εὐκλείας λαβεῖν) it is better to accept Lenting's dative.

'to avenge the insult offered to H.'s marriage'. This participle has been called (Monro, *Hom. Gr.*[2] § 245) the participle of implied predication. Much commoner in Latin (e.g. *mortuus Caesar* = *mors Caesaris*) than in Greek, where it is found almost exclusively in Homer (e.g. *Il.* 13. 38 νοστήσαντα ἄνακτα = the lord's return) and Hdt. (e.g. i. 34 μετὰ Σόλωνα οἰχόμενον = after Solon's departure). μετέρχεσθαι = *to go in search of*, then *to prosecute* (with acc. of person). In E. *Cyc.* 280, 1 (οἳ μετῆλθεθ' ἁρπαγὰς | Ἑλένης . . . Ἰλίου πόλιν) we get both accusatives. Influenced by this Markland suggested Ἑλένην. But vengeance was taken not so much on Helen as on Troy.

15. Cf. A. *Ag.* 188 ἀπλοίᾳ κεναγγεῖ; E. *IA.* 88 ἥμεσθ' ἀπλοίᾳ χρώμενοι κατ' Αὐλίδα. No convincing correction of this difficult line has yet been made. We must accept Barnes' δ' for the MSS. τ' to secure connexion, for the τε after δεινῆς must look forward to that after πνευμάτων, and even if it did not we want 'but' (δέ), not 'and' (τε), to begin this sentence. But 'getting dread non-sailing weather and not getting winds' is impossible, and the alternative, to take δεινῆς ἀπλοίας as gen. absol. understanding οὔσης, is worse. Witzschel's τε for the MSS. τ' οὐ, printed in our text, is better: 'getting dread non-sailing weather and ⟨unfavourable⟩ winds' (cf. Thuc. 2. 85. 6 καὶ ὁ μὲν . . . ὑπ' ἀνέμων καὶ ἀπλοίας ἐνδιέτριψεν οὐκ ὀλίγον χρόνον); or, as a hendiadys, 'dire straits caused by winds'. Nauck's δεθεὶς δ' ἀπλοίᾳ gives good sense, but it is hard to see how the corruption occurred, and the same may be said of Dindorf's σχεθεὶς δ' ἀπλοίᾳ,

Weil's δεινῆς δ' ἀπλοίας πνεύμασιν συντυγχάνων, and Wecklein's δεινῆς δ' ἀπλοίας πνευμάτων τυχὼν κακῶν. Simpler and better is Madvig's δεινῇ δ' ἀπλοίᾳ, a causal dat. joined to a causal participle, as at E. *Andr.* 805 πατρός τ' ἐρημωθεῖσα συννοίᾳ θ' ἅμα. Prof. Housman (*CR.* 1887, p. 240) ingeniously suggests νήστει δ' ἀπλοίᾳ = because of famine-causing ἄπλοια (cf. A. *Ag.* 192 πνοαὶ . . . νήστιδες), supposing a confusion of letters, i.e. νηστ-ει-δ becoming δ-ει-νηστ.

16. ἔμπυρα: divination from flames, ἐμπυροσκοπία. Homer mentions θυοσκόοι in *Il.* 24. 221 who may have had such functions. Aesch. (*Pr.* 498) has φλογωπὰ σήματα. Cf. Teiresias' account in S. *Ant.* 1005 sqq. where ἐκ . . . θυμάτων |Ἥφαιστος οὐκ ἔλαμπεν. 'It was a bad sign, if the fire was smothered in smoke, or played feebly around the flesh without consuming it' (Jebb). The obscure passage in E. *Ph.* (1254–8) refers to divination by means of the shape of the sacrificial flame. Cf. also A. *Th.* 25 πυρὸς δίχα ('without divination from fire'), E. *Supp.* 155 μάντεις δ' ἐπῆλθες ἐμπύρων τ' εἶδες φλόγα; and *ib.* 212, *Hel.* 747, *Ba.* 257.

18. ἀφορμίσῃ: the compound does not occur elsewhere. On the analogy of ὁρμίζω 'to bring to anchor', ὁρμίζομαι 'to come to anchor', it might be advisable to accept Kirchhoff's ἀφορμίσῃς.

20. ἐνιαυτός: i.e. the year of Iph.'s birth. As Iph. was of marriageable age at the time of the prospective start of the expedition from Aulis, we must suppose that Ag.'s vow, the full import of which he did not realize at the time of his making it, had remained unfulfilled for at least fifteen years. In E. *IA.* (ll. 528–31) Ag. pictures Odysseus as saying of him ὡς ὑπέστην θῦμα, κᾆτ' ἐψευδόμην.

21. φωσφόρῳ = Artemis as the moon-goddess. Cf. E. *IA.* 1570, 1 ὦ θηροκτόνε, | τὸ λαμπρὸν εἱλίσσουσ' ἐν εὐφρόνῃ φάος; Cic. *ND.* ii. 27. 68 Dianam . . . et Lunam eandem esse putant ⟨Graeci⟩. See introduction, p. viii.

For the vow cf. Cic. *de off.* iii. 25. 95 quid? Agamemnon cum devovisset Dianae quod in suo regno pulcherrimum natum esset illo anno immolavit Iphigeniam, qua nihil erat eo quidem anno natum pulchrius.

22. Notice οὖν = 'well'; 'proceeding to a new point' (Denniston, *Greek Particles*, p. 426). Clytemnestra is spelt correctly in Greek without the 'ν' and is so found in an inscription (IG. xiv. 930). This spelling agrees with the old Latin Clutemestra (Livius Andron., *Aigisthus*, fr. 6) and conforms to the derivation ἡ κλυτὰ μηδομένη (*EM.* 521. 18 παρὰ τὸ κλυτὸν . . . καὶ τὸ μήδω (i.e. μήδομαι)). At A. *Ag.* 1100 Cassandra, punning on C.'s name, asks τί ποτε μήδεται;

A 'ν' sometimes attaches itself to μ; e.g. δίδυμνος = δίδυμος (Pi. *O.* 3. 35), ἀπάλαμνος = ἀπάλαμος (cf. παλαμναῖος fr. παλάμη), etc. There may even have been a definite intention to connect the second part of the name with the verb μνηστεύω (cf. l. 208 below and note). The '*αι*' of Κλυταιμήστρα may be explained on the analogy of, e.g., μεσαιπόλιος (*Il.* 13. 361) = μεσοπόλιος, or may be due to a form of the adjective *κλυταῖος (Brugmann, *Griech. Gram.*[4], p. 202).

23. Notice the common historic present **τίκτει** = is the mother of; cf. E. *Ba.* 2 Διόνυσος, ὃν τίκτει ποθ' ἡ Κάδμου κόρη. Homer uses the present only of the father; in later Greek it could be used of either parent.

The subject of the parenthesis is Calchas and its verb is λέγει understood from l. 16; '⟨said Calchas⟩, referring the title of fairest to me'.

24. The subject, i.e. the Greeks, must be supplied if the MSS. are correct. Many editors, however, accept Lenting's τέχναι which gives a subject to παρείλοντο.

27. Cf. A. *Ag.* 234 λαβεῖν ἀέρδην of Iphigenia. So Lucr. 1. 95 sublata virum manibus. **ἐκαινόμην**, possibly an inceptive, but more probably a conative imperfect (cf. ἔσφαζον, l. 360, etc.); more easily understood had it been in the active: *they were for killing me.*

29. There is no need to suspect the dat. Ἀχαιοῖς (going with ἀντιδοῦσα), though Nauck would read Ἀχαιούς (with ἐξέκλεψεν) on the analogy of κρύπτειν τινά τι. No such construction is actually found with ἐκκλέπτω.

31. There are three possible explanations of **οὗ γῆς ἀνάσσει βαρβάροισι**: (1) γῆς partitive gen.; οὗ γῆς = ubi terrarum, in which case ἀν. governs βαρβ.; (2) ἀν. governs γῆς with βαρβ. as dat. of advantage (cf. E. *Or.* 1690 ναύταις μεδέουσα θαλάσσης); (3) γῆς ἀνάσσει as one idea with βαρβ. as object. Such compounds are common in Greek, e.g. E. *Rh.* 781–3 ἵππους . . . εἶδον . . . λύκους ἐπεμβεβῶτας . . . ῥάχιν, where the last two words, forming one idea (*to back-ride*), govern ἵππους. Emendation (e.g. Nauck's γύαις δ') is unnecessary. Against (1) and (3) is the fact that Eur. uses ἀνάσσειν + gen. elsewhere fifteen times and never with the dat.

32. This punning derivation of **Θόας** from θοός is quite in the tragic manner; cf. E. *Hel.* 13, 14 where Θεονόη is so called τὰ θεῖα γὰρ | τά τ' ὄντα καὶ μέλλοντα πάντ' ἠπίστατο; *Ion* 661–3 Ἴωνα δ' ὀνομάζω σε . . . ὁθούνεκ' ἐξιόντι μοι . . . ἴχνος συνῆψας πρῶτος; *Ph.* 26, 7 σφυρῶν . . . ὅθεν νιν Ἑλλὰς ὠνόμαζεν Οἰδίπουν; *ib.* 636, 7 ὄνομα Πολυνείκη πατὴρ | ἔθετο . . . νεικέων ἐπώνυμον; *Ba.* 367 Πενθεὺς δ' ὅπως μὴ πένθος εἰσοίσει δόμοις; *ib.* 508 ἐνδυστυχῆσαι τοὔνομ' (i.e. Pentheus) ἐπιτήδειος εἶ; *IA.* 321 μῶν τρέσας οὐκ ἀνακαλύψω βλέφαρον, Ἀτρέως γεγώς; *Rh.* 158, 9 ἐπώνυμος . . . Δόλων (i.e. from δόλος); *fr.* 181 τὸν μὲν κίκλησκε Ζῆθον· ἐζήτησε γὰρ . . .; *fr.* 517 Μελέαγρε, μελέαν γάρ ποτ' ἀγρεύεις ἄγραν. Aeschylus plays on the name Prometheus: ψευδωνύμως σε δαίμονες Προμηθέα | καλοῦσιν· αὐτὸν γάρ σε δεῖ προμηθέως (*Pr.* 85, 6); on Helen's in the well-known passage in the Agamemnon (688 ἑλένας, ἕλανδρος, ἑλέπτολις), and at *Ch.* 949 explains Δίκη as Δι[ὸς] κ[όρ]η. So, too, Sophocles derives Ajax' name (Αἴας) from αἰαῖ (*Aj.* 430) and Odysseus' from *ὀδύσσομαι (1st aor. infin. ὀδύσασθαι) (*fr.* 965), this last borrowed from Homer (*Od.* I. 62). Aristoph. in the Lemnians (*fr.* 357) produces a *lucus a non lucendo* pun upon the name: Θόας, βραδύτατος ὢν ἐν ἀνθρώποις δραμεῖν.

For **πόδα τιθεὶς** cf. E. *Andr.* 545, 6 δέδορκα . . . Πηλέα . . . | σπουδῇ τιθέντα δεῦρο γηραιὸν πόδα, and *Supp.* 171, 2 ξένον πόδα | θεῖναι. Better therefore taken lit. 'setting a swift foot equal to wings' than 'equating a swift foot to wings' (i.e. τιθεὶς ἴσον = ἰσῶν) as some have taken it.

34. The subj. of **τίθησι** (historic present) is Artemis, not Thoas. ἱερέα (not ἱέρεια or ἱερία) is the correct Attic form and should be read at E. *Or.* 261, *Ba.* 1114, and l. 1399 of our play. In all these passages the MSS. offer the corrupted forms (cf. Meisterh.[3] p. 40).

35–6. Difficult lines. If we are to keep them (some edd. do not) we must accept the correction **τοῖσιν** for τοῖσιδ' in L and P, for we need the relative. Except in lyric Eur. seldom uses the article = relative; there are, however, definite instances, e.g. κτείνουσα τοὺς οὐ χρὴ κτανεῖν (*Andr.* 810); πελέκει τῷ πατὴρ ἀπώλετο (*El.* 279). The gen. ἑορτῆς may go either with **νόμοισι** or with **τοῖσιν**; but it is better to put a comma at νόμοισι and take it with the former. The ἧς of the aposiopetic relative clause has for its antecedent ἑορτῆς and not Artemis. It is true that Artemis was called Καλή and Καλλίστη; but we cannot suppose that her priestess would say anything so derogatory as that Artemis was fair only in name.

One mitigation of the difficulty is to suppose Ἄρτεμις a gloss on θεά and to replace it by χρώμεσθ' (Weil), 'whence we use rites such as the goddess loves in our feasts, of which', etc.

But whether or not we accept Weil's emendation the double relative is offensive and the logic of ὅθεν suspect. The *type* of rites does not depend on the *installation* of the priestess. (Some edd. take ὅθεν = 'ever since which time'. But such a temporal use of ὅθεν would be unique.) Any emendation on the lines of ὅθ' (i.e. ὅθι = οὗ)—and there have been many (e.g. Canter's ὅθ' ἐννόμοισι)—may be ruled out at once as never in trag., except in the doubtful S. *El.* 709, is ὅθι found in iambics, and even when it occurs in lyric the iota is never elided. Prof. Housman (*CR.* 1887, p. 241) suggests νόμοις ἵν' ὀθνείοισιν, supposing that here, as at l. 15, there has been a confusion of letters.

38–41. If 38 and 39 are genuine we can only suppose that Iph. finds the *silence* she has announced impossible. It is more likely that these two lines have been inserted by some over-knowledgeable scribe. (Or possibly by an actor; so Mr. D. L. Page, *Actors' Interpolations in Greek Tragedy*, p. 76.)

If we keep the lines, and if θύω—the reading of L—is to be accepted, we get a strange asyndeton after the end of l. 39. But the θυ of P and its correction θείου suggest the taking of 38, 9 as a clause, not a main sentence. θείου itself would do and might be translated: 'for the custom being hallowed . . . I begin the rite in the case of any Greek who . . .'. Kvičala would read θύειν, i.e. τοῦ νόμου ὄντος θύειν = 'the custom being to sacrifice'; cf. A. *Eu.* 448 ἄφθογγον εἶναι τὸν παλαμναῖον νόμος.

κατάρχομαι (a technical word in ritual, like ἀπάρχομαι) refers to the sprinkling of the victim's head with water (cf. ὑδραίνειν, l. 54; δρόσον, l. 443; χερνίψομαι, l. 622).

If τῶνδ' ἀνακτόρων θεᾶς of l. 66 is genuine (and there is no reason to suspect it) the same phrase is at least a little awkward here. It is possible that ll. 40, 1 also should be excised.

43. **ἄκος**: the telling to the bright day of the visions of the dark night is regarded as their 'healing'. Cf. S. *El.* 424, 5 Ἡλίῳ | δείκνυσι τοὔναρ, on which passage the schol. comments: ἔθος ἦν τοῖς παλαιοῖς ὁπότε καθ' ὕπνους ὄναρ δεινὸν θεάσαιντο, ἅμα πρωῒ πρὸς τὸν ἥλιον λέγειν, ἵνα, ἐπειδὴ ἐναντίος οὗτός ἐστι τῇ νυκτί, ἀποτροπὴν ἐργάσηται τούτου. Cf. also E. *Med.* 56 sqq. εἰ δή, which may be either sceptical or confident (see Denniston, p. 223 note), is probably here the latter and so almost = εἴπερ = 'since'.

45. In the face of E. *Ba.* 221 θιάσοις ἐν μέσοισιν, *ib.* 259 ἐν βάκχαισι . . . μέσαις and *Rh.* 486 ἐν μέσοισι συμμάχοις, Musgrave's παρθενῶσι (*women's quarters*) δ' ἐν μέσοις is needless.

46. L & S[9] explain σάλος as 'any unsteady, tossing motion'; usually = sea-wave, here = earth-wave. Cf. A. *Pr.* 1081 χθὼν σεσάλευται. With σεισθῆναι we can understand ἔδοξε from ἔδοξα of l. 44. In this case with l. 47 we return to the first person. Alternatively we can take ἔδοξα = 'I thought' rather than 'I seemed', in which case νῶτα σεισθῆναι is parallel to ⟨ἐγὼ⟩ εὕδειν.

48. **ἐρείψιμον**: predicative with βεβλημένον = fallen in ruin. The σταθμός is properly the bearing pillar of the roof, generally used in the singular (e.g. *Od.* 1. 333, etc.). Cf. Virg. *Aen.* 2. 290 ruit alto a culmine Troia.

Reiske's ἐρέψιμον = 'roofing' (attributive) is not impossible.

50–4. Porson's emendation, received into our text, gives good sense though the asyndeton is strange. It is perhaps better to take Victorius' δ' ἐλείφθη . . . ὡς ἔδοξε which preserves the connexion. In this case καθεῖναι and λαβεῖν are constructed with ἔδοξε understood out of ὡς ἔδοξε.

ἐπίκρανον: usually = a head-dress; here (as at Pi. *fr.* 78–9. 14, ἂν δ' ἐπικράνοις σχέθον πέτραν . . . κίονες) = κιονόκρανον, a capital: cf. Eustath. (701. 1 = 852, 53) ἐπίκρανον, ὅπερ ἐστὶ κεφαλὴ κίονος. Note the so-called *epic* lengthening of the ι (cf. Descroix, *Trim. iamb.*, p. 16: Tucker in *C.R.* 1897, pp. 341 sqq.). Hermann's ἐκ δέ γ' ἐπικράνων is unnecessary. Weil would read μόνος δὲ λειφθεὶς στῦλος εἷς . . . ἐκ μὲν ἐπῑκράνων, but the 'correction' is needless and the introduced antithesis ἐκ μὲν ἐπικράνων

. . . φθέγμα δέ forced and unnatural. For the metaphor cf. A. *Ag.* 897, 8 where Clyt. calls Ag. ὑψηλῆς στέγης | στῦλον ποδήρη.

With ὑδραίνειν understand ἔδοξα from ἔδοξε.

54. τιμῶσ', 'in due observance of'; cf. τιμάς in ll. 748 and 776 below, and τιμᾶν l. 960.

55. For συμβάλλειν = interpret, cf. E. *Med.* 675 σοφώτερ' ἢ κατ' ἄνδρα συμβαλεῖν ἔπη. So at A. *Pr.* 775 εὐξύμβλητος = easy to interpret, and at S. *Tr.* 694 ἀξύμβλητος = incomprehensible.

56. The main sense is in the relative clause. She means: Or. is the reference of my dream and he must be dead.

57. As Artemidorus, Stobaeus, and Menander all quote this line as στῦλοι . . . παῖδές εἰσιν most edd. give this order for that of the MSS. εἰσὶ παῖδες.

59, 60. Iph. does not know of the existence of Pylades, son of Strophius, king of Phocis, and of Anaxibia, sister of Agamemnon (cf. ll. 249 and 920). What she says here is in effect: 'My dream can refer to no one but Orestes, there having been no other στῦλος δόμων at the time of my supposed death'. But there might have been, and in fact there was, one subsequently; and Iph. could not have been so illogical, not to say stupid, as not to realize this fact, supposing her to envisage any possible alternative to Orestes at all. These two lines were evidently inserted by some scribe who perceived that, had Iph. known of the existence of Pylades, her dream would have had an uncertain reference; cf. Page, *Actors' Interpolations*, pp. 76, 7.

Besides this ἐς φίλους is almost meaningless. To bear any sense at all φίλους must = relatives other than my brother.

64. The acc. Ἑλληνίδας γυναῖκας is attracted from the dat. into the case of the relative ἅς. A common idiom.

65. Our text accepts Markland's τίνος for the MSS. τινός, and so gives us two sentences: a question and a statement. Keeping τινός and putting a comma at πάρεισιν we get a causal clause followed by the main sentence: 'but since for some reason . . ., I will go . . .'. In this case ἀλλά = ἀλλὰ . . . γάρ This construction, though rare, is well attested. It is usually followed by an imperative; e.g. S. *Ph.* 1153 ἀλλ' ἀνέδην ὅδε χῶρος ἐρύκεται . . . ἕρπετε; E. *Ph.* 99, 100 ἀλλ' οὔτις ἀστῶν τοῖσδε χρίμπτεται δόμοις | κέδρου παλαιὰν κλίμακ' ἐκπέρα ποδί. εἶμι is here almost a self-command. However, futures also are found; e g. E. *Alc.* 136, 7 ἀλλ' ἥδ' ὀπαδῶν ἐκ δόμων τις ἔρχεται | δακρυρροοῦσα, τίνα τύχην ἀκούσομαι;

Heidel (*Class. Philol.* 1915, p. 81) suggests οὐ γάρ for οὔπω, but the distance between ἀλλά and γάρ makes this impossible.

The reading of the MSS. εἰς μ' suggests that Eur. possibly wrote . . . πάρεισ'; ἔσειμ' or . . . πάρεισ', ἔσειμ'.

66. ἀνακτόρων: descriptive gen.: 'in which (house) consisting of the temple of the goddess here'. Iph. lives in the temple as does Ion (E. *Ion* 314, 5). There is no need to accept any

emendation, e.g. Bergk's ἀνακτόρων πέλας. The phrase occurs again at E. *Andr.* 380.

67. i.e. φυλάσσου μὴ ⟨ἤ⟩; ἤ is sometimes omitted as at E. *Hipp.* 659, 60 νῦν δ' ἐκ δόμων μέν, ἔστ' ἂν ἔκδημος χθονὸς | Θησεύς, ἄπειμι. But it is probably better to understand ἐστί and take it with ὅρα, φυλάσσου being parenthetical. ὅρα with μή + indic. is not uncommon, cf. e.g. E. *Or.* 208 ὅρα . . . μὴ . . . λέληθ' ὅδε (Kühner-Gerth, *Griech. Gram.* II. ii, p. 395). Observe too that Pylades takes up ὅρα, not φυλάσσου.

68. Our text accepts Monk's πανταχῇ for MSS. πανταχοῦ. Probably the right correction is πανταχοῖ, cf. Ar. *Lys.* where Brunck substitutes it for the MSS. πανταχοῦ.

70. ἔνθα = whither (cf. ὁδοιποροῦμεν ἔνθα χρήζομεν, S. *El.* 1099). Some edd. have needlessly excised this line as spoiling the otherwise exact stichomythia. Burges put it after 76, where it would form an indirect question. ἔνθα is rare in such cases, but cf. S. *El.* 1101. Hermann put 76 after 71, thus securing two initial couplets. The attribution of 76 to Pyl. (the MSS. give it to Or.) helps to give a pattern to the passage, though in any case exact stichomythia is occasionally broken as at E. *Ion* 937, a line which is vital to the sense of the passage.

72. οὗ probably gen. of relat. pron. rather than adv. καταστάζειν takes acc. of thing dropped and gen. of that dropped upon, e.g. E. *Hec.* 760 νεκρὸν . . . οὗ καταστάζω δάκρυ.

73. τρίχωμα = a head of hair. It is hard to see how this could be applied to an altar, and we should possibly accept Ruhnken's θριγκώματα, regarding τριχώματα either as a pure corruption or as the 'correction' of a scribe anxious to justify the ξανθὰς κόμας of Iph.'s dream (ll. 51, 2).

If θριγκώματα be the correct reading it refers, as does θριγκοῖς in the next line, to the projecting top of the altar. Musgrave's suggestion τοιχώματα is palaeographically likely, as is Seidler's τροχώματα = abacus (cf. *EM.* 455, 52 θριγκῷ· τῷ τροχώματι παρὰ τὸ θρέξαι· ὁ περιτρέχων κυκλόθεν οἷον στέφανος). The σκῦλα were doubtless the severed heads of the victims (cf. Amm. Marc. 22. 8. 33 Tauri . . . caesorum capita fani parietibus praefigebant).

75. Notice Hermann's γε for MSS. τά. γε is idiomatic, though not absolutely necessary, for the affirmative answer to the question. Cf. E. *Alc.* 201 Ἦ που στενάζει . . .; κλαίει γε (Denniston, p. 130). No γε is found in similar cases at E. *HF.* 615, *Ion* 278, *ib.* 295, *Andr.* 586, *Ph.* 745; in the last three cases, however, the metre admits of ⟨γε⟩ and various scholars have suggested its addition.

76. Understand με. Pyl. examines the temple during Or.'s monologue. L & S give ἐγκυκ. as from ἐγκυκλόω. This verb means 'to surround'. Its simple form is not infrequently confused with κυκλέω, e.g. E. *Or.* 632 (where the O.C.T. reads κυκλεῖς) and *ib.* 1379, and it may be that here ἐγκυκ. comes from ἐγκυκλέω.

77–84. This long and loosely strung sentence may be punctuated in various ways, and has suffered needless emendation (e.g. Markland's *χρήσας*; *ἐπεὶ γὰρ πατρὸς* . . .; *διαδοχαῖς γ'* . . .). Our text is to be taken: 'into what new snare hast thou . . ., since I avenged . . . and (*δέ*) was driven . . . and (*τε*) fulfilled . . . and (*δέ*) asked . . .?'

ποῖ should not be translated 'why'. It here almost = *τίνα*.

αὖ: the first 'snare' was the oracular command to slay his mother. We seem to hear the sceptical Euripides speaking through Orestes' mouth.

διαδοχαῖς . . . Ἐρινύων. 'by relays of Furies' seems strange. It means, as Weil said, *μεταδρομαῖς Ἐρινύων διαδεχομένων ἀλλήλας*, and should not be altered to *μεταδρομαῖς* (Mähly—from S. *El.* 1387 and l. 941 below) or *διαδρομαῖς* (Monk).

For the expression **ἔξεδροι χθονός** cf. *σκήνης ὕπαυλον* (S. *Aj.* 796); *Κρήτας* (= *-ης*) *ἔξορμος* (E. *Hipp.* 155); *δωμάτων ἔκδημος* (E. *IA.* 419); and *ἑδράνων . . . ἔκτοπος* (S. *OC.* 233).

τροχηλάτου = that keeps one constantly on the move, as a rotating wheel would a chariot. Eur. is fond of this metaphor; he uses it at *Or.* 36, 7 *τὸ μητρὸς . . . αἷμά νιν τροχηλατεῖ* | *μανίαισιν*; and *El.* 1252, 3 *δειναὶ δὲ κῆρές* ⟨*σ'*⟩ . . . | *τροχηλατήσουσ' ἐμμανῆ πλανώμενον*.

For *ἐκπίμπλημι* = fulfil, accomplish, cf. below l. 90 and E. *Hel.* 735 *μοχθήματ' ἐξέπλησας*. **δρόμους καμπίμους** may be a metaphor from the race-course = *διαύλους*.

Line 84 so nearly equals l. 1455 that many edd. reject it.

86. The MS. reading *σύ* is untranslatable. A second hand in P corrected it to *σή*, and grammatically this is unobjectionable since *σύγγονος* can be used as a substantive—and, indeed, is in lines 795 and 805 of this play. Kirchhoff's *σοι* gives a more orthodox caesura, but Eur. 'a énormément développé la coupe entre le possessif *σός* et le substantif' (Descroix, *le trimètre iambique*, p. 283; he cites many instances, e.g. l. 1399 of our play). *σή*, therefore (an easier change than *σοι*), is metrically possible.

The change of the MSS. *ἔχει* to *ἔχοι* is quite unnecessary. The indicative is constantly retained in clauses in *oratio obliqua* (cf. K.-G. II. ii, p. 553).

87. Many edd. accept the suggestion *οὑνθάδε* (= *οἱ ἐνθάδε*) made independently by Markland and Hermann. However, though *ἐνθάδε ἐς τούσδε ναούς* is somewhat tautological, it is better to keep it, for *οὑνθάδε* suggests that the heavenly provenance of the *ξόανον* is a theory of the Tauri about which Orestes is sceptical.

91. 'Beyond that nothing further was *ordered*' (not 'said'; cf. *εἶπας* of l. 85). *τὸ ἐνθένδε*, adverbial: 'as to what was to follow'.

96. **τοίχων** is a descriptive or defining gen., = the walls which encircle. Cf. E. *Ph.* 1357 *τειχέων περιπτυχαί*.

97. Or. has just called Pyl.'s attention to the height of the walls.

He then (with the MSS. reading δωμάτων) suggests walking up the steps of the temple or (l. 99) forcing the doors. Now these are not true alternatives; the second suggested course of action implies the first, and the first is pointless without the second. Further, the suggested 'frontal attack' does not fit in well with the observation upon the height of the walls.

In E. *Ph.* 1173 and A. *Th.* 466 we find κλίμακος προσαμβάσεις, and in E. *Ba.* 1213 and *Ph.* 489 κλιμάκων προσαμβάσεις. Kirchhoff has therefore suggested that we read here κλιμάκων for δωμάτων. The sense is then: 'see how high the walls are. We should need a ladder. But we should be seen. Shall we try to force the door?'

There seems no parallel for ἐκβαίνειν = to mount. ἐκπερᾶν κλίμακα is found in E. *Ph.* 100, but that scarcely justifies the present passage. It is tempting to read Blomfield's ἐμβησόμεσθα or Markland's ἐσβησόμεσθα. Elmsley admits the difficulty; his citation from Hesych. ἐκβῆναι ὅρος, ποταμὸν διαβῆναι is not illuminating, and he himself admits that we should possibly emend ὅρος to ὅρον.

Kayser, accepting Kirchhoff's κλιμάκων, added the line ⟨λαβόντες ἀρούμεσθα πρὸς δόμον θεᾶς⟩ and for ἐκβ. read κἀσβησόμεσθα. This gives good sense, but his line is not necessary.

98-100. Keeping the MSS. μάθοιμεν we can only take it with ὧν οὐδὲν ἴσμεν. This means cutting out 99 or putting it after 100 where it would go not inaptly. But 'how should we learn facts about which we know nothing?' meaning something like 'how are we to find out where the ladders are kept?' is very frigid. With δωμάτων it could mean nothing at all, for the steps of the temple must have been obvious, and any forward reference to the difficulty of opening the doors is precluded by οὖν which must be retrospective. Hermann's μή for ἤ (i.e. μὴ . . . λύσαντες = εἰ μὴ λύσαιμεν) would save the necessity of excising or transposing 99, but the addition of a protasis does not really help the meaning.

Accepting Sallier's λάθοιμεν we get good sense whether we read δωμάτων or κλιμάκων in 97: 'how could we escape notice mounting the steps?' or '. . . climbing the ladder?' But with this reading ὧν οὐδὲν ἴσμεν is deprived of its construction, and we can only (as does our text) suppose a definite anacoluthon. 'Or ⟨shall we enter by⟩ forcing the doors?—⟨what! doors of the mechanism⟩ of which we know nothing'.

A third line of approach is to read λάθοιμεν and emend ὧν οὐδὲν ἴσμεν in such a way that it can be taken with 99. Many such emendations have been proposed, and most exhibit in common the change of ὧν to ὧδ' and ἴσμεν to ἔσιμεν (both palaeographically reasonable). For the middle word we can choose between Badham's οὐδόν; unlikely, for the tragedians do not use the Ionic form οὐδός nor is εἰσιέναι the right verb for it;

Köchly's ἱερόν and Wecklein's ἄδυτον—both giving good sense but not very near the MSS.; 'or having burst open . . . shall we so enter the temple?'

Among other suggestions may be cited: Weil's ἀν' οὖδας ἔσιμεν which could only mean '. . . shall we enter ⟨and walk⟩ over the ⟨temple⟩ floor?'; and, as an alternative to the MSS. μάθοιμεν, England's πῶς ἄρ' ἐγκαθείμεθ' ἄν; 'How then (i.e. supposing we scaled the wall) could we let ourselves down'.

In spite of the not infrequent conjunction of κλῇθρα and μοχλοί (e.g. E. *Andr.* 951; Ar. *Lys.* 264) for the bars and bolts of a door it is better to take μοχλοῖς here as = crowbars. Orestes suggests force, not cunning, as his second alternative.

101. **εἰσβάσεις μηχανώμενοι**: referring back to the δωμάτων (or, better, κλιμάκων; see note on l. 97) προσαμβάσεις, just as ἀνοίγοντες πύλας refers to κλῇθρα λύσαντες. The arrangement is chiastic.

102. ἀλλά = 'nay'. Some edd. try to save Or.'s reputation for courage by putting a note of interrogation at the end of l. 103 and so taking φεύγωμεν as = 'would you like us to fly' rather than 'let us fly'. There is something to be said for this, though nothing for Hartung's ἀλλ' ἦ (for MSS. ἀλλά) which is not used to ask an alternative question whereas ἀλλά is (cf. Denniston, pp. 9 and 27).

105. The δέ of the MSS. is unobjectionable and Kirchhoff's τε unnecessary. δ' in 106 = ἀλλά. 'We must not be cowardly nor impious; no, we must hide till nightfall . . .'

κακιστέον is odd. κακίζειν normally means 'to reproach' and once 'to make cowardly' (E. *IA.* 1435); κακίζεσθαι = 'to play the coward'. The meaning we want is 'play the coward in face of the oracle', but it is scarcely possible to extract it from the Greek. L & S give 'one must ⟨not⟩ bring reproach on', but even this is doubtful, for the verbal adjective should mean 'one must ⟨not⟩ reproach', which is not the same thing. Of emendations φλαυριστέον (Rauchenstein) 'one must not hold cheap' (φλαῦρος) has neither good authority as a word nor is it near the MSS.; αἰκιστέον (Vogel, *ap.* Wecklein), though near the MSS., is too violent in sense ('to damage') nor is the verbal adj. found; *ἀτιστέον = ἀτιμαστέον (Valckenaer) is not impossible.

107. Cf. *Od.* 4. 359 μέλαν ὕδωρ; Hor. *Sat.* 2. 2. 16 atrum mare—of the stormy sea.

108. It is hard to see why retirement from the ship should cause the *ship* not to be seen, and Musgrave may be on the right track in emending to πόλεως ἄπωθεν . . . σκοπός. We can only make logic of the text if we suppose all the stress to lie on μὴ . . . ληφθῶμεν βίᾳ. Hiding would secure a (temporary) security.

109. **βασιλεῦσιν**: the general, allusive, or rhetorical plural. Cf. S. *Ant.* 10 τοὺς φίλους (= Polynices) . . . τῶν ἐχθρῶν (= Creon); E. *IA.* 1015 τέκνα = Iphigenia; E. *Med.* 823 δεσπόταις = Medea. (Löfstedt, *Syntactica* I, p. 34.)

110. 'The eye of night' = 'night' (*not* 'the moon') is a commonplace: cf. A. *Pers.* 428 κελαινῆς νυκτὸς ὄμμα; E. *Ph.* 543 νυκτός τ' ἀφεγγὲς βλέφαρον.

λυγαῖος, fr. λύγη = twilight; cf. E. *Heracl.* 855 λυγαίῳ νέφει.

112. **προσφέροντε**, not, as might be expected, -όντοιν, as the verbal adj. can have either dat. or acc. of the agent. In one passage Thuc. uses both in one sentence (8. 65. 3) οὔτε μισθοφορητέον ἄλλους ἢ τοὺς στρατευομένους οὔτε μεθεκτέον τῶν πραγμάτων πλείοσιν ἢ πεντακισχιλίοις. The acc. construction probably comes from a false analogy with that of δεῖ.

113–14. The general meaning is clear. Pylades points out to Orestes the spaces between the triglyphs—in later temples filled by metopes—through which they may climb in. The Phrygian slave in the Orestes (1372) escapes in this way from the temple. As the text stands it is almost untranslatable. ὅποι is impossible; if it *could* be taken with δέμας καθ. (i.e. ὅρα . . . κενόν, ὅποι δέμας καθεῖναι) it should be ὅπῃ (suggested by Kirchhoff) 'by which way we might let ourselves down', but the position of κενόν makes it certain that the construction is rather 'where the inter-triglyph spaces ⟨are⟩', and we should therefore emend to ὅπου. We could then translate the passage 'see where between the triglyphs ⟨is⟩ an empty ⟨space through which⟩ to let ourselves down.' But this is open to three objections: (1) can εἴσω = between? (2) can κενόν = an empty space? (3) can we understand before δέμας κ. ⟨ὥστ' ἐκείνῃ⟩, or even ⟨τοσοῦτον ὥστ' ἐκείνῃ⟩? (1) No real case of εἴσω = 'between' seems to occur, unless it be at E. *Cyc.* 62 Αἰτναίων εἴσω σκοπέλων: (2) both Hippocrates and Aristotle use τὸ κενόν as a substantive: (3) this appears to me impossible.

One line of emendation we can at once rule out. Blomfield suggested ὅρα δὲ γεῖσα, for which word cf. E. *Ph.* 1158 and S. *OT.* 876, where it is plausibly conjectured. But whether we take γεῖσα with τριγλύφων or not, and whatever we suppose to be the consequent construction of the sentence, we do not want the word γεῖσα at all, for it means the raking cornices of the pediment (γεῖσα αἰέτια or καταιέτια) and has nothing to do with the inter-triglyph spaces. Elmsley's γείσων (taking τριγλύφων as an adj. 'three grooved') gives a better construction, but it is open to the same fatal objection.

A better kind of emendation replaces ὅρα δέ γ' εἴσω by words which will give a construction to δέμας καθεῖναι. [One would have thought it unnecessary to warn the reader against taking ὅρα with καθεῖναι, 'see that you let down . . .', had it not actually been suggested.]. Such emendations are (1) Köchly's ῥᾷστον δέ γ' εἴσω; (2) Weil's ὅρα δ'· ἔνεστι, . . . Both read ὅπου for ὅποι and understand ἐστί. Neither of these is palaeographically very likely. As to the sense, Weil's is distinctly preferable; indeed, to say that the suggested feat is easy is ridiculous in itself and contradicted by πόνους. Bergk's ἄριστα δ' εἴσω (i.e. 'our best course is to let ourselves down where . . .') deserves mention, but no really satisfactory emendation has yet been made.

It is just possible that a line has fallen out from between 113 and 114 of the type ἄραρε χάσμα Δωρικῶν, ὅπῃ πάρα |, trouble being caused by ὅπου . . . ὅπῃ. 'See, where (reading ὅπου) a gap is set between . . . by which it is possible to . . .'

Or again ὅποι may conceal some case of ὀπή, the meaning of which is particularly suitable: e.g. . . . ὀπάς, ὅπῃ [κενόν], i.e. 'see the holes between the triglyphs where ⟨it is possible⟩ to . . .' It must be supposed in this case that κενόν entered the text as a gloss on ὀπάς.

116–17. These two lines are given by the MSS. to Orestes. They are awkward here, but Markland's attribution of them to Pylades does not help matters. Some edd. have inserted them after l. 103. If so they must form the first couplet of Pylades' remark, not the last of Orestes'; the latter could scarcely utter them so hard on the heels of his suggestion of flight. Wecklein, with some probability, puts them after 105. Dindorf and others rejected them as spurious. Badham suggested οὕτω for οὔ τοι, with a mark of interrogation at the end of 117.

Note the relative position of οὐ and μέν: 'it is not the case that we have come and shall return . . .' **ἐκ τερμάτων** = short of our goal.

119. = ἐκεῖσε χθονὸς ὅπου. A good instance of adverbial attraction and contraction, the relative adverb ὅπου being attracted into the *form* of the demonstrative (ἐκεῖσε . . . ὅποι) and then coalescing with it. Valckenaer's ὅπου should not be accepted.

120. It is difficult to extract much sense from the MSS. reading. For though 'God will not be the cause of his ⟨own⟩ oracle's perishing uselessly' makes sense of itself, it does not make sense in the context. It is themselves, not the god, who are likely to let the oracle down. Read, then, with Weil, οὐ γὰρ τὸ τοῦδέ γ', i.e. οὐ τό γ' ἐμόν. τὸ τοῦδε : τὸ ἐμόν :: ὅδε : ἐγώ. This suggestion was made independently by Wilamowitz in his *Analecta Euripidea*. Some edd. (e.g. Seidler, Schöne) explain αἴτιον as = 'deserving of' (with πεσεῖν ἄχρ.), but this is in itself impossible, and even if it were possible the fut. γενήσεται would make nonsense of it. To take τὸ τοῦ θ. θέσφατον together, too, is awkward.

122. σκῆψιν φέρει: lit. brings an excuse = justifies shirking. For the sentiment cf. E. *fr.* 461 αἰσχρὸν . . . μοχθεῖν μὴ θέλειν νεανίαν.

123–235. The πάροδος of the chorus of Greek captive women, fifteen in number. At line 143 the πάροδος proper turns into a κόμμος, i.e. a θρῆνος κοινὸς χοροῦ καὶ ἀπὸ σκηνῆς, as Aristotle (*Poet.* 12. 1452^b 24) defined it. It is written in free anapaestic rhythm and is not antistrophic. Most of the lines are acatalectic dimeters, but a certain number are catalectic, and these are as a rule spondaic in character as befits the dirge-like nature of the choric song and Iph.'s monody. Whether we consider these lines as catalectic anapaestic dimeters or as paroemiacs is immaterial. Ll. 126, 7 are spondaic dochmiacs.

123–5. *Favete linguis.* The customary injunction to silence at the beginning of a religious ceremony. The address is presumably made to any natives within hearing (not, as Monk, to the birds!).

συγχωρούσας πέτρας = the Symplegades; the clashing rocks which guarded the entrance to the Euxine and through which the Argo passed (E. *Med.* 2; Pi. *P.* 4. 208). After the passage of the ship they remained in place. Hence 'inhabitants of the Symplegades' = 'dwellers on the coast of the Euxine'.

127. **Δίκτυνν⟨α⟩**, cult-name of Artemis. Probably to be derived from δίκτυον, hunting or fishing net; not from Mt. Dicte in Crete, though the worship of the goddess was connected with that island (cf. E. *Hipp.* 145 and 1130). Notice the un-Greek form of the name; the goddess is of Minoan origin (cf. Nilsson, *Minoan-Mycenaean Religion*, p. 439).

129. Cf. Milton, *PL.* i. 713–15. Built like a temple, where pilasters round | Were set, and Doric pillars overlaid | With golden architrave.

130. It is almost impossible to believe in the two lengthenings *in arsi* (παρθένιōν ὅσιōν) necessary to make this line scan as an anapaestic dimeter. Seidler's rearrangement ὁσίας ὅσιον πόδα παρθ. should possibly be accepted, or else we may regard the line as a resolved paroemiac, i.e. ⏑⏑ – ⏑⏑ ⏑͡⏑ ⏑⏑ ⏑͡⏑ –. Alternatively we might suppose ὅσιον ὁσίας a gloss and read πόδα παρθ. ζάθεον ζαθέας (Wecklein). For πόδα παρθένιον cf. παρθένῳ χερί (E. *Ph.* 838), γέροντι . . . ποδί (E. *Or.* 456).

131. The priestess is the key-holder, the guardian of the goddess' temple; cf. Io, the κληδοῦχος Ἥρας (A. *Supp.* 291). Whether or not we accept Rauchenstein's ⟨σᾶς⟩ κληδ. we must translate 'thy key-holder'.

135. The MSS. **Εὐρώπαν** is sound. The chorus has left (ἐξαλλάξασα = ἀμείψασα = λιποῦσα) Europe with its (lit. 'of the') wooded pastures; for this gen. of quality cf. S. *Aj.* 1004 ὄμμα . . . τόλμης πικρᾶς. For the early wooded state of Europe cf. Hdt. 7. 5 Εὐρώπη . . . δένδρεα παντοῖα φέρει. Barnes' Εὐρώταν is worse than needless. Why should all the chorus come from Sparta? Wecklein's θεράπνας ('dwellings') is no better. If any alteration is to be accepted that of Bergk is perhaps the best: εὐρωπὰ ('broad'; cf. l. 626) νάπη. But why should -απη have got lost?

137. At this point the coryphaeus addresses Iph. who comes out of the centre door of the temple. ἔμολον = 'I have come ⟨at your command⟩'.

139–41. With the MSS. χιλιοναύτα μυριοτεύχοις Ἀτρειδᾶν τῶν κλεινῶν we can get neither metre nor grammar out of the passage. Our text keeps the first two words (with Seidler's necessary μυριοτευχοῦς for MSS. μυριοτειχοις), corrects Ἀτρειδᾶν to Ἀτρείδα (Altenburg), and excises τῶν κλεινῶν (because of the proximity of κλεινᾷ in 140). This gives a form of sentence almost exactly like that in S. *El.* 1, 2 ὦ τοῦ στρατηγήσαντος ἐν Τροίᾳ ποτὲ | Ἀγαμέμνονος παῖ. But the two adjs. are more applicable to κώπᾳ than to Ἀτρείδα; cf. A. *Ag.* 45 στόλον Ἀργείων χιλιοναύτην. Nor need we hesitate to accept τῶν κλεινῶν following so soon upon κλεινᾷ (cf. notes on ll. 339, 686, 722, 760, 763, and 1352. Euripides' constant repetition of words may give offence but should not invite emendation). We should, I think, rather read κώπᾳ | χιλιοναύτᾳ μυριοτευχεῖ | ⏑⏑– Ἀτρειδᾶν τῶν κλεινῶν. The lacuna can be filled by some word in apposition to παῖ such as θάλος (Bergk), γένος (Dindorf), or σπέρμ' (Schöne)—the latter word would account for the σ at the end of μυριοτεύχοις. Grégoire's τέκος might account by haplography (-τευχεῖ τέκος) for (μυριο)τεύχοις. Alternatively (but less well) we can suppose that some genitive in appos. to τοῦ ἐλθόντος has fallen out and read e.g. Monk's τῶν Ἀτρειδᾶν μέγ' ἀρίστου (cf. E. *Alc.* 899 μετ' ἐκείνης (i.e. Alcestis) τῆς μέγ' ἀρίστης).

143–7. **ὡς** may give the reason for her cry ἰώ, or may be itself exclamatory. Dindorf's ⟨ἴδεθ'⟩ ὡς would give good sense and produce an acatalectic anapaestic dimeter. But it may be noticed that in the *Ion* Creusa starts her monody (l. 859) with three spondaic paroemiacs.

ἔγκειμαι = to be busied with; cf. E. *Andr.* 91, 2 ἐγκείμεσθ' ἀεὶ | θρήνοισι καὶ γόοισι καὶ δακρύμασι.

Our text keeps the MSS. reading, altering only ἓε ἐν to αἰαῖ, αἰαῖ and excising βοάν. In this case both ἐλέγοις and οἴκτοισιν are in apposition to θρήνοις.

δυσθρηνήτοις . . . θρήνοις: a common form of paronomasia; cf. l. 203 δυσδαίμων δαίμων, and νύμφαιον δύσνυμφον l. 216; also E. *Ph.* 1047 γάμους δυσγάμους, *Hec.* 194 δυσφήμους φήμας, *Tr.* 75 δύσνοστον νόστον, etc. In all these the adjective produces an oxymoron; here it intensifies the meaning of the substantive as in S. *Ant.* 1276 πόνοι δύσπονοι and *ib.* 587 δυσπνόοις πνοαῖς.

βοάν (βοᾶν L) can only be kept if we insert before it some participle such as μέλπουσα (Wecklein), ἰεῖσα or ἱστᾶσα, and even then we have to alter τᾶς . . . εὐμούσου to τὰν . . . εὔμουσον. In his third edition Wecklein gives [μολπᾶς] μέλπουσα βοᾶς ἀλύρους ἐλέγους. But 'hymning unlyrical elegies ⟨in the form⟩ of a (lit. "the") musicless cry' is impossibly harsh and but a poor bargain at the cost of so much emendation.

ἀλύροις = 'unfit for the ⟨joyful⟩ lyre', not necessarily (as England) 'fit for the gloomy pipe'. ἀλύροις ἐλέγοις: a common Graecism; the actual phrase occurs again at E. *Hel.* 185 and cf. E. *El.* 310 ἀνέορτος ἱερῶν; *Ph.* 324 ἄπεπλος φαρέων; *ib.* 791 κῶμον ἀναυλότατον; *Or.* 319 ἀβάκχευτον . . . θίασον; *Ph.* 1028 ἄλυρον μοῦσαν: also A. *Ag.* 990 τὸν . . . ἄνευ λύρας . . . θρῆνον Ἐρινύος; *Supp.* 681 ἄχορον ἀκίθαριν . . . Ἄρη; S. *OC.* 1221 μοῖρα . . . ἄλυρος. As the common Greek derivation of ἔλεγος was ἒ ἒ λέγειν (*EM.* 326. 49), the correction αἰαῖ, αἰαῖ cannot be regarded as at all certain. Nor, indeed, should the MSS. ἐν be disregarded. ἒ ἕ, ἐν κηδείοις οἴκτοις forms by itself a possible anapaestic dimeter catalectic. For the hiatus cf. E. *Hipp.* 594.

148. MSS. αἵ. The relative is feeble and Greverus' οἷαι [μοι]—exclamatory—should probably be read, or, better, Badham's οἷαί μοι . . . which will give us an acatalectic line. αἵ (or οἷαι) . . . ἆται is best regarded as a parenthesis, κατακλαιομένα going directly with ἔγκειμαι; though οἷαί μοι συμβαίνουσι might be taken as = οἵας ἔπαθον which gives a κατὰ σύνεσιν construction to the nominative participle. Barnes suggested the obvious κατακλαιομένᾳ, which certainly regularizes the grammar and which should perhaps be accepted, as it is by, e.g., Grégoire (ed. Budé).

150. If **ζωᾶς** is correct we must take it as a sort of causal gen., common after verbs expressing emotion (cf. K.-G. II. i, p. 388) 'because of his ⟨lost⟩ life'. The euphemism is not un-Greek. However, Schöne's ζωᾶς ⟨ἀπλακόνθ'⟩ = 'deprived of (= ἀμπλακόντα) life' is in itself attractive and completes the metre.

οἵαν = ὅτι τοιαύτην; cf. A. *Pr.* 907–9 ἦ μὴν ἔτι Ζεύς . . . ἔσται ταπεινός, οἷον ἐξαρτύεται | γάμον γαμεῖν; E. *HF.* 816, 7 ἆρ' ἐς τὸν αὐτὸν πίτυλον ἥκομεν φόβου, | . . . οἷον φάσμ' ὑπὲρ δόμων ὁρῶ; (cf. K.-G. II. ii, p. 371).

151. Some edd. bracket **ὀνείρων** as a gloss. This would render Hermann's second οἵαν unnecessary as the lines would run

ζωᾶς, οἵαν ἰδόμαν ὄψιν
νυκτός, τᾶς ἐξῆλθ' ὄρφνα.

152. **νυκτός** might be taken with ὀνείρων = of the dreams of the night, but it is more probably gen. of time within which. 'In the night the darkness of which (τᾶς = ἧς; cf. l. 35 and note) has ⟨just⟩ passed.' An uncommon use of ἐξέρχεσθαι; L & S cite Hyp. *Eux.* 35 τοῦ ἐξελθόντος μηνός. Commoner in this sense is the perf., e.g. S. *OT.* 735 χρόνος . . . οὑξεληλυθώς.

157. The MSS. ὃς τὸν μόνον με is unmetrical. Either Prof. Murray's or Heath's emendation (which makes two full acatalectic dimeters) will mend the line (see *app. crit.*).

158. **ᾧ** refers to **κασίγνητον**. **χοὰς . . . κρατῆρά τε**, a hendiadys.

160. For **τὸν φθιμένων** = devoted to the dead, cf. S. *Ant.* 601 φοινία θεῶν τῶν νερτέρων κόνις (if the MSS. are correct. The O.C.T. prints Jortin's κοπίς).

161. **ὑδραίνειν** here = 'to sprinkle'. In Greek verbs of moistening usually take an acc. of the thing which moistens; cf. S. *Tr.* 848 τέγγει δακρύων ἄχναν, *Aj.* 376 ἐρεμνὸν αἷμ' ἔδευσα, Pi. *N.* 10. 75 τέγγων δάκρυα. No alteration (e.g. Bergk's ῥαίνειν) is to be tolerated.

162. Milk, wine, honey, and water were, severally or together, poured upon the ground as a libation to the dead. Cf. *Od.* 10. 518 χοὴν χεῖσθαι πᾶσιν νεκύεσσι | πρῶτα μελικρήτῳ, μετέπειτα δὲ ἡδέϊ οἴνῳ | τὸ τρίτον αὖθ' ὕδατι. In A. *Pers.* 611–15 all four elements are mentioned; in S. *OC.* 481 water and honey only; in E. *Or.* 115 milk, wine, and honey; in S. *El.* 895 milk only. This being the case there is no need to suspect any lacuna, and such suggestions as Köchly's πηγάς ⟨θ' ὑδάτων κρηναίων | γάλα⟩ τ' should be rejected. πηγάς, λοιβάς, and πόνημα are all in explanatory apposition to χοάς, the τ' after πηγάς merely looking forward to the other two.

166. Nauck's χεῖται is attractive, but κεῖται here = νενόμισται; cf. the common νόμοι κεῖνται. (E. *Med.* 494 καινὰ κεῖσθαι θέσμια.)

167–8. Addressed to one of her attendants. **τεῦχος καὶ λοιβάν** another quasi-hendiadys; i.e. the vessel containing the libation for (lit. 'of') the god of the underworld.

For **ἔνδος** cf. E. *Cyc.* 510 ἀσκὸν ἔνδος μοι.

171. As England remarks, Iph. means 'to you as being dead' though the audience may understand 'as though you were dead'. In English 'send' connotes the separation of sender and thing sent; there is no such implication in the Greek πέμπειν; see its use at ll. 590, 604, and 1440 (ἐσπέμπειν) below and cf. E. *Andr.* 966. Hence its meaning of 'accompany' and (as here) 'bring'; and hence the possibility of such phrases as πέμπειν πόδα (l. 130). See note on ἐκπέμπειν (l. 1467).

173. For the cutting of the hair as a sign of mourning cf. *Il.* 23. 135, 141. The locks were placed on the tomb; cf. A. *Ch.* 167, S. *El.* 901, E. *Alc.* 101, *El.* 515, *Or.* 96, and below l. 703.

176. The MSS. give the unmetrical and nonsensical δοκίμα, corrected by Porson to the almost certain δοκήμασι; cf. ὡς δοκεῖ of l. 8 and E. *Tr.* 411 τὰ σεμνὰ καὶ δοκήμασιν σοφά. Prof. Murray suggests ἔνθα δόκημα | σφαχθεῖσ' ἁ τλάμων κεῖμαι—Hermann had suggested δοκήματα—but these appositional nominatives are difficult. The δόκημα of E. *HF.* 111 is not parallel as it is helped by ὥστε.

δοκήμασι = ⟨ἀνθρώπων⟩ δοκήμασι = 'as men suppose'.

178–81. ἀντιψάλμους· ἀντιστρόφους· Εὐριπίδης, Ἰφιγενείᾳ τῇ ἐν Ταύροις; Hesych. There is, however, no exact metrical correspondence between the chorus's song and that of Iph. which precedes it. The word means merely 'answering'.

The MSS. reading ὕμνον τ' ἀσιήταν (i.e. Ἀσιήταν) may be right —it is found in Hib. Pap. 24, and is indeed kept by several edd. In this case βάρβαρον ἀχάν is in apposition to ὕμνον Ἀσ.

If we keep the MSS. voc. δέσποινα we must for metrical reasons accept Weil's δέσποιν', ἀντεξαυδάσω as does Wecklein.

183. Markland's μελομέναν ('dear to') is an almost certain correction of the impossible μέλεον of the MSS. Cf. E. *Ph.* 1301 στενακτὰν ἰαχὰν μελομέναν νεκροῖς, and below l. 645 and note.

Other suggestions are: νέκυσιν μελέων (Schöne), i.e. 'the music of songs in dirges for the dead', and ν. μεδέων (Kviçala). The first of these is very weak and leaves νέκυσιν almost without a construction, while the second involves transferring the comma after μελομέναν to the end of l. 182, and taking νέκυσιν μεδέων in apposition to Ἅιδας; 'which Hades, ruler among the dead, sings'.

τάν, relative. The joyful paean has no connexion with the funeral dirge, though both are *sung* (ἐν μολπαῖς). Cf. A. *fr.* 161 μόνος θεῶν γὰρ θάνατος οὐ δώρων ἐρᾷ, | . . . οὐδὲ παιωνίζεται.

187. 'the sceptre-brilliance of ⟨your⟩ ancestral home'. Besides the awkward double gen. we have the difficult omission of τῶν σῶν. Some edd. have therefore added τῶν σῶν to l. 188, while others have cut out the line altogether on the ground that it is a mere repetition of Ἀτρειδᾶν οἴκων above. Grégoire (ed. Budé) thinks that the MSS. had originally in l. 189 ἀκτίς, which by a transposition of syllables became τισακ and so τινεκ to τίν' ἐκ. He prints the passage

οἴμοι, τῶν Ἀτρειδᾶν οἴκων
ἔρρει φῶς σκήπτρων, οἴμοι,
πατρῴων οἴκων ἀκτίς,
⟨καὶ⟩ τῶν εὐόλβων Ἄργει
βασιλέων ἀρχά.

This gives good sense whether we take τῶν Ἀτρ. οἴκ. as gen. of exclamation (as Grégoire seems to do in his translation) or as double gen. with σκήπτρων. But it is difficult to see why τις should have become τιν where there is no other accusative to corrupt it, and the addition of καί is somewhat arbitrary. Another, and perhaps a better, way is, with England, to give 186–91 to Iph. (the MSS. give her 186–235) and to read ἔρρει φῶς σκήπτρων, ἔρρει (or οἴμοι), | οἴμοι πατρῴων οἴκων. This avoids all the above-mentioned difficulties, for τῶν ἐμῶν can easily be understood where, in the chorus' mouth, τῶν σῶν could not. In this case the ἀντιψάλμους ᾠδάς promised by the chorus must be taken as beginning at l. 192.

189. Ἄργει is probably a locative, though it might be dat. of advantage.

τίν' ἐκ τῶν (the reading of the MSS.) is impossible. Prof. Murray's ἦν ('once existed': Latin, 'fuit') is palaeographically likely. Of other more arbitrary emendations may be mentioned Wecklein's οὐκ ἔστιν ἔτ' [τῶν]; and Köchly's οὐκέτι τῶν (both of which have the merit of getting rid of the difficult ἐκ); Badham's τίνος ἐκ τῶν (which is near the MSS.), and Hermann's τίς ἔτ' ἐκ τῶν can only be accepted if we suppose a considerable lacuna after 190 which contained some word like κακῶν (ἀρχά here meaning 'beginning') and answered the question so posed by 'Pelops', whose story then follows.

If ἐκ is kept it must mean 'consisting of'—a rare use, cf. X. *Smp.* 8. 32 στράτευμα . . . ἐκ παιδικῶν.

192 et sqq. A difficult and probably very corrupt passage. The chorus traces the troubles of the royal house of Argos back to the theft from King Atreus by his brother Thyestes of the golden-fleeced lamb, the symbol and earnest of sovereignty. Atreus avenged this theft and the seduction of his wife Aerope which made it possible by serving up to Thyestes his own children as food. In horror at such deeds the sun, which up to that time had risen in the west, reversed its orbit and rose in the east. The cause of the quarrel between the brothers is mentioned below (l. 813) and in E. *Or.* 812 (χρυσείας ἔρις ἀρνός), and the action of the sun in l. 1001–2 of the same play (ὅθεν Ἔρις τό τε πτερωτὸν | ἁλίου μετέβαλεν ἅρμα); see also E. *El.* 737–42. Plato tells the story in the Politicus (269 A).

ἵπποισι: this word has been taken as referring (1) to the horses with which Pelops won the race for Hippodamia, or to those with which he subsequently engineered the death of Myrtilus, the charioteer; (2) to the horses of the sun. Though at E. *Or.* 988 sqq. the curse of the house is said to come from (ὅθεν ἦλθε) the ποτανὸν δίωγμα πώλων of Pelops, I am inclined to think that, from the *immediate* mention of the sun, it is to *his* horses that reference is here made.

Prof. Murray, however, in our text takes the other view. Here ῥιφαί (a rare word found only in Lycophron and meaning 'hurlings'; i.e. the hurling into the sea of Myrtilus by Pelops) and (δέ) ἅλιος ἀλλάξας (= ἡλίου ἀλλαγή) are in explanatory apposition to μόχθος (= μόχθοι).

The corrections πταναῖς, from πτανοῖς (Hermann) and ἐξ ἕδρας, from ἐξέδρασ' (Seidler) may be considered certain. At l. 192 apparently a new sentence begins which has neither connecting particles nor main verb. As to the first point we should, I think, either (1) with Weil suppose a lacuna before the line; or (2) with Wecklein remove the δ' after ἀλλάξας and read ἵπποισιν ⟨ἐπεὶ⟩ πταναῖς, putting a comma only after ἄσσει and supplying a verb (he suggests μετέβαλλ' after ἱερόν) for the clause [ἐπεί = 'ever since']; or (3) shift the δ' after ἀλλάξας which in its own place is impossible, and put it after δινευούσαις; this also will necessitate the importation of μετέβαλλ', a very likely verb here as it is used both by Plato and by Euripides in the passages to which reference has been made. (The imperf. is metrically preferable to the aor. μετέβαλεν, suggested by Hermann.) Another possible verb is Paley's μετέβασ' (i.e. μετέβησε) though it is *not* supported by an appeal to E. *El.* 727, μετέβασ' being there an emendation of Musgrave for the metrically impossible MSS. μεταβάλλει.

Some edd. have objected to ὄμμα, and Köchly proposed ἱερᾶν ἅρμ' αὐγᾶν on the strength of E. *Or.* 1001 πτερωτὸν ἁλίου . . . ἅρμα, but see Ar. *Nu.* 285, 6 ὄμμα . . . αἰθέρος . . . σελαγεῖται | μαρμαρέαις ἐν αὐγαῖς. ἱερὸν ὄμμ' αὐγᾶς = the divine light (lit. eye) of his beam⟨s⟩.

195. With the MSS. ἄλλοις the passage must mean 'different troubles have come upon different branches of the family as a result of the golden-fleeced lamb'. But both ἄλλοις and μελάθροις are difficult. For the first Seidler's ἄλλαις (which our text adopts) is possible, and the causes of corruption would be obvious, but ἄλλαις ἄλλη προσέβη ὀδύνη = 'one trouble after another

has come upon' is dubious Greek. Easier, if less palaeographically likely, is ἄλλοτε: 'at different times different troubles.' For μελ. Wecklein proposes the attractive γενέθλοις.

197. φόνος and ἄχεα are in explanatory apposition to ὀδύνα.

ἄχε' ἄχεσιν is unmetrical and the hiatus ἄχεα ἄχεσιν impossible. We might accept something like Barnes' ⟨τ'⟩ or Brodaeus' ⟨ἐπ'⟩. As far as the *grammar* of the passage is concerned ἐπί, from ἐπὶ φόνῳ, might be understood with ἄχεσιν. δάκρυσιν seems to be used as = ἐπὶ δάκρυσιν at E. *Or.* 1308 and *Hel.* 195; cf. *Or.* 1257 πήματα πήμασι.

In a series of anapaests we must take this line (if correct) as an anapaestic tripody with the long syllable of each anapaest resolved and the ω of φόνῳ short before ἄχεα. As Prof. Murray pointed out in his first edition the emendation ἄχεά τ' ἐπ' ἄχεσιν would give us a proper paroemiac. It should probably be accepted.

For the form of the phrase cf. E. *Hel.* 365, 6 ἄχεά τ' ἄχεσι, | δάκρυα δάκρυσιν, and for the general sense of the passage *Or.* 816 φόνῳ φόνος ἐξαμείβων . . . οὐ προλείπει δισσοῖσιν Ἀτρείδαις.

For ἐπί + dat. = (practically) 'in addition to' cf. E. *Cyc.* 424, 483, 670; *Alc.* 1032, etc.

198. i.e. the nemesis springing (ἐκβαίνει) from the misdeeds of Pelops and others of the family still haunts the house of their descendants. τῶν δμαθέντων = the murdered children of Thyestes. The genitive particularizes and explains ἔνθεν.

200. Many edd. have objected to the rather pointless γε: Hartung suggested ποίναμ'—an easy change; Wecklein in his old ed. ἐκβαίνει ποινὰ Τανταλιδᾶν, in his new ποινὰ | σοῖς οἴκοις. Verrall (*CR.* 1913, p. 225) defends γε: 'punishment, yes; but to visit it on Iph. is going too far'.

201. The phrase σπεύδειν ἀσπούδαστα (internal acc.) occurs also in E. *Ba.* 913 though in a different sense. Here it means 'to be zealous with an evil zeal' (England).

203. Iph., catching up the chorus' remarks, traces her ill-fortune to the night of her conception—ζώνας ⟨λυθείσης⟩ καὶ νυκτός is a hendiadys. The δαίμων is further particularized by λόχιαι Μοῖραι, and ξυντείνουσί μοι has both for subjects, the second ἐξ ἀρχᾶς being anaphoric. Alternatively we might understand ⟨ἐστί⟩ with δαίμων as subject and δυσδαίμων as predicate, in which case a new sentence starts with the ἐξ ἀρχᾶς of l. 205.

Eur. often uses δαίμων in the sense of 'luck', e.g. *Alc.* 561 τὸν παρόντα δαίμονα, *ib.* 935 γυναικὸς δαίμον' εὐτυχέστερον, *Andr.* 98 στερρὸν . . . δαίμονα, *IA.* 1136 ὦ πότνια μοῖρα καὶ τύχη δαίμων τ' ἐμός; at *Ion* 1374, 5 he contrasts it with the gods τὰ τοῦ θεοῦ μὲν χρηστά, τοῦ δὲ δαίμονος | βαρέα. For Sophoclean examples (rarer) cf. S. *OC.* 76, *ib.* 1337, and *fr.* 210 l. 37. The word corresponds in this sense to the Latin 'genius'.

λόχιαι is Hermann's necessary correction of the MSS. λοχείαν, and preferable to Elmsley's λοχίαν. 'My birth-Fates' = 'the Fates at my birth'.

208. The MSS. give ἁ μναστευθεῖσ' ἐξ 'Ε. This is next door to impossible as it involves (1) an awkwardly postponed relative (ἅν in 209), and (2) a hiatus between ll. 207 and 208—suspicious where there is no full stop or at least colon. The first—which can be paralleled in E. *Hel.* 317, 8 ἢ τὰ πάντ' ἐπίσταται, τῆς . . . κόρης—we may avoid by the simple transposition (suggested by Paley and followed by England) of 208 and 209. The reference of the line in either position is to Clytemnestra, the 'famously wooed'; cf. note on l. 22 above.

Elmsley's τᾷ μναστευθείσᾳ 'ξ 'Ε. adopted in our text avoids both difficulties, but gives unsatisfactory sense, for the dat. must refer to Iph. herself, and to say that she was wooed by all Hellas is untrue. Even if the phrase means merely 'wooed in Hellas' it is here pointless and should probably be inserted in the nominative form, as Scaliger suggested, after 220. There the contrast 'once wooed in Hellas, now banished to the Euxine' is to the point. Still more point would be got if we put ἁ μνασ. ἐξ 'Ελλ. after 220 and took it, as does Grégoire, as = 'summoned from Hellas for marriage'. The end of Iph.'s journey from Mycenae was not marriage with Achilles at Aulis but a virgin priesthood in Tauris.

The hiatus θεαὶ | ἅν which would be caused by either shifting of l. 208 can be avoided by reading τάν for ἅν as Wecklein does.

211. **πατρῴᾳ λώβᾳ** = ὥστε ὑπὸ πατρὸς λωβᾶσθαι. The reference is to Agamemnon's rash vow (cf. εὐκταίαν of l. 213) and its intended fulfilment.

σφάγιον = the victim slaughtered; **θῦμα** = the slaughtered victim burnt.

213. This line as it stands in the MSS. needs a syllable to complete the catalectic dimeter. Kirchhoff's εὐκταίαν, ⟨ἅν⟩ is palaeographically likely and is necessary to the construction unless we accept, as Prof. Murray does, Monk's ἱππείοις ⟨δ'⟩ in the next line. Prof. Murray's own suggestion ⟨θεοῖς⟩ ἔτεκεν gives good sense (θεοῖς going with εὐγάθητον) and avoids the rare short syllable (-τŏν) at the end of l. 212; see note on l. 220 below. Hermann suggested ἔτρεφεν, ⟨εὖτ'⟩ εὐκταίαν. εὖτ' might easily have dropped out by haplography.

215. Note the very rare conjunction of dactyl + anapaest — Αὐλῐ́δŏς | ἐ̆πῐ́βᾱ |.

For **ἐπέβασαν** + gen. = to disembark (some one) on, cf. Od. 7. 223 ἐμῆς ἐπιβήσετε πάτρης. The subject is 'the Greeks' understood. With Monk's ⟨δ'⟩ in 214 ἐπέβασαν is the verb of a main sentence; with Kirchhoff's ⟨ἅν⟩ or Hermann's ⟨εὖτ'⟩ in l. 213 the verb of a clause. Canter's simple ἐπιβᾶσαν would render such emendations unnecessary from the point of view of construction.

But we have seen that l.213 lacks a foot, and in any case the sentence so formed would be intolerably long and rambling.

216. The MSS. νύμφαιον will only scan if we take the word as a dactyl; cf. the scansion of παλαιός in S. *Ph.* 421 (O.C.T.); *fr.* 956; E. *El.* 497. So, too, δείλαια at S. *El.* 849, E. *Supp.* 279. Scaliger suggested νύμφαν; England (better) νύμφαν μ'; Weil νύμφευμ' (cf. E. *Tr.* 420 καλὸν νύμφευμα).

219. **δυσχόρτους**, pastureless, barren, is an odd epithet for οἴκους, and Köchly may be right in emending to συγχόρτους = bordering, marching with. For the gen. cf. E. *Andr.* 16, 7 πόλεως Φαρσαλίας | σύγχορτα . . . πεδία.

220. There is no need to regard this line as an anapaestic tripody with resolved long syllables, i.e. ◡ ◡ ◡́ ◡ ◡ ◡ ◡́ ◡ ◡ ◡ ◡́ ◡ or to prefix ⟨ἰώ,⟩ (see crit. note), for we can suppose an epic lengthening of ἄτεκνος, and so get a catalectic dimeter. For the short syllable of the catalectic foot, very rare where no strong stop follows, see E. *Ion* 898. [Wilamowitz, *Verskunst*, p. 267, apparently regards this line and l. 232 below as resolved trochaics.]

For the type of phrase cf. S. *Ant.* 876 ἄκλαυτος, ἄφιλος, ἀνυμέναιος; E. *Or.* 310 ἀνάδελφος, ἀπάτωρ, ἄφιλος; *Andr.* 491 ἄθεος ἄνομος, ἄχαρις; and *Hec.* 669 ἄπαις ἄνανδρος ἄπολις; and for the scansion cf. E. *Ion* 889.

221. Hera, tutelary goddess of Argos, is naturally mentioned by Iphigenia; the reference in the next few lines to the πέπλος woven by Athenian women for the summer festival of the Athenian Pallas is made by the poet for the sake of his audience. The same matter is mentioned again at greater length in E. *Hec.* 466–74. Cf. [Virg.] *Cir.* 28, 9 Ergo Palladiae texuntur in ordine pugnae; | Magna Giganteis ornantur pepla tropaeis.

223. **καλλιφθόγγοις** refers not, as has been sometimes thought, to the song of the weavers but to the clatter of the loom. Edd. compare Ar. *Ra.* 1316 κερκίδος ἀοιδοῦ μελέτας (quoted, according to the scholiast on the passage, from the Meleager of Euripides), and *AP.* 6. 288. 5 (Leonidas of Tarentum) κερκίδα, τὰν ἱστῶν μολπάτιδα. If Virgil had the passage in mind when he wrote *G.* 1. 293, 4 Interea longum cantu solata laborem | Arguto coniunx percurrit pectine telas he accepted both explanations. We should expect the adj. to qualify κερκίδι rather than ἱστοῖς, but the transference is not unnatural and Badham's ἱστοῖσιν καλλιφθόγγῳ is unnecessary.

226. The easiest emendation of this nonsensical and unmetrical line is Matthiae's rejection of βωμούς as a gloss. βωμούς would be indeed the natural object of αἱμάσσουσα; ἄταν is a sort of internal acc. The sense is 'inflicting on strangers a bloody fate'. Other more elaborate and less likely emendations are: (1) Wecklein's ἁγνίζουσ' ἄταν [βωμούς], i.e. dedicating the fate of strangers; (2) Madvig's αἱμορράντῳ (note the MSS. give αἱμορράντων; our αἱμόρραντον is due to Monk) δυσφόρμιγγας ξείνων στάζουσ' ἄτᾳ βωμούς; (3) Köchly's τέγγουσ' ἄταν βωμοῖς. This last is very improbable, for, granting one can say τέγγουσ' ἄταν αἱμόρραντον = shedding fateful blood (cf. note on l. 162), yet the dat. (locative) βωμοῖς is slightly awkward; (4) Prof. Murray's πάσσουσ' for αἱμάσσουσ' (see *app. crit.*). πάσσω is found with the acc. both of the thing sprinkled and of that with which it is sprinkled. Here we should get both together.

δυσφόρμιγγα gives a good antithesis to καλλιφθόγγοις. There is nothing 'musical' about Iph.'s present rites.

230. **δμαθέντᾱ κλαίω** is metrically doubtful; cf. Descroix, Trim. iamb. p. 18. We might accept Weil's δμαθέντ' ἀγκλαίω (= ἀνα-κλαίω).

231–2. As our text stands we are left with the first line ending in a tribrach, **-τίδιὄν**, instead of an anapaest, and the second consisting of three resolved anapaests. Wecklein's τότε (for the first ἔτι) or Heath's ἐπιμαστίδιόν ⟨γ'⟩ saves l. 231 without helping 232. Prof. Murray's ⟨σύγγονον⟩ ἔτι would mend both lines, giving us two resolved acatalectic dimeters. It, or something like it, should probably be accepted. Homoeocatarcton would account for the falling out of the second σύγγονον.

[We might possibly read [ἔτι] β., ἔτι ν., ἔτι θάλος ἐν χερσὶν | ματρὸς . . . Ἄργει | ⟨— —⟩ σκ. Ὀρ., or (l. 235) σκηπτ. ⟨— ⏑⟩ Ὀρ.]

236–391. First episode.

(*a*) Iphigenia and the herdsman, 236–343.

(*b*) Iphigenia's monologue, 344–91.

240. Not (as Wecklein and others) 'what is it that scares me from my present conversation?', which would almost necessitate Markland's τό με for τοῦ. Nor do Musgrave's μόγου or Lenting's γόου (for λόγου) help matters. The meaning is rather 'what is there ⟨so⟩ alarming in your news?' Cf. l. 773 below.

241. The singular is curious, but it occurs again in the MSS. at E. *Andr.* 794. (The O.C.T. there accepts, however, Hermann's ποντιᾶν Ξυμπληγάδων, and there is much to be said for Bentley's plural here; see *app. crit.*)

243. With **πρόσφαγμα καὶ θυτήριον**, cf. ll. 211, 12 σφάγιον . . . θῦμα. θυτήριον is strange, = θῦμα. It is used elsewhere (by Aratus (403) and Quintus Smyrnaeus (4. 554)) as = the constellation Ara. The προ- of πρόσφαγμα has here little or no meaning as at A. *Ag.* 1278 and E. *Tr.* 628, unless indeed we accept ll. 258, 9 as they stand (see notes on them). In this case πρόσφαγμα would = πρῶτον σφάγμα. If we may argue from the προθύσων of E. *Ion* 805 the προ- of πρόσφαγμα = ὑπέρ, so that the word means a sacrifice on behalf of some one; here of the Taurians.

246. If the MSS. ὄνομ' is right (and it is the reading of the papyrus) it cannot be taken with γῆς. Strangers do not bear the name of their (or of any) country. Follow Verrall, therefore, and punctuate: ποδαποί; τίνος γῆς; ὄνομ', κτλ.; 'have the strangers a name?', i.e. 'did you learn their names?' But Monk's σχῆμ' saves an awkward mixed question, and is better answered by Ἕλληνες. (For this use of σχῆμα cf. E. *Ion* 237, 8 τρόπων τεκμήριον | τὸ σχῆμ' ἔχεις τόδ'; *fr.* 476 Τευθράντιον δὲ σχῆμα Μυσίας χθονός and S. *Ph.* 223, 4 σχῆμα μὲν γὰρ Ἑλλάδος | στολῆς ὑπάρχει.)

249. Pylades was not yet born at the time of Iph.'s attempted sacrifice (cf. l. 920 below and l. 59 above) and the name would mean nothing to her. It is natural that the more excitable Or. should twice address Pyl. by name (ll. 285 and 321) while the more phlegmatic Pyl. makes no reply—and it is of course dramatically imperative that Or.'s name should not be mentioned.

250. It is almost impossible to make **τοῦ ξένου** (adj.) qualify **τοῦ ξυζύγου**, 'of the stranger companion'. Better take it 'of the stranger's companion' (i.e. of Orestes). This is awkward and Elmsley's τῷ ξυζύγῳ is tempting. Weil's δὲ λέξον αὖ τί gives good sense and is palaeographically not improbable.

252. Musgrave's ποῦ for MSS. πῶς is attractive considering the oxherd's answer, but it should involve the alteration of the πῶς in 256, since in that line Iph. bids the oxherd 'return' to her former question. If, further, we regard l. 253 as an interrupted recital by the oxherd, his failure to answer the question immediately is natural enough.

Pap. Hib. 24 confirms Reiske's conjecture κἀντυχόντες for MSS. καὶ τυχόντες.

253. The Hib. pap. has Εὐξείνου (as does Plu. 2. 602 a), but ἀξείνου is probably the right reading (cf. l. 125 and *app. crit.* there).

254. It would have been more natural, as Grégoire points out, if one of the murex-gatherers (l. 263) had been the ἄγγελος at this juncture, but Eur. no doubt wished to introduce the picturesque incident of the slaughter of the cattle, perhaps in imitation of the well-known scene in the *Ajax*.

258–9. These two lines as they stand in the MSS. will scarcely translate. (*a*) **χρόνιοι . . . ἥκουσι** lacks a subject and we have to understand one out of **νιν** (l. 256); (*b*) **γάρ** is illogical, and (*c*) the statement that the altar has not (i.e. never) yet been stained by Hellene blood is, I think, false. [True Iph. never 'expressly says' it has (see *app. crit.*), but if not (1) what was the fate of the αἰχμάλωτος (l. 585) and why did he not deliver, as well as write, Iph.'s letter? (2) how did Iph. placate the goddess or satisfy Thoas when Greeks fell into her hands? Further, I do not believe that ἡνίκ' in l. 347 (see crit. note) *can* = εἴ ποτ', or that that line can refer to any time but the past.] Seidler's οἶδ' ἐπεί for οὐδέ πω (where ἐπεί = ἀφ' οὗ as, e.g., at E. *Med.* 26 and *Or.* 78), with no stop at ἥκουσ', = 'these men have come at a long interval of time since the altar was ⟨last⟩ stained . . .', gets over difficulties (*a*) and (*c*); and (*b*) can be solved if, with Wecklein, we put the lines after 245, giving them to the βουκόλος. This should probably be done, unless, with Monk, we excise the lines altogether.

The use of the adj. χρόνιοι where in English we should use an adverbial phrase is common in Greek; e.g. Thuc. I. 141. 7 χρόνιοι . . . ξυνιόντες; for Euripidean examples cf. *Cyc.* 249, *Andr.* 84, *Ion* 403, etc.

260–3. The illogicality of 'when we had plunged . . . there was a cave' can be almost exactly paralleled in Athena's ῥῆσις (ll. 1449, 50 below), ὅταν . . . μόλῃς, | χῶρός τις ἔστι, and in the messenger's speech of E. *Hipp.* (1198, 9) ἐπεὶ δ' ἔρημον χῶρον εἰσεβάλλομεν, | ἀκτή τις ἔστι . . .; cf. also S. *Tr.* 750–3 ὅθ' εἵρπε . . . ἀκτή τις . . . ἐστίν. This proves Bothe's ᾗ τις unnecessary. The transitive use of εἰσβάλλειν with a bare accusative of direction is rare. Mähly's ἐπεὶ ⟨'s⟩ may be right. ἐσρέοντα is odd in view of the fact that the water flows not into but out of the Euxine, and Elmsley's ἐκρέοντα may be textually as well as geographically correct. Little stress, however, can be laid on any geographical argument, for Eur. throughout seems to confuse the Thracian Bosporus (the 'real' position of the Symplegades) with the Cimmerian Bosporus which lay near the scene of the play.

ὑλοφορβοῦς: edd. cite Hes. *Op.* 591 καὶ βοὸς ὑλοφάγοιο κρέας. [The adj. is a ἅπ. λεγ. and its accentuation uncertain; but, being passive in sense ('fed on tree-leaves') it should probably be proparox. on the analogy of εὔφορβος.]

ἀγμός (transmitted correctly by L only) fr. ἄγνυμι occurs again in the plural in E. *Ba.* 1094 = crag.

κοιλωπός (note Eur.'s fondness for adjs. so formed) should be taken with the instrumental dat. σάλῳ = worn hollow by the waves.

πορφυρευτικαί = τῶν πορφυρέων. The purple-fishers would use the cave while watching the floats of their traps (see Pollux (I. 47–9) for a description).

265. Though ἀναχωρεῖν is commoner than ἀποχωρεῖν in the sense of 'retreat', 'withdraw' there is no need to accept Blomfield's suggested emendation. For πορθμεύειν = convey, cf. l. 936 π. πόδα, etc. England notes that this verb, rare elsewhere, is used eight times in this play.

270. When Athamas, king of Thessaly, killed his son Learchus in a fit of madness his wife Ino leapt into the sea with the surviving son, Melicertes. Ino and Melicertes were subsequently turned by Poseidon into sea deities under the names respectively of Leucothea and Palaemon.

272. Understand ἵλεω γένεσθον.

εἴτε . . . ἤ for εἴτε . . . εἴτε cf. E. *El.* 896, 7. Wecklein's suggested ἐπ' ἀκτῆς is unnecessary: ἐπ' ἀκταῖς is found in Eur. almost as often. At E. *Hec.* 28 (see *app. crit.*) the MSS. vary between ἐπ' ἀκταῖς and ἐπ' ἀκτῆς.

273. Whatever be the explanation of this rather puzzling line it is *not* that the θεοσεβής, overcome by religious awe, mistook Orestes and Pylades for two of the Nereids as some edd. have strangely thought. Either Nereus had, besides fifty daughters, at least two sons, or the ἀγάλματα (= *deliciae*, darlings) referred to are his grandsons. In S. *Ant.* 1115 Dionysus is called Καδμείας ἄγαλμα νύμφας; and cf. E. *Supp.* 370 and 1164 ματέρος ἄγαλμα and *fr. trag. adesp.* 126. 3 Αἰτωλίδος ἀγάλματα ματρός. Schenkl arbitrarily excised this line and the next.

275. μάταιος = scoffer. We see here the touch of 'Euripides the rationalist'. As Weil remarks: 'L'esprit fort, qui ne veut pas croire à une théophanie, finit par avoir raison.'

277. For θάσσειν with acc. of place where cf. E. *Ion* 91 θ. τρίποδα and *Andr.* 117 θ. δάπεδον καὶ ἀνάκτορα (L & S).

278. Tournier's οὑνθάδε (οἱ ἐνθάδε) may be right; cf. l. 87 (note).

280. ἔδοξε is to be understood with θηρᾶν, but in an impersonal sense: 'he seemed . . . and it seemed good . . .'

283. Except in this passage the verb ἀποστενάζω does not occur. Indeed it is not cited at all in L & S[9]. Hence Monk's κἀνεστέναξεν.

284. If the κυναγός of the MSS. is correct we must suppose the oxherd to mean that Orestes shouted to Pylades as a hunter might shout to warn a companion of the approach of some beast. This would be quite satisfactory but for the fact that Orestes is usually depicted as hunted by, not as hunting, the Furies. Hence such suggested emendations as Hermann's βοᾷ· "κυναγὸν ὥς, Π., . . . τήνδε;" or Weil's βοᾷ· "κυναγὸν οὔ, Π., . . . τήνδε;". Nauck went further and rejected κυναγὸς ὥς altogether in favour of κυνώπιδα (similarly in the oratio recta and agreeing with τήνδε). Wecklein, too, would eject καὶ . . . ὥς, regarding it as a gloss which has ousted some such phrase as κἀπιθωύσσει φίλῳ.

The phrase μανίαις ἀλαίνων occurs also at E. *Or.* 532.

287. ἐστομωμένη: στόμα (= *acies*) is used for the edge of a weapon or the front of an army. The participle here means 'having brought herself into line against me with her vipers'; i.e. 'forming into line against me the vipers which compose her hair'. For this use of στομόω edd. cite Plut. *Ant.* 42 ἀκοντισταῖς καὶ σφενδονήταις . . . τὰς πλευρὰς ἑκατέρας στομώσας. Cf. further the common phrase κατὰ στόμα; e.g. E. *Heracl.* 800, 1 ἐπεὶ γὰρ ἀλλήλοισιν ὁπλίτην στρατὸν | κατὰ στόμ' ἐκτείνοντες ἀντετάξαμεν.

288. If χιτώνων is right we must suppose that a line has dropped out between it and πῦρ, e.g. νυκτὶ προσφερῶν ἰδεῖν | ἐμοὶ στομωτόν (Heinisch). If there is no lacuna χιτώνων is almost certainly wrong. It cannot be taken as = 'slough', as L & S[8]. We may set aside a host of emendations not worth the paper they are written on and accept Kirchhoff's very probable ἐκ τρίτων αὖ = thirdly. Cf. E. *Or.* 1178 σωτηρίαν σοὶ τῷδέ τ' ἐκ τρίτων τ' ἐμοί. For the triad of Furies cf. E. *Or.* 408 ἔδοξ' ἰδεῖν τρεῖς νυκτὶ προσφερεῖς κόρας and *ib.* 1650 Εὐμενίσι τρισσαῖς. This emendation becomes even more plausible if we could accept Hermann's τήνδε δ' αὖθ' ὁρᾷς in l. 285.

[Matthiae's suggestion that ἐκ χιτ. πτεροῖς ἐρέσσει is to be taken together = (apparently) 'rows with wings ⟨projecting⟩ out of her garments' is unlikely to command respect. The passage in A. *Eu.* (404) where Athene flies using the κόλπον αἰγίδος as wings is no real parallel.]

290. The MSS. πέτρινον ὄχθον has been taken as acc. of the end of motion with πτεροῖς ἐρέσσει, 'wings her way to the rocky eminence'. But (1) it is badly misplaced; (2) ὄχθος is an odd word for the cliff which contained the cave. Much the same objections might be urged against Hirzel's περὶ τὸν ὄχθον, except that the presence of the preposition eases the difficulty of word-order. Further πέτρινον has an air of genuineness about it, and a sounder line of emendation is to correct not it but ὄχθον (a thing which even in a madman's words cannot be 'thrown') into ὄγκον (Heimsöth) or ἄχθος (Greverus), taking these words as in apposition to μητέρα and so the object of ἔχουσα. The apposition of πέτρινον ἄχθος to μητέρα is not surprising in the mouth of the mad Orestes.

ὡς ἐπεμβάλῃ, scil. 'her on me'; not 'dash her on the ὄχθος', as L & S. Verrall (*CR.* 1913, p. 225) would keep the text, taking ὄχθον = grave or barrow, as at A. *Pers.* 647, 659: 'it seems to him (Orestes) as if, in some way, the cold corpse of his murdered mother were to be or become the stone which is to crush and imprison him.' It is doubtful, however, whether without a more suitable context ὄχθον could or would be so understood.

292–4. Wecklein, doubting μορφῆς σχήματ', accepts Heimsöth's οὐ ταὖτ' ἄμορφα, but E. *Ion* 992 ποῖόν τι μορφῆς σχῆμ' ἔχουσαν ἀγρίας; suggests that the MSS. here are right. If anything in the line is reasonably suspect it is the word μορφῆς itself. We should certainly have expected something like Markland's φωνῆς or Burges' ταὖτ' ἄρ' ὀμφῆς. It is what he *hears*, not what he *sees*, that Or. misinterprets. Perhaps the best line to take is to postulate, with Bruhn, a lacuna after ἠλλάσσετο and to suppose the sense (reading ταὐτά and ἃ φάσκ') 'one could see him not keep the same attitude but change it ⟨according to the visions which he said he saw. Then, when he approached us he heard⟩ the lowing of our cattle and the barking of our dogs, which he swore were the cries of the Furies imitating such sounds.'

ἀλλ' . . . μιμήματα. At least the ungrammatical ἃς of the MSS. must be altered. The correction involving the least change is Badham's ἃ ᾽φασκ': 'he misinterpreted the lowing of cattle and the barking of dogs which he imagined the Furies were emitting as an imitation', i.e. he thought what he heard was an imitation by the Furies of lowing, etc. Prof. Murray's δόξας gives much the same sense, and that sense is not bad. But ἀλλάσσεσθαι = 'to alter in imagination' is surely impossible. Better (if the crasis of καὶ ἅ be legitimate) is Heimsöth's χἅ φασ': 'he confused the lowing . . . and (i.e. "with") what imitations men say the Furies emit'. We should expect a genitive (μιμημάτων ἅ φασι . . .), but the καί construction is not impossible. But though to a diseased imagination the Furies may seem to imitate cattle and dogs, it is nonsense to say that men say they do, and this emendation necessitates something like Nauck's μυκήματα. Herwerden's βριμήματα would be more attractive were the word itself better attested (it occurs only in *APl.* 103, if the reading is correct; and at A. *Th.* 461 we get ἐμβριμωμένας).

295. Some edd. have regarded the superscript μβ in L (see *app. crit.*) as an attempt of the scribe to 'correct' θανούμενοι to θαμβούμενοι. Hence its inclusion in our text. Badham held that this μβ meant 'second future' (μέλλων β') and was therefore no more than a grammatical note on θανούμενοι. However this may be we can scarcely welcome θαμβούμενοι as a reading since (1) the middle of θαμβέω is not classical; (2) ὡς in this case has no meaning (nor is ὥς much better). θανούμενοι is unsatisfactory, for the oxherds are in no danger. Wilamowitz' θανουμένου is good: 'shrinking back from him as being about to die'. We can take the gen. as either one of separation or as absolute, understanding τούτου. Cf. E. *Alc.* 191 ὡς θανουμένη.

298. The MSS. will translate, 'He pierced their flanks with his iron sword, thrusting it into their ribs'. But Reiske's ⟨θ'⟩ is easier. The construction is ⟨εἰς⟩ λαγόνας εἴς τε πλευρὰς ἱεὶς ⟨αὐτόν⟩; cf. E. *Ph.* 284 μαντεῖα σεμνὰ Λοξίου τ' ἐπ' ἐσχάρας, *IA.* 210 αἰγιαλοῖς παρά τε κροκάλαις, etc. The loss of Θ after C is not unusual.

299. *Not*, as Seidler, 'thinking that such things could ward off the Furies'. τάδε stands for the internal acc. τάσδε τὰς ἀμύνας. It can, however, be translated simply 'thus'.

300. Again (cf. l. 298) Θ may have fallen out after C and Markland's ὥσθ' for MSS. ὡς be correct. Still, ὡς + inf. = ὥστε is not uncommon in the tragedians, e.g. S. *Ant.* 292, *ib.* 303, E. *Cyc.* 647, etc.; cf. K.-G. II. ii, p. 501.

πέλαγος ἁλός = 'the sea' is odd, though Aesch. uses ἅλς πελαγία (*Pers.* 427, *ib.* 467), and Eur. himself ἅλιον πέλαγος (*Andr.* 1011). If Housman is right (*Journ. Phil.* 25, p. 244) there is a Latin parallel in Lucr. 5. 1442 maris . . . pontus. Wecklein adopts the correction in P, πέλανον (i.e. πελανόν), which is no improvement. Keep πέλαγος with αἱματηρόν as proleptic: 'the sea was coloured blood-red'. ἐξανθεῖν should be taken not of foam but of colour. For ἄνθος so used cf. Pl. *R.* 429 D ὅπως δέξεται (the wool) ὅτι μάλιστα τὸ ἄνθος (here = ἁλουργόν), also A. *Pr.* 23 χροιᾶς ἀμείψεις ἄνθος. For ἀνθέω cf. X. *Cyr.* 6. 4. 1 ἤνθει φοινικίσι . . . ἡ στρατιά (L & S). [Aesch. uses ἀνθέω in a different sense at *Ag.* 659 ὁρῶμεν ἀνθοῦν πέλαγος Αἰγαῖον νεκροῖς. Here, as Verrall says, 'the sea is a plain or field which in the morning is seen to have broken out in flowers after the rain'.]

303. **κόχλος**, the primitive trumpet. Edd. cite Hesych. *κόχλοις τοῖς θαλαττίοις ἐχρῶντο πρὸ τῆς τῶν σαλπίγγων εὑρέσεως.* Cf. Theoc. 9. 27 *ὁ δ' ἐγκαναχήσατο κόχλῳ*, *id.* 22. 75 *Ἄμυκος . . . κόχλον ἑλὼν ἐμυκήσατο κοῖλον.*

306. **ἐν μακρῷ χρόνῳ** seems weak, and seemed so, apparently, to the corrector of L who wrote in *μικρῷ*. Nauck's [*ἐν*] *οὐ μακρῷ* is possible; *οὐ μακρῷ χρόνῳ* = soon, appears at S. *Ph.* 360, and cf. *O. C.* 1648 *χρόνῳ βραχεῖ.* Wecklein quotes instances from Homer, Theognis, and the tragedians of the antithesis *πολλοί—παῦροι* and boldly reads here *ἐν παύρῳ*. It is possible that *οὐ μακρῷ* was a gloss on this, of which *μακρᾷ* only got into the text.

πολλοί is used proleptically, 'our numbers were filled up so that we became many'; cf. E. *Andr.* 1097 *ἀρχαὶ ἐπληροῦντο*—if this, the MSS., be the right reading (the O.C.T. here accepts an emendation of Verrall's); and *Or.* 884 *ἐπεὶ δὲ πλήρης ἐγένετ' Ἀργείων ὄχλος.*

307. **μανίας πίτυλον**, 'the pulse of madness'. Another nautical metaphor, *πίτυλος* being used particularly for the rhythmic beat of oars. For this metaphorical use cf. E. *HF.* 1189 *μαινομένῳ πιτύλῳ πλαγχθείς*, and in the same play (l. 816) *πίτυλον φόβου.*

308. **γένειον** is not a direct but an internal acc. Cf. A. *Eu.* 42 *αἵματι στάζοντα χεῖρας* and S. *Aj.* 10 *κάρα στάζων ἱδρῶτι* (L & S).

309. **προύργου** (= *πρὸ ἔργου*) = suitably ⟨for us⟩. Eur. uses the adv. again at *Hel.* 1379.

πόνον ἔχειν = to be busy. Cf. E. *Hec.* 572 *οὐδεὶς τὸν αὐτὸν εἶχεν Ἀργείων πόνον*: i.e. they were busy in various ways. Theoc. 7. 139 *τέττιγες λελαγεῦντες ἔχον πόνον.* The aor. is odd. Perhaps *εἶχεν* should be read.

310. Eur. seems fond of this particular combination, cf. *Andr.* 1153, 4 *τίς οὐ σίδηρον προσφέρει, τίς οὐ πέτρον | βάλλων, ἀράσσων*; and *Hec.* 1173–5 *θὴρ ὣς διώκω . . . βάλλων, ἀράσσων.* Soph. used such asyndeton participles at the start of a line in *Ph.* 11 *βοῶν, στενάζων* and *Tr.* 787 *βοῶν, ἰύζων*; and Eur. at *HF.* 602 *ἕλξων, φονεύσων* and *Or.* 951 *κλαίοντες, οἰκτίροντες.*

311. *ψάω* contracts in *η*, and in spite of the testimony of Lucian—or rather of the Lucian MSS. (the passage is quoted with *ἀπέψα* in Luc. *Am.* 47)—we should read *ἀπέψη.*

If the MSS. are to be trusted at E. *IA.* 731 *τημελεῖν* takes an acc., as it does at Moschio trag. 6. 12 (with Salmasius' certain emendation *ὀρχάτους ἐτημέλει*), but it is possible that in the *IA.* passage *παρθένων* should be read for *παρθένους.*

312. In the above mentioned passage of Lucian we find *πέπλου . . . εὐπήκτους*—an indication not of what we should read here so much as of the dangers of unverified citation. *εὐπήνους* (*πήνη*) is far preferable to *εὐπήκτους* (*πήγνυμι*) as an epithet of *ὑφάς*, cf. below ll. 814 and 1465.

For καλύπτειν with the acc. of the screen cf. Il. 5. 315 πρόσθε δέ οἱ πέπλοιο φαεινοῦ πτύγμ' ἐκάλυψεν and 17. 132, 3 ἀμφὶ Μενοιτιάδῃ σάκος εὐρὺ καλύψας | ἑστήκει.

313. **καραδοκῶν** here in its original and literal sense, practically = 'dodging'.

320. οὗ δή = 'at which point'; παρακέλευμα seems the older form (so L & S[9]), but Eur. may have written παρακέλευσμα.

321. While **ὅπως** with the 2nd person of the fut. in commands is common (and colloquial), its use with the first person is rare. Cf. Ar. *Ec.* 297 ὅπως . . . πλησίοι καθεδούμεθα; cf. K.-G. II. ii, p. 376.

323. **δίπαλτα.** Not as L & S 'brandished with two hands', though the adj. has that meaning at E. *Tr.* 1102 δίπαλτον . . . κεραυνοφαὲς πῦρ. Here it means 'the two brandished swords'; cf. δίκροτος in l. 408.

325. **τις** = 'one or two'. **εἰ φύγοι** here is frequentative: cf. E. *Hec.* 1166, 7 εἰ δὲ κινοίην χέρας | πλήθει γυναικῶν οὐδὲν ἤνυον τάλας.

In this construction εἰ and ὅτε (or ὁπότε) are interchangeable; cf. E. *Supp.* 897, 8 ὁπότ' εὖ πράσσοι πόλις | ἔχαιρε, λυπρῶς δ' ἔφερεν, εἴ τι δυστυχοῖ; see K.-G. II. ii, p. 476.

326. **αὐτούς** = Or. and Pyl. **εἰ δέ, κτλ.** 'But if they (i.e. Or. and Pyl.) thrust these (ἅτεροι) back, in their turn the but recently (νῦν) yielding party . . .' Notice Eur.'s use of the so-called 'vocalic ν' (ὠσαίατο for ὤσαιντο) for metrical reasons.

327. **τὸ ὑπεῖκον** being virtually a plural (cf. τις in l. 325) the plural verb of the MSS. (ἤρασσον) is probably correct.

328–9. Tournier suggested ἕν γ' for ἦν, which gives good sense. But there is no need to suspect the MSS.

μυρίων ἐκ χερῶν goes with βαλών, as though Eur. had been going to write after it βαλλόμενοι, ὑπ' οὐδενὸς ἐτρώθησαν. Badham's ηὐστόχει is quite unnecessary, and Mekler's εὐχερῶν for ἐκ χερῶν ('no one out of countless skilled aimers') improbable though ingenious. Or. and Pyl. were indeed under the protection of the gods as the oxherd thought, but for a different reason. According to Meisterhans (p. 171) ηὐτύχει is the better form.

θύματα = the ⟨destined human⟩ victims; cf. A. *Ag.* 1118 θύματος λευσίμου.

330. The constr. is μόλις χειρούμεθά νιν, οὐ τόλμῃ ἀλλά . . . Mähly's τέλος for μόλις is unnecessary.

331. κλέπτειν has here the sense of 'to wrest unfairly' (in modern English 'unsportingly'). Cf. Theoc. 22. 151 γάμον ἐκλέπτετε δώροις. There is no need to emend, though Bothe's ἐξεκόψαμεν gives good sense. Hermann's ἐξελέψαμεν ('we peeled'), though very near the MSS., will not commend itself to many; still less Köchly's ἐξεκλέψαμεν | πέπλοισι; i.e. 'with our garments'.

335. Some correction must be made of the impossible MSS. **τε χέρνιβας.** Our text accepts Valckenaer's ἐς. Hartung's ἐπί would do; but perhaps best Prof. Housman's πρός, supposing this preposition to have been written πρ and so corrupted into τε.

σφαγεῖ' is Musgrave's emendation of the unmetrical σφάγι'. There is MSS. confusion between σφάγιον and σφαγεῖον at E. *El.* 800; and σφάγια may have been the 'correction' of a scribe ignorant of metre whose eye fell on σφάγια in l. 337. σφαγάς (Heath) gives better sense, but σφάγιον, properly = victim, is not infrequently used for σφαγή = slaughter (e.g. in l. 40 of this play); and σφαγεῖον too, properly = bowl for catching sacrificial blood, may well be so used. The word occurs with χέρνιβες at Lyc. 196 σφαγείων ἠδὲ χερνίβων πέλας. ἐς (or πρός) is purposive. Understand νιν from l. 334 as object both of ἐσιδών and ἔπεμπε.

336. Keeping the MSS. εὔχου (imperative) we must understand ἄλλα with τοιάδε or even emend to σοι θαμὰ [ξένων] (Stadtmüller) or πολλά σοι [ξένων] (Paley and Barthold), regarding ξένων as a gloss. Our text accepts Mekler's ηὔχου (imperf.). The sense then is 'you have often prayed for such victims'.

[Though σοι is not emphatic the accentuation should rather be ὦ νεᾶνι, σοί; cf. Chandler, *Greek Accentuation*², p. 270.]

337. The present stem ἀναλίσκω is not found elsewhere in tragedy and Mekler's ἀναλώσῃς may well be right.

338. (ἀπο)τείσει, not (ἀπο)τίσει (Meisterhans, p. 180).

339. τίνουσα need not surprise after ἀποτείσει of the previous line. Köchly would read διδοῦσα; Nauck ejects the line as spurious.

340. It may be that θαυμαστὰ λέγειν τινά is an extension of the common εὖ λέγειν τινά construction. Edd. cite E. *Ph.* 200, 1 ἡδονὴ δέ τις | γυναιξὶ μηδὲν ὑγιὲς ἀλλήλας λέγειν. But it is at least equally likely that the construction is: θαυμάστ' ἔλεξας τὸν (= this) μανέντ' ἐλθεῖν, ὅστις ποτ' ἐστὶν ὃς ἦλθεν; 'You have spoken a marvel that this madman has come, whoever, &c.' Our text accepts Kähler's μανέντα for the MSS. φανέντα = this man who has appeared. Wecklein's suggested σφαλέντ' is nearer the MSS. but gives less good sense. Cf. l. 3 of Hypothesis to the play and note.

341. Elmsley's Ἑλληνίδος γῆς is unnecessary; as Ἕλλην, though usually masc. ()(Ἑλληνίς) is sometimes used with feminine substantives, e.g. A. *Ag.* 1254 Ἕλλην(α) . . . φάτιν, E. *Heracl.* 130 στολὴν . . . Ἕλληνα, and below l. 495 πατρίδος Ἕλληνος (where (again) Elmsley suggested Ἑλλήνων).

343. The MSS. text is objectionable for two reasons: (1) οἷα = οἷα ἔσται is impossible; (2) the fut. mid. of φροντίζειν is not elsewhere used. Prof. Murray's aposiopesis (with Reiske's ὅσια) saves (1), and (2) may be no more than a chance. For the sake of the sceptical some other emendations may be mentioned (though it is hard to see how the supposed corruption arose): φροντιοῦμεν οἷα χρή (Badham); οὐκ ἀφροντιστήσομεν (Madvig); ἔσμεν οἳ

φροντίζομεν (Wecklein—who urges, unconvincingly, that ἐσμεν might have fallen out after ἡμεῖς).

346. ἐς τὸ ὁμόφυλον = (almost) τῆς ὁμοφυλίας ἕνεκα. This passage surely supplies convincing proof that Greeks *had* already been sacrificed; that Iph. *wept* does not imply that she did *not* sacrifice; see ll. 258, 9 and notes.

349. δοκοῦσα after ἠγριώμεθα (as if it had been ἠγρίωμαι) is not unusual; cf. 579 (and note) ἥκομεν . . . σπεύδουσα (if Musgrave's emendation is accepted), and E. *HF.* 858 ἥλιον μαρτυρόμεσθα δρῶσ' ἃ δρᾶν οὐ βούλομαι. But, as Wecklein says (and Nauck thought), the line has rather the air of an interpolation. Also it is hard grammatically to justify μηκέτι which should be οὐκέτι.

351. MSS. ἠχθόμην: L. Dindorf ᾐσθόμην which all edd. accept. But surely we should emend to ᾔσθημαι? Cf. *E. Hipp.* 1403.

352–3. Misfortune, says Iph., has made me cruel. The παροιμία as it stands in the MSS. can only mean 'the unfortunate when themselves in trouble are not well disposed towards the more fortunate'. To this there are two objections: (1) αὐτοὶ κακῶς πράξαντες is redundant (also we should expect πράσσοντες); (2) Or. and Pyl. cannot be referred to as εὐτυχέστεροι.

Reiske's αὐτοῖς κ. πράξασιν gets over these two difficulties, but 'the more fortunate when they themselves (as well as the normally δυστυχεῖς) are in trouble' is odd. This emendation Wecklein now introduces into his text to the neglect of his own better one which our text accepts—τοῖσι δυστυχεστέροις. Even so αὐτοὶ κ. πράξ. is objectionable. An added point is gained if the δυστυχεῖς were once εὐτυχεῖς, and this can be effected if we read Dindorf's πάλαι καλῶς πράξ. or Rauchenstein's αὐτοί ποτ' εὖ πράξ. Further, this justifies the *aor.* participle. Weil's reading

τῷ δυστυχεῖ γὰρ οἱ πρὶν εὐτυχέστεροι
αὐτοὶ κακῶς, κτλ.,

gives good sense, but is too far from the MSS. to command acceptance.

354. The thought continues from l. 350. 'I shall deal harshly with these strangers undeserving of harshness though they are, for I cannot avenge myself on the real culprits.'

οὔτε . . . οὐ is common in trag. Cf. E. *Med.* 1348, 9, *Tr.* 934. Because, in ll. 438 sqq., the chorus express a wish that Helen should arrive among the Tauri there is no need to accept here Kirchhoff's emendation ἀλλ' εἴθε . . . ἡ πορθμίς. ἵνα with the past tense of the indic. in l. 357 is as idiomatic after a negative statement as after a wish, though doubtless less common; e.g. S. *OT.* 1387–9 οὐκ ἂν ἐσχόμην | τὸ μὴ ἀποκλῇσαι τοὐμὸν ἄθλιον δέμας, | ἵν' ἦ τυφλός, and Pl. *Tht.* 161 C, τεθαύμακα ὅτι οὐκ εἶπεν . . . ὅτι πάντων χρημάτων μέτρον ἐστὶν ὗς . . . ἵνα . . . ἤρξατο . . . If a wish (in the form of a question) *were* needed Enger's τί δ' for ἀλλ' would produce it more easily, cf. S. *OT.* 1391, 2 τί μ' οὐ λαβὼν | ἔκτεινας . . ., ὡς ἔδειξα μήποτε . . .; See K.-G. II. ii, p. 388.

356. Unless there is some quasi-legal sense in ἀπάγω here—'to hale away to justice' (cf. ἀπαγωγή)—it is an unlikely verb. Badham proposed κατήγαγε, Wecklein (better) ἐπήγαγε, and Matthiae (still better) ἂν ἤγαγε. The aor. is assimilated to ἦλθε the sense being almost ὥστ' ἀπαγαγεῖν.

358. For Iph. Aulis is the place of sacrifice. By metonymy she uses it here = sacrifice. The gen. with ἀντιτίθημι when it means 'to set off against', 'to make to compensate for' is analogous to one of price; cf. Th. 2. 85. 2 οὐκ ἀντιτιθέντες τὴν Ἀθηναίων . . . ἐμπειρίαν τῆς σφετέρας . . . μελέτης. Markland's τῇ γ' ἐκεῖ should not be accepted.

359. **χειρούμενοι** as well as ἔσφαζον (conative imperf.) governs με.

362. **ὅσας χεῖρας** = ὁσάκις χεῖρας. Edd. cite Call. *Dian.* 27 πολλὰς δὲ μάτην ἐτανύσσατο χεῖρας. γενείου and γονάτων are genitives of the thing aimed at and are governed by ἐξηκόντισα, while the participle ἐξαρτωμένη goes probably with γονάτων only and helps to define the action more closely.

367. **αὐλεῖται**, passive = 'sounds with flutes', cf. E. *Heracl.* 401 θυηπολεῖται δ' ἄστυ μάντεων ὕπο. Pacuvius (*Dulorestes*, fr. 1), perhaps translated or imitated this passage: hymenaeúm fremunt | aequáles, aula résonit crepitu músico: see Introduction, p. xiii.

370. The MSS. προσεῖπας is impossible. Hartung's προειπών is possible, but Badham's προτείνας (accepted by most edd.) is better, though not so good as Bothe's προσείσας; cf. Pl. *Phdr.* 230 D, where προσείειν θαλλόν = to wave a branch to lure cattle on. (Prof. Margoliouth suggested προσείει for the MSS. προσῄει at A. *Ag.* 817, and Eur. may well have written προσείσασ' at *Hel.* 28—indeed this seems to have been the original reading of P. Other MSS. give προτείνασ'.) It is quite possible to understand με as object of ἐπόρθμευσας out of the dat. μοι, but as the Aldine ed. has δ' after ἁρμάτων Nauck may be right in reading μ' at that place. This δέ, however, is more likely to have been put in by a scribe who read προσεῖπας—in order to connect that verb with ἐπόρθμευσας—than to be a corrupted με. The redundant phrase ἁρμάτων ὄχος occurs again at E. *Hipp.* 1166.

372. **ὄμμα διὰ καλυμμάτων ἔχουσα** = looking out from behind. Cf. A. *Ag.* 1178, 9 ὁ χρησμὸς οὐκέτ' ἐκ καλυμμάτων | ἔσται δεδορκὼς νεογάμου νύμφης δίκην; S. *Ph.* 1013, 4 ἡ κακὴ σὴ διὰ μυχῶν βλέπουσ' ἀεὶ | ψυχή. **λεπτῶν** does not imply that the bridal veil was thin—it means it was of fine material, and the whole phrase means that Iph. could or would *not* see *openly* to give her brother and sister a final embrace. It is logically with this part of the sentence that ὑπ' αἰδοῦς (l. 375) goes.

373. **ἀνειλόμην**, for Or. was still a βρέφος ἐπιμαστίδιον (cf. l. 231). Note the rare τ' οὐκ . . . οὐ = οὔτε . . . οὔτε involved in Hermann's emendation.

376. **ἀποτίθεσθαι** = to defer. Here almost a synonym for ἀποβάλλειν. The phrase εἰσαῦθις ἀπ. occurs in Pl. *Grg.* 449 B. For *αὖθις* = later, cf. ll. 1312 and 1432 below and A. *Ag.* 317: the Scotch say 'I'll see you again' = 'I'll see you later'.

378. **πατρός** goes both with *καλῶν* ('fair fortunes'—note Reiske's palmary emendation) and *ζηλωμάτων* ('enviable lot'): cf. A. *Ag.* 589 *ἅλωσιν Ἰλίου τ' ἀνάστασιν*, and E. *Med.* 986, 7 *εἰς ἕρκος . . . καὶ μοῖραν θανάτου*. Iph. does not yet know of Ag.'s fall, so the exclamation is natural enough. Kviçala needlessly proposed *πάρος* for *πατρός*.

380. There is no need to postulate a lacuna here as do Monk and Nauck. No doubt there was a pause after l. 379 before Iph. turns to the temple and philosophizes on its rites. *σοφίσματα* = subtleties, quibbles.

382. Some edd. have objected to this line partly because of the odd dual **χεροῖν**, but see E. *HF.* 1342. The sense also seems redundant, for *νεκροῦ θίγῃ* = *ἅψηται φόνου*—unless indeed we suppose that the latter phrase = 'engages in murder' as it does at, e.g., A. R. I. 999. Its more natural sense would be simply 'touches blood'. Eur. may, however, intend to make a definite distinction between 'blood' and 'corpse'.

383. **μυσαρὸν ὡς ἡγουμένη**: the phrase is pleonastic. Logically Eur. should have written either *ὡς μυσαρόν* or *μυσαρὸν ἡγουμένη*. Cf. S. *OT.* 1178, 9 *ὡς ἄλλην χθόνα* | *δοκῶν ἀποίσειν* which = either *δοκῶν ἀποίσειν* or *ὡς ἀποίσοντι*. Cf. also in Latin the 'quod diceret' construction. So Wecklein and others; but the translation may rather be 'pretending to think it *μυσαρόν*'; i.e. a *σόφισμα* of the goddess.

384. Cf. E. *IA.* 1524, 5 *θύμασιν βροτησίοις* | *χαρεῖσα*.

385. The sense of the MSS. is good enough (*pace* Wecklein and others) but the metre is ugly, not to say impossible; cf. Descroix, *Trim. iamb.*, p. 161. The simplest emendation is **ἂν ἔτεκεν** (Hartung). Edd. who object to the potential emend to *ἔτικτεν* (Porson); *ποτ' ἔτεκεν* (Hermann); *ἄρ' ἔτεκεν* (Bothe).

386. **ἀμαθίαν** (Nauck, needlessly, *ἀνομίαν*—better Wecklein's *ἀλογίαν*) = *ἀμαθῆ*; cf. E. *Heracl.* 459 where *ἀμαθὲς φρόνημα* = *ἀμαθής*. Weil compares Cat. 17. 21 iste meus stupor = iste stupidus (so 'scelus' often for 'scelerosus'). This use of abstract for concrete is rarer in Greek, but cf. below 525 *ὦ μῖσος*, and, for an almost exact parallel, S. *Ant.* 533 *τρέφων δύ' ἄτα κἀπαναστάσεις θρόνων*. Sophocles, indeed, affects this idiom frequently, e.g. *μῖσος* (*Ant.* 760), *λάλημα* (*ib.* 320), *δούλευμα* (*ib.* 756), *μίσημα* (*El.* 289), *βλάβη* (*ib.* 301).

387. Without Hermann's *τε*'s the constr. is *ἐγὼ μὲν κρίνω τὰ Τ. . . . ἄπιστα, δοκῶ δὲ τοὺς ἐνθάδε, κτλ.*; perfectly normal Greek for the more logical *κρίνω τὰ μὲν Τ. . . . ἄπιστα, τοὺς δ' ἐνθάδε ἀναφέρειν . . .* But we do not want an *antithesis* between the gods who took pleasure in Tantalus' offered banquet and the Taurian Artemis. Iph. is trying to clear both of the charge of cruelty and to suggest that men are merely attributing their own cruel habits to the gods. Hence Hermann's Ταντάλου ⟨τε⟩ and τούς τε (389) should probably be accepted. (τε for δέ is not so necessary since τε is often so answered; cf. note on 1415. On the other hand δέ may well have been 'corrected' by a scribe whom μέν *solitarium* offended.) ἡσθῆναι (sc. τοὺς θεούς) is in loose apposition to ἑστιάματα. The dat. θεοῖσιν is caused by the verbal force of ἑστιάματα (ἑστιᾶν τι τινί); cf. S. *Tr.* 668 τῶν σῶν Ἡρακλεῖ δωρημάτων, Ar. *Nu.* 305 οὐρανίοις . . . θεοῖς δωρήματα.

391. For the sentiment cf. E. *HF.* 1341 sqq. ἐγὼ δὲ τοὺς θεοὺς οὔτε λέκτρ' ἃ μὴ θέμις | στέργειν νομίζω . . . ἀοιδῶν οἵδε δύστηνοι λόγοι, and the famous line of the Bellerophon (*fr.* 292) εἰ θεοί τι δρῶσιν αἰσχρόν, οὐκ εἰσὶν θεοί. Pindar similarly clears Tantalus' character in *O.* I. 35 sqq., prefacing his revised myth with the line ἔστι δ' ἀνδρὶ φάμεν ἐοικὸς ἀμφὶ δαιμόνων καλά, 'it is seemly for a man to tell fair things about the gods'.

Nauck's οὐδὲν for MSS. οὐδένα is probably right. The neut. makes the expression more forceful. A similar corruption occurs at S. *OT.* 1195, 6 where the MSS. read βροτῶν | οὐδένα μακαρίζω (against the metre) which Hermann emended to οὐδέν. For this neut. for masc., cf. S. *fr.* 724. 4 Ἄρης γὰρ οὐδὲν τῶν κακῶν λωτίζεται.

At this point Iph. retires into the temple and the chorus sing their first stasimon.

393. σύνοδοι θαλάσσας. i.e. the Thracian Bosporus which joins the Euxine and the Propontis. Βόσπορος is derived here (as usually in antiquity) from βοὸς πόρος; that is the strait over which passed Io, turned by Hera into a cow and pursued by a gadfly (οἶστρος). Io fled from Argos, across the Bosporus into Asia, and ultimately into Egypt. Cf. A. *Pr.* 561 sqq. and 732–4 ἔσται δὲ θνητοῖς εἰσαεὶ λόγος μέγας | τῆς σῆς πορείας, Βόσπορος δ' ἐπώνυμος | κεκλήσεται. Some modern scholars derive Βόσπορος from φωσφόρος, this district being the seat of the worship of Ἑκάτη Φωσφόρος.

394–5. To get exact correspondence we should here read either *l*'s ποτώμενος or, preferably, (as England), Bergk's νότια (for πόντια) in l. 409. In P l. 395 ends with διεπέρασεν; *l* has διεπέρασέν ποτε. Metrically speaking we need – –, not ⏑ ⏑, to complete the line. Such emendations as Kirchhoff's Ἰώ, or Weil's πόρτιν, ignore the fact that there is no evidence for διαπερᾶν = 'to make to pass over' until Lucian. (The citation from Eubulus in L & S is due to an error in the interpretation of the passage.) It is moreover odd to make the οἶστρος rather than Io the subject of the sentence. It is best to take Ehrfurdt's Ἰοῦς, observing the similarity between ΙΟΥϹ and ΠΟΤϾ, and regarding οἶστρος Ἰοῦς as = Ἰὼ οἰστροπλήξ, as at E. *Hipp.* 1298–1300 ἐκδεῖξαι . . . σῆς γυναικὸς οἶστρον = σὴν γυναῖκα οἰστροπλῆγα γενέσθαι. Wecklein's διεπόρευσε ⟨τὰν βοῦν⟩ is possible but less likely.

If the line-division of our text is retained, l. 394 (= 409) seems to be an anapaestic tripody (a thing questionable in itself and out of place here) and 395 (= 410) a combination of cretic +

syncopated choriambic dimeter (⏖ ⏑ – | ⏖ ⏑⏑ – | ⏑ – · ⏑). It is probably better to divide after Ἀργόθεν (and κύματα). We then get in l. 394 (= 409) a lecythion (⏖ ⏑ ⏖ ⏑ – ⏑ ⏑) and in 395 (= 410) a syncopated iambic trimeter with dactyl for iambus in the first foot (– ⏑⏑ | ⏑ – | ⏑ ⏖ | ⏑ – | ⏑ – | · –). The non-observance of synaphaea in the lecythion (Ἀργόθεν) is rare but not without parallel; e.g. E. *HF.* 134, *Hipp.* 350, *Hel.* 230.

397. **Ἀσιῆτιδα . . . διαμείψας** = having taken Asia in exchange for Europe; i.e. having crossed from Europe to Asia. (The aor., where we might have expected a present, is attracted by the aor. of the main verb; cf. E. *Med.* 431, 2 ἔπλευσας . . . ὁρίσασα.) The participle is easy if Ἰοῦς οἶστρος (= Io) is subject; with Ἰώ as acc. ('the gadfly caused Io to cross') we must emend to διαμεῖψαι (i.e. ὥστε διαμεῖψαι)—a further reason for preferring Erfurdt's emendation.

399. The chorus speculates on the identity of the strangers.

δονακόχλοα. If this form is correct (note L's δονακόχλοον) it must be formed on the (false) analogy of adjs. in -χρους = χροος; e.g. ταμεσίχροα χαλκόν (*Il.* 4. 511), γλαυκόχροα κόσμον (Pi. *O.* 3. 13), ἁπαλόχροα γένυν (E. *Hel.* 373): Nicander (*Ther.* 676 and 885) has ἔγχλοα = ἔγχλοον. The long syllable at the end of the corresponding line of the antistrophe suggests that δονακόχλοον is the right reading. But l. 413 is so uncertain that we cannot lay much stress on this argument. 'Reedy' is a stock epithet for the Eurotas; cf. E. *Hel.* 210 δονακόεντος Εὐρώτα, *ib.* 349 δόνακι χλωρόν, *ib.* 493 καλλιδόνακος . . . Εὐρώτα, *IA.* 179 Εὐρώτα δονακοτρόφου.

402. **ἄμεικτον** = here 'unmixing' in the sense of 'unsociable', 'inhospitable'. Odysseus applies the epithet to the Cyclops (E. *Cyc.* 429), Heracles to the Centaurs (S. *Tr.* 1095); and for a similar use cf. E. *Alc.* 542 and *HF.* 393. It should be spelt ἄμεικτον (Meisterhans, p. 181 note), rather than ἄμικτον.

402–6. Note Elmsley's emendation. Dindorf proposed κούρα Δία making it subject of τέγγει, but Artemis herself did not perform human sacrifice (cf. l. 40 above). Better therefore retain the dat. making αἷμα β. subject. For the adj. Δῖος = Διός cf. l. 1272 below (note) and E. *Ion* 200 and 1144 where Herakles is Δῖος παῖς.

περικίονας ναούς; cf. E. *fr.* 369 πρὸς Ἀθάνας περικίοσι . . . θαλάμοις, S. *Ant.* 285, 6 ἀμφικίονας | ναούς and ll. 128, 9 of this play εὐστύλων ναῶν. Pollux (1. 78) says εἴποις δ' ἂν τὸν περίστυλον τόπον περικίονα.

407. In the first antistrophe the chorus continues its speculations upon the strangers' motive in coming. Are they merchants urged by greed of gain?

407–10. **ῥόθιος**, properly an adj. = rushing, always used in tragedy as neut. substantive ῥόθια = surges (see on l. 1133). δίκροτα ῥ. = the waves cast up by the oars on each side of the ship; cf. l. 323 δίπαλτα. For ἐπὶ = over cf. *Il.* 2. 159 ἐπ' εὐρέα νῶτα θαλάσσης, 13. 27 βῆ δ' ἐλάαν ἐπὶ κύματ', and above l. 395.

For νάϊον ὄχημα cf. E. *Med.* 1122, 3 ναΐαν . . . ἀπήνην and S. *Tr.* 656 πολύκωπον ὄχημα ναός.

Our text sticks to the MSS. 'Did they sail the pine-wood oars with double surge over the sea waves, the ship-chariot with sail-wafting breezes?'

There are, however, many objections to this. (1) πλέω, though it can take an acc. of that which is sailed over, is not transitive; (2) though νάϊον ὄχ. might well be in apposit. to κώπας, the dat. αὔραις has no construction (it certainly can't in any sense qualify ὄχημα); (3) for antistrophic correspondence a short syllable is needed between λινοπόροις and αὔραις. (1) and (2) can be got over by accepting Rauchenstein's ἔπεμψαν or Dindorf's πόρευσαν for ἔπλευσαν and taking εἰλ. κώπας as a genitive. 'Did they by means of sail-wafting breezes send the ship-chariot over . . . with double surge of pine-wood oar⟨s⟩?' As to (3), not only the metre but also the sense is improved if we read Wecklein's λινοπόροις σὺν αὔραις—better than Monk's λινοπόροισί τ' αὔραις, as we do not want αὔραις parallel to ῥοθίοις. The ἅπ. λεγ. λινοπόροις = sail-wafting seems an odd compound, and Rauchenstein's suggested *λινοτόνοις = sail-spreading, may well be right.

[It is possible with our text to regard εἰλ. κώπας as gen. sing. 'with double surge of (i.e. caused by) pinewood oar', but if we do so we leave νάϊον ὄχημα with no construction.]

411. As at E. *Med.* 557 a ἅμιλλα πολύτεκνος = a competition in children, so here a ἅμ. φιλόπλουτος = a competition in wealth. But αὔξοντες is odd. It seems to mean 'engaging in a competition for the increasing of wealth.' Musgrave's ᾄξαντες is no improvement. μελάθροισιν is dat. of advantage 'for their homes'.

413. γάρ = I am reasonable in suggesting this motive, for . . .

413–18. As our text stands it may be translated: 'for hope is fond and to their hurt insatiable to men who seek to bear away the burden of wealth . . .' But βροτῶν . . . ἀνθρώποις is tautological and l. 413 does not correspond with l. 398 as it should. The passage is hopelessly corrupt and no suggested emendation can claim to be more than a makeshift. For metrical reasons Monk's transposition ἐγένετ' ἐλπίς (MSS. ἐλπὶς γένετ') may commend itself, and (pragmatically) we may adopt England's ἔν τε ποθήμασιν [βροτῶν] which will at least scan and translate.

The line will then run φίλα γὰρ ἐγένετ' ἐλπίς, ἔν τε ποθήμασιν which corresponds exactly with 398: 'hope is fond, and insatiable in desires for men who . . .'

Prof. Housman's ἔν τ' ἐπιπάμασιν (in J. P. xvi, p. 276) postulates a word *ἐπίπαμα (*not* the Doric form of ἐπίπημα) = property. πᾶμα = property occurs in a fourth-century inscription and in Theoc. *Syrinx* 12 (where there is a v.l. πῆμα). So here ἐν ἐπιπάμασιν ἄπληστος = 'insatiable in acquisitions'.

ἐπί, as though πλάνητες had been πλανώμενοι.

κεινᾷ δόξᾳ going, if there is a comma at περῶντες, with φίλα ... ἄπληστός ⟨τ' ἐστί⟩ = *consensu omnium* is intolerably weak. Elmsley's κεινᾷ should be accepted or perhaps (considering *l*'s κεναὶ (sic)) κενᾷ, though it would not correspond so exactly with l. 403; 'with empty expectation'. κενᾷ, not because riches do not come, but because of their 'deceitfulness' when they do. Heath's κενόδοξοι is plausible. If we read κεινᾷ or κενόδοξοι there should be no comma at περῶντες.

419–20. This may be, and has been, taken: 'the judgement of some ⟨traders⟩ fails to hit the right moment for acquiring wealth, while ⟨wealth⟩ comes in others' way'; i.e. taking ⟨ὄλβος⟩ as subject of ἥκει. It is, however, better to take γνώμα as subj. of both clauses. ἄκαιρος then means 'in season and out of season' and μέσον = virtually τὸ μέτριον, as at E. *HF.* 58 μέσως εὔνους (and cf. the phrase οἱ διὰ μέσου = the moderates). Tucker would read μέτρον, unnecessarily. 'The thought of wealth comes to some in season and out of season, but to others in moderation'. As to ἐς + acc. of adj. = adv. cf. l. 477 ἐς ἀφανές = ἀφανῶς, and S. *OT.* 50 ἐς ὀρθόν = ὀρθῶς, *ib.* 78 ἐς καλόν = καλῶς, etc. etc. For the gen. ὄλβου cf. Pl. *R.* 619 πόνων ἀγύμναστοι. For οἷς μέν = τοῖς μέν cf. Men. *fr.* 428 οἷς μὲν δίδωσιν οἷς δ' ἀφαιρεῖται θεός; and for the mixture of articular and relatival forms cf. Phocyl. *fr.* 1 Λέριοι κακοί· οὐχ ὁ μέν, ὃς δ' οὔ. The δ' of l. 419 = γάρ. If any emendation is to be made something like Bruhn's ἄκληρος for MSS. ἄκαιρος might be admitted. In this case δέ = ἀλλά and two classes, οἷς μέν and τοῖς δέ, are contrasted with the greedy trader: i.e. those who have no thought of wealth at all (ἄκληρος) and those who have reasonable desires for it. Hermann, it may be remarked, opens up a new line of interpretation by reading οἷς μενέκαιρος: 'but for those who await a suitable occasion for getting wealth it comes ready to hand.' In this case in l. 420 τοῖς = τούτοις and δ' is apodotic.

422. The chorus expresses surprise at the strangers' survival of the rocky and stormy coast of Salmydessus, i.e. the coast between the promontory of Thynias and the Bosporus. For its dangers cf. A. *Pr.* 726, 7 τραχεῖα πόντου Σαλμυδησσία γνάθος | ἐχθρόξενος ναύταισι, μητρυιὰ νεῶν, and Xen. *An.* 7. 5. 12 εἰς τὸν Σαλμυδησσόν, ἔνθα ... πολλαὶ (i.e νῆες) ὀκέλλουσι καὶ ἐκπίπτουσι· τέναγος γάρ ἐστιν ἐπὶ πάμπολυ τῆς θαλάττης. Phineus, king of Salmydessus (cf. S. *Ant.* 967–71), was the husband of Cleopatra, daughter of Boreas and Oreithyia; his visitations by the Harpies (= whirlwinds) further connect him with storms. περᾶν here = to pass *by*, not *through.* If ἀΰπνους is right it must mean that the waves which beat on the shore were sleepless, i.e. unceasing, but we might well accept Wilamowitz' λιγύπνους, though the form λιγύπνοος = λιγὺ πνείων (cf. Od. 4. 567) is late.

Φινεΐδᾶν. The reference of the word is to the Ἅρπυιαι, the tormentors of Phineus, but its form is a matter of some uncertainty.

On the analogy of e.g. Νηρηΐς = Νηρεΐς the change of η to ε (see *app. crit.*) is easy, but Rauchenstein's -ιδᾶν, the masculine patronymic, for -ίδας involves two difficulties: (1) the Harpies were not the *children* of Ph.; (2) they were female. Though a greater change, -ίδων would be preferable. I believe myself that Φινεΐδᾶς (fr. Φινεΐς) is the right reading and that something like Wilamowitz's λιγύπνους followed it, making the final syllable long. In A. *Eu.* 1026 Athens is called the χθὼν Θησηΐς, which gives us an exact analogy to ἀκταὶ Φινεΐδες here.

424–5. With the MSS. παράλιον we could regard π. αἰγιαλόν as in apposition to ἀκτάς, but it is better to accept Seidler's παρ' ἅλιον, taking it with δραμόντες. ἀκτὰς ἐπέρασαν... παρ' ἅλιον αἰγιαλὸν... δραμόντες is, it is true, tautological; but there is no need to accept any emendation such as Wecklein's ἀλίμενον, the epithet applied by Strabo (7. 6. 1) to this coast. He himself later discarded it.

426. ἐπὶ . . . ῥοθίῳ = 'amid the surge'. Wecklein would read ῥόθιον = 'over the surge'.

428. A dibrach or trochee (according as we read χερί or χειρί in l. 445) is needed before χοροί to complete the metre. Wecklein's ὄπα gives μέλπουσι (= 'they dance-and-sing') an internal acc. as at E. *Med.* 149, 50 ἀχὰν . . . μέλπει; E. *Tr.* 547 βοὰν ἔμελπον; Hermann's ποσί an instrumental dat. Better, as giving — ⏑, would be Wilamowitz' (*Verskunst*, p. 567) ποσσί—a form which occurs in drama at S. *Ichn.* 67. And cf. E. *Alc.* 756 χείρεσσι. If we accept either of these last it is advisable to let the MSS. ἐγκυκλίοις stand; if ὄπα, then take Heath's ἐγκύκλιοι. But with the added dibrach the metre is, as Prof. Murray says, very strange. He suggests ⟨δῆλα⟩, or Νηρέως ἔκδηλα (in which case Νηρῄδων would be a gloss).

430–3. ὅπου . . . ἐγκύκλιοι has been a parenthesis; at συριζόντων we return to the main sentence, the verb of which is still ἐπέρασαν (l. 423). This is awkward, and Rauchenstein's anaphoric ⟨πῶς⟩ should probably be accepted at the beginning of l. 430. Grégorie (ed. Budé) takes Bergk's almost equally good ⟨ᾗ⟩. Notice (*app. crit.*) (?) *l*'s καί. As to metre: ⟨πῶς⟩ πλησιστίοισι πνοαῖς would correspond with ἀδίσταν δ' ἀγγελίαν (l. 447) if we regard -τίοισ- as a synizesis, or with τάνδ ἄδιστα δ' ἀγγελίαν (see note on l. 447) if we take it as disyllabic. With the reading of our text there is no exact corresponsion. πλησ. πνοαῖς is best taken as an instrumental dat. with ⟨ἐπέρασαν⟩, though it might be a causal dat. with συριζόντων. συριζόντων . . . πηδαλίων in either case is a gen. absolute; 'the rudder at the stern creaking'. The plural, πηδάλια, is used because the Greeks often employed as a rudder two long oars joined together by means of cross-pieces. The rudder would 'creak' because so constantly thrust over to sail the boat straight. If εὐναίων is right it can only mean 'couched' in the sense of 'in its groove or rowlock', with the suggestion that the rudder-oar, unlike the ordinary oars, was never unshipped. As possible emendations may be mentioned Wecklein's εὐθύνων = directing (Hesych. εὔθυνος· εὐθυντήρ, κυβερνήτης; cf. A. *Supp.* 717 οἴακος εὐθυντῆρος); Herwerden's εὐπάκτων (= εὐπήκτων) or his εὐπαγῶν = stout; Bergk's εὔδιον = gently (lit. fair-weather-ly, an adv. going with συριζόντων); Weil's εὐαγῶν = mobile, or his εὐηρῶν = well-fitted (cf. l. 1050).

αὔραις must be corrected for metrical reasons. Wecklein's σύν is preferable to Kirchhoff's αὔραισιν as avoiding another pure dative. Wilamowitz (*Verskunst*, p. 567) suggested ⟨ὑπ'⟩ which is also possible.

435. The construction of ἐπέρασαν is still continued. The uninhabited island of Leuce (mod. Phidonisi, opposite the mouth of the Danube) was so called, either because of the many white sea-birds which rested there (so Dionys. *Perieg.* 542), or because of its white cliffs (so Arrian, *Peripl.* 21). A tradition going back to the epic poet Arctinus regarded it as haunted by the shade of the dead Achilles; cf. E. *Andr.* 1260–2 (Thetis speaking to Peleus) τὸν φίλτατον σοὶ παῖδ' ἐμοί τ' Ἀχιλλέα | ὄψῃ δόμους ναίοντα νησιωτικοὺς | Λευκὴν κατ' ἀκτὴν ἐντὸς Εὐξείνου πόρου. For races run there by the ghosts of Ach. and other dead heroes cf. Schol. Pi. *N.* 4. 79 καὶ δρόμους τινὰς δεικνύουσι διὰ τὰ τοῦ ἥρωος γυμνάσια.

ἐπ' presumably = 'to', though this island was not their goal. It is mentioned perhaps as a potential port of call on the way to the Taurian land (i.e. Crimea).

438. **κατά** may go with ἐπέρασαν and mean 'over', or (more probably) with αἶαν and mean 'in', sc. κειμένην.

439. Neither Iph. (see l. 521) nor the chorus knew of Helen's return to Greece. These εὐχαί are general and need not refer to l. 354 (see note there).

443–6. **δρόσον** here = lustral water. αἱματ., because it prepares the victim for slaughter. ἑλιχθεῖσα (a correction in L for the MSS. εἱλιχ., the ionic form, which may be right; cf. ll. 1103 and 1145 below, and Ar. *Ra.* 1314—a parody of Euripides) here = crowned—the lustral water being poured on the victim's head with a circular motion; cf. below, l. 622 χαίτην ἀμφὶ σὴν χερνίψομαι, also S. *Ant.* 431 χοαῖσι τρισπόνδοισι τὸν νέκυν στέφει, and E. *Hec.* 126, 7 τὸν Ἀχίλλειον τύμβον στεφανοῦν | αἵματι χλωρῷ. As the active would be ἑλίσσειν δρόσον ἀμφὶ χαίτᾳ, so where, as here, the passive is used the acc. remains. It must, however, be admitted that the verb is a strange one, and Köchly's ἁγνισθεῖσα or Bergk's χερνιφθεῖσα is attractive.

Metrically χειρί—instrumental dat., as though θάνοι were, as it virtually is, a passive—is preferable to χερί (cf. note on l. 428). The MSS. θάνῃ is grammatically possible, for τύχοι is primary in meaning though not in form. The chorus is not saying 'would that not these strangers but Helen *had* come' (which would need ἔτυχε), but 'would that Helen *would* come'. But as a rule what is potentially a subjunctive in such a final clause becomes *by attraction* an optative: cf. S. *Ph.* 324, 5 θυμὸν γένοιτο χειρὶ πληρῶσαί ποτε | ἵν' αἱ Μυκῆναι γνοῖεν . . .; S. *Tr.* 953–5 εἴθε . . . γένοιτο . . . αὔρα, ἥτις μ' ἀποικίσειεν; S. *Aj.* 1217–21 γενοίμαν ἵν' . . . προσείποιμεν. The subjunctive is kept in S. *Tr.* 1109, 10 προσμόλοι . . . ἵν' ἐκδιδαχθῇ, E. *Or.* 982–4 μόλοιμι . . . ἵν' . . . ἀναβοάσω, E. *Suppl.* 617–21 πῶς ἱκοίμεθ' ἂν . . ἵνα . . . μόλω. See K.-G. II. i. 256–9.

447. The MSS. ἥδιστ' ἂν τήνδ' ἀγγ. does not correspond as it should with l. 430 and involves an awkward asyndeton. All edd. excise τήνδ'. If this is the right line to take, then the reading of our text is as good as any. δεξαίμεσθ', being rather more a pure than a conditional optative, needs no ἄν. The particle may well have been supplied by a too-little-learned scribe. Some, however, retain the ἄν, e.g. Teuffel, who reads ἁδίσταν δ' ἂν ἀγγ. This would necessitate reading ⟨πῶς⟩ or the like in l. 430 (see note). ἄν is also kept by Hermann who gives ἥδιστ' ἂν δ' ἀγγ. (for the unusual position of the particle cf. below, l. 1217 ἡνίκ' ἂν δέ and Th. 2. 63. 3 τάχιστ' ἄν τε). Either of these is better than Badham's ἥδιστ' ἂν ἀγγ., the asyndeton of which is intolerable.

I cannot help thinking the universal ejection of τήνδ' somewhat arbitrary. We rather want the sense 'I wish Helen would come, but *this* is what I should most welcome, viz. if . . .' We might therefore read here τάνδ' ἅδιστα δ' ἀγγ. | (corresponding to ⟨πῶς⟩ πλησιστίοισ|). Alternatively, if ἄν is to be kept, we might read τὰν (quasi-demonstrative) δ' ἅδιστ' ἄν. The rare demonstrative use of the article (e.g. S. *Ant.* 1035, *Tr.* 549) often leads to MSS. corruption; cf. E. *Ph.* 9 where, after τοῦ (demonstr.) in l. 8, L reads ἐκ δὲ τοῦ, and A ἐκ τοῦδε. For the demonstrative article followed by an appositional substantive, cf. Pi. *N.* 4. 9–11 τό μοι θέμεν Κρονίδᾳ τε Δί . . . ὕμνου προκώμιον εἴη.

450. **δουλείας . . . παυσίπονος**, i.e. παύσων τοὺς πόνους τῆς δουλείας; cf. S. *Tr.* 1021 λαθίπονος ὀδυνᾶν, Ar. *Nu.* 1163 λυσανίας κακῶν.

452–5. A monosyllable is missing in the MSS. before γάρ. *l* supplies καί. Our text gives Herwerden's κἂν followed by Fritzsche's ὀνείροισι συνείην (for the unmetrical and difficult ὀνείρασι συμβαίην of the MSS.), together with Hermann's ὕπνων for MSS. ὕμνων. 'For if only in dreams (κἂν γάρ = καὶ γὰρ κἂν) may I be in my home . . ., the enjoyment of sweet dreams'. The same sense can be got from Hermann's καὶ γὰρ ὀνείροις ἐπιβαίην δόμοις . . . 'For ⟨even⟩ in dreams may I set foot in my home . . .'; or from Wilamowitz' (*Verskunst*, p. 567) κἂν γὰρ ὀνείροισι δόμοις συμβαίην . . . (i.e. ἐν ὀνείροις συμβ. δόμοις πόλει τε). He defends συμβ. δόμοις = 'be in' on the analogy of Τίρυνθι συμβέβηκεν (S. *Tr.* 1152—but here the verb is helped out by ὥστ' ἔχειν ἕδραν). In all these cases ἀπόλαυσιν must be taken as in apposition to the sentence—unless indeed we suppose τερπνῶν a corruption of δρέπουσ' as did Badham.

But the γάρ is difficult; it must explain ἀδίσταν ἀγγ. δεξαίμεσθα: 'I should be delighted to hear . . . for I pray even in dreams to be back at home.'

Wecklein reads ὡς γὰρ ὀνείροις ἀνυσαίμαν . . . ὕμνων ἀπόλαυσιν. 'For would that in dreams I might gain at home the enjoyment of song'.

But, as Weil well says, 'Le souhait de revoir la patrie en songe, quelque touchant qu'il puisse être, ne convient pas ici. Les vœux du chœur sont plus positif.' He suggests τὰν γὰρ ὀνείροις ἀποβαίη, . . . ὕμνων ἀπολαύειν (the reading of *l*); i.e. 'may what we ⟨so often⟩ dream of come true, viz. the enjoyment at home of song . . .' With this reading and interpretation it is best to take κοινὰν χάριν ὄλβου as in apposition to ⟨τὸ⟩ ὕμν. ἀπολ., and as meaning 'a pleasure which the wealthy (ὄλβου = τῶν ὀλβίων) enjoy in company.' But it must be admitted that this phrase is rather pointless, and that ὕπνων with the meaning 'a pleasure (i.e. dreaming) common to ⟨us and⟩ the wealthy' would be better: cf. Pi. *N.* 1. 34 κοιναὶ γὰρ ἔρχοντ' ἐλπίδες πολυπόνων ἀνδρῶν. Such a meaning, however, can only be admitted with some interpretation of the earlier part of the sentence other than Weil's.

A suggestion has been made (*Phil. Wochenschr.*, 1930, p. 1201) to read ὕπνων . . . ὄρφνας (for ὄλβου); i.e. 'dreams, the gift which night gives to all in common'.

456–66. The κορυφαῖος intones the anapaests which lead up to the second epeisodion. They greet the entry of Or. and Pyl. still in charge of the oxherd—dramatically speaking, of a παραχορήγημα who wears the oxherd's dress, for the actor who took the part of the oxherd must have taken that of Orestes also. All are accompanied by Iph.

459. ἀκροθίνια (by derivation 'top of the heap') = choicest piece of anything offered or sacrificed; cf. E. *Ph.* 202, 3 Τύριον οἶδμα λιποῦσ' ἔβαν | ἀκροθίνια Λοξίᾳ and *ib.* 282 Φοίβῳ μ' ἔπεμψαν ἐνθάδ' ἀκροθίνιον. The κορυφαῖος is struck, as was the oxherd, with the noble appearance of the strangers.

460. Note the comparatively rare dat. with πέλας, which usually takes a gen.

466. With Ἕλλησι διδούς these lines are nonsensical; for Grégoire's attempt to take the οὐχ with both ὁσίας and διδούς (i.e. ἃς ὁ . . . νόμος οὐχ ὁσίας ἀναφαίνει, (οὐ) διδοὺς ⟨αὐτὰς⟩ Ἕλλησι) is surely hopeless. All modern edd. follow Bergk in excising them. Ἑλλ. looks like a gloss on ἡμῖν and διδούς may well have been put in to complete the metre after the introduction of the gloss.

Kirchhoff (less well) would read Ἕλλησι δοθεὶς ἀποφαίνει, but the νόμος against human sacrifice was not 'given' to the Greeks. T. W. Allen (*CR.*, 1905, p. 198) νόμον, with ὁ . . . διδοὺς = 'our law-giver'. But who is he?

The two lines should probably be arranged ἂς ὁ παρ' ἡμῖν | νόμος οὐχ ὁσίας ἀναφαίνει.

469. Animals destined for sacrifice were allowed to run free in the τέμενος of the God; Io is allowed ἄφετον ἀλᾶσθαι (A. *Pr.* 666), cf. also S. *Aj.* 1214 and S. *Ph.* 947. Such were called ἄφετα (cf. E. *Ion* 822) ἀνειμένα or (later) ἄνετα.

470. It seems unsuitable to send the oxherd with the others to prepare for the ceremony, but for dramatic purposes the stage must be left clear for Iph., Or., and Pyl.

472. Iph. takes Or. and Pyl. for brothers; cf. below l. 497.

475. i.e. τίς οἶδ' ὅτῳ τοιαίδε τύχαι ἔσονται;

477. For ἐς ἀφανές = ἀφανῶς see note on l. 419. The MSS. κακόν reduces the line to nonsense; for Grégoire's 'personne ne sait le malheur qui l'attend' is not a fair or possible translation of the Greek. Either a lacuna, e.g. ⟨ὁπηνίχ' ἥξει χὠπόθεν κἀφ' ὅντινα⟩ has occurred, the completion of which would make κακόν intelligible, or the last word only of this line has been corrupted. On the latter supposition many somewhat arbitrary emendations have been proposed: e.g. Weil's τέλος (cf. E. *Or.* 1545, 6 τέλος ἔχει δαίμων βροτοῖς, | τέλος ὅπᾳ θέλῃ), Wecklein's σαφῶς, Kirchhoff's βροτῶν (with οὐδείς—much too wide a statement), Köchly's ὅποι, and, perhaps best, F. W. Schmidt's ἄκος. The fact that l. 478 says the same as 477 is an argument in favour of the first view. Indeed some who hold the second excise l. 478 on the score of its tautology (e.g. England).

480. ὡς might be exclamatory, but more probably = καὶ γάρ and gives the reason both for her question and for her use of the word ταλαίπωροι.

481. The ἀεί of the MSS., even when printed as in Wecklein's text with a preceding dash, is worse than tautological after μακρόν. It is an intolerable dotting of the i. Elmsley suggested ἐκεῖ, Herwerden γῆς (which is better), but the best is Dobree's δή, for (1) it gives good sense ('La particule δή marque que la chose n'est que trop évidente', Weil); (2) ΔΗ and ΑΕΙ might easily be confused.

Hirzel's χθονός (with κάτω) for χρόνον and μακράν (adv. of time) for μακρόν may be an improvement on Euripides; it can scarcely rank as an emendation.

482. We may keep the MSS. reading as our text does. Lit. 'why trouble ⟨us⟩ on the ground of evils about to come to us?' λυπεῖν is so often used absolutely (e.g. S. *Aj.* 589 ἄγαν γε λυπεῖς, and the same phrase in S. *Ant.* 573) that Porson's νώ is unnecessary; nor, *pace* Wecklein, is there any objection to the dat. with μέλλουσι. [νῷν *might* be gen. on the analogy of E. *IA.* 1117, 8 οἶσθα γὰρ πατρὸς | πάντως ἃ μέλλει.] But λυπεῖν is scarcely the polite or the just word to apply to Iph.'s sympathetic interest and it should probably be corrected. Markland's λυπεῖ γ', i.e. λυπῇ γ' is simple, or Cobet's λυπῇ κακοῖσιν, and either is preferable to

more complicated emendations such as Bergk's κακοῖς ἀλύεις (too strong a word), or Musgrave's κ. ἀλυκτεῖς, which (being the Cretan for 'bark' = ὑλακτεῖς) is unsuitable both in form and meaning.

In a pencilled *marginale* Prof. Housman once made the suggestion κακοῖς σε λυπεῖς—a simple and attractive emendation. The reflexive use of the personal pronoun is rare but well attested; cf. E. *Andr.* 256 οὐδ' ἐγὼ μὴν πρόσθεν ἐκδώσω μέ σοι, *IA.* 1186 τί σοι κατεύξῃ τἀγαθόν . . .; (cf. K.-G. II. i, p. 559).

484–7. There are two difficulties in the MSS. reading: (1) οὐχ in l. 486 must (to avoid a very awkward asyndeton) be corrected, as it was by Hermann, to οὐδ'; (2) Orestes is made to say exactly the same thing twice. To avoid this tautology our text (tolerating the asyndeton) accepts Seidler's κτενεῖν. But the cure is worse than the disease, for (1) it ignores the fact that Stobaeus (8. 6) quotes l. 484 as ending in θανεῖν; (2) it puts into Orestes' mouth what Weil reasonably calls 'un langage fort déplaisant'; (3) it involves translating τὸ δεῖμα νικᾶν as 'to overcome ⟨the victim's⟩ fear'; and (4) it introduces a sentiment inconsistent with the following sentence, ὡς δύ', κτλ.

It is better to let θανεῖν of l. 484 stand, and cut out l. 486 as a parallel passage cited in the margin and thence introduced into the text.

We can take οἴκτῳ δεῖμα νικᾶν either as 'to drown his fear in pitiful cries' or 'to overcome his fear by the help of others' pity.' The latter is preferable, and the sense of the whole passage (cutting out l. 486) is: 'why should you lament my coming fate? ⟨It does no good⟩; indeed I think him a fool who accepts the doubtful comfort of another's pity, when that pity cannot save him from a certain doom.'

σοφόν may be masc. or neut.; cf. note on l. 606.

487–8. δύ' ἐξ ἑνὸς κακὼ συνάπτειν is, as it were, a mixture between δύο κ. ἐξ ἑνὸς ποιεῖν and συνάπτειν δύο κ. There is no need to accept Wecklein's suggested ἀνθ' for ἐξ, nor yet his συνάπτων for συνάπτει.

490. *Not*, as Weil and England, 'So do not weep for us' (i.e. δέ = (practically) δ' οὖν). This would only be possible with κτενεῖν in l. 484, and then only if ἡμᾶς δὲ . . . immediately followed l. 485. Besides, with this rendering, the pronouns lose all their force. The meaning is: 'I think it folly to lament my own fate, and do not you lament it for me.' In prose the sentence would have run σὺ δὲ μὴ θρήνει ἡμᾶς.

491. This somewhat strange tautology occurs again at E. *Hipp.* 380; cf. S. *El.* 131 οἶδά τε καὶ ξυνίημι τάδ(ε).

492. ἐνθάδ' ὠνομασμένος Πυλάδης = lit. 'having been addressed as Pyl. ⟨on the shore⟩ here': Πυλ. is used ἀπὸ κοινοῦ with ὠνομ. and κέκληται. The ref. is to ll. 249 and 285. But ἐνθάδε is odd and is not (*pace* Wecklein) paralleled by the ἐνθάδε of l. 932 which means 'here in my presence' as opposed to ἐπ' ἀκταῖς. Weil in his first edition suggested εἶπατ(ε), but this leaves ὠνομ. tautological. Usener rewrites Euripides Πυλάδης ἄρ' ὑμῶν πότερος ἦν κεκλημένος, excising l. 492.

494. ἐν ἡδονῇ = ἡδύ occurs at Hdt. 7. 15 εἰ (θεῷ) ἐν ἡδ. ἐστι γενέσθαι στρατηλασίην; cf. l. 762 ἐν ἀσφαλεῖ (and again at E. *Hipp.* 785), and E. *Ph.* 1276 ἐν αἰσχύνῃ, E. *IA.* 969 ἐν εὐμαρεῖ, *Hel.* 1277 ἐν εὐσεβεῖ.

495. Ἕλληνος: cf. note on l. 341.

496. τί, either adverbial, 'in what way', or with πλέον, 'what advantage'.

498. Our text keeps the MSS. reading, but γύναι here after that of l. 496 (which probably caused it) is a little awkward. We might read with Nauck φιλότητί γ' ἐσμέν, οὐ κασιγνήτω γένει. (The γένει is Köchly's; Nauck himself suggested φύσει.)

It may further be observed that though the MSS. reading answers πότερον ἀδελφὼ ἐστον; it does not well answer that question when μητρὸς ἐκ μιᾶς is added.

500. τὸ δίκαιον is prob. adverbial; cf. τὸ ἐναντίον, etc., though Wecklein would have it an internal acc. after καλοίμεθ' ἄν, understanding ὄνομα.

One of the Paris MSS. has, for καλοίμεθ', κεκλήμεθ' which Hermann corrected to κεκλῄμεθ' and adopted—quite possibly rightly.

MSS. Δυστυχεῖς. Greek idiom would admit of either sing. or plur. in such a case; but the (strictly) ungrammatical sing. is more likely to have been 'corrected', and Barthold is probably right in replacing it.

For the thought, cf. Plaut. *Pers.* 4. 4. 94, 5 Quid illum miserum memorem qui fuit? | Nunc et illum Miserum et me Miseram aequomst nominarier; Hor. *Epp.* 1. 7. 92, 3 pol me Miserum, patrone, vocares, | Si velles, inquit, verum mihi ponere nomen.

501. τοῦτ'; i.e. I do not ask what you think your name *ought* to be, but what it is.

502. To any Greek, and above all to *tristis Orestes*, the thought of an enemy's exultation in his death would be bitterer than the thought of death itself. But no personal exultation is possible where the name of the dead is not known. Euripides is therefore psychologically as well as dramatically justified in making Or. here and at l. 504 refuse to give his name.

504. θύσεις almost = 'your business is to sacrifice'; cf. the common use of the fut. for the imperative.

506–7. i.e. ⟨οὐκ ἂν φράσαιμι·⟩ ζητεῖς γὰρ ⟨ὃ⟩ οὐδὲν κέρδος ⟨ἐστὶν ἐμοὶ⟩ ὡς θ. Iph. admits that the information will not *benefit* him but urges that it will *oblige* (χάριν) her. Or. politely yields the point.

509. For πρὸς θεῶν in a surprised question cf. E. *Med.* 670 πρὸς θεῶν ἄπαις γὰρ δεῦρ' ἀεὶ τείνεις βίον; *Ion* 265 πρὸς θεῶν ἀληθῶς . . .; *Hel.* 660 πρὸς θεῶν, δόμων πῶς τῶν ἐμῶν ἀπεστάλης;

511. ἀπῆρας, sc. ναῦν; cf. E. *Cyc.* 131 ἀπαίρειν χθονός. Sometimes with an acc. added, e.g. E. *Tr.* 944 Σπάρτης ἀπῆρας νηὶ Κρησίαν χθόνα, where the original constr. is so far forgotten that νηί appears for ⟨ναῦν⟩. (On this analogy Monk needlessly conjectured here φυγαῖς for φυγάς.) φυγάς is a nominative substantive.

512. A good Euripidean σόφισμα. Or. was not exiled by his city; to this extent he goes ἑκών: he goes οὐχ ἑκών as driven out by the Furies. For other similar expressions cf. E. *Or.* 904 Ἀργεῖος οὐκ Ἀργεῖος; *Alc.* 521 ἔστιν δὲ κοὐκέτ' ἔστιν; *Hel.* 138 τεθνᾶσι καὶ οὐ τεθνᾶσι; and for the jingle *Or.* 397 σοφόν τοι τὸ σαφές, οὐ τὸ μὴ σαφές. Aristophanes ridicules such turns of phrase in *Ach.* 395, 6 Δι. ἔνδον ἔστ' Εὐριπίδης; | Κη. οὐκ ἔνδον ἔνδον ἐστίν, εἰ γνώμην ἔχεις.

513–17. When in l. 514 Or. gives a grudging consent to answer we do not expect or want a greeting from Iph. but the question she was anxious to put, viz. l. 517. Almost all edd. follow Badham and Kirchhoff in putting ll. 513, 4 after 516.

This is better but still not entirely satisfactory. If instead we put ll. 515, 6 after 510 we should not only bring l. 514 next to 517 (an imperative change) but also bring Iph.'s reference to Argos (515) next to Orestes' (510) where we should expect it—and get a reason for Iph.'s question (l. 511) which is asked because of Orestes' disgruntled remark οὔκουν ἐμαυτῷ γε. In this case ⟨γ'⟩ might be preferable to Scaliger's ⟨δ'⟩.

514. Hermann's ὥς ⟨γ'⟩ is attractive (see note on l. 75 above); though in this idiom γε seldom, if ever, comes immediately after ὡς (see Denniston, p. 143). πάρεργον is often used with a gen. = secondary consideration in; e.g. E. *Or.* 610 πάρεργον . . . πόνων; *Hel.* 925 πάρεργον . . . τῆς τύχης; *HF.* 1340 πάρεργα . . . κακῶν; *El.* 509 πάρεργα ὁδοῦ. So here Or. means '⟨very well (γε);⟩ to answer you is troublesome, but a detail as compared with my present misfortune.' Wecklein's θήσομαι (the verb is used in the passage from E. *Or.* quoted above) for τῆς ἐμῆς is utterly unnecessary, as is Bauer's θείς for τῆς.

515–16. Iph. uses ποθεινός merely in the sense of 'welcome'. μολών is causal. Or. replies that he sees nothing 'desirable' in his arrival. If she finds it so, well and good. The MSS. σὺ τοῦτ' ἔρα is difficult but possible. τοῦτο is an internal acc. and the phrase = τοῦτον τὸν πόθον ἔχε (Wecklein); i.e. keep your pleasure in my arrival to yourself. Barnes' σὺ τοῦδ' ἔρα = *you* may be as pleased as you like at my arrival; τοῦδε = τοῦ ἐμὲ ἐλθεῖν. For ἐρᾶν = 'to be pleased with' England cites the well-known frag. of Aeschylus' Niobe (A. *fr.* 161) μόνος θεῶν γὰρ θάνατος οὐ δώρων ἐρᾷ; cf. also l. 530 below. Jacobs suggested, with some plausibility, σὺ τοῦθ' ὅρα = (colloquially) that is your affair. Maltby's σύ γ' οὖν ἔρου introduces 517 well, but is, with the MSS. order of lines, too far from its reference, viz. τι in l. 513. With the revised order of lines it becomes pointless.

517. **Τροίαν . . . οἶσθα.** To have knowledge of a thing is usually *εἰδέναι τινός*, not *τι* (if there is no preposition), but see E. *Hec.* 1266 *οἶσθα μορφῆς μετάστασιν* and *Ion* 987 *οἶσθα γηγενῆ μάχην.*

518. The constr. is **ὡς** (exclamatory) *ὤφελον μήποτ' εἰδέναι αὐτήν*; cf. Ar. *Ra.* 955 *ὡς πρὶν διδάξαι γ' ὤφελες μέσος διαρραγῆναι*, and for *μή* in front of *ὤφελον* see E. *Cyc.* 186, 7 *μηδαμοῦ γένος ποτὲ | φῦναι γυναικῶν ὤφελε.* Scaliger's *ἰδεῖν* for *ἰδών* is attractive. *ὄναρ*, as so often, adverbial = in a dream.

519. **οὐκέτ' οὖσαν** goes closely with *οἴχεται* as in the common phrase *οἴχεται θανών.* The three words together = *ὀλέσθαι*—hence the instrumental *δορί.*

520. Cf. E. *Ba.* 1231 *οὐδ' ἄκραντ' ἠκούσαμεν.*

521–4. **δῶμα** is awkward at first sight, for, the 'home' of Menelaus and Helen being Sparta, Or.'s affirmative answer to the question in l. 521 might be expected to preclude Iph.'s further question in l. 523. At E. *Med.* 140 the MSS. L and P (i.e. our two MSS.) bowdlerize *λέκτρα* (the reading of another MS. family) into *δῶμα.* On the theory that a similar change was made here Weil 'replaces' *λέκτρα.* The question then only means 'has Helen rejoined Menelaus?', and the following query 'where is she ⟨now⟩?' becomes more reasonable.

We can, however, take *δῶμα* = household, in which case the MSS. reading gives good sense. Iph. may well have imagined what was actually the case, viz. that Menelaus did not return home at once (cf. *Od.* 3. 305–12; E. *Hel.* 776).

Bruhn's *λῦμα* M. = the bane of M. (on the analogy of *λῦμ' Ἀχαιῶν*—i.e. Priam, in E. *Tr.* 591) is possible though less likely.

522. **τινι** = *Ἀγαμέμνονι.* Or. regards the return of Helen as = the object, and therefore the end of the war, which led to the murder of A. This is much better than to take it as referring to Or. himself, as some have done, citing as parallel l. 548 below and Haemon's remark (S. *Ant.* 751) *ἥδ' οὖν θανεῖται καὶ θανοῦσ' ὀλεῖ τινα.*

523. The *προ* of **προυφείλει** suggests, as England puts it, that the debt in Iph.'s case was of longer standing.

[**προυφείλει**, not *προὐφείλει* (as it is occasionally printed) for this reason. The mark of crasis is not a breathing, smooth or rough, but the *coronis*, which in MSS. had much the same shape as the smooth breathing. From which it follows, incidentally, that such printings as *χἡ* (for *χὠ*) are incorrect. But whereas crasis is always marked by the *coronis*, internal contraction is not so marked. *προὐφείλει* would be about as reasonable as *ποιεῖ̓*.]

525. **μῖσος εἰς Ἕλληνας**: cf. E. *Ba.* 779 *ψόγος ἐς Ἕλληνας μέγας*; *Or.* 21 *ἐπίσημον εἰς Ἕλληνας* and *ib.* 30 *πρὸς οὐχ ἅπαντας εὔκλειαν φέρον.* For *μῖσος* personified cf. E. *Andr.* 261 *ὦ . . . σκληρὸν θράσος* (of Andromache) and l. 385 (note) above.

526. **ἀπολαύειν** here used of bad things; cf. E. *Ph.* 1204, 5 *ἔοικε τῶν ἐμῶν νυμφευμάτων | τῶν τ' Οἰδίπου δύστηνος ἀπολαῦσαι κακῶν.*

γάμων: the plur. refers only to Helen's 'marriage' with Paris.

528. συλλαβοῦσα governs *πάντα*, **ἀνιστορεῖς** governs *με*.

529. τοῦδ' = the answering of my questions. But Paley's *τοῦτο* (with the same meaning) understanding *σου* = 'from you' is very likely right. For the double constr. cf. A. *Pr.* 28 *τοιαῦτ' ἐπηύρου τοῦ φιλανθρώπου τρόπου.*

Semitelos' (cited by Weil) *τοῦτ' ἔτ' ἀνερέσθαι* would give good sense.

531. For **Κάλχας τις**, 'a certain C.': cf. S. *Ph.* 442 *Θερσίτης τις ἦν* and l. 545 below; also E. *Hel.* 98 *τιν' Ἀχιλλέα*; *HF.* 748; *Ion* 330; *ib.* 1311 where *τις* = quidam.

532. Lenting's *ὥς γ' ἦν* is possible (cf. l. 514 note). *ὡς . . . λόγος* suggests that there were various stories about C.'s death. According to Strabo (14. 1. 27) he died near Colophon *διὰ λύπην, περιτυχὼν ἑαυτοῦ κρείττονι μάντει, . . . Μόψῳ.* This competition in prophecy between Calchas and Mopsus seems to have formed a scene in Soph.'s *Ἑλένης ἀπαίτησις* (see S. *fr.* 180 and Pearson's note, vol. i, p. 122).

533. ὡς εὖ (note Musgrave's palmary emendation), for Calchas had demanded her sacrifice (cf. l. 16).

For this use of *γάρ* cf. S. *Aj.* 101, *εἶέν· τί γὰρ δὴ παῖς ὁ τοῦ Λαερτίου*; *ib.* 983, 4 *τί γὰρ τέκνον | τὸ τοῦδε.* See Denniston, p. 82.

534. The news of Odysseus' wanderings would have been spread in Greece by Menelaus who had it from Proteus in Egypt (*Od.* 4. 555–60).

537. Most edd. accept Elmsley's **δέ** for the MSS. *δ' ὁ* on the ground that the MSS. reading must mean 'Is Achilles still a boy?' Certainly *Θέτιδος* is badly placed and *δέ* would be more normal Greek. Monk proposed to regard Θ. as a gloss on *Νηρῇδος* and to read *Ἀχιλεὺς δ' ὁ*, but Eur. always uses λλ in this word in dialogue. We should rather expect, too, that Iph. would suppress the actual name of Achilles, nor is it fair to argue from l. 663 below that she must have used it.

538. ἄλλως = to no good purpose, to no useful end. Weil needlessly emends to *οὐκ ἔσθ' ὃς ἄλλως.*

540. τἀφ' may be *τὰ ἐφ'* Ἑλλ. = the things in Greece, or, with more probability, *τὰ ἀφ'* Ἑλλ. on the analogy of such phrases as *τἀκεῖθεν* = the things there (Ar. *Av.* 1304), and A. *Th.* 68 *εἰδὼς τὰ τῶν θύραθεν*; cf. also ll. 1182 and 1410 below and E. *Supp.* 182 where *οἴκοθεν* = *οἴκοι.* It is as though knowledge of events at a distance physically came from the place concerned. Because at E. *Or.* 867, 8 we find *πυθέσθαι δεόμενος τά τ' ἀμφὶ σοῦ | τά τ' ἀμφ' Ὀρέστου* there is no need to write here *τἀμφ'* as Wecklein does.

541. The meaning of **ἀπωλόμην**, lit. 'I was destroyed ⟨from it⟩', is best seen where it occurs in the active as at l. 1363 below and E. *Hec.* 946–8 *ἐπεί με γᾶς ἐκ πατρῴας ἀπώλεσεν . . . γάμος.* It should not be altered to *ἀπῳχόμην.* A further difficulty in the present passage is that we have no *ἐκ* + gen. expressed; we have to understand ἐκεῖθεν. For this reason it is probably better to accept Hermann's παῖς ⟨δ'⟩ which binds both parts of the sentence better together; i.e. = ἐκεῖθέν εἰμι μέν, ἀπωλόμην δέ.

φθείρεσθαι is used in a similar manner; cf. E. *Andr.* 708 εἰ μὴ φθερῇ τῆσδ' ὡς τάχιστ' ἀπὸ στέγης, *HF.* 1290 γῆς . . . ἀποφθαρήσεται.

543–4. Iph. means by εὐδαίμων rich (cf. l. 551 τὸν ὄλβον) and famous; Or. means fortunate. The constr. is οὐ γὰρ ⟨οὗτός γε⟩, ὃν ἐγῷδα, τῶν εὐδαιμόνων ⟨ἐστίν⟩. Markland suggested εὐδαίμονα for εὐδαιμονεῖν, in which case λέγουσ' would mean 'call'.

548. τινα = himself, as (possibly) at S. *Ant.* 751, cf. note on l. 522.

550. τοῦτο ⟨τὸ στέναγμα⟩; not ⟨τὸ πρᾶγμα⟩.

552. Or. answers the question put in 549 ποίᾳ συμφορᾷ; though γάρ does not 're-establish the broken connection' (England). It rather gives a reason or a justification for ἀναστένω. 'You rightly lament for . . .'

ἐκ γυναικός = at a woman's hands. The ambiguity γυνή = wife and γυνή = woman is intentional, and any 'correction' such as Heimsöth's ἰδίας γάρ or Köchly's δάμαρτος is fatal. Iph. does not realize yet that Clytemnestra is the murderess, as is clear from her next two inquiries. Full knowledge comes only after l. 558. Hence her exclamation at that point.

553. Wecklein's ᾗ for MSS. ὦ may well be right; cf. the MSS. confusion at l. 930 between ᾗ and οὐ.

If κτανών (the reading of P) is right Iph. must, as Prof. Murray suggests in the critical note, be thinking of Ag.'s attempt to kill her at Aulis. But in favour of θανών (second hand in L) is the frequent conjunction of κτανεῖν and θανεῖν, e.g. S. *Ph.* 336 ἀλλ' εὐγενὴς μὲν ὁ κτανών τε χὠ θανών, S. *Ant.* 1263, 4 ὦ κτανόντας τε καὶ θανόντας βλέποντες ἐμφυλίους, *OC.* 1388 θανεῖν κτανεῖν θ'.

555. i.e. ⟨παύσομαι,⟩ τοσόνδε γ' ⟨ἐρωτήσασα⟩.

556. There is no need to suspect οὗτος on the ground that ὅδε is generally used of the speaker. The statement is impersonal—'the child she bare, he killed her'. Hartung's ἔτεκ', αὐτός is needless. Cf. l. 763 (note).

558. It is difficult to see what is wrong with τήνδε—unless, indeed, one holds the persistent but erroneous view that in tragedy ὅδε must be used of persons present on the stage. [For the sceptical the following instances may be cited from Euripides: *Hipp.* 48, *Andr.* 1116, *Or.* 771, *IA.* 72, *Rh.* 588, cf. S. *Tr.* 718.] 'Avenging on her the death of his father'; the constr. is the normal one. Weil's remark that the MSS. reading 'implique antithèse entre τήνδε et πατρός' is true. But why should it not? His own suggestion (see crit. note) involves a strange, not to say impossible, use of τιμωρεῖν. His other suggestion τῇδε (as printed in the last (3rd) edit.) gives good sense ('thus') and is very near the MSS. Emendations are legion. We may mention Blomfield's ἀντιτιμωρούμενος, Köchly's σφ' ἀντιτιμωρούμενος (both excellent in sense), Elmsley's αἷμα (for τήνδε; this acc. after τιμωρεῖσθαι, though rarer than the acc. of the person on whom the vengeance is wreaked, is correct—cf. E. *fr.* 559 αἷμ' ἐτιμωρησάμην), and Semitelos' τὴν δίκην ἀρούμενος (but αἵρεσθαι means rather 'to undertake', which is scarcely the sense we want).

559. ⟨τὸ⟩ **δίκαιον** is here the substantive, not κακόν (as some edd.), and almost = δίκην. Lit. 'how well he exacted an evil justice'.

At A. *Ag.* 812 we get δικαίων . . . ὧν ἐπραξάμην πόλιν = the just penalty I exacted from the city.

Eur. does not elsewhere use εἰσπράσσειν (a prose word) and Elmsley suggested ἐξέπραξεν (cf. E. *HF.* 42, 3 μὴ . . . ἐκπράξωσιν αἵματος δίκην). His κακήν ('exacted a just penalty from an evil woman') is ingenious but unnecessary.

There is, as England points out, a double oxymoron here, between εὖ and κακόν, and again between κακόν and δίκαιον.

560. This line might be taken as = ἀλλ' οὐκ εὐτυχεῖ ⟨καίπερ⟩ δίκαιος ὢν ⟨εὐτυχεῖν⟩, 'though deserving to prosper'. There are clear cases of this use of δίκαιος in Eur., e.g. *Alc.* 1147 and *Heracl.* 776 (at *Hipp.* 1081 and *Med.* 724 it means rather 'as is your duty'); but it gives better sense—and fits in better with the preceding line—to translate 'though a just man'.

England's ἀλλ' οὔ τι involves the dubious use of πρὸς θεῶν = μὰ τοὺς θεούς, nor can one agree with his remark that 'εὐτυχεῖ seems stronger by itself, and the mention of the gods' agency is hardly in place here'.

For εὐτ. τὰ πρὸς θεῶν cf. S. *Ph.* 1441 εὐσεβεῖν τὰ πρὸς θεούς, where the acc. is used because the εὐσέβεια is directed *towards* the gods, while here the εὐτυχία would come *from* the gods (cf. below, l. 692 ἃ πράσσω πρὸς θεῶν). Flagg translates the two lines well: *Iph.* Ah! an evil deed of justice right well done. *Or.* Yet Heaven does not well by him, just though he be.

562. In E. *Or.* (l. 23) a third daughter, Chrysothemis, is mentioned, and the number is given as three in *IA.* 1164. Sophocles, in the Electra (l. 157) names even a fourth, Iphianassa. In *Il.* 9. 145 the three daughters are Χρυσόθεμις καὶ Λαοδίκη καὶ Ἰφιάνασσα. Lucr. (1. 85) gives the name Iphianassa to the victim at Aulis.

566. 'For the sakeless sake of a bad woman (Helen)' is impossible in English; but in Greek χάριν, though used prepositionally, is still half a substantive, and can, as such, be adjectivally qualified. Cf. S. *Aj.* 176 νίκας ἀκάρπωτον χάριν = lit. 'for the fruitless sake of victory' = 'for the sake of a fruitless victory'. Seidler's Latin trans. gives the sense well 'ob causam, quae causa esse non debebat'. For the oxymoron cf. A. *Pr.* 545 = *Ag.* 1545 ἄχαρις χάρις, *Ch.* 42–6 τοιάνδε χάριν ἀχάριτον . . . μωμένα μ' ἰάλλει δύσθεος γυνά, E. *Ph.* 1757 χάριν ἀχάριτον ἐς θεοὺς διδοῦσα.

568. i.e. he cannot be said to live anywhere; he is driven (by the Furies) here, there, and everywhere. England aptly quotes from a letter of Sir Thomas More to Erasmus 'The heretic Tyndale . . . who is in exile nowhere and everywhere'.

570. οὐδ' here = 'not . . . either'. Dreams, says Or., are, I agree, liars, but gods and their oracles are no better, as I know well who have suffered from them.

572. The asyndeton is strange and Wilamowitz may be right in reading ταραγμὸς ⟨δ'⟩, or Mekler in supposing a lacuna after 571 ⟨κείνῳ δὲ μὴ 'πίχαρμ' ὀνειδίσῃς, ἐπεί⟩.

573–5. There are four methods of dealing with this difficulty. (1) We may, with Monk and Dindorf, suppose a lacuna after l. 573. This is not so arbitrary as it might seem, since *l*'s λείπεται (see *app. crit.*) is very possibly no more than a 'correction' of λείπει, the usual marginal gloss signifying that something has fallen out. (2) We can take λυπεῖται as impersonal 'there is but one cause of grief'. This is objectionable because (*a*) it is very dubious Greek (Schöne's λυπεῖ τοι would give the meaning correctly); (*b*) it would naturally be followed by an infinitive (e.g. τὸ ἐμὲ ὀλωλέναι). The temporal relative ὅτε (MSS.), still more the personal relative ὅς (our text, from Wecklein), follows it awkwardly; (*c*) the statement is ludicrously untrue. This world unfortunately contains many ills besides a misplaced confidence in oracles. (The same criticism applies equally to emendations such as Köchly's ἓν δὲ λυπηρόν μ. and Hermann's ἓν δὲ λυπεῖσθαι μ., the latter of which is also objectionable because ἓν = ἔνεστι will not stand in iambics—and it should be πάρεστι.) (3) We can take λ. as personal, ἓν then being an internal acc. In this case the subject of the verb is either 'a man', somehow understood out of βροτείοις, and we must keep ὅτ': 'but a man is hurt only in this when . . .'; or, reading ὅς, the subject is ⟨οὗτος⟩ = ἐγώ: 'but he (= I) is (= am) hurt only in this, who . . .' Both these involve not only the palpable untruth mentioned above (to a modified degree in the latter case, it must be admitted), but also a *non sequitur*. (4) We can emend to Heimsöth's ἓν λελάμπρυνται (? better δεδήλωται) μόνον· ὅδ'. This at least gives good sense: 'all is confusion; one thing only is clear, ⟨viz. that⟩ he (= I) . . . having trusted . . . is (= am) undone.' The lacuna before -ται in P justifies a correction which does not, when we consider the reading of L, look palaeographically likely.

For ὄλωλεν ὡς ὄλωλε cf. E. *Tr.* 630. εἰδόσιν is an ethic dat.; cf. A. *Ag.* 39 (the watchman) μαθοῦσιν αὐδῶ κοὐ μαθοῦσι λήθομαι, E. *Rh.* 973 σεμνὸς τοῖσιν εἰδόσιν θεός, and Ar. *Nu.* 1241 Ζεὺς γελοῖος ὀμνύμενος τοῖς εἰδόσιν.

Or.'s attack on oracles is due to that one which bade him kill his mother, but some have thought that Eur. is here voicing his own sentiments with regard in particular to the Sicilian expedition. In the Helen (produced in 412) we read (ll. 744, 5) ἀλλά τοι τὰ μάντεων | ἐσεῖδον ὡς φαῦλ' ἐστὶ καὶ ψευδῶν πλέα, and disparaging remarks are not infrequent in other of Eur.'s later plays, e.g. *IA.* 520, *ib.* 956-8, *Rh.* 65, 6. Thuc. (8. 1. 1.) notes the subsequent anger of the people: ὠργίζοντο δὲ καὶ τοῖς χρησμολόγοις τε καὶ μάντεσι καὶ ὁπόσοι τι τότε αὐτοὺς θειάσαντες ἐπήλπισαν ὡς λήψονται Σικελίαν; cf. Introduction, p. xiv.

579. The MSS. σπουδῆς (v. l. σπουδαῖς) is surely impossible: 'a benefit of attention alike to . . .' in the sense of 'a subject, attention to which will be a benefit alike to . . .' We must read Musgrave's σπεύδουσ'. This mixture of sing. and plur. (ἥκομεν . . . σπεύδουσα) is very common; cf. ll. 348, 9 (and note). For other instances in Eur. see *Hipp.* 244 αἰδούμεθα . . . τὰ λελεγμένα μοι; *Ion* 1250, 1 διωκόμεσθα . . . κρατηθεῖσα; *Ph.* 497, 8 ἐμοὶ μέν, εἰ . . . | τεθράμμεθ', ἀλλ' . . . μοι.

580. The MSS. involve a violation of the final cretic rule. We may possibly regard οὕτω as a gloss (which has got into the text) on some such word as ὧδε or τῇδε (Heimsöth, with [γ']), though, it must be admitted, neither word stands in need of a gloss. Wecklein suggests τὸ κοινὸν δ' εὖ μάλιστα γίγνεται.

Instances of broken fifth-foot spondees in Eur. (other than prepositions and articles in agreement) may be classed as follows:—

(1) the article not in agreement with the cretic that follows: e.g. *Ph.* 886 τῶν Οἰδίπου.

(2) the relative (not very common): e.g. ᾧ πείσομαι (*El.* 572).

(3) certain monosyllabic particles: καί, μή, οὐ, ὡς, ἤ, εἰ (if followed by μή).

(4) elided demonstratives; generally parts of ὅδε. (Elmsley emends *Hel.* 281 τοῦτ' ἐσ|τι to τόδ' ἐσ|τι.)

(5) a few other elided dissyllables: ὥστ', ἐστ', οὔτ'.

(6) article or monosyllabic preposition followed by elided δέ. (*Or.* 1035 δεῖ δ' is unique.)

(7) elision before ἄν.

(8) the following monosyllabic nouns: παῖς (*Suppl.* 1098), νοῦς (*Ba.* 271), τρεῖς (*IA.* 49)—all going closely with the following cretic.

(9) five inexplicable cases: οὐδεὶς βούλεται (*Alc.* 671), νώτοις οὐρανόν (*Ion* 1), κεῖνον δεῖ (*IA.* 1455—Porson δεῖ κεῖνον), οὐδὲν δεῖ (*HF.* 1338), οὐδὲν θάτερον (*Ph.* 747).

[I take no account of the frequent cases which occur in the corrupted end of the *IA.*]

τὸ δ' εὖ = τὸ δ' εὖ ἔχειν = a good state of affairs.

582. σῴσαιμι. When has σῴζω and its parts an iota subscript? L & S (9th ed.) say 'with ι wherever ζ follows ω'. But they admit that the ι is often rejected even before ζ, while on the other hand some inscriptions (early as well as late) show σῳσ- in the form σωισ-; cf. Meisterhans, p. 181.

585. An Athenian audience would not well have understood a woman of the heroic age who could write. Hence Eur.'s care to have the letter written for Iph. It is to be remarked, however, that in the *Hippolytus* Phaedra herself writes a letter (856 sqq.).

586–7. 'And that the victims of the goddess, who thinks such things right, die beneath the law.' The τά of the papyrus (the τ is not quite certain) confirms a conjecture of Hermann's. Grenfell and Hunt suggest ἡγουμένου, i.e. 'beneath the law which considers this right'. But can νόμος be said ἡγεῖσθαι? Besides correcting the impossible γε of the MSS. to τά Hermann also read ἡγούμενος; i.e. 'thinking this the lawful action (δίκ. here a substantive) of the goddess'. But the direct object τάδε coming in the middle of the predicative phrase τὰ τῆς θεοῦ δίκαια is very doubtful. Markland's σφε for γε (with a comma after it and none after θεοῦ) gives good sense: 'and that he dies beneath the law, the goddess holding this to be right'.

φονέα here adjectival and predicative. The meaning is that the captive, realizing that his impending sacrifice was not a murder but a matter of νόμος, bore no ill-will to his destined sacrificer.

588–90. Our text adheres to the MSS., except for the insertion of τ' (Elmsley, δ'), taking L's optative (ἀγγεῖλαι), not P's infin. This gives fair sense. It is clear from the present situation that while *single* strangers must be sacrificed, *one* of a larger number might be spared. Presumably the writer of the letter was single, and no Greek pair, or larger number, had since arrived in Tauris. But αὖθις is, as the text stands, rather pointless, and either Musgrave's Ἀργόθεν or Wecklein's Ἀργεῖος (with no τ') for ἀγγεῖλαι is good. Weil similarly suggested Ἀργείαν μολὼν | εἰς γαῖαν. An Argive might more reasonably be expected to deliver a letter in Argos than, say, a Theban.

τινι = 'one', not 'any' which would be οὐδενί. Dindorf and Monk rejected these three lines. They are, however, found in Pap. Hib. 24.

591–3. Many edd. adopt L's δυσγενής, so introducing the idea of *noblesse oblige*; cf. l. 609 ἀπ' εὐγενοῦς ῥίζης.

οὔτε . . . καί is very suspicious; Denniston quotes no instances of it. οὔτε . . . τε is not uncommon (cf. Denniston, p. 508).

Keeping the MSS. reading as in our text we can construe: 'You, for you know M. and those whom I too wish ⟨you to know⟩, be saved, you too receiving a fair reward, your life for ⟨the carrying of⟩ a light letter'. But this is open to many objections: (1) the καί with ἐγώ is meaningless; (2) to understand ⟨τούτους τοὺς ἀνθρώπους⟩ οὓς ⟨εἰδέναι σε⟩ θέλω is almost impossible—nor does it give particularly good sense. It is useless to cite E. *Heracl.* 791 φόβος γάρ εἴ μοι ζῶσιν οὓς ἐγὼ θέλω, sc. ζῆν, for it is not a true parallel; (3) the καί before σύ is pointless.

Markland's ἐγώ (for κἀγώ) and Musgrave's φιλῶ for θέλω are excellent, but they still leave the καὶ σύ difficulty. The same may be said of England's χοἰς κἀγὼ (? better ἐγὼ) μέλω, of Badham's δοὺς ἁγὼ θέλω (with the parenthesis ending at οἶσθα), of Kirchhoff's γ' ὥστε μ' ὠφελεῖν (too far from the MSS.), and even of Weil's οἶσθ'· ἄγ', ὡς κἀγὼ θέλω, σώθητι καὶ σύ (with the idiomatic γάρ (= ἐπεί) . . . ἄγε . . . σώθητι, and understanding σωθῆναι with θέλω—the καί of κἀγώ is here to the point, for obviously Or. wishes for his own safety); 'since thou knowest . . ., come, as I, too, wish ⟨thee to be saved⟩, be thou, too, saved . . .'

But to avoid the καὶ σύ difficulty we must adopt Bothe's σύθητ' ἐκεῖσε or Wecklein's σύθητι κεῖσε, 'hasten thither', or perhaps more simply σώθητι κεῖσε; cf. E. *Ph.* 725 εἴπερ σφαλείς γε δεῦρο σωθήσῃ πάλιν. The latter is rendered the more likely by Pap. Hib. 24 which confirms the reading σώθητι. For another case where ἐκεῖσε has *possibly* been corrupted into καί, cf. E. *Ion* 828.

Reiske's σώθητι καὶ σοῦ (citing Hesych. σοῦ· ὅρμα) is worth mention as an example of misplaced ingenuity.

598. Lucian (*Am.* 47) quotes this line with τόνδ' ἐμοί for our MSS. τόνδε μοι, and this reading should probably be adopted, not because it occurs in Lucian, but because the sense demands ἐμοί rather than μοι.

599–600. **ναυστολεῖν** = to convey by sea. συμφοραί, Or. means, form the cargo of the ship of which he is master; Pyl. has joined him out of pity for his troubles. This is better than to regard, as some have done, ναυσ. as intrans. and συμφοράς as acc. of the goal. F. W. Schmidt conjectured τοῦδ' ἑκὼν μοχθῶν χάριν. τοῦδε = ἐμοῦ might have been glossed τῶν ἐμῶν.

602. **χάριν τίθεσθαί** ⟨σοι⟩ = lit. to invest gratitude in you; i.e. to do something to ensure your gratitude.

605. For ὁ χρῄζων cf. E. *Suppl.* 440, 1 καὶ ταῦθ' ὁ χρῄζων λαμπρός ἐσθ', ὁ μὴ θέλων | σιγᾷ, and Xen. *Cyr.* 2. 1. 18 ὁρᾶτε τὰ ὅπλα· ὁ μὲν χρῄζων λαμβανέτω ταῦτα. Aristophanes uses ὁ βουλόμενος in the same way, cf. *Pl.* 918.

606. **αἴσχιστον ὅστις** by a common Greek idiom for αἴσχιστός ἐστιν εἴ τις or αἴσχιστόν ἐστι with infin. It occurs as early as Hom.; *Il.* 14. 81 βέλτερον ὃς φεύγων προφύγῃ κακὸν ἠὲ ἁλώῃ, and Theognis (743–6) πῶς ἐστι δίκαιον | ἔργων ὅστις ἀνὴρ ἐκτὸς ἐὼν ἀδίκων | . . . μὴ τὰ δίκαια πάθῃ. For instances in Eur. cf. ll. 1064, 1121 of this play (σοφόν in l. 484 is ambiguous) and *Ph.* 509, 10 ἀνανδρία γάρ, τὸ πλέον ὅστις ἀπολέσας | τοὔλασσον ἔλαβε; further *Tr.* 648, 9; *ib.* 1156; *El.* 815, 6; *Hel.* 267, 8; *ib.* 271, 2; *ib.* 941, 2.

607. The better form seems to be σέσωται (Meisterh., p. 185, and Photius agrees: οἱ παλαιοὶ ἄνευ τοῦ σ.).

610. For ὀρθῶς **φίλος**, a true friend, cf. S. *Ant.* 99 τοῖς φίλοις . . . ὀρθῶς φίλη; E. *Andr.* 376, 7 φίλων γὰρ οὐδὲν ἴδιον, οἵτινες φίλοι | ὀρθῶς πεφύκασ', ἀλλὰ κοινὰ χρήματα.

613. **πλὴν ὅσα**, more usually ὅσον (for ὅσα cf. Pl. *R.* 456 A), 'except in so far as' can be followed by a finite verb, by a participle as here, or, elliptically, by neither, e.g. S. *OT.* 1509 πάντων ἐρήμους, πλὴν ὅσον τὸ σὸν μέρος.

616. It is best to keep the MSS. προθυμία and to take τοῦδε = τοῦ θανεῖν. Some edd. however take Tournier's προμηθία and explain τοῦδε as = Πυλάδου.

618. Prof. Murray has returned to the MSS. τῆσδε; but surely

Bothe's τήνδε (a conjecture confirmed by Pap. Hib. 24) is right? Certainly προστροπήν = (properly) prayer or supplication, here in the sense of 'service' is very strange. The papyrus has συμ[φο]ράν, from which Weil conjectures προσφοράν; lit. 'this offering' = (?) 'the duty of offering this'. This is not likely to commend itself.

619. Bothe's ἄζηλον [γ'] is attractive, especially as (1) Γ and N are not infrequently confused; (2) some scribe might have taken εὐδαίμονα as a neut. plur. and altered ἄζηλον to ἄζηλα. On the other hand (1) a plur. in apposition to a singular (and this is in effect appositional) is not uncommon; cf. S. *Ph.* 35, 6 ἔκπωμα, φλαυρουργοῦ τινος | τεχνήματα, and l. 650 below; (2) the two adjs. need not refer specifically to προστροπήν but to the general situation.

620. **κεῖμαι** = (as often) τέθειμαι = here (almost) πέπτωκα. Hence εἰς; and cf. εἰς with such verbs as παρεῖναι and ὑπεκκεῖσθαι.

621. **θῆλυς** for θήλεια frequent in trag.; cf. E. *Ba.* 828, 836; *Hec.* 659; *Med.* 1084.

Hib. Pap. 24 gives κτείνουσα for the MSS. θύουσα. Before its discovery Mähly had conjectured θείνουσα. θύουσα, however, may be right; cf A. *Ag.* 137 where Aesch. uses the verb (in the middle voice) of eagles killing hares.

622. **ἀμφί**: cf. note on l. 443 above.

626. Hesychius gives two explanations of the word εὐρωπός: (1) = σκοτεινός, in which case it is to be connected with the substantive εὐρώς, mould (cf. the Homeric adj. εὐρώεις, dank); (2) = πλατύς, and so connected with εὐρύς. The latter is certainly right; the word is formed like στενωπός and κοιλωπός. Oppian, who uses the word occasionally, always uses it with the meaning of 'broad' (e.g. *Hal.* 4. 526 ἐν εὐρωποῖσιν ἁλὸς λαγόνεσσι).

Diodorus (20. 14), describing a bronze statue of Baal-Moloch (whom he calls Κρόνος) at Carthage, a statue into the arms of which children were so placed ὥστε ἀποκυλίεσθαι καὶ πίπτειν εἴς τι χάσμα πλῆρες πυρός, thinks that Eur. had this in mind when he wrote this passage. There being no mention of a statue here it is hard to see the connexion; besides it is fairly clear that here the victims were first burned in the temple and their remains then hurled into the chasm. (Others, e.g. Wecklein, picture the fire as burning at the bottom of the chasm.)

631. Notice the rare division of **οὐ μὴν . . . ἀλλά**, and cf. Ar. *Ra.* 1180 where the similar οὐ γὰρ ἀλλά is so divided—οὐ γάρ μοὖστιν ἀλλ' ἀκουστέα (see Denniston, p. 28).

Nauck's ὅσων for ὧν would destroy the ἀλλά and substitute for οὐ μήν . . . ἀλλά the equally idiomatic οὐ μήν . . . οὐδέ. This is, however, unnecessary.

Markland's 'λλείψω is probably right (= 'omit'). The constr. is οὐκ ἐλλείψω χάριν τούτων γε ἃ δυνατόν ἐστι χαρίζεσθαι.

οὐδέ = not either; i.e. no more than your sister would have omitted . . .

632. Supposing the fire and the chasm to be in two separate places, the τάφῳ may = the chasm (so England). It is more likely that it means the fire, it being the habit of the Greeks of the heroic age to burn the dead man in his clothes; cf. Od. 24. 67, 8 καίεο δ' ἔν τ' ἐσθῆτι θεῶν καὶ ἀλείφατι πολλῷ | καὶ μέλιτι γλυκερῷ: E. *Rh.* 959, 60 τεῦξαι τάφον | καὶ ξυμπυρῶσαι μυρίων πέπλων χλιδήν.

633. Most commentators have pointed out that oil poured on a burning corpse would, so far from extinguishing it, make it burn the fiercer. Some have gone so far as to suggest that Iph. actually means by 'extinguishing' this speeding-up of combustion. If the text is sound we should rather suppose that by σῶμα Iph. here means the ashes left smouldering after the fire had gone out. T. W. Allen (*CR.* 1905, p. 199) suggests that the verb here = to smother (i.e. to coat) with oil—i.e. after the execution and before the cremation.

Musurus, however, in the Aldine ed., excised the line, and many emendations have been offered of which we may mention Geel's κατασκεδῶ (very near the MSS.), but the constr. with this verb should be κ. ἔλαιον σώματος); Musgrave's καταστελῶ (but to 'equip' is an odd verb for ἔλαιον) and Köchly's κατακλύσω (again, to 'deluge' is scarcely the word we want). Better sense would be given by Wecklein's σὸν καταπείσω δέμας (cf. E. *Or.* 1239 δακρύοις καταπένδω σε and *ib.* 1187 χοὰς καταπείσουσ' ὑπὲρ μητρὸς τάφῳ)—but it is difficult to see how the text should have been corrupted.

637. With Reiske's 'μοί we must take the sentence as 'do not be angry with me'. This may be right, but it is scarcely a necessary change from the MSS. μου (which, however, should be corrected to 'μοῦ) = 'do not take the cruelty ⟨of your fate as coming⟩ from me'. Kirchhoff's μή μου 'γκαλῇς = 'do not bring my cruelty as a charge' is awkward with μου in that position. Perhaps μὴ 'μοὶ 'γκαλῇς might stand = 'do not bring the cruelty of your fate as a charge against me'.

μέντοι in what Denniston (p. 399) calls the 'affirmative' or 'emphatic' sense. 'μέν denotes objective certainty, while τοι brings the truth home to another person: "really, you know".'

641. Wecklein suggests χὴ δέλτος.

642. If πιστάς is right, then we do not want καί in 641 but ἀλλά; ἄελπτα . . . καὶ . . . πιστάς is nonsense.

In the sixteenth century Aemilius Portus suggested λέγουσ' ἀπίστους for λέγουσα πιστάς, but four hundred years have not proved sufficient to ensure its general acceptance.

Wecklein's δηλοῦσα for MSS. λέγουσα is certainly what one would have expected Eur. to write, but that is no proof that he wrote it.

644–56. This short κόμμος or dirge has caused endless discussion, the two main questions being (1) how is it to be divided among speakers; (2) how is it to be scanned?

(1) The whole chorus may sing all the lines assigned in our text to them; or some (or even all) the lines may be sung by individual members of the chorus; or (it was Hermann's view) the chorus may be divided into two halves, one of which addresses Or. (644, 5 and 652), the other Pyl. (647–9 and 651)—he attributes 653–6 to the whole chorus. 651, 2 were in the MSS. given to Pyl., but a correction in L attributed them (rightly) to the chorus.

Hermann's view seems to me the most likely, but it is impossible to dogmatize.

(2) Our text reproduces the MSS. arrangement of lines, an arrangement which admits no antistrophic responsion, and which introduces some very strange lines (e.g. 645 and 649) into what is clearly a dochmiac system. Hermann first attempted to (?) restore both responsion and metrical normality, and almost all edd. have followed him. He read

κατολοφύρομαι σὲ τὸν χερνίβων — str.
ῥανίσι ⟨— ∪ —⟩
μελόμενον αἱμακταῖς.
σὲ δὲ τύχας, μάκαρ· σὲ δ', ὦ νεᾶνία, — antistr.
σεβόμεθ', ἐς πάτραν
ὅτι ποτ' ἐπεμβάσῃ.

It will be seen that very little (an introduced cretic after ῥανίσι and ΣΕΔ for MSS. ΟΣ in 647) is needed to regularize this system metrically, and there is little doubt that it should be so regularized.

As to details, various words have been suggested for ⟨— ∪ —⟩; Hermann himself proposed ἐν κάρᾳ, Elmsley βαρβάρων, Weil ὦ μέλεος, Wecklein ὦ τάλας or παρθένου, etc. etc.

Some alternative suggestions for 647 are Wecklein's μακαρτέρας, νεᾶνία; Kirchhoff's μακαίρας, ὦ, Schöne's μακάριος, ὦ, etc. etc.

Weil adopts this last and alters κατολοφύρομαι in l. 644 to κατολοφυρόμεθα. This secures exact corresponsion (κατολοφυρόμεθα | = σὲ δὲ τύχας μακάρι |); but it is unnecessary, for, for a partially unresolved dochmiac to correspond with a resolved one (∪∪∪ – ∪ – = ∪∪∪ – ∪ ∪͡∪∪) is perfectly regular.

If we keep the O.C.T. we get in l. 645 a (resolved) iambic metron + a syncopated dochmiac (∪ ∪͡∪∪ ∪ ∪͡∪∪ | ∪ — — . –). (For this form of dochmiac see Wilamowitz, *Verskunst*, p. 405). 647 is a partially resolved cretic dipody (∪͡∪∪ ∪ – | ∪͡∪∪ ∪ –); 648 a syncopated iambic dimeter (∪ – | ∪ – | ∪∪ ∪ | .—); 649 another (partially resolved) iambic metron + syncopated dochmiac (∪ – | ∪ ∪͡∪∪ | ∪ — — . –).

645. μελόμενον = 'an object of care to'; personifying, as it were, the lustral sprinkling; cf. E. *Hel.* 196, 7 Ἰλίου κατασκαφαὶ | πυρὶ μέλουσι δαΐῳ; *Ph.* 1301 ἰαχὰν μελομέναν νεκροῖς, and above l. 182 μοῦσαν νέκυσι μελομέναν. Thus it comes almost to = 'doomed'; so E. *Hel.* 1161 Ἅιδᾳ μέλονται κάτω.

646. A curious inversion of ἀλλὰ . . . γάρ = ἀλλ' οὐ γὰρ οἶκτος . . . χαίρετε; see Denniston, p. 71.

647–8. Notice **μάκαρος** = μακαίρας, and cf. E. *Hel.* 375; *Ba.* 565, etc. (L & S). **σέβομαι** here takes the constr. (gen. (causal) + acc.) of μακαρίζω or **εὐδαιμονίζω.** For this use of σέβειν cf. A. *Ag.* 833 **τὸν εὐτυχοῦντα . . . σέβειν.**

For **νεανία** trisyllabic cf. E. *Ph.* 147; *IA.* 615 (νεάνιδες); Ar. *V.* 1069, etc. The following instances of synizesis may be found in Eur.: *Cyc.* 144 νεώς, *Hipp.* 56 ἀνεῳγμένας, *Ion* 390 ἐᾶν, *ib.* 1563 ἀνεῴχθη, *Rh.* 881 λεωφόρου (see note on l. 1486 below).

649. **ποτε** of the future (except when negative) is not common, but it is well enough attested, e.g. S. *OC.* 385, 6 ἔσχες ἐλπίδ' ὡς ἐμοῦ θεοὺς | ὤραν τιν' ἕξειν, ὥστε σωθῆναί ποτε: E. *HF.* 1294 ἐς τοῦτο δ' ἥξειν συμφορᾶς οἶμαί ποτε: so, though Elmsley's πόδ' is good idiomatic Greek (e.g. E. *Heracl.* 168 ἐς ἄντλον ἐμβήσῃ πόδα) there is no need to receive it into the text.

Seidler's ὅς is no improvement in sense on ὅτι (though perhaps more idiomatic) and it spoils the corresponsion.

650. **ἄζηλα**: either ἄζηλα ⟨ἐστι⟩ = ἄζηλόν ἐστι (cf. E. *El.* 1026 = *Med* 491 συγγνώστ' ἂν ἦν), or else ἄζηλα is in apposition to the previous sentence = τὸ ἐς πάτραν ἐπεμβαίνειν. Cf. note on l. 619.

651. **πομπαί** = νόστος. Cf. *Od.* 6. 290 πομπῆς καὶ νόστοιο (τυχεῖν).

652. Many alterations of this line have been suggested. They mostly take the form of removing φεῦ φεῦ (which is given a separate line and made to correspond with αἰαῖ [αἰαῖ]), and reading something like σὺ δὲ διόλλυσαι (Monk) or τὸ σὲ διόλλυσθαι (Wecklein). With either of these we should get a dochmiac. Except, however, for supposed metrical reasons there is no need to interfere with the MSS. reading. If any correction be accepted it should perhaps be Weil's ingenious πομπαί, φεῦ φεῦ, δύ' ὀλλῦσαι = (lit.) 'a home-sending destroying two'.

651–3. If the κόμμος is to be regarded as antistrophic, the epode may begin at l. 651 (so Weil) or at πότερος—so Hermann, who gives:

— ὦ σχέτλιοι πομπαί.	στρ. β'
— φεῦ, φεῦ, διόλλυσαι	ἀντ. β'
— αἰαῖ	στρ. γ'
— αἰαῖ	ἀντ. γ'

The MSS. ὁ μέλλων makes nonsense unless, with Dindorf and others, one postulates a lacuna. For it is really impossible to interpret with some edd. πότερος ὁ μέλλων ⟨ὡς ἀληθῶς διολλῦσθαι;⟩. Köchly's πότερος ὁ μέλεος ὤν; is only possible if μέλεος could be translated '*really* miserable'. We must have a comparative. Hermann's ὁ μᾶλλον is, textually speaking, the simplest emendation, i.e. πότερος ⟨ἐστὶν⟩ ὁ μᾶλλον ⟨διολλύμενος⟩; Wecklein's πότερος ὁ μέλ⟨εος μᾶλ⟩λ⟨ον⟩ ὤν; is good; or, if we accept Weil's above-mentioned suggestion, his πότερος ὃν μᾶλλον; i.e. πότερος ⟨ἐστὶν⟩ ὃν ⟨ὑμεῖς πομπαὶ⟩ μᾶλλον ⟨ὄλλυτε⟩;

655–6. **μέμονε** = (properly) 'wishes'; here apparently = 'debates'. But it is strange. A similar constr., though not similar sense, occurs at *Il.* 16. 435 διχθὰ δέ μοι κραδίη μέμονε φρεσὶν ὁρμαίνοντι. πάρος = *potius*, not *prius*, is Homeric (e.g. *Il.* 8. 166, 16. 629), though it is occasionally found in lyrics, e.g. E. *Or.* 345, 6 τίνα ... πάρος οἶκον ἕτερον ἢ τὸν ἀπὸ | θεογόνων γάμων;

657. **πέπονθας**, sc. mentally. In effect, 'has the same thought struck you as has struck me?'

πρὸς θεῶν, as in l. 509, because virtually = πρὸς θ., εἰπέ μοι.

658. The third Episode (lasting till 1088) begins. It consists of

(*a*) dialogue between Or. and Pyl., 653–724.

(*b*) the ἀναγνώρισις: Or., Pyl., and Iph., 725–1088.

662. A rare use of ἐν = in the matter of; cf. *Il.* 23. 671 ἐν πάντεσσ' ἔργοισι δαήμονα.

663. **ὄνομα.** Unless Monk's Ἀχιλεύς be accepted in l. 537, Iph. had not mentioned Achilles' *name*. But ὄνομα can, and here does, = title or style, i.e. παῖς Θέτιδος.

664. We can keep the MSS. ᾤκτιρεν with [ἂν] ἠρώτα τε (as Markland), but Heath's ᾤκτιρ' ἀνηρώτα τε which our text adopts is better. ἐρωτᾶν can be followed by a double acc., but it is generally in the sense of asking a person a question (e.g. Ar. *Nu.* 641 οὐ τοῦτ' ἐρωτῶ σε) rather than asking a person about a thing. This is rather ἀνερωτᾶν, cf. Ar. *Pl.* 499 and l. 661 above (the proximity of which has caused some, e.g. Weil, to prefer ἠρώτα).

666. With ordinary adjectives τις expresses a 'type'; e.g. E. *Hipp.* 424 θρασύσπλαγχνός τις = one of the bold-hearted type: with proper nouns it is either contemptuous (e.g. Θερσίτης τις, S. *Ph.* 442) or vague (e.g. A. *Ag.* 1233 Σκύλλαν τινά = Scylla or some one like her). With an adj. like Ἀργεῖος it is odd. Perhaps Nauck's Ἀργειῶτις should be adopted.

668. i.e. ὡς κοινῇ καλῶς πράσσουσα = as one who shares the good fortunes of Argos. MSS. πράσσει; Hermann proposed πράσσοι and most edd. have followed him. In primary sequence we should in fact expect ἐὰν πράσσῃ, but this use of the indic. in general conditions (= indefinites) is not uncommon, e.g. S. *Tr.* 943–5 ὥστ' εἴ τις δύο | ἢ κἄτι πλείους ἡμέρας λογίζεται, | μάταιός ἐστιν, and there is no reason why, in this case, the so-called 'vivid' primary should not stand; cf. Goodwin, *Moods and Tenses*, § 467.

669. Taking P's φράσας we might emend with Bergk ταὐτὰ δ' ἐκφράσας ἔχεις ('and you have expressed the same view'), but L's φθάσας is perhaps better.

670–1. Take ἕν as explained by τὰ γάρ τοι, κτλ. (Hermann's τοι for MSS. τῶν should be accepted). γάρ is the redundant γάρ common after phrases like τεκμήριον δέ.

ὧν may have for its antecedent either βασιλέων or πάντες: if β., then ἐπιστρ. = attention, regard, and the phrase means 'all know the fortunes of kings such as have won regard for themselves'—in this case Kirchhoff's ὧν ⟨τ'⟩ is attractive: 'of kings and of such as ...'; if π., then ἐπιστρ. = visitation⟨s⟩, and the sense is rather 'all who have given and received visitations know', etc.; i.e. all who have not lived out of the world. The latter is preferable; as parallels may be cited *Od.* I. 177 ἐπεὶ καὶ κεῖνος ἐπίστροφος ἦν ἀνθρώπων; E. *Hel.* 439, 40 κατθάνῃ | Ἕλλην πεφυκώς, οἷσιν οὐκ ἐπιστροφαί.

As the relative clause is indefinite we might have expected ᾖ, and Hartung's suggested correction may well be right. If we keep ἦν we must regard it as a perfect (= 'has ever been') and explain the indic. mood as we have that of πράσσει in l. 668.

672. **διῆλθον**, sc. mentally.

The sense of the four lines is: 'You have only just anticipated my appreciation of the priestess's words. I object only to your surprise at her questions about Agamemnon and the others. Any one is well enough informed to be able to ask intelligent questions about such as they. But (changing the subject completely) I have been considering another point.' The MSS. reading διῆλθε is impossible; for even if we could supply a subject (who must be Iph.) (1) Or.'s exhortation (l. 673) to 'publish' the λόγος would be meaningless; (2) Iph. would be made out as having said something (i.e. l. 674) which she never did say.

673. i.e. you will clarify your own ideas in communicating them. Edd. cite various passages from Plato where this not very striking thought is exemplified.

675. The MSS. τ' is impossible unless we suppose an aposiopesis at ἔπλευσα and a change of constr., as Prof. Murray does. Alternatively we might read καί με δεῖ κοινῇ θανεῖν. But both of them are rather unsatisfactory. Neither Elmsley's δ' (= 'no! I sailed ...') nor Reiske's γ' is much better. Departing a little further from the MSS. we might accept Elmsley's δὲ πλεύσας in spite of its bad grammar—cf. below, l. 947 and note, or, better, Weil's πέπλευκα (ΠΕΠΛΕΥΚΑ to ΤΕΠΛΕΥϹΑ). Badham's [τ'] ξέπλευσα is also palaeographically likely.

Wecklein's κοινῇ πλέοντα δεῖ gives good sense but is too far from the MSS.

676. i.e. δόξαν δειλίας καὶ κακῆς; cf. E. *Med.* 218 δύσκλειαν ἐκτήσαντο καὶ ῥᾳθυμίαν; S. *Ant.* 924 τὴν δυσσέβειαν εὐσεβοῦσ' ἐκτησάμην; E. *Hel.* 1097 κάλλος ἐκτήσω ('you got your reputation for beauty'—of Aphrodite). So, too, with φέρομαι; e.g. S. *El.* 968, 9 εὐσέβειαν ... οἴσῃ.

678. **πολλοὶ γὰρ κακοί**, i.e., 'I can say "to the majority" for the malicious-minded form the majority'. E. *IA.* 1357 supplies a good parallel: τὸ πολὺ γὰρ δεινὸν κακόν.

679. The MSS. προδούς σε σώζεσθ' will not do, for -αι cannot be elided in tragedy. (For βούλομ' in E. *IA.* 407 see Prof. Murray's note in the *app. crit.*) Erfurdt's σε σωθείς will not do either as we need a parallel infin., not a participle, to ῥάψαι of l. 681.

This we could get by accepting also Hartman's *μολεῖν* for *μόνος*. True, either a participle (e.g. *σωθείς*) or an infin. (e.g. *ῥάψαι*) is possible after *δόξω*, but *δόξω . . . σωθεὶς . . . ἢ . . . ῥάψαι* is impossible. Elmsley's other suggestion (see crit. note) *σε σωθείς τ'* might stand, for in this case we should have the one infin. (*ῥάψαι*) after *δόξω* attended by three participles *προδοὺς . . . σωθείς τ' . . . ἢ καὶ φονεύσας*. But these participles are not logically parallel, and grammatically *τε . . . ἢ καί* is clumsy. Elmsley's later suggestion *σεσῶσθαί σ'* is far better. Many parallels can be cited for the misplaced *σε*, e.g. E. *Ion* 293 *καὶ πῶς ξένος σ' ὢν ἔσχεν οὖσαν ἐγγενῆ*.

680. **ἐπί** = 'taking advantage of'. **νοσοῦσι**: because of the murder of Agamemnon and the madness of Orestes.

φονεύσας is odd in conjunction with **ῥάψαι μόρον**. We should probably adopt either Lobeck's *ἢ καφεδρεύσας* (ΚΑΦΕΔΡΕΥ to ΚΑΙΦΟΝΕΥ) or Bergk's *φονεῦσαί σ' . . . ῥάψας*.

682. **γαμεῖν** can mean 'be the husband of' (cf. l. 2 and E. *Tr.* 962) just as *τίκτειν* can mean 'be the father or mother of'. We know from ll. 696 and 915 that Pyl. is already husband of Electra. It is therefore little short of perverse to take *γαμῶν* here as a fut., though even Porson did so.

For **ἔγκληρον** cf. E. *Hipp.* 1011 *ἔγκληρον εὐνὴν προσλαβών*.

Flor. 1 (a copy of L) reads *ἄκληρον*, which Hermann oddly enough adopted. **ἔγκλ.**; i.e. *ἔγκλ. γενησομένην* after Or.'s death. Many edd. (e.g. Dindorf, Nauck, Bergk) reject the line. It is true that *ἐπίκληρος* is the correct technical term for one who is an heiress in default of male issue. But *ἐπίκληρος*, perhaps for metrical reasons, is not a tragic word, and *ἔγκληρος* may well have been used as a substitute.

685. Prof. Murray writes the MSS. *συσφαγῆναι* as two words because the *σύν* goes also with *πυρωθῆναι* = *συμπυρωθῆναι*. A similar line occurs at S. *Ant.* 537 *καὶ ξυμμετίσχω καὶ φέρω τῆς αἰτίας*, and cf. Ar. *Ra.* 687 *ξυμπαραινεῖν καὶ διδάσκειν*.

686. Wecklein needlessly suggests *πεφευγότα* for *φοβούμενος*. *φοβοῦμαι* of 683 is far enough away, and see note on l. 139.

687. Porson's *ἐμέ* for *κακά* (regarded as a gloss) should not be accepted (it is by Wecklein). The sense is not '*I* must bear my own troubles' but 'My *own* troubles I *must* bear': a thought continued in the next line 'I won't bear *yours*'.

690. With Dindorf's *ταὔτ'* and *ἔστιν* paroxytone we can only construe 'what you call . . ., that same exists for me'. The correction is scarcely necessary as *ταῦτ' ἐστιν* gives equally good (if not better) sense: 'what you call . . ., that (i.e. *τόδε* understood and explained by the *εἰ* clause which = *τὸ σὲ κτείνειν*) is these things (i.e. *λυπρὸν κἀπονείδιστον*) to me'.

691–2. The constr. is *τὸ εἰς ἐμέ*, adverbial, 'as far as I am concerned' with ⟨*τόδε*⟩ as subject of *ἔχει* and explained by ⟨*τὸ*⟩ . . . *λῦσαι βίον*.

Schenkl's *λῦσαι* (see crit. note) is as good an emendation as any for the impossible futures of the MSS. which can scarcely be defended on the analogy of e.g. S. *Ph.* 596, 7 οὗτος γὰρ πλέον | τὸ θάρσος εἶχε θατέρου δράσειν τάδε (Hermann), where the fut. infin. is justified by θάρσος = confidence of success.

695–6. As our text (= MSS.) stands there are two slight difficulties: (1) the asyndeton participles σωθείς and κτησάμενος; (2) the 'nominativus pendens' (σωθεὶς . . . κτησάμενος . . . ὄνομα γένοιτ' ἄν.). But (1) is not unusual; cf. l. 824, 5 πάλλων . . κτανών and E. *Ph.* 77 ὁ δ' Ἄργος ἐλθών, κῆδος Ἀδράστου λαβών. Moreover, here σωθείς is really subordinated to κτησάμενος. (2) is too common to need exemplification. Logically he would have continued ὄνομά τ' ἐμοῦ διασώσεις . . . There is no need, therefore, to accept either Markland's παῖδάς ⟨τ'⟩ or Wecklein's κτήσαι' ἄν. Ellis's γένοι' ἄν is scarcely possible. If it could mean anything it would mean either (1) your son will take my name—which would not be the case (see following note); or (2) you would become me—which is more or less nonsense; and ὄνομα . . . ἐμοῦ = ἐγώ can scarcely be paralleled, even though at E.*Ph.* 1702 ὄνομα Πολυνείκους (if that is the right reading) *may* = Πολυνείκης.

697. ὄνομα. Pyl. would not call his son Orestes, but would, by having married the ἔγκληρος Electra, continue the family of the Atridae, not that of Strophius. The importance to a Greek of having his family continue is a matter of religion; for naturally where there are no descendants there can be no ancestor-worship.

For the rare τε . . . οὐδέ (= καὶ οὐ) see Denniston, p. 192. Lenting's γ' . . . οὐδέ is unnecessary, and his τ' . . . οὔτε next door to impossible (see Denniston, p. 509).

γένοιτ' ἄν is strange. We should expect rather a word = survive, continue; Herwerden's διαγένοιτ' would do, though it is not a tragic word; better Markland's μένοι γ' ἄν (F. W. Schmidt suggested ὄνομα γένους μένοι τ' ἄν, which is attractive). Tournier's σέβοιτ' ἄν is also possible.

699. πατρός = of ⟨my⟩ father.

701. ἐπισκήπτειν in the sense of 'enjoin' is usually followed by the dat. of the person. But the acc. is sometimes used on the analogy of the acc. after κελεύειν; e.g. S. *Tr.* 1221 τοσοῦτον δή σ' ἐπισκήπτω, τέκνον.

702. τύμβον, sc. a cenotaph; cf. *Od.* 4. 584 where Menelaus says that in Egypt χεῦ' Ἀγαμέμνονι τύμβον, 'I heaped up a mound for A.'

705. 'Having been purified ⟨by her⟩ at the altar ⟨with lustral water⟩ for the sacrifice'. This is better than 'purified with ⟨lustral water which typifies⟩ sacrifice' (cf. δρόσον αἱματηράν of l. 443).

Monk needlessly read φόνου; i.e. cleansed of the murder (of Clytemnestra).

707. κήδη καὶ δόμους is a hendiadys. 'The family into which you have entered by marriage.' ἔρημα is predicative.

712. τέχνην . . . θέμενος = τεχνησάμενος, δόλῳ χρησάμενος: 'setting his cunning to work'.

Notice the ionic form *προσώτατα* for attic *-άτω*; cf. S. *El.* 391 ὅπως ἀφ' ἡμῶν ὡς προσώτατ' ἐκφύγω. Nauck's [ὡς] Ἑλλάδος προσωτάτω is unnecessary. Thucydides (if we may trust the MSS.) uses both ἐγγύτατα (e.g. 1. 13. 2) and ἐγγυτάτω (e.g. 3. 38. 1).

714. Sc. καὶ ⟨οὔ⟩ πεισθεὶς λόγοις. Wilamowitz (*Anal. Eur.*, p. 245) thinks this line and the next spurious, and certainly Or.'s admission of matricide before the ἀναγνώρισις is odd (see Page, *Actors' Interpolations*, p. 78).

717–8. Several attempts have been made to ruin these beautiful lines: Weil (though he later repented) ἐπεὶ οὔ σ' ἐγὼ | βλέποντα μᾶλλον ἢ θανόνθ'; Vitelli βλέπονθ' ὁμοίως καὶ θανόνθ'.

Wecklein's ἄξω = 'value' is possible (cf. S. *Ant.* 34, 5 τὸ πρᾶγμ' ἄγειν | οὐχ ὡς παρ' οὐδέν).

719. The old edd. which kept L and P's με, supposed Pyl. to refer to his impending parting from Or. Nauck's σ' οὐ . . . γε is preferable to the Paris apograph, the stress being rather on διέφθορεν than on τοῦ θεοῦ.

If we follow Herwerden in rejecting 720, L and P's με would give tolerable sense; but in and by itself there is no need to suspect 720, except on the ground that μάντευμα may have been a gloss on τὸ τοῦ θεοῦ, introduced into the text and expanded into a line.

720. Following Porson's dictum that γε could not immediately follow καίτοι, Elmsley proposed καίπερ . . . ἑστῶτος. If σε were the reading cf l. 719 an ignorant scribe might well have 'corrected' the idiomatic σε . . . ἑστῶτός (σου). Erfurdt suggested καίτοι κἀγγύς. But καίτοι γ', though rare, is all right (see Denniston, p. 564).

721–2. λίαν is generally used with *verbal* substantives, cf. A. *Pr.* 123 τὴν λίαν φιλότητα = τὸ λίαν φιλεῖν. So this = τὸ λίαν δυσπραγεῖν. ἔστι . . . διδοῦσα = δίδωσι; sometimes called the σχῆμα Χαλκιδικόν.

ὅταν τύχῃ = when things so fall out. A common expression; cf. e.g. E. *El.* 1169 νέμει τοι δίκαν θεός, ὅταν τύχῃ.

Objections have needlessly been raised against the effective repetition of λίαν, and such alterations as δεινάς, τάχ' αὖ, and πάλιν suggested.

723. If δ' is here right and we should not rather read γ', then it must be δέ = γάρ; see Denniston, p. 169.

Phoebus' μάντευμα which bade Or. kill his mother implied that if Or. obeyed all would be well with him. On seeing the priestess return Or. thinks that all *cannot* now be well with him, that there is going to be no μεταβολή, that Phoebus has definitely betrayed him. The sense is 'speak no more; Phoebus' commands have undone me' (οὐδὲν ὠφελεῖ is a meiosis).

F. W. Schmidt's μ' ἔτι . . . ἤδη (for ἥδε) is plausible.

725. Iph., or rather Euripides, gets rid of the guards on the same pretext as at 470. Dramatically they must not be present during the recognition scene.

727. Luckily Aristotle in the *Rhetoric* (see crit. note) quotes this line with the correct reading **πολύθυροι**. The MSS. πολύθρηνοι is unmetrical.

πολύθυροι = πολύπτυχοι = of many folds. Pollux (4. 18 and 10. 57) remarks Ἡρόδοτος μὲν λέγει δελτίον δίπτυχον, οἱ δὲ Ἀττικοὶ γραμματεῖον δίθυρον, καὶ θύρας τὰς πτύχας ἄχρι δύο.

730. **πίπτειν** is not necessarily used of falling into a *worse* state (cf. E. *Or.* 1141 ἐπὶ τὸ βέλτιον πεσῇ). Wecklein's proposed προβῇ is unnecessary.

731. **ἀπονοστεῖν** more unusually + acc. of the place reached than + gen. of the place left. But see E. *Hel.* 474 Λακεδαίμονος γῆς δεῦρο νοστήσασ' ἄπο.

There is no need to read Kirchhoff's χθόνα, i.e. Argos (χθών in Iph.'s mouth *must* mean Tauris), or Köchly's δόμον; still less Semitelos's ἔξω δὲ ταρβῶ μὴ πόδα στήσας χθονός.

736. Badham rejected this line as spoiling the stichomythia. It has also been remarked that without it we get two sets of nine lines each (734–43 and 744–52), the first a colloquy of Iph. and Or., the second one between Iph. and Pyl. (At 753 the subject changes.) It would, moreover, be quite in Eur.'s manner to make 735 an aposiopesis, if indeed we require an acc. of the end to which. But cf. 812 (below), *El.* 651, *ib.* 966, *Hel.* 1198, *Ba.* 1270, &c.

737. **τοὺς αὐτοὺς λόγους**, i.e. the same sworn assurance. Nauck conjectured τῶνδε (sc. λόγων) for **τῷδε**, governed by the ἀντί of ἀντιδώσεις.

738 = E. *Med.* 748. Here put in for the sake of the stichomythia.

739. **μή** should logically be οὐ for it qualifies only θανόντα, but the force of the understood verb of swearing has affected it.

740. **δίκαιον εἶπας** = 'I can't object to that' (England). But δίκαιον is not the word one would expect, and Wecklein's ἀχρεῖον or μάταιον, or Madvig's εἰκαῖον (= 'useless') may be right. Still better is a suggestion of Prof. Housman (*Camb. Phil. Soc. Proceedings*, 1890) ἀρχαῖον = silly; cf. E. *fr.* 1038 ἀρχαῖον εἴρηκας, where Suidas, who cites the fragment, glosses ἀντὶ τοῦ εὔηθες. Cf. also E. *Hel.* 1056 παλαιότης γὰρ τῷ λόγῳ γ' ἔνεστί τις.

πῶς γὰρ ⟨ἄλλως⟩ ἀγγ.

741. **τύραννος ταῦτα συγχωρήσεται;** = 'will the king concede this?' There is no need to suspect the reading, though the *active* voice is used elsewhere with this meaning. Kirchhoff's τυράννοις (dat. of agent) with συγχ. middle for passive is certainly no improvement.

742. The extra-metrical **ναί** (cf. S. *Tr.* 425) shows a hesitation on the part of Iph. Thoas, she feels, might well object.

εἰσβήσω ⟨αὐτόν, i.e. Pyl.⟩ **σκάφος**. For εἰσβαίνειν (trans.) with no object expressed and a plain acc. of that into which, cf. E. *Alc.* 1055 θάλαμον ἐσβήσας (sc. αὐτήν). Markland (unnecessarily) **καὐτόν**. From E. *Cyc.* 467 νεὼς μελαίνης κοῖλον ἐμβήσας σκάφος Wecklein conjectures ἐμβήσω. P's εἰσθήσω or εἰσφρήσω is not impossible.

743. ὄμνυ addressed to Pyl.; σὺ δ', κτλ., to Iph. For ἔξαρχε cf. E. *Med.* 745 ἐξηγοῦ θεούς.

744. The MSS. δώσω . . . τοῖς ἐμοῖς is clearly impossible. We must alter either to τοῖσι σοῖς (Bothe) keeping δώσω, or to δώσεις (Lindau) keeping τοῖς ἐμοῖς. δώσειν is a possibility (with τοῖς ἐμοῖς), though it seems better to regard λέγειν χρή as parenthetic.

747. ἐπόμνυμι takes an acc. of the witness and a dat. of the thing witnessed.

748. τιμὰς ἔχω: not 'am held in honour', but 'hold holy office', as at l. 776; cf. τιμῶσ(α) l. 54 above, E. *HF.* 845, and *Hel.* 15.

749. The γε signifies, as Wecklein says, that Pyl. will be contented with no one less than Ζεὺς ὅρκιος. Nauck's ἀνάκτορ' οὐρανοῦ is needless—or worse.

754. Our text keeps the MSS. reading except for the change of αὖτις (an epic form which often finds its way into the MSS. of tragedy) to αὖθις. Grégoire, who reads the same, translates: 's'il le faut, nous pouvons changer cette formule'. But this gives little sense and is (perhaps necessarily) a paraphrase rather than a translation. In his first edition Prof. Murray accepted Kirchhoff's κακῶς for MSS. καλῶς. This is certainly better; but λόγον in l. 753 means 'consideration', 'subject', whereas λόγος in this line (where it is understood with καινός) and with this reading must mean 'conversation'; and the sense of the line must be: 'we will certainly renew the conversation, if what we have said so far is not satisfactory'. (Kirchhoff's ὅ τι π. λόγου in l. 573 would preserve the sense of 'conversation' in both lines.) This meaning is not easy to extract and not particularly good when extracted. Prinz and Wecklein mention eighteen proposed emendations, only one of which has won general acceptance, viz. Bothe's ἀλλ' οὔτις ἔστ' ἄκαιρος, i.e. 'why, no suggestion is ἄκαιρος (here = too late) if it is a good one'.

756. Needless exception has been taken to χρημάτων which here, as at A. *Ag.* 1007 = 'things or chattels on board'. Most of the suggested emendations are bathetic, e.g. σελμάτων (Köchly), γραμμάτων (Markland). F. W. Schmidt's κυμάτων ἄγρα gives excellent sense but it is too far from the MSS.

758. ἔμπεδον = binding, cf. l. 790 ἐμπεδώσομεν. Prof. Housman's suggestion (*AJP.* ix, p. 325) ἐμποδών = obstructive, is attractive but perhaps unnecessary.

759. For the constr. οἶσθ' ὃ δράσω cf. E. *Hec.* 998 οἶσθ' οὖν ἃ λέξαι . . . θέλω. (This construction is usually followed by the *imperative*, but the indicative is well attested (cf. K-G. II. i, p. 239), and why the great Scaliger proposed δρᾶσον—in which he was followed by several edd.—passes comprehension.)

Beware of translating 'Do you know what I shall do?' It is 'I will do you-know-what'; οἶσθ' ὅ, like ἔστιν ὅς, etc., forms a substantive. Cf. the English 'what's-his-name' which is not the same as 'what is his name?' Strictly speaking this phrase should be printed without a mark of interrogation.

πολλὰ γάρ; clearly a proverbial saying='many precautions ensure much success'. In English 'it pays to have more than one string to your bow'. German 'Viel hilft viel'.

On the analogy of ἄλλα δ' ἐξ ἄλλων κυρεῖ (l. 865) Markland proposed πολλὰ δ' (or γ') ἐκ.

Any such 'emendations' as Musgrave's πλοίῳ, Hermann's πολλοῖς, or Herwerden's πόντῳ (in all of which κυρεῖ = 'happen') are to be eschewed.

760. Wecklein's κἀντεταλμέν' = enjoined, commanded, is a needless alteration of the MSS. κἀγγεγραμμέν'. The recurrence of the word in 763 is quite in Eur's. manner; cf. note on 139.

761. The constr. is ⟨ὥστε σ' (understood from σοι)⟩ ἀναγγεῖλαι ⟨δυνήσεσθαι⟩. ἀναγγ. = to carry back a message, cf. A. *Pr.* 661; it is exactly the right word—yet Elmsley would read ἀπαγγεῖλαι.

762. i.e. ⟨οὕτω⟩ γὰρ ⟨ἔσται⟩ ἐν ἀσφαλεῖ ⟨τὰ ἐμοὶ ἐπεσταλμένα⟩.

763. Some edd. keep the MSS. αὕτη which gives quite good sense; cf. E. *Med.* 1225–7 . . . ἂν εἴποιμι τοὺς σοφοὺς βροτῶν | δοκοῦντας εἶναι . . . | τούτους μεγίστην ζημίαν ὀφλισκάνειν, and l. 556 above.

Monk proposed τἀπεσταλμένα (i.e. what it is commanded to tell) on the ground of the proximity of γραφή. The Greeks did not feel such repetitions as tautological; cf. note on 760 above.

765. England suggests that Eur. wrote ἐμοί as being unwilling to add to the sibilants by writing ἐμούς. I do not think that Eur. would have hesitated to end this line with τοὺς ἐμοὺς σώσεις λόγους, for he seems to have cared no more about sibilants than did Aeschylus when he wrote ὁ πρῶτος νύχιος ἄγγελος πυρός (*Ag.* 588). That others were more sensitive is clear from Plato Comicus' well-known parody (*fr.* 30 ἔσωσας ἐκ τῶν σῖγμα τῶν Εὐριπίδου) of E. *Med.* 476 ἔσωσά σ', ὡς ἴσασιν Ἑλλήνων ὅσοι. But ἐμοί is weak, and we might well adopt Badham's ὁμοῦ or Heimsöth's ἅμα.

766. It is hard to extract any real sense out of τῶν θεῶν; we should emend. Bothe's τῶν θ' ἑῶν, which looks ingenious, is simply impossible. ἑός is not used in tragic iambics, and the reference in the *app. crit.* to E. *El.* 1206 is to a line of lyric in which the MSS. ἑῶν πέπλων has been corrected by Seidler into ἔξω πέπλων, which correction has been adopted in the O.C.T.

On the other hand, Haupt's τῶν τε σῶν is almost palmary (τῶν σῶν = σοῦ, as τὰ σά = σύ). The meaning is: 'Your suggestion benefits us both'.

767. Neither the relatival constr. (indica eum cui debeo . . .) followed by the indirect question (indica quae debeam . . .), nor the repetition of χρή should offend, though many efforts have been made to 'emend' one or both; e.g. Badham's σήμαιν' ὅτῳ δή, Elmsley's σήμαινε τῷ (= τίνι) χρή, and Monk's σήμαινε δ' ᾧ με.

771. **τοῖς ἐκεῖ = τοῖς ἐν Ἄργει.** For this dat. cf. S. *Ph.* 1030 οὐδέν εἰμι καὶ τέθνηχ' ὑμῖν πάλαι, and l. 575 above (note).

772. **ἥκει πάλιν.** England compares the French *revenir* and *un revenant*, a ghost.

773. **λόγοις ἔκπλησσέ με.** = 'interrupt me with ⟨your⟩ words'. But Seidler's λόγων = 'interrupt (lit. drive me out of) ⟨my⟩ words' is very likely right. Cf. l. 240 above.

775. Toup's θέας is ingenious; 'move ⟨me⟩ from the sight of the sacrifices', but the text should not be altered.

776. P's unmetrical ξενοκτόνους may derive from l. 53 **τέχνην . . . ξενοκτόνον. τιμάς** = holy office (cf. l. 748).

777. **ποῦ** = 'in what situation'. **ὄντ⟨ε⟩.** The mixture of dual and plural is too common to need comment.

778. Iph. continues the recitation of her letter. Line 777 is an aside and ἔχω (776) should be followed by a comma. For **ἀραία δώμασιν** cf. E. *Med.* 608 ἀραία . . . δόμοις and S. *OT.* 1291 δόμοις ἀραῖος.

779. The words of the MSS. are clear and undisputed. Only the attribution of them is confused. L gives 778 to Iph., 779, 80 (to ὦ θεοί) to Pyl., and the rest of the line to Iph., and 781, 2 to Pyl. A corrector of L, *l*, erased ΠΥΛ before 779 and wrote it in in front of 780.

It is clear that **ἵν' . . . μάθῃς** cannot be spoken by Pyl. and must belong to Iph.

It seems to me that we must take the whole of 779 as being Iph's., putting a comma at γενήσομαι. Iph. must say Ὀρέστα, otherwise what is Pyl. hearing twice? Taking it in this way "ἢ σοῖς . . ., Ὀρέστα" is Iph's recitation of the letter; ἵν' . . . μάθῃς is a remark made to Pyl. to explain why, having said Ὀρέστῃ in 769, she says Ὀρέστα here. It is to impress the name on Pyl.'s memory.

The further (and less important) question, the attribution of **ὦ θεοί** and lines 781, 2, is less easy to settle. Either Pyl. or Or. might utter the exclamation, but it seems more natural for Pyl. to apologize and bid Iph. continue, as it is with him that she is speaking. At the same time it was Or. who interrupted at l. 777 and there is something to be said for keeping Pyl. silent until l. 788. This was the view of Hermann, who gave also ll. 781, 2 to Or. Grégoire follows him.

780. **ἐν τοῖς ἐμοῖς**: 'in matters which concern *me*'.

781. **οὐδέν**: 'for no reason' just as τί = 'for what reason?' Cf. E. *Med.* 922–5 Ια. τί χλωροῖς δακρύοις τέγγεις κόρας; . . . Μη. οὐδέν: *Ion* 255, 6 Ιω. τί χρῆμ' . . . δυσθυμῇ, γύναι; | Κρ. οὐδέν. So, too, after ποῖ (= 'to what end . . . ?'), e.g. A. *Ag.* 1138, 9 ποῖ . . . με δεῦρο . . . ἤγαγες; οὐδέν ποτ' εἰ μὴ . . .

ἐξέβην . . . = 'my thoughts had strayed . . .'

782. We can do one of three things with this puzzling line: (1) keep it where it is (with emendation); (2) transpose it; (3) excise it.

(1) Prinz and Wecklein mention some twenty proposed emendations, most of which are re-writings of the line. Two may be considered: (a) Prof. Murray's οὐκ for MSS. οὖν. In this case the line is an aside by Pyl. intended to justify his interruption of Iph. But Pyl. cannot be said to have asked any question, so it is doubtful to what ἐρωτῶν refers, unless it be to the question which, taking the O.C.T. reading, he was about to ask in l. 780. (b) Weil's τάχ' οὖν ἐρωτῶν σ' . . . ἀφίξεται, giving the line to Iph. = 'perhaps in interrogating you he, Or., will come to a point at which he won't believe you. ⟨In that case⟩ tell him that, etc.', continuing the letter.

This is possible but for the rather violent change of ἀφίξομαι to ἀφίξεται. This change, however, will seem less violent when we remember that, once the attribution goes wrong, the change of person is almost bound to follow.

(2) Hartung suggested Iφ. τάχ' οὐκ ἐρωτῶσ' εἰς τὰ πίστ' ἀφίξομαι (ἐρωτῶσ' being the uncorrected reading of P) to come after l. 809; Hermann Iφ. τάχ' οὐκ ἐρωτῶσ' εἰς ἄπιστ' ἀφίξομαι to come after l. 811. Neither of these can be said definitely to spoil the sense of the passages into which they are respectively intercalated, but certainly neither *improves* the sense. Of the two Hartung's suggestion is preferable, though Hermann's would 'restore' the strict stichomythia of 805–22.

(3) Dindorf, Monk, and Nauck all rejected the line, and this is probably the wisest course.

784–5. The antecedent of ἥν is ἔλαφον, not με. Not seeing this caused Paley to alter ἔθυσ' to ἔθυ' (conative imperfect); ἔθυσ' = ἀντέθυσ'. **δοκῶν,** κτλ., 'thinking that it was into *me* he had . . .'

789. κάλλιστα δ' ⟨ἡμῖν⟩ ὀμόσασα, viz. to send me home. We do not, however, want any reference to *Iph.*'s oath. There is a v. l. in L, ὀμόσας, which Markland adopts, putting a colon at the end of 788. κάλλιστα will have a meaning very like that of ῥᾳδίοις = easy to fulfil. Hermann objected to the δ' after κάλλιστα in this case, but it is difficult to see what other particle Eur. could have used. δ' = 'and indeed'.

790. Instead of **δ'** we might have expected after **σχήσω** (= refrain, check myself) either a τὸ μὴ οὐ or a πρίν construction; but the parataxis is not unnatural; cf. S. *OT.* 717–9 οὐ διέσχον ἡμέραι | τρεῖς, καί νιν . . . ἔρριψεν, and A. *Supp.* 368, 9 ἐγὼ δ' ἂν οὐ κραίνοιμ' ὑπόσχεσιν πάρος, | ἀστοῖς δὲ πᾶσι . . . κοινώσας = 'I pledge no promise before I have communicated' (if indeed, this, the reading of the O.C.T., be correct).

791. ἀποδιδόναι = to give what is due, as ἀπαιτεῖν = to ask for one's property back (cf. S. *Ph.* 362 τά θ' ὅπλ' ἀπῄτουν (of Neoptolemus) and E. *Ph.* 80 πατρῷ' ἀπαιτεῖν σκῆπτρα), and ἀπολαμβάνειν = to get one's due.

793. γραμμάτων διαπτυχάς is merely a synonym for δέλτον. If we accept Badham's attractive ἀναπτυχάς it would mean 'the opening of the letter'.

794. **οὐ λόγοις** ⟨ἀλλ' ἔργῳ⟩; the common Greek antithesis. Or. means he will not waste time reading the letter (λόγοις) but will embrace his sister (ἔργῳ).

796. **ὅμως** in this common use, where it strengthens a participle whose sense is sharply opposed to that of the verb, originally (logically speaking) belonged to the verb and not the participle; i.e. here ⟨καίπερ⟩ ἐκπεπληγμένος, ὅμως εἶμι. Later it attached itself to the participle as though it equalled καίπερ.

From the MSS. ἀπιστῶ we can either take Markland's σ' ἀπίστῳ ('clasping you in incredulous arms', an easy transference of epithet) or Döderlein's ἀπίστω π. βραχίονέ ⟨σοι⟩. Powell's (*CR.* 1903, p. 266) [σ'] ἀπιστῶν . . . βραχίονε is possible, though the string of participles is ugly. Madvig's σε πιστῷ, which Wecklein adopts, is a very inferior emendation, whether we take πιστῷ as = 'loyal', or as = 'secure', 'definite', 'undoubted')(θαυμαστά.

[**ἀπιστῷ** in our text is a misprint for ἀπίστῳ.]

802. **δοκοῦσ'** is, as England points out, an historic present. **ποτε** goes half with **δοκοῦσ'** and half with **ἕξειν**: 'though you never thought you would ever have him ⟨again⟩'.

804. To say that Argos and Nauplia are 'full of' Or. must mean either (1) that he is 'at large' there, which is in this context pointless, though E. *Ion* 1107, 8 (πανταχῇ . . . ἄστεως | ζητῶν νιν ἐξέπλησα) offers a vague parallel; or (2) that he is 'the big man' there (so England; but it is hard to get it out of the Greek); or (3) that these places are full of his fame—perhaps the best explanation, though even this does not seem very pertinent in the context. So, e.g., Grégoire: 'c'est A. et N. que remplit sa grandeur'.

Emendations (of which many have been suggested) are not happy. The best are Bergk's αὐτὸν ἴστον, 'know him', i.e. he is a well-known figure there; Heimsöth's αὐτοῦ μέτοχον (sc. ἐστί), 'is a sharer in him'; and Weil's μέλετον, 'have a care for him'.

The first and third of these involve a σχῆμα 'Αλκμανικόν, i.e. a dual or plur. verb with a singular subject (τὸ δ' A. ἥ τε N. μέλετον would be regular); cf. *Od.* 10. 513, 4 ἔνθα μὲν εἰς 'Αχέροντα Πυριφλεγέθων τε ῥέουσιν | Κωκυτός τε. (K-G. II. i. p. 80.)

Another line of emendation is to take αὐτοῦ = here, and read something like Kvičala's τὸ δ' (? better τόδ') Ἄργος αὐτοῦ μοι (ethic dat.) 'στὸν ἥ τε Ναυπλία;—i.e. 'are A. and N. *here*, then? For that is where Or. is': or, putting it as a loose syllogism, 'You say Or. is here: I know he is in A.: therefore A. is here'. A rough parallel may be found in E. *Heracl.* 193–6 οὐ γάρ τι Τραχίς ἐστιν οὐδ' 'Αχαιικὸν | πόλισμ', ὅθεν σὺ τούσδε . . . ἤλαυνες. As an alternative to μοι Herwerden suggested μή = 'surely . . .

not . . . ?' We might, perhaps, take the μή as one of cautious assertion, and, reading τόδ', translate 'perhaps this here is Argos . . .' ; the words would be spoken ironically.

It must be admitted, however, that wlth αὐτοῦ = 'of him' l. 805 fits better.

806. ἀλλ' ἦ : Monk read ἦ for MSS. ἡ = 'do you mean to say . . . ?' ἀλλ' ἦ introduces an incredulous question ; cf. S. *El.* 879 ἀλλ' ἦ μέμηνας ; and E. *Heracl.* 425, 6 ἀλλ' ἦ πρόθυμον οὖσαν οὐκ ἐᾷ θεὸς | ξένοις ἀρήγειν τήνδε χρήζουσιν πόλιν ;

809. It is better to take τι as cognate acc. ('ask some question') rather than acc. of the direct object ('ask about something') ; cf. note on l. 664 above.

See note on l. 782 for its possible insertion here.

810. This seems to mean 'it is your business to make statements, ⟨not to answer questions⟩, mine to gather information from you ⟨not to interrogate you⟩'.

But οὐκοῦν is strange. Possibly οὔκουν . . . ἐμέ ; would be better, or even, supposing a confusion of syllables, λέγειν μὲν οὖν οὐ χρὴ σέ . . . ;

811. The line runs better with no comma at ἄν. Or. will first tell what he knows from Electra, then ἃ εἶδεν αὐτός (l. 822).

Just as one would say in Greek ἀκούω 'Ηλέκτρας = 'I hear from E.', so one can say ἀκοῇ 'H. = 'by hearing from E.', i.e. 'from E.'s report'.

813. Our text adopts Mekler's ἦν νείκη for MSS. ἡνίκ' ἦν. It might well have gone a step further and read his ἤκουσ' ἃ χρυσῆς . . . νείκη . . .

Many other emendations have been proposed, the most generally accepted of which is Barnes' οὕνεκ' ἦν πέρι, sc. ἔρις ; (οὕνεκα = that). Porson's ἥτις ἦν and Markland's ἣν εἶχον are both quite possible. All these involve the removal of the colon at ἤκουσα. But when all is said and done there is no need to alter the MSS. at all. The translation is '⟨it was⟩ when there was ⟨an ἔρις⟩ about the golden lamb'. An almost exact parallel occurs at E. *Tr.* 69, 70 Aθ. οὐκ οἶσθ' ὑβρισθεῖσάν με καὶ ναοὺς ἐμούς ; Πο. οἶδ', ἡνίκ' Αἴας εἷλκε Κασάνδραν βίᾳ.

815. If κάμπτεις (Blomfield, for MSS. κάμπτῃ) be what Eur. wrote we must take it as a metaphor from racing : 'you turn close round the turning-post of my memory'. But there seems to be no exact parallel to this use. Wecklein's χρίμπτῃ is better. In English we should say 'you touch a chord in my memory'.

816. Both εἰκώ and μετάστασιν are governed by ⟨οἶσθ' ὑφήνασα⟩, μετ. being in apposition to εἰκώ. We should rather say 'a picture *of*'. Cf. E. *Ph.* 1135 ἑκατὸν ἐχίδναις . . . γραφῇ.

818. In Greece both bride and bridegroom bathed themselves ceremonially on the morning of their marriage. The water used for this purpose came, where possible, from some sacred spring or river : e.g. at Athens from Callirrhoe (cf. Thuc. 2. 15. 5), at Thebes from Ismenus (cf. E. *Ph.* 347, 8 ἀνυμέναια . . . 'Ισμηνὸς ἐκηδεύθη λουτροφόρου χλιδᾶς; i.e. Ismenus had no part in supplying the bath for your marriage. So, too, in E. *HF.* (480–2) Megara says of her sons' prospective marriage μεταβαλοῦσα δ' ἡ τύχη | νύμφας μὲν ὑμῖν Κῆρας ἀντέδωκ' ἔχειν | ἐμοὶ δὲ δάκρυα λουτρά.) Iph's. marriage was to take place at Aulis, but her mother sent her holy water from a spring in Argos for the ceremony.

οἶδ' (l. 819) is no answer to 'did you receive . . . ?', and all Or.'s questions concern not fact but Iph.'s *memory* of fact. Read therefore Kirchhoff's suggestion ἁδέξω (= ἃ ἐδέξω), or ὅτ' ἐδέξω (Wecklein), which would give a good parallel to ἡνίκα in l. 813.

819. The object of ἀφείλετο has been taken to be λουτρά, and the line explained: 'the marriage was too good a one to deprive me of that'. But (1) the order of words is against this, and (2) it is a question not of Iph.'s having *received* λουτρά but of her *remembering* the fact. A note in L gives the right explanation: τοῦτο, τὸ μὴ εἰδέναι, the construction being in full οὐκ ἀφείλετο τοῦτο, τὸ [μὴ] εἰδέναι ἃ ἐδεξάμην; and the meaning is 'I remember it; for my marriage, not being a happy one, has not robbed me of the recollection'. i.e. 'had I had a happy marriage I should have forgotten all the preliminaries; as it is, all are stamped on my memory'. οὐ goes both with ἐσθλὸς ὢν and ἀφείλετο; cf. E. *Alc.* 296 οὐκ ἂν μονωθεὶς σῆς δάμαρτος ἔστενες, *Ion.* 579, 80 οὐδὲ θάτερον νοσῶν | . . . κεκλήσῃ. Bruhn's εἰ γάρ = 'would that . . .' gives the same sense and avoids the awkward double negative. It may well be right.

ἐσθλός is certainly odd, and we might accept Wecklein's ὀρθός or Heimsöth's τέλεος.

820. τί γάρ; proceeding to a new point (cf. Denniston, p. 83). **κόμας,** κτλ. = ⟨οἶσθα⟩ δοῦσά ⟨τινι⟩ κόμας σὰς ⟨ὥστε⟩ τῇ μητρὶ φέρειν ⟨αὐτάς⟩;

821. τάφῳ = for my cenotaph. Iph., about to be burned in sacrifice at Aulis, knowing that she could not be buried in Argos, sent to her mother a lock of her hair ἀντὶ σώματος. Edd. compare the passage in Stat. *Theb.* 9. 900–3, where Parthenopaeus, mortally wounded, sends to his mother, Atalanta, a lock of his hair: 'Hunc tamen, orba parens, crinem' (dextraque secandum | Praebuit), 'hunc toto capies pro corpore crinem. | . . . Huic dabis exsequias'. Cf. also A. *Th.* 49, 50 μνημεῖά θ' αὑτῶν τοῖς τεκοῦσιν ἐς δόμους | πρὸς ἅρμ' Ἀδράστου χερσὶν ἔστεφον.

825. According to the usual story Oenomaus was killed by a fall from his chariot in the race in which Pelops strove for the hand of O.'s daughter Hippodameia, the accident being caused through the removal by O.'s charioteer Myrtilus (at Pelops' instigation) of the lynch-pins of the chariot. This passage suggests another version in which P. kills O. with his spear.

Nauck's Οἰνομάου κόρην does not avoid the difficulty, for no one brandishes a spear *in order to* drive a chariot (indeed the race is not here mentioned), and 'the spear brandishing which he gained H.' can only mean 'the spear, killing some one with which, he ...' So that even on this showing Οἰνόμαον κτανών is implied.

With a proper noun the anapaest in the fifth foot is all right; cf. Descroix, *Trim. iamb.*, p. 194 sqq. We need not accept Elmsley's ἑλών for κτανών; though these two verbs seem sometimes to be confused in MSS., as at E. *Med.* 385 where one 'family' reads ἑλεῖν and the other κτανεῖν. Cf. below l. 1457.

827. For οὐδὲν ἄλλο (which is better than Markland's ἄλλ', ὁ φ.) cf. E. *Med.* 465 ὦ παγκάκιστε, τοῦτο γάρ σ' εἰπεῖν ἔχω.

828. The sense and derivation of the Homeric word τηλύγετος are both uncertain; but the word does *not* in Homer mean 'distant', and it is very unlikely that Eur., if he wished to use it for the one and only time in tragedy, would so use it. Wecklein transposes it so as to precede βρέφος in l. 834, where at least it has its customary meaning of 'only son'—it is certainly awkward with that meaning in its present position; others emend: e.g. Elmsley τηλόθεν, Rauchenstein τηλέπορον (the latter preferable if we remove χθονός and regard the line as a senarian). Köchly wished to remove τηλ. and insert some such participle as φανέντα or μολόντα, a suggestion adopted and perhaps improved upon by England who proposes τηλικόνδ' (= now grown so big), ἀπὸ χθονὸς | πατρίδος, Ἀργόθεν | πλανῶντ', ὦ φίλος.

831. δοξάζεται, historic present = 'as was supposed'; cf. δοκῶν (l. 785).

832. The MSS. reading adopted in our text may be right, κατά going with νοτίζει by tmesis. But the Aldine ed. reads δάκρυα δάκρυα which Musgrave altered to δάκρυ' ἀδάκρυα, tears which are no tears, tears of joy. Further, though anaphora with μέν ... δέ is possible (cf. *Il.* 23. 798, 9 κατὰ μὲν δολιχόσκιον ἔγχος | θῆκ' ... κατὰ δ' ἀσπίδα and Ar. *Lys.* 262, 3) it is rare with δέ ... δέ. (But see Denniston, p. 163.) Seidler, therefore, removed the second δέ. A combination of these two emendations (adopted both by Weil and Wecklein) gives us, for what it is worth, a senarian of which all the feet but the last are resolved into tribrachs; and it is noticeable that Or., unlike his more excitable and excited sister, speaks throughout in iambics. So, too, Helen and Menelaus use respectively dochmiacs and iambics at E. *Hel.* 663 sqq., Antigone and the paedagogus at E. *Ph.* 103 sqq., and the (female) chorus and Danaus at A. *Supp.* 736 sqq. The line can of course be made into a senarian without these emendations; e.g. Dindorf's κατὰ δὲ δάκρυ⟨α⟩, κατὰ δὲ γόος χαρά θ' ἅμα, or Badham's ... δάκρυ⟨α⟩ ... γόος ἅμα καὶ χαρά.

834. Or., as he stands before Iph., is not a βρέφος, and Barnes' τόδε (see *app. crit.*) is only possible if we can suppose τόδε = τόνδε by gender-attraction from βρέφος. Bergk's τόν is better and the change is very slight. The constr. is ⟨ἔχω σε⟩ τὸν (= ὅν).

ll. 835, 6 are dochmiacs; 834 is nothing. But it can be made into a resolved dochmiac by the addition of Fix's ⟨ἔλιπον⟩ (see *app. crit.*), an addition which should almost certainly be made.

For the repetition of the same word in dochmiacs (⟨ἔλιπον⟩ ἔλιπον . . . νεαρὸν . . . νεαρόν) cf. E. *Hipp.* 836, 7 τὸ κατὰ γᾶς θέλω, τὸ κατὰ γᾶς κνέφας | μετοικεῖν σκότῳ, *Med.* 1273 ἀκούεις βοὰν ἀκούεις τέκνων, and below l. 852.

837–40. Our text takes the simplest emendation εὐτυχοῦσά μου for MSS. εὐτυχῶν ἐμοῦ. But we may well ask how εὐτυχῶν arose, and wonder at the metre of 838.

Of the almost innumerable emendations suggested I believe that of Wecklein to be the best. He holds that ἐμοῦ ψυχά was originally a gloss on θυμέ (cf. E. *Med.* 1056 μὴ δῆτα, θυμέ), a vocative which explains, while ψυχά does not, the presence of the masc. εὐτυχῶν, and reads accordingly ὦ θυμέ, κρεῖσσον ἢ λ. εὐτυχῶν | τί φῶ ; . . ., thus reducing 838 to a dochmiac monometer.

A simpler way is to consider that εὐτυχῶν refers and is addressed to Or. Hermann conjectures ὦ κρείσσον' . . . εὐτυχῶν [ἐμοῦ] ⟨τύχαν,⟩ | [ψυχά,] τί φῶ ; But apart from the arbitrariness of the introduction of τύχαν, and the removal of ἐμοῦ and ψυχά, one does not want a comment by Iph. on *Or.'s* happiness, but on her own.

κρεῖσσον ἢ λόγοισιν εὐτυχοῦσα might mean (as England thinks) ἔργῳ εὐτ. (cf. l. 794), but it is better to take the expression as = κρεῖσσον ἢ λόγοισι ⟨φάναι οἷόν τ' ἐστίν⟩. Hartung's ἢ λέγοι τις, cf. E. *Hipp.* 1186 θᾶσσον ἢ λέγοι τις, is unnecessary. Cf. E. *Supp.* 844, 5 εἶδον γὰρ αὐτῶν κρείσσον' ἢ λέξαι λόγῳ | τολμήματα, *Hipp.* 1217 κρεῖσσον θέαμα δεργμάτων.

For **θαυμάτων πέρα** cf. E. *Hec.* 714 ἄρρητ' ἀνωνόμαστα, θαυμάτων πέρα, *Ba.* 667 δεινὰ δρῶσι θαυμάτων τε κρείσσονα, and below l. 900 μύθων πέρα.

Weil transposes πρόσω to the end of the line to get the unresolved antepenultimate of the dochmiac there: ⏑ ⏖ – ⏑ – for ⏑ – ⏖ ⏑ –.

843. In the face of 837 and 845 there is no need to suspect this senarian or to accept Blomfield's δέδια δ' . . . μή με . . . which would give us a dochmiac dimeter.

For the sentiment cf. E. *Med.* 439, 40 αἰδὼς . . . αἰθερία . . . ἀνέπτα and Aristophanes' parody in *Ra.* 1352 ἀνέπτατ' εἰς αἰθέρα (referring to a rooster).

844. ἀμπτάμενος (= ἀναπτ.) sc. 'Ορέστης—unless, indeed, we accept Markland's ἀμπταμένα (sc. ἡδονή). With the masc., which seems odd in the 3rd person, we might read Burges' φύγῃς.

845. The stages of MSS. corruption are probably . . . Κυκλωπὶς ἑστία· ἰὼ . . . : . . . Κυκλωπὶς ἑστίαι· ὦ . . . : Κυκλωπίδες ἑστίαι· ὦ. Notice the rare hiatus between fourth and fifth foot.

For 'Cyclopean' Mycenae cf. E. *IA.* 152 ἐπὶ Κυκλώπων ἱεὶς θυμέλας, *ib.* 265 Μυκήνας . . . τᾶς Κυκλωπίας, and *El.* 1157, 8 εἰς οἴκους Κυκλώπειά τ' οὐράνια τείχεα.

847–9. ζόας, sc. 'Ορέστου; the phrase is expanded in the ὅτι clause.

φάος δόμοις is in apposition: for *φάος* = light, salvation, cf. S. *Ant.* 599, 600 *ἐσχάτας ὑπὲρ | ῥίζας ἐτέτατο φάος ἐν Οἰδίπου δόμοις.*

As our text stands 848 is an anapaestic dimeter, and 849 a cretic dipody. These seem out of place in a dochmiac, or dochmiac-iambic, system. If we accept Blomfield's *ὅτι δόμοισι τόνδε συνομαίμον' ἐξ-|* we get three dochmiacs.

850. **γένει**; not, as Weil, 'lucky *for* our race in that we can perpetuate it'. Rather *γένει* = *εὐγενείᾳ* and is parallel to *εἰς συμφοράς* (= *συμφοραῖς*): '⟨though⟩ lucky in our good birth, yet ⟨when you look⟩ at what we have suffered . . .' 'Nous devons au destin une noble naissance, mais au destin, aussi, des jours riches en malheurs' (Grégoire).

852–3. We need between the **ἐγώ** and **μέλεος** of the MSS. a long syllable to complete the metre. Seidler's ⟨*δή*⟩ or Wecklein's ⟨*μέν*⟩ would do, but Bruhn's emendation, accepted in our text, is preferable with its repetition of *οἶδα* (cf. note on l. 834 above). For *οἶδ' ὅτε* cf. E. *Hec.* 110 *οἶσθ' ὅτε χρυσέοις ἐφάνη σὺν ὅπλοις.* (The constr. is not exactly that of l. 813.)

Elmsley's *'φῆκέ* (= *ἐφῆκέ*) is tempting, aud even Jacob's *'θηγέ*, but **τιθέναι φ. δέρᾳ** is all right for 'set the sword at my throat'.

855. Nil mutandum. F. W. Schmidt's *γάρ τοι* for *γὰρ οὐ* ruins alike metre and sense. *οὐ παρών* = ⟨*καίπερ*⟩ *οὐ παρών*—the participle being an imperfect one.

856–8. The constr. continues from l. 853; i.e. ⟨*οἶδ'*⟩ *ὅτε* . . . Take **κλισίαν** *λέκτρων* together; as we say 'bed-chamber'.

δόλιος is an adj. of either two or three terminations. The MSS. *δολίαν* may therefore be all right. But if we keep it as an epithet of *κλισίαν* (which seems sufficiently qualified by *λέκτρων*) we must, if we are to save the dochmiac, take *ἀγόμαν* as unaugmented (◡◡͞ – ◡◡͞ ◡ –). It is probably better to regard the word as adverbial and read Hermann's *δόλι' ὅτ' ἀγόμαν.* Hartung's *δόλιον* (which might easily have been altered to **δολίαν**) [*ὅτ'*] *ἀγόμαν* sacrifices the necessary *ὅτε.*

Weil's *εἰς κλισιᾶν ἀλέκτρων δόλον ὅτ' ἀγόμαν* is excellent in sense but metrically impossible, unless we could arrange it *εἰς κλισιᾶν ἀλέκ|τρων δόλον ὅτ' ἀγόμαν.*

For Prof. Murray's suggestion see *app. crit.*; lit. 'to the deceitful bed-lying of. . . .' The comparatively rare *κλίσιν* (a word which goes much better with **λέκτρων** than does *κλισίαν*) might well have been corrupted into **κλισίαν**, especially in the presence of the similar sounding *δολίαν.*

861. Seidler's ⟨*τῶν*⟩ completes sense but not metre. It is better to accept some suggestion that does both, e.g. Wecklein's *χ. ἐκεῖ* ⟨*φοινίων*⟩, or Kirchhoff's ⟨*τῶν ἐμῶν*⟩ (perhaps better *φεῦ φεῦ* **τῶν** *ἐμῶν ἐκεῖ χερνίβων*), or Schröder's ⟨*ἀνοσίων*⟩ *ἐκεῖ* (cited in his Eur. *Cantica*, p. 102).

862. **ᾤμωξα** with present sense, as at E. *Med.* 791; cf. *ἥσθην* = I rejoice at.

863. The metre changes in this and the following two lines, and we get a resolved iambic dimeter followed by two lecythia. Iph. means that her father treated her in no fatherly fashion; so at S. *El.* 1154 Electra refers to her mother as μήτηρ ἀμήτωρ. Hartung's suggestion (see *app. crit.*) is attractive, though metrically difficult. For πότμον ἄποτμον cf. E. *Hipp.* 1143 δάκρυσι διοίσω πότμον ἄποτμον.

865–7. Cf. E. *Hec.* 690 ἕτερα δ' ἀφ' ἑτέρων κακὰ κακῶν κυρεῖ. Iph. means that even after her experiences at Aulis her life has been a succession of evils; to which Or. answers '⟨it would indeed have been⟩ if you had killed me, your brother'. ll. 865 and 867 form, in any case, one sentence. Whether we keep the MSS. order and suppose that Or. interrupts with this remark, or accept, as our text does, Monk's transposition, is immaterial.

Herwerden's suggestion of τέχνᾳ for MSS. τύχᾳ is unnecessary in face of e.g. Pi. *O.* 8. 67 (τύχᾳ . . . δαίμονος) and *P.* 8. 53 (τύχᾳ θεῶν); cf. also E. *IA.* 351 τῇ τύχῃ τῇ τῶν θεῶν, *Rh.* 728 δαίμονος τύχα βαρεῖα, and *fr.* 37 δαιμόνων . . . τύχας.

868. **τόλμας**, gen. of cause, common after such exclamations; cf. E. *Med.* 96 δύστανος ἐγὼ μελέα τε πόνων; *Ion* 960 τλήμων σὺ τόλμης.

872. Logically speaking **δαϊχθείς** makes nonsense. Iph. should have said τὸ δαϊχθῆναι. The sense, however, is clear. παρ' ὀλίγον ἀπέφ. ὄλ. = παρ' ὀλίγον κατέθανες; cf. Th. 7. 71. 3 παρ' ὀλίγον ἢ διέφευγον ἢ ἀπώλλυντο.

873–4. As they stand in our text (= MSS.) these two lines look like irregular trochaics. But l. 873 can only so be scanned if we take it as a doubly syncopated trochaic catalectic trimeter (ἁ δ' ἐπ' | αὐτ· | οῖσι | τίς τελ|ευ· | τά) = a most improbable type of line (see Wilamowitz, *Verskunst*, p. 264 (note)), while l. 874 contains a vicious spondee in the third foot. This latter can be cured by Bothe's συγκυρήσει (= 'will befall'), a change demanded not only by metre but by sense, for συγχωρήσει μοι (= 'will yield to me') is not the meaning we want. As to l. 873, αὐτοῖς[ι] (Wilamowitz, *op. cit.*, p. 268) would do metrically, giving us a trochaic dimeter. But ἐπ' αὐτοῖς is, to say the least, questionable Greek for ἐπὶ τούτοις, no word of possible reference having preceded. We might accept F. W. Schmidt's ἁ δὲ τούτοις or Weil's ἁ δὲ πάντως (πάντως = 'in any case', i.e. even now that I have avoided killing my brother). But in both these the order of words is awkward with τίς between the article and its substantive. We might perhaps read τὰ δ' ἐπὶ τούτοις, taking this phrase adverbially = 'as to what happens after this': cf. A. *Ag.* 255 πέλοιτο . . . τἀπὶ τούτοισιν εὖ πρᾶξις. [Schröder perversely takes the lines ἁ δ' ἐπ' αὐτοῖσι τίς τελευτά (two cretics followed by a bacchius) [τίς τύχα] μοι συγχωρήσει (dochmiac).]

875–7. These lines will construe if we understand, as we well may, σε, from σοι, as the object of πέμψω. But metrically l. 875 needs something to complete the anapaestic dimeter. The simplest emendation is something like ⟨ξείνας⟩ after εὑρομένα. But πόλεως has not unnaturally caused suspicion. The wilds of Tauris would scarcely be so designated by a Greek. (Cf. πόλει, l. 38 above, a line which we have seen reason to suspect on other grounds. πόλις in l. 595 = the people.) Köchly suggested ἀπὸ ξένας, taking πόλεως as a (bad) gloss on ξένας. (There is a fairly definite case of such a gloss at A. *Supp.* 634 where πόλιν glosses τάνδε Πελασγίαν.) If we accepted this we should have to complete l. 875 in some other way. It seems more likely that πόλεως conceals some such word as πελέκεως (Reiske) or πελάνων (Orelli), either of which words would fit in better with φόνου. Wecklein adopts the former but does not complete l. 875. We might possibly read

τίνα σοι πόρον εὑρομένα πέμψω
πάλιν ἀπὸ πελέκεως, ἀπὸ φόνου ⟨πάλιν⟩

remembering Eur.'s fondness for repeating words in dochmiacs (see l. 834, note). In Bergk's πάλιν ἀποστελῶ σ' the introduction of σε is good, but we want the repeated preposition, and the asyndeton ἀποστελῶ . . . πέμψω is awkward.

Markland's suggestion (see *app. crit.*) seems to me to solve none of the difficulties.

880. **ἐπὶ . . . πελάσαι** by tmesis. The verb is intrans. here (as is πελάσεις at l. 886) with ξίφος as its subject; there is now no question of *Iphigenia's* sacrificing Or.

ἐπιπελάζειν not being found elsewhere, Hartung proposed ἔτι and Bergk ἔσω (cf. E. *Hel.* 356 αὐτοσίδαρον ἔσω πελάσω διὰ σαρκὸς ἅμιλλαν—where πελάσω, however, is trans.).

From P's παλαῖσαι Scaliger conjectured παλάξαι (which gives bad sense) and Nauck πελάσσαι (a form which both Weil and Wecklein receive into their editions), but both these ruin the anapaests.

882. **ὦ μελέα ψυχά**; she addresses not herself but Or.

883. The hiatus **ναΐ** | **ἀλλά** is suspicious. Either we must suppose a lacuna which we can fill up with ναΐ⟨ῳ στόλῳ⟩, as Wilamowitz, or preferably with something that does not cause another hiatus, such as Badham's simple ναΐ⟨ος⟩; or we can emend, taking Monk's ναυσίν or Badham's ναός. This latter gives a good antithesis to ποδῶν, but necessitates the removal of the mark of interrogation from the end of l. 883 to a position after **στείχων**, as πότερον . . . στείχων in this case forms one sentence.

886–7. ἄρα = if so; i.e. if you go ποδῶν ῥιπᾷ. Markland's ἀνά is unnecessary, φῦλα is governed by διά equally with ὁδούς; cf. E. *Hec.* 144 ἀλλ' ἴθι ναούς, ἴθι πρὸς βωμοὺς = ἴθι ⟨πρὸς⟩ ναούς; *Ph.* 284 μαντεῖα σεμνὰ Λοξίου τ' ἐπ' ἐσχάρας; *IA.* 210 αἰγιαλοῖς παρά τε κροκάλαις; S. *Ant.* 367 τοτὲ μὲν κακόν, ἄλλοτ' ἐπ' ἐσθλὸν ἕρπει, and *ib.* 1176 πότερα πατρῴας ἢ πρὸς οἰκείας χερός; The MSS. διόδους (see crit. note) may be all right, it being the substantive and ἀνόδους the adjective. In this case στείχων governs both accusatives, which we can regard either as internal or as accusatives of extent.

889–91. It is possible to take this sentence in two ways: either (1) 'but on the other hand (μήν) the way by (lit. of) the Symplegades is long for flight by ship', or (2) 'no (μήν), ⟨it must be by⟩ the long journey *via* the S. by means of flight on shipboard'.

In this second case μακρὰ κέλ. is acc. and parallel to φῦλα and ὁδούς (or διόδους); a verb of motion must be understood.

895. This line as it appears in our text (= MSS.) is almost impossible; τάδε has no construction unless we take it as object of φαίνοι with ἔκλυσιν in apposition.

As L reads φανεῖ it is as well to accept this and clear away these ἄν's, taking some such emendation as Badham's τίς ἄρ' οὖν, τάλαν, ἤ or Rauchenstein's τίς ἄρ' οὖν νῷν ἤ (νῷν having δυοῖν . . . 'Ατρείδαιν in apposition to it), or Mähly's τίς ἄρ' οὖν τῶνδ' ἤ (τῶνδ' going with κακῶν).

896–7. Lit. 'what of unlooked-for agencies'; i.e. what being, half god, half man; cf. E. *Hel.* 1137 ὅ τι θεὸς ἢ μὴ θεὸς ἢ τὸ μέσον and A. *Pr.* 115, 6 τίς ἀχώ, τίς ὀδμὰ προσέπτα μ' ἀφεγγής, | θεόσυτος, ἢ βρότειος, ἢ κεκραμένη; But τί τῶν ἀδοκ. is an odd expression.

πόρον ἄπορον ἐξανύσας: i.e. 'bringing about a solution which is no solution'. This is no κακῶν ἔκλυσις. The phrase cries out for emendation. Hermann's second suggestion πόρον εὔπορον would do, but it is far inferior to his first πόρον ἀπόρων = 'finding a way out where no way is'; cf. A. *Pr.* 59 δεινὸς . . . εὑρεῖν κἀξ ἀμηχάνων πόρον and Ar. *Eq.* 758, 9 ποικίλος γὰρ ἀνὴρ | κἀκ τῶν ἀμηχάνων πόρους εὐμήχανος πορίζειν.

If the partic. ἐξανύσας is correct we must supply some main verb, or accept *l*'s φανεῖ which gives good sense. Alternatively we may take Nauck's ἐξανύσει and reject φανεῖ (a word missing in P)—or Kirchhoff's ἐξανύσαι (optat.) if we keep an ἄν in 895. In either of these cases ἔκλυσιν would be in apposition to πόνον.

The scansion of the passage is very uncertain, but τίς ἄρ' οὖν, τάλαν, ἤ . . . | τί τῶν . . . | πόρον ἀπόρων ἐξανύσας, | δυοῖν τοῖν μόνοιν 'Ατρείδαιν φανεῖ | κακῶν ἔκλ. would give us an anapaestic dimeter, a dochmiac, a choriambic dipody (with first long syllable resolved), a dochmiac dipody, and a simple dochmiac.

It is tempting in view of the stereotyped ending to five of Eur.'s plays in which the words ἀδοκήτων πόρον occur together (τῶν δ' ἀδοκήτων πόρον ηὗρε θεός, e.g. E. *Alc.* 1162) to take them together here. Weil does so, adding ⟨τρίτον⟩ after τί. Bruhn's τί ⟨μέσον τῶνδ' ὄν⟩ gives the same meaning. It may be observed that by taking Bruhn's reading and excising ἄπορον (Schröder) we get good sense and a more regular metre:

τίς ἄρ' οὖν, τάλαν, ἢ θεὸς ἢ βροτὸς ἢ	anap. dim.
τί μέσον τῶνδ' ὂν τῶν ἀδοκήτων	anap. dim.
πόρον ἐξανύσας,	anap. monom.
δυοῖν τοῖν μόνοιν 'Ατρείδαιν φανεῖ.	doch. dim.

In spite of the apparent boldness of Bruhn's addition I believe that this is the best solution.

898. **μόνοιν.** Electra is still alive and Iph. knows the fact (cf. l. 562 above). She is, however, thinking only of herself and Or. just as at S. *Ant.* 941 Antigone, forgetting Ismene, calls herself τὴν βασιλειδᾶν μούνην λοιπήν. Markland's δυσδαιμόνοιν (for metrical reasons it should be τοῖν δυσδαιμόνοιν) 'Ατρ. is quite unnecessary, nor does it meet the point. The predicative position of δυοῖν is analogous to that of ἄμφω (K.-G. II. i, p. 634).

900. **μύθων πέρα**: cf. E. *Hipp.* 437 ἔξω λόγου and l. 840 above.

901. We want an antithesis between εἶδον and κλύουσα, and must therefore accept Hermann's κοὐ for MSS. καί; cf. E. *Tr.* 481, 2 καὶ τὸν φυτουργὸν Πρίαμον οὐκ ἄλλων πάρα | κλύουσ' ἔκλαυσα, τοῖσδε δ' εἶδον ὄμμασιν.

If the MSS. ἀπαγγελῶ is to be kept it must be taken 'and since I have not ⟨merely⟩ heard them I shall ⟨be able to⟩ speak ⟨of them⟩'. But Hermann's ἀπ' ἀγγέλων should almost certainly be accepted. The καί here, though grammatically speaking it is superfluous, joins αὐτὴ ⟨ἰδοῦσα⟩ and the rest of the sentence. Hartung's κοὐκ ἀπ' ἀγγέλων κλύω and still more England's κοὐ κλύω παρ' ἀγγέλων are unnecessary.

ἐν τοῖσι θαυμαστοῖσι and **μύθων πέρα** are both secondary predicates.

902. The constr. is εἰκός ⟨ἐστι⟩ τὸ . . . λαβεῖν. It is odd to find εἰκός between article and infin.

904. **ἐκεῖνο** is explained in the ὅπως clause which follows. οἴκτων is at first sight odd. We might expect a word = manifestations of joy, not sorrow. But Pyl. means that both mutual embraces and expressions of self-pity must be postponed to making plans for escape.

905. **τῆς**, as Prof. Murray says, is suspicious and **ὄνομα** almost impossible. ὄνομα Πολυνείκους = Πολυνείκης (E. *Ph.* 1702) is no real parallel. Musgrave's πνεῦμα (for ὄνομα) would be good but for κλεινόν, which is an unsuitable epithet. On the whole the Paris apograph ὄμμα is the best; cf. S. *Tr.* 203, 4 ὡς ἄελπτον ὄμμ' ἐμοὶ | φήμης ἀνασχὸν τῆσδε νῦν καρπούμεθα, and E. *Or.* 1082 ὦ ποθεινὸν ὄμμ' ὁμιλίας ἐμῆς (where there is MS. confusion between ὄμμα and ὄνομα).

Enger's σῆς will not do; Pyl. must include himself in the plans for escape.

907–8. These lines as they stand in our text (= MSS.) are perilously like nonsense, and it is possible that Dindorf was right in expelling them as the interpolation of some scribe whose inclination towards moralizing was stronger than were his powers of expression. At the same time they seem to offer a forward reference to τύχη in l. 909, and they can be made to yield some meaning, viz. 'it is the part of a wise man not to fly in the face of fortune and, though he may get the opportunity of doing so, seize pleasures foreign to his true good'. (μή, in this case, goes both with ἐκβάντας and λαβεῖν.)

At least we must alter λαβόντας . . . λαβεῖν. Heimsöth's λιπόντας might do; the lines would then = μή, λαβόντας ἡδ. ἄλλ., καιρὸν λιπεῖν. Much better is Weil's λαχόντας (same sense as λαβόντας and an easy corruption). In both these cases, however, we are left with the awkward 'κβάντας τύχης = (?) overstepping fortune.

Bothe keeps the MSS. reading (except that he accepts Scaliger's ἄλλως), putting commas not at τύχης and λαβόντας but at καιρόν and ἡδονάς. This gives definitely better sense and does away with both the 'κβάντας τύχης and the λαβόντας . . . λαβεῖν difficulty: 'it is the part of a wise man not to lose an opportunity given by chance and ⟨thus⟩ not, in grasping pleasures, find he has grasped them in vain'. This is probably the best solution, though he perhaps need not have taken ἄλλως for ἄλλας. The adj. can bear the same meaning as the adverb (cf. the Homeric οὐκ ἂν ἐγώ γε | ἄλλα παρὲξ εἴποιμι παρακλιδὸν, οὐδ' ἀπατήσω Od. 4. 347, 8 and 17. 138, 9).

909. δέ = and indeed. Not adversative. τῇ τύχῃ = τὸ θεῖον. Cf. l. 911.

910. τοῦδε = τοῦ ἡμᾶς σῴζεσθαι. F. W. Schmidt's τόδε ξυνέρδειν for τοῦδε ξὺν ἡμῖν is unnecessary.

911. μᾶλλον probably with σθένειν: England takes it, less well, with εἰκότως. Countless 'emendations' of σθένειν have been proposed: αἰνεῖν, στέργειν, σπεύδειν, συνθεῖν, etc. All are possible, none very likely.

For the sentiment ('Heaven helps those who help themselves') cf. E. *fr.* 432 αὐτός τι νῦν δρῶν, εἶτα δαίμονας κάλει and S. *fr.* 407 οὐκ ἔστι τοῖς μὴ δρῶσι σύμμαχος τύχη, etc.

εἰκότως ἔχει = it is reasonable to suppose.

912. Prinz and Wecklein cite twenty emendations of this line, and, as England says, every word in it except λόγου has been 'corrected' by some one. Fortunately the sense is clear: Iph. will not be hurried out of an inquiry into the fate of her sister. λόγου is explained by πυθέσθαι. Grégoire keeps the MSS. (with ἐπίσχει, for which he claims MS. authority, and P's ἀποστήσει) = 'nothing hinders me nor shall prevent me from . . .' But the present tense is awkward—something, or, rather, some one, *is* hindering her—and particularly awkward in conjunction with the future. Kviçala suggested οὐ δεῖ (= 'you ought not to') μ' ἐπισχεῖν οὐδ' ἀποστῆσαι which is paleographically likely. Otherwise emendations fall into two classes: (1) those which make οὐδέν the subject and supply 3rd person verbs; (2) those which make Or. subject and give 2nd person verbs, οὐδέν being taken adverbially. Of class (1) may be cited Enger's (see *app. crit.*) 'stay! nothing shall hold me from this question', and Hermann's οὐδέν με μὴ σχῇ γ'· οὐδ' ἀποστήσῃ; of class (2) Monk's suggestion given in the *app. crit.* Prof. Murray's emendation makes Iph. appeal to Or. against Pyl.'s attempt to hurry her. This is good,

as any possible thwarting of Iph. is more likely to come from Pyl. than from Or.

S. *OC.* 450–2 οὔ τι μὴ λάχωσι τοῦδε . . . οὐδὲ . . . ὄνησις ἥξει illustrates alike οὐ μή . . . οὐδέ (Hermann and Monk) and the conjunction of subjunctive and future (Murray).

914. φίλα γάρ: the phrase is a little reminiscent of E. *Or.* 1192 πᾶν γὰρ ἓν φίλον τόδε, where Electra is stressing the unity of interest of herself, Or., and Pyl. But the ἔσται of the MSS. is unmetrical and their πάντα very difficult. All that can be said for Vitelli's ἔστε (read in our text) is that it is very near the MSS. But 'you are all dear [things] to me' seems incredibly weak, and the translation 'you two are all that I have to love' is scarcely justifiable. Of the mass of corrections the best is probably Schöne's ἐστι τἄμ' ἐμοί (where τἄμα = οἱ ἐμοί). Wecklein's φίλα δὲ (= γάρ) τἄμα πάντ' ἐμοί is also good.

917. Not 'his father is called . . .', which would necessitate ⟨ὁ⟩ πατήρ, but 'Strophios is . . .' For κλῄζεται = ἐστί cf. S. *OT.* 1451, 2 ἔνθα κλῄζεται | οὑμὸς Κιθαιρὼν οὗτος.

918. θυγατρός: sc. Anaxibia, sister of Agamemnon and mother of Pyl.

919. ἀνεψιός γε: sc. σοί.

926. 'The reason why' not 'the cause for which', for ὅτου is necessarily masc. or neut. and cannot = ἥστινος; cf. below l. 1071 (note).

927. οὐδέ, as though something like οὐ βούλομαι ἐγὼ λέγειν had preceded.

930. οὔ που (interrogative) is not so common as οὔ τί που (cf. S. *Ph.* 1233, Ar. *Ra.* 522) or οὐ δή (cf. S. *OT.* 1472, *Ant.* 380), but it is correct (cf. E. *IA.* 670, *Med.* 695, *El.* 235) and is preferable to Kviçala's οὕτω νοσοῦντας . . . ;

931. Ἐρινύων is trisyllabic; the υ is consonantal, almost = our 'w', cf. ll. 970 and 1456.

932. ἆρ', as often, = ἄρ'. ταῦτα may be taken as = διὰ ταῦτα or as an internal acc. with μανείς: '*that* was the madness you were announced as suffering from, was it (ἄρα)?'

καὶ (with ἐνθάδε))(ἐν Ἄργει, understood from χθονός of 931: 'here too'. Bothe reads [καὶ] ἐνθάδ'.

ἠγγέλης; this 2nd aor. pass., formerly thought a solecism in fifth-cent. Attic (see Porson on E. *Hec.* 672), has been found on an inscription from Eleusis of the year 439 B.C. (Meisterh., p. 187). ἠγγέλθης may, however, be right (see *app. crit.*).

934–5. ἡλάστρουν being a metaphor from horse-driving, the reference to 'bits' is natural. However, two objections have been urged against the line: (1) that ἐμβάλλειν is the usual word for inserting a bit, and the ἐπί here has no force; (2) that nowhere else are the Furies depicted as 'driving' their prey, always as 'pursuing' it. Hence Weil, comparing A. *Eu.* 137–9 σὺ δ' αἱματηρὸν πνεῦμ' ἐπουρίσασα τῷ, | ἀτμῷ κατισχναίνουσα, νηδύος πυρί, | ἕπου, reads αἱματηρὰν ἀτμίδ' ἐμβαλεῖν, Herwerden αἱματηρὸν ἆσθμά γ', etc. Some edd. seek to cure only one 'fault', e.g. Elmsley στόμιά γ' ἐμβαλεῖν; Wecklein, αἱματηρὸν πνεῦμ' ἐπεμβαλεῖν.

But there is no need to change: ἐπεμβάλλειν is a common enough word, and it means 'to insert'. As to στόμια—the pursuit of the Furies is in any case metaphorical. Why should not Or., following his sister's lead (ἠλάστρουν), slightly change the metaphor? The word occurs in the same context at l. 971.

We might expect a γε in answer (cf. l. 919 and 75 note), but it is often omitted, e.g. S. *Tr.* 629 ὥστ' ἐκπλαγῆναι τοὐμὸν ἡδονῇ κέαρ and E. *Alc.* 1084 ὥστ' ἄνδρα τόνδε μηκέθ' ἥδεσθαι βίῳ.

Some edd. following Monk (Wecklein for one) put 932, 3 after 935. This gives good sense, but not so much better as to justify the transposition.

938. τί χρῆμα δράσειν occurs again in the MSS. at E. *Ion* 1348 where Musgrave's suggestion δρᾶσαι is accepted in the O.C.T. It is probable that Elmsley's similar suggestion should be accepted here. (Monk's δράσων is possible.)

σιγώμενον: the pres. partic. has here a modal force, almost = σιγητέον: cf. S. *Ant.* 61, 2 γυναῖκε . . . πρὸς ἄνδρας οὐ μαχουμένα = 'who cannot fight with . . .'

939. αἵδε, attracted as usual into the gender of the predicate, ἀρχαί, may refer back to θέσφατα (= τάδε τὰ θέσφ.), but more likely = simply τάδε and looks forward, as ὅδε generally does, to his story.

940–1. = after my mother's punishment had devolved on me.

942–3. The MSS. δή γ' is not impossible; cf. E. *Heracl.* 632, but it is to be suspected here (cf. Denniston, p. 247). With it or with Scaliger's δῆτ' the MSS. reading, kept in our text, will just translate: 'when . . . had devolved . . . I was driven . . . ; next (ἔνθεν) Loxias directed my steps . . .' (Elmsley's μου for μοι would be a slight improvement—or Hermann's ἔνθ' ἐμόν.) But this is very awkward, and we should almost certainly emend. Bauer's μεταδρομαῖς ⟨τ'⟩ is simple, but one feels that even so ἔνθεν or ἔνθα is wrong.

Emendations exist in plenty: they follow one of two lines: (1) that of replacing ἔνθεν by ἔστε (Badham, Köchly (ἔστ' ἐμόν), Paley (ἔστε δή, with ἐξέπεμψε in 943)); (2) that of replacing ἐς τάς by ἔστ' εἰς and regarding ἔνθεν μοι as the corruption of some epithet qualifying πόδα such as ἐμμανῆ (Weil. See *app. crit.*). In this case, ἔπεμψε having lost its object (for πόδα has become an internal acc. with ἠλαυνόμεσθα—no comma at φυγάδες), we must read δή μ' for the MSS. δή γ'.

This second method seems decidedly the better.

944. i.e. ⟨ὥστε⟩ δίκην ὑπέχειν = so as to stand my trial. For the nameless goddesses cf. S. *OC.* 128 ἃς τρέμομεν λέγειν.

945–6. ψῆφος = tribunal. ἐκ = as the result of. The crime of Ares was the murder of Halirrhothius, son of Poseidon, for the violation of his daughter Alcippe. Cf. E. *El.* 1258 sqq.; the story is told in Apollod. 3. 14. 2.

This account of the founding of the Areopagus is not really inconsistent with that of Aeschylus (*Eu.* 681 sqq.), as England points out. Zeus may have tried Ares there, but Athene was the first to establish it as a court for human beings.

947. ἐλθὼν . . . με; cf. ll. 675, 695, and 964. Almost exact parallels are furnished by E. *fr.* 579 πάλαι δή σ' ἐξερωτῆσαι θέλων | σχολή μ' ἀπεῖργε, and *Hipp.* 22, 3 τὰ πολλὰ δὲ | πάλαι προκόψασ'—οὐ πόνου πολλοῦ με δεῖ.

Demosthenes (20. 158) quotes a law of Draco ordering τὸν ἀνδροφόνον εἴργεσθαι σπονδῶν, κρατήρων, ἱερῶν, ἀγορᾶς; cf. S. *OT.* 238–40 (proclamation against the murderer of Laius) τὸν ἄνδρ' ἀπαυδῶ . . . μήτ' ἐνδέχεσθαι μήτε προσφωνεῖν τινα, | μήτ' ἐν θεῶν εὐχαῖσι μηδὲ θύμασιν | κοινὸν ποεῖσθαι, μήτε χέρνιβας νέμειν.

949. i.e. 'those who felt compunction' or 'those who showed mercy'. For αἰδώς = mercy, cf. S. *OC.* 1267, 8 ἀλλ' ἔστι γὰρ καὶ Ζηνὶ σύνθακος θρόνων | Αἰδώς, E. *Alc.* 981 οὐδέ τις ἀποτόμου λήματός ἐστιν αἰδώς, etc.

951. 'And by their silence they kept (lit. "framed", "contrived") me speechless'. For this treatment of a murderer cf. A. *Eu.* 448 ἄφθογγον εἶναι τὸν παλαμναῖον (τὸν φονέα, schol.) νόμος. It is, however, very doubtful whether ἀπόφθ. can mean speechless, since, as Weil points out, it is only when compounded with substantives that ἀπό = ἀ privative (e.g. ἀπόθεος, ἀπόπολις). Hermann's ἀπρόσφθεγκτόν μ' should probably be accepted, or perhaps Wilamowitz' προσφθεγκτόν meaning 'they kept me addressed in silence', i.e. 'not spoken to'. Mekler's ὄπ' ἄφθεγκτον is palaeographically likely, but 'rendered me a speechless voice' is an odd expression.

952. Scaliger's αὐτῶν, accepted by Hermann, should probably be read; but in any case γενοίμην is odd and a suggestion of Professor Housman's, δαιτός τ' ὀναίμην, is very attractive.

953–4. i.e. instead of the communal bowl each had his own χοῦς. Cf. A. *Ch.* 291, 2 οὔτε κρατῆρος μέρος | εἶναι μετασχεῖν, οὐ φιλοσπόνδου λιβός. εἶχον ἡδ. = 'took their pleasure', i.e. 'feasted'.

Schöne's transposition of these two lines after 950 has been almost universally accepted. In the first place it gives further point and explanation to μονοτράπεζα, in the second it causes πώματος to *follow* μέτρημα βακχίου as it almost certainly should. Weil adopts the transposition and reads σιγῇ τ', ἐτεκτήναντό τ' ἄφθεγκτόν μ', with no stop at ἡδονήν, i.e. 'both themselves feasted in silence and kept me speechless'; but the τε after σιγῇ (= αὐτοί τ' εἶχον ἡδονήν) is badly misplaced.

For this aetiological myth see Ath. 10. 437 c (it is mentioned also in a schol. on Ar. *Eq.* 95). It is intended as an explanation of the feast of Χόες, held on the second of the three days of the larger festival of the Anthesteria. At this feast apparently each participant had his own table (μονοτράπεζα) and a separate χοῦς of wine in place of the communal κρατήρ.

μέτρημα πληρώσαντες: a curious use of πληρόω (cf. l. 306 above). An English (or ? Scots) parallel may be seen in Stevenson's *New Arabian Nights* (*The Suicide Club*): 'the Prince signified in the affirmative, and the other immediately filled some of the spirit into a tumbler'.

957. There is no point in Wecklein's μεταστενάζων—a non-existent verb which he coins on the analogy of μεταστένειν.

For Herwerden's excision of the whole line there is much to be said; Or.'s outspokenness contrasts strangely with his previous euphemisms. It may well have been inserted by a scribe desirous of (wrongly) particularizing εἰδέναι.

οὕνεκ' with **εἰδέναι**, *not* **στενάζων**; 'pretending not to have it on my conscience that I was . . .' Köchly's λάθρα for μέγα would greatly help the sense. Without the line εἰδέναι would have a backward reference and mean 'pretending not to notice their treatment of me'.

958–60. Many have thought these lines spurious. They certainly seem a little unnecessary to an Athenian audience.

960. **χοῆρες ἄγγος** = a pot holding a χοῦς. A χοῦς (which equals about 5½ pints) contained 12 κοτύλαι. 12 χόες = a μετρητής or ἀμφορεύς (about 9 gallons).

For this use of τιμᾶν cf. l. 54.

961. MSS. δίκην τ'. If this be the correct reading it is the one and only case in which Eur. elides at the end of the line. Soph. avails himself of this licence some eight times. Paley would read δίκην | ἔστην τ'; i.e. 'when I came . . . and stood . . . Phoebus saved me' (with no stop after Ἐρινύων). But Elmsley's correction, [τ'] ἔστην . . . εἰπὼν ⟨δ'⟩, with a full stop at Ἐρινύων, should probably be accepted as it is in our text.

962. The two βάθρα here mentioned are the λίθοι ἀργοί on one of which (the λίθος ὕβρεως) stood the accused, while the accuser stood on the λίθος ἀναιδείας = the stone of implacability (Paus. 1. 28. 5).

963. ⟨λαβοῦσα⟩ as though ἔστημεν, not ἔστην, had preceded. A similar constr. occurs at E. *Ph.* 53, 4 γαμεῖ δὲ τὴν τεκοῦσαν, οὐκ εἰδὼς τάλας, | οὐδ' ἡ τεκοῦσα (εἰδυῖα) παιδὶ συγκοιμωμένη. Markland's ἢ παρῆν is attractive.

964. For **εἰπὼν . . . με** cf. l. 947 and note. (It will be observed that with Paley's δίκην | ἔστην τ' (see note on l. 961) this grammatical peculiarity would not occur, as l. 964 would fall within the ὡς (l. 961) clause.) For **εἰπὼν . . . ἀκούων θ'** cf. E. *Heracl.* 181, 2 ἄναξ, ὑπάρχει μὲν τόδ' ἐν τῇ σῇ χθονί, | εἰπεῖν ἀκοῦσαί τ' ἐν μέρει πάρεστί μοι. Some have taken Apollo as subject of these participles which must refer to the accused, not to his advocate.

965. **μαρτυρῶν** = being my advocate. We might say 'witness to character'.

966. Seidler's **διερρύθμιζε** = arranged in order, scarcely gives the meaning we want, and except for its possible use in this passage it is a late word. If, however, it is not right here, it is difficult to understand P's corrupt reading. L's διηρίθμησε certainly gives good sense.

ὠλένῃ = χερί is, I believe, impossible. E. *Ba.* 1125 quoted as a parallel is a line of very uncertain reading and meaning (MSS. ὠλέναις, Kirchhoff ὠλένης), and citations from the notorious Lycophron (e.g. 205 and 1183) are pointless where Euripides' practice is in question. Mähly's ἡγεμών or F. W. Schmidt's εὐμενής are possible, though feeble. Better is Kvičala's Παλλάς· ὧδε δὴ | νικῶν [δ'] ἀπῆρα.

For **ἴσας ψήφους** cf. E. *El.* 1268, 9 νόμος . . . νικᾶν ἴσαις ψήφοισι τὸν φεύγοντ' ἀεί.

967. 'I came off victorious in my murder trial'. **πειρατήρια** is an internal acc. going with νικῶν.

The whole story of the trial and the consequent acquittal is to be found in A. *Eu.* 566–753.

969. Lit. 'marked out for themselves a holy place by the very scene of the voting'. Markland's ὥρισάν γ' (on the ground that Eur. uses the active, not the middle, in this sense) is unnecessary. The middle is so used in E. *fr.* 696, 1, and in any case one wants the middle here—'marked out for themselves'.

ψῆφος = place of voting. Cf. l. 945 and such common Grecisms as ἰχθῦς = fish-market.

ἔχειν is epexegetic.

Note that Eur. here, in order to provide a reason for Or.'s journey to Tauris, departs from Aeschylus' version, according to which *all* the Erinyes δίκῃ ἐπείσθησαν.

970. **νόμῳ** much the same as δίκῃ in 968. Wecklein suggests θεᾷ. For **'Ερινύων** trisyllabic cf. 931 and 1456.

971. ἀϊδρύτοισιν ('vagabond') seems the better form. For **ἠλάστρουν** cf. l. 935 above (and note).

972. **Φοίβου πέδον**, i.e. the τέμενος of Apollo at Delphi; cf. A. *Ch.* 1036, Ar. *Pl.* 772.

αὖ, not 'again', but, as usual, 'in turn', almost 'next'.

973. **νῆστις βορᾶς**; cf. l. 80 above and note.

984. No difference of meaning is intended between **σῷσον** and **ἔκσῳσον**. Eur. often couples the simple and the compounded verb without change of sense, cf. *Andr.* 459 κτείνεις μ'· ἀπόκτεινε; *Hec.* 982 φίλη μὲν εἶ σύ, προσφιλὲς δέ μοι τόδε; *Ion* 1533, 4 ἐκπεφυκέναι; πεφυκέναι μὲν οὐχί; *Tr.* 892 αἱρεῖ γὰρ ἀνδρῶν ὄμματ', ἐξαιρεῖ πόλεις; *El.* 1096 εἰ γὰρ δίκαι' ἐκεῖνα, καὶ τάδ' ἔνδικα; *Or.* 181 διοιχόμεθ', οἰχόμεθα. So, also, Soph.: e.g. *OT.* 133 ἐπαξίως γὰρ Φοῖβος, ἀξίως δὲ σύ; *Ant.* 898 φίλη μὲν ἥξειν πατρί, προσφιλὴς δὲ σοί.

986. **θεᾶς.** Synizesis is rare in the fifth foot, cf. Descroix, *Trim. iamb.*, p. 33.

987–8. Taking Canter's ἄγει, as our text does, we must suppose either that ἐπιζέω here uniquely governs an acc. in the sense of 'boils up against' for which the dat. is the usual case, cf. E. *Hec.* 583 δεινόν τι πῆμα Πριαμίδαις ἐπέζεσεν, or that the τε is badly misplaced (for τό τε Ταυτ.)—so badly, indeed, as to be impossible.

Alternatively we might accept Hartung's δεινήν τις ὀργὴν . . . | . . . διὰ πόνων [τ'] ἄγων (with ἐπέζ. *transitive*, as at E. *Cyc.* 392); or even Rauchenstein's ἐπέζεσ' ἐς. For such a division cf. S. *Ph.* 626, 7 εἶμ' ἐπὶ | ναῦν. Eur. seldom ends a line with a preposition governing the first word of the following line, though in three places he ends a line with a genitive governed by a prepositional adverb at the beginning of the next line (*Or.* 1216, 7 δόμων | πάρος; *IA.* 610, 1 ὀχημάτων | ἔξω; *ib.* 1532, 3 δόμων | ἔξω); but in face of *El.* 852, 3 ὑπὸ | γέροντος this division cannot be called impossible. Herwerden would read ἐπιζαρεῖ (ἐπιζαρέω = ἐπιβαρέω, oppress—a word which occurs at E. *Ph.* 45, 6 ὡς δ' ἐπεζάρει | Σφὶγξ ἁρπαγαῖσι πόλιν and *Rh.* 440, 1 ἀλλ' οἷα πόντου Θρῄκιον φυσήματα | κρυσταλλόπηκτα Παιόνας τ' ἐπεζάρει (MSS. ἐπεζάτει).

989 sqq. The μέν is answered by the δέ in 995. 'I have the *will*, and had it before your arrival, to be . . . but I fear I may not be able to elude . . .' ἔχω here is (*pace* Weil) the correct tense. That Iph. should state in combination a wish to be in Argos (which she is not) and to see her brother (which she is doing) is not particularly strange, especially as, until its fulfilment, she *had* the latter wish.

The δ' in 991 is purely copulative.

Editors have, however, taken great exception to the whole passage.

Weil proposes ποθεινόν for πρόθυμον and translates 'Ce que je souhaitais avant ta venue, je le tiens', which makes Iph. say that she is in Argos.

Köchly's transposition (in which he was followed by Nauck) of 999–1003 after 993 gives good sense *as far as 1003*, but leaves the thought-sequence of 1003 and 994 unintelligible.

Wecklein supposes a lacuna after 993 in which occurred a passage with the sense 'But I do not know how it could be done. I will certainly steal the image for you and help you in your escape.'

He points out that there is a lacuna after 1014, which, supposing a lacuna here, makes it look as though the archetype had had 21 + (say 24) lines to a page and one page (i.e. two sides) had been torn at the bottom. For the theory of a 24-line archetype see note on l. 1380 below.

Markland's 'γγενέσθαι (for γενέσθαι in l. 990) would be a very slight change. It might well be adopted. [But see E. *HF.* 729 βρόχοισι . . . γενήσεται.] Otherwise *nil mutandum.*

992. England keeps the MSS. κτανοῦντι, believing it to be an alternative pres. form 'with a desiderative force'; cf. E. *Ph.* 765, *Or.* 940, and *IT.* 291 (as quoted in Long. περὶ ὕψ. 15—κτανεῖ).

If it is to be emended there is little to choose between Hermann's τοῖς κτανοῦσι (generalizing plur.), Elmsley's τῷ κτείνοντι, and Heath's τῷ κτανόντι.

993. Most edd. alter either this **θέλω** (to e.g. Paley's ποτε or Markland's πάλιν: cf. S. *Ant.* 163 ὤρθωσαν πάλιν), or that of 991 (to e.g. Musgrave's ἄλλως), but the MSS. are almost certainly right. The repetition of a word is quite in Eur.'s manner: cf. E. *Hipp.* 327 κάκ', ὦ τάλαινα, σοὶ τάδ', εἰ πεύσῃ, κακά; *Ba.* 963 μόνος σὺ πόλεως τῆσδ' ὑπερκάμνεις, μόνος; *IA.* 1026 ποῦ σ' αὖθις ὀψόμεσθα, ποῦ; *Rh.* 579 θρασὺς γὰρ Ἕκτωρ νῦν, ἐπεὶ κρατεῖ, θρασύς.

994. This is not nonsense as many edd. have thought. Iph., in helping Or. to escape, *would* 'free' her 'hand from his slaughtering', because, if Or. remained in Tauris, she would be obliged by the king to sacrifice him. England, taking further exception, oddly enough, to the mixture of number in ἀπαλλάξαιμεν . . . σώσαιμι, reads ὀρθῶσαι πάλιν. σφαγῆς . . . χεῖρ' ἀπαλλάξαι θέλω | σῶσαί τ' ἐς οἴκους; taking γάρ as = 'to wit', and the infinitives as explanatory of the preceding ones, μεταστῆσαι and ὀρθῶσαι. I cannot see how this solves what he feels are the main difficulties, viz. (1) what Iph. means by 'freeing her hand from Or.'s slaughtering'; (2) the 'tautology' of νοσοῦντά τ' οἶκον ὀρθῶσαι θέλω and σώσαιμί τ' οἴκους.

995. **ὅπως λάθω δέδοικα** seems to stand for οὐκ οἶδα ὅπως λάθω καὶ δέδοικα μὴ οὐ λάθω. England's τὴν θεὸν δὲ πῶς λάθω; or Wecklein's οὐκ οἶδα for δέδοικα, are both good.

996–7. **κενάς** with ἀγάλματος. **κρηπῖδας** = pedestal. An odd plural. England suggests that the pedestal took the form of steps.

998. 'And then of course I shall die.' But the δέ is odd. Köchly omits it.

ἔνεστι = in sense ἐνέσται, which Badham wishes to read.

λόγος = explanation or excuse; cf. Dem. 1. 6 οὐδὲ λόγος οὐδὲ σκῆψις ἔθ' ὑμῖν . . . ὑπολείπεται, and below, l. 1358.

999. If we keep the MSS. and introduce no parenthesis the literal translation must be 'but if this (the acquisition of the statue and my escape) is one thing all together', i.e. if we succeed in both these things together. τοῦτο, though referring to a plural (or strictly speaking a dual) subject, viz. τὸ ἄγαλμα φέρειν καὶ ἐμὲ ἄγειν, is correct and Markland's ταῦτα should not be accepted. It is only another case of the assimilation of the subject into the number of the predicate, ἕν τι (cf. E. *Or.* 1192 πᾶν γὰρ ἓν φίλον τόδε for πάντες γὰρ οἵδε ἓν φίλον). But of ἕν τι, in this sense, and ὁμοῦ one is redundant.

With Prof. Murray's parenthesis we should presumably translate 'but if—it is one possibility—this (i.e. these two things) occur(s) at the same time'. In this case surely ταῦθ' should be accepted ?—unless indeed we take it ‘but—if one thing, namely this occurs . . .’, which would be even worse.

Several likely emendations have been proposed ; e.g. F. W. Schmidt’s ἀλλ’ εἰ μὲν ἡμῖν ταῦθ’, or Wecklein’s ἀλλ’ εἰ μὲν ἔσθ’ ᾗ ταῦθ’, i.e. if there is a possibility of these things happening together, or Paley’s ἀλλ’ εἰ μὲν εἰς ἓν ταῦθ’ (less well—for εἰς ἓν = ὁμοῦ).

1000–1. The futures of the MSS. are parallel to τοῦτο (or ταῦτα) γενήσεται in 999, and must fall within the protasis ; the apodosis does not begin till τὸ κινδύνευμα. But futures where we should expect explanatory infinitives are strange and Bothe proposed οἴσειν . . . ἄξειν. Alternatively there is much to be said for Weil’s ἄγαλμά τ’ εἰ σύ ; we do not need both οἴσεις and ἄξεις.

1002. τούτου = τοῦ ἐπὶ νεὼς ἄγεσθαι. The sentence is something of a truism. Weil proposed τούτω δὲ χωρισθέντ’(ε), accus. absolute = ‘these two things (i.e. acquisition of the statue and escape of Iph.) being inconsistent’. This gives good sense if the Greek can really mean this, which is doubtful.

1004–5. Kirchhoff’s first suggestion (see *app. crit.*) restores the grammar and gives good sense, though σ’ is rather far separated from σώσασαν which governs it. His second suggestion involves putting a comma at χρεών also and taking σῶσαι as governed by φεύγω. For φεύγω + infin. = to shrink from, cf. E. *HF.* 1072–4 τὸ φάος ἐκλιπεῖν . . . οὐ φεύγω, *Andr.* 56, 7 τοὔνομ’ οὐ φεύγω τόδε | καλεῖν σε, *Tr.* 891 ὁρᾶν δὲ τήνδε φεῦγε. With our text φεύγω may be taken as absolute = I do not shrink (cf. S. *Ant.* 580 φεύγουσι γάρ τοι χοἱ θρασεῖς), or as governing θανεῖν understood.

οὐ γὰρ ἀλλ’ = ‘for ⟨I need⟩ not ⟨trouble about my death⟩ ; no (ἀλλά), a man . . .’

θανών has sometimes been taken as a gloss on φροῦδος, but cf. E. *fr.* 736. 6 ὅταν τις ἐκ δόμων ἀνὴρ θάνῃ.

For the sentiment cf. E. *IA.* 1394 εἷς γ’ ἀνὴρ κρείσσων γυναικῶν μυρίων ὁρᾶν φάος.

1008. Cf. E. *Or.* 1039 ἅλις τὸ μητρὸς αἷμ’ ἔχω· σὲ δ’ οὐ κτενῶ.

κοινόφρων σοι = no more than κοινῇ σύν σοι ; cf. E. *Ion* 577 στεῖχε κοινόφρων πατρί.

1009. Musgrave’s ζῶν for ζῆν and Dunn’s θανεῖν λαχών are quite unnecessary. The slight variation in the construction is easy and natural.

1010–11. The MSS. reading (taking L P’s εἰ in 1011 ; see *app. crit.*) can only be translated by regarding οἶκον as = not Argos but Ἅιδης, the last ‘home’, and ἐνταυθοῖ as referring proleptically to it. ‘And indeed I shall be coming “home” ⟨even⟩ if I come there by violence (lit. “fall thither”), if I stay here with you in death.’ This has a definite meaning and is not tautological ; but the double protasis is awkward and ἐνταυθοῖ πέσω next to impossible. Taking οἶκον = Argos we at once have a tautology with the preceding sentence. For this reason, if for no other, the lines were rejected—probably rightly—by Dindorf and others. If, with this, the natural, interpretation of *οἶκον* and the reading *ἤ* in 1011, *ἐνταυθοῖ* is kept, we must accept Hermann's *περῶ* (as our text does) and Canter's *ἄξω . . . σ'*. Apart from the tautology mentioned above this gives good sense. But *ἐνταυθοῖ*, though used several times by Aristophanes and therefore presumably Attic—Elmsley said it was not—is nowhere else used in tragedy, and is, as Prof. Murray suggests, suspect. It is better, therefore, to alter not *πέσω* but *ἐνταυθοῖ*; e.g. Weil's *ἤνπερ . . . ἔνθεν ἐκπέσω* = 'if I escape hence' (cf. A. *Eu.* 147 *ἐξ ἀρκύων πέπτωκεν . . . ὁ θήρ*). But all these three lines of interpretation involve a common difficulty, viz. the *καί* in *καὐτός* which has no point at all. Much better, therefore, is Markland's *μαὐτός* (= *μὴ αὐτός*), with the easy change of K to M. Adopting this, and taking *ἐνταυθοῖ πέσω* = die here, Hermann made no further change, and it is true that with *ἤξω* we can understand *μετά σου* from the *ἤ* clause. 'No (*δέ*); I will come home ⟨with you⟩, if I do not die here, or. . .' But even if *ἐνταυθοῖ* is correct as a form it cannot (*pace* Hermann) mean 'here'. We should therefore accept in its place something like Goram's *ἐν Ταύροις* or possibly *ἐν ταύτῃ* or *ἔνθ' αὐτοῦ* (cf. *Il.* 8.207 *αὐτοῦ . . . ἔνθα* and S. *OC.* 78 *ἐνθάδ' αὐτοῦ*). The best reading, then, if we keep the lines, is *ἄξω δέ σ'* (or possibly *ἤξω δέ γ'*—understanding ⟨*μετά σου*⟩) *ἤνπερ μαὐτὸς* (?) *ἐν ταύτῃ πέσω . . . ἤ σοῦ . . .* But the two lines may well have been put in by a scribe or an actor 'to augment the nobility of Orestes' (Page, *Actors' Interpolations*, p. 78).

1014. See *app. crit.* *ἐς* Π. does not, of course, violate the final cretic rule; on the other hand *κομίζειν* and other such verbs are often used by the tragedians with an acc. of the end to which. Kirchhoff first showed that there was here a lacuna. *ἐθέσπισε* cannot govern *εἰσιδεῖν* for Apollo had given no such order. Musgrave's *ἦγ' ἰδεῖν* (= *καὶ πῶς ἄν μ' ἦγεν ὥστ' ἰδεῖν*) is possible but unlikely. The contents of the lacuna must have consisted of further proofs that the gods were on the would-be fugitives' side in thus allowing Or. to reach Tauris and see Iph. once more. From the words *ἅπαντα συνθείς* we may imagine the lacuna to have been a considerable one. (See note on l. 993.)

1018. *τῇδε νοσεῖ* (Markland's excellent correction of the MSS.'s nonsensical *νόει*) = 'suffers from this'. Cf. E. *IA.* 965, 6 *εἰ πρὸς Ἴλιον | ἐν τῷδ' ἔκαμνε νόστος*, and *ib.* 1403 *τὸ τῆς τύχης δὲ καὶ τὸ τῆς θεοῦ νοσεῖ*. The stress falls on *λαβεῖν θ'*: *escape* may be comparatively simple; the real difficulty will be *escape with* the image.

1019. The MSS. *ἡ δὲ βούλησις*, kept in our text, is intolerably weak: 'the wish is here'. We may accept Markland's convincing emendation *ἥδε βούλευσις*: i.e. *τόδε ἐστὶν ἡ β.*, with the usual assimilation of gender in the subject (see note on l. 939): 'this is what we now have to discuss'.

1020. Markland's ἆρ' οὖν gives a smoother start to the stichomythia and may be right. Wecklein accepts it.

1021. **ἐπήλυδας** is the subject. **ξενοφονεῖν** here = 'to murder one's host'. The king is, according to Greek ideas, Iph.'s 'host' if not also Or.'s.

1023. Or. has said 'if the king's murder will save us it must be *dared*'. Iph. answers in effect 'yes, but it is not *decent*—though I recognize and admire the daring of your suggestion'. **οὐκ ἂν δυναίμην** = 'I couldn't do it'. For δύναμαι in a moral sense cf. S. *Ant.* 686 οὔτ' ἂν δυναίμην . . . λέγειν. Any change like Stadtmüller's σθένοιμεν or Wecklein's δύναιο is one for the worse.

1025–6. To render 1025 even intelligible we must accept Brodaeus' ἐκσωθεῖμεν (see *app. crit.*) and probably Dindorf's σκότον (the 2nd decl. form of this word being the one used in trag.). But σκότον λαβόντες = 'taking advantage of darkness' is odd. 1026 is frigid and the cynicism of κλεπτῶν (despite the κλοπαῖς of l. 1400) intolerable. Further, the couplet divides 1024 awkwardly from 1027. It should almost certainly be regarded as an actor's insertion and excised as such. So Markland and others.

1027. The **φύλακες** themselves can scarcely be called ἱεροί, though in Homer we find φυλάκων ἱερὸν τέλος (= band), *Il.* 10. 56 and ἱεροὺς πυλαωρούς, *ib.* 24. 681. We had better read Markland's ἱεροφύλακες [the word occurs in an inscription and is used by Dionysius Halic. (L & S)] or Dobree's ἱεροῦ φύλακες.

1030–1. These two lines have been before now suspected as an interpolation. Certainly 1032 would follow after 1029 more easily than it does after 1031.

Many emendations have been suggested for the MSS. ἀνίαις (= 'your troubles'), e.g. ἀτυχίαις (Kayser), ἄλαισι (Goram), σαῖσι μανίαις (Kirchhoff). The latter two, though both Weil and Wecklein accept μανίαις, are not only unnecessary but deleterious. Iph. proposes to turn to good account not Or.'s madness but his bloodguiltiness.

σοφίσμασιν is either an adverbial dat. = 'cunningly', or more probably it is in apposition to σαῖς ἀνίαις = 'as a trick'.

1032. For the thought Wecklein cites E. *Hipp.* 480, 1 ἦ τἄρ' ἂν ὀψέ γ' ἄνδρες ἐξεύροιεν ἄν, | εἰ μὴ γυναῖκες μηχανὰς εὑρήσομεν.

For this use of **γάρ** (= 'clearly') see Denniston, p. 75, 'your suggested σοφίσματα do not surprise me, for . . .'; or, if we excise 1030, 1, 'I am not surprised that you have an ἐξεύρημα, for . . .'

1035–7. i.e. λέξομεν ὡς οὐ θέμις ⟨ἐστὶ⟩ θύειν ⟨σε⟩ . . . οὐ καθαρὸν ὄντα. Reiske's σε for γε and χὡς for ὡς may be right.

τίν' αἰτίαν ἔχουσ'; may mean 'urging what excuse?' though ἔχειν is scarcely the verb we expect. I believe myself that Reiske's ἔχονθ' is what Eur. wrote = 'as open to what charge'. ἔχονθ' might well not be understood by a careless or stupid scribe, and so altered to the simple ἔχουσ'. If we adopt this, we *must* also take his σε for γε.

Such emendations as Weil's *τίν' αἰτίαν σχοῦσ'; ὡς ὑπ. τι δή* are no improvements on the MSS., while Markland's ... *σχοῦσ'; οὐχ ὑπ. τι γάρ* (= for I cannot imagine anything that would be a reasonable *αἰτία*) is even less likely.

τὸ δ' ὅσιον δώσω φόβῳ. Though kept by the far from conservative Wecklein this *φόβῳ* seems to me impossible. It is generally explained by taking *δώσω φόβῳ* = 'I will alarm' (lit. 'give to fright'; cf. E. *Ph.* 994 *δειλίᾳ δίδωσι* = 'gives to cowardice' and so 'makes cowardly') and *τὸ ὅσιον* = 'religious scruples' (cf. E. *Hipp.* 656 *τοὐμὸν ... εὐσεβές* = 'my holiness'). With this we must supply ⟨*τῶν Ταύρων*⟩. It has also been taken as = 'I will attribute ⟨my⟩ scruples to the fear ⟨of causing an *ἄγος*⟩'. This gives good sense, but it is scarcely justifiable as a translation of the Greek.

The simplest emendation is the Aldine ed.'s *φόνῳ* '⟨I shall say (*λέξομεν* understood from above) that⟩ I shall (= can) devote ⟨only⟩ what is pure to sacrifice'.

Other emendations are either not very satisfactory in sense like Tyrwhitt's *ὄντα σ', ἀνόσιον δὲ τῷ φόνῳ* or Musgrave's *ὄντα, τόδε σ' ὀνειδίσω, φόνῳ*, or else they depart too far from the MSS. like Mähly's *θύσω μόνον*.

1038. μᾶλλον = the more, i.e. the easier, for your suggested line of action. **ἁλίσκεται** is another present with fut. meaning (e.g. *φεύγω* in l. 1004).

1039. βουλήσομαι = '⟨I shall say⟩ I shall require ...' For this use of *βούλεσθαι* cf. E. *Med.* 259 *τοσοῦτον οὖν σου τυγχάνειν βουλήσομαι*.

1040. Or. means '*that* will not help us to get the statue; for it will still be in the temple'. With **ἐν δόμοισι** we must understand *ἐστί* = *ἔσται*.

Many editors have altered **ἐφ' ᾧ πεπλ.** to e.g. *ἐφ' ὅπερ ἐπλεύσαμεν* (so Weil—though he prints the MSS. reading in his actual text), or *ἐφ' οὐκπεπλεύκαμεν* (= *ἐφ' ὃ ἐκπεπλ.*) (Herwerden), or *δόμοισιν ἐφ' ὃ πεπλεύκαμεν βρέτας* (Wecklein). It is true that it is good Greek to say *πέπλευκα ἐπί τι* = 'I have sailed to get something', but it is also good Greek to say *πέπλευκα ἐπί τινι* = 'I have sailed with the idea (or intention) of getting something'.

1041. ἐρῶ νίψαι must mean 'I will say I have washed it', and to make it stand for *ἐρῶ βούλεσθαι νίψαι* is awkward. Madvig's *νίψειν* is better. But I believe, with F. W. Schmidt, that *ἐρῶ* is a gloss (e.g. *ἐρῶ ὅτι βουλήσομαι ἁγνίσαι καὶ νίψαι*) which has got into the text and ousted some such word as *χερί*. If we accept this, the comma after *ὡς* must be deleted.

1042. ποῖ, the usual pregnant construction 'whither will you take it to wash it?' Cf. S. *Ph.* 1211 *ποῖ γᾶς*; after *πατέρα ματεύων*.

πόντου, κτλ., 'do you mean the spray-swept (lit. wet) inlet of the sea?' But *πόντου* in this emphatic position after the *πόντου* of 1039 is awkward. Iph. has already said she means the sea. Also ἔκβολον = creek (= outbreak of sea into the land) is without parallel and in any case unlikely. Eustathius' remark (1405. 49 = 40. 44) that Eur. uses the word as = ὀξὺ ἀκρωτήριον, even if it applies here, does not help without our having recourse to emendation, for one does not wash an image or anything else on a promontory. If we are to pin our faith to Eustathius we must accept some correction of εἶπας like ἦ παρ' ('at the foot of the sea-cliff?'). Weil suggests τόνδε (he thinks πόντου has got in from 1039) νοτερὸν ἦ παρ' ἔκβολον; Wecklein, more boldly, ποῦ δῆτα πόντου νίπτρον; ἦ παρ' ἔκβολον; 'where in the sea (cf. ποῦ γῆς) is this washing place? Near the promontory?'

Discarding Eustathius' statement (at least as applying to this line) we must emend ἔκβολον to e.g. ἔμβολον and read something like Tournier's ποῦ δῆτα; πόντου νοτερὸν ἧπερ ἔμβολον; though πόντου ἔμβολον = 'a tongue of the sea' is very doubtful.

For εἶπας = 'do you mean' cf. E. *Alc.* 520 πότερα θανούσης εἶπας ἢ ζώσης ἔτι; and *Supp.* 602 διὰ δορὸς εἶπας, ἢ λόγων ξυναλλαγαῖς;

1043. 'Yes, where ...' without γε. Cf. l. 75 note.

1046. ἡμῖν: ethic dat. φόνου may be right, 'what part will he be supposed to have taken in the murder?' Many alternatives have been suggested: e.g. πόνου, δόλου, τόπου; but by far the best is Winckelmann's χοροῦ, as we might say 'what part in the game will he be supposed to have played?' Cf. Pl. *Euth.* 279 B τὴν δὲ σοφίαν ποῦ χοροῦ τάξομεν; cf. E. *El.* 668 where Wecklein suggests a similar χοροῦ for the MSS. φόνου.

1047. λέξεται used as a passive. ἔχων: there is no need to take Kirchhoff's ἔχειν. Verbs of speaking are often used with participles in the sense of to speak of a person as being or doing something; e.g. A. *Ch.* 682 τεθνεῶτ' Ὀρέστην εἰπέ, S. *OC.* 1580 λέξας Οἰδίπουν ὀλωλότα, E. *El.* 687 μηδέ με ζῶσαν λέγε, *Hel.* 537 νιν εἶπε σεσωσμένον.

1048. ἄνακτος has a double constr.: (1) after λάθρα (cf. S. *OT.* 787, 8 λάθρα δὲ μητρὸς καὶ πατρὸς πορεύσομαι | Πυθῶδε), (2) as subject of the gen. absol. ἄνακτος εἰδότος.

1049. The Aldine ed. has σε for γε whence Canter conjectured σφε. This is unmetrical. We might read οὔ σφε γὰρ λάθοιμί γ' ἄν. Blomfield νιν for γε.

1051 sqq. These few lines have been variously attributed by some editors, while others (e.g. Weil) have supposed a lacuna after 1051, giving 1052 to Iph. and 1053–5 to Or.

There seems to me no need to tamper with the MSS. attributions, or to suspect the text. Or. says (1050) 'my ship is ready'. Iph. answers 'yes, indeed (δή), the rest (i.e. everything that has to be done after I have got you and the image on board) *you* must look after'. Or. then remarks 'there is one thing we must do: secure the silence of the chorus (τάσδε)'. He then turns to Iph. and asks her to see to this. For such a fear of betrayal by the chorus cf. E. *Or.* 1103, 4 Πυ. σίγα νυν· ὡς γυναιξὶ πιστεύω βραχύ. Ορ. μηδὲν τρέσῃς τάσδ'· ὡς πάρεισ' ἡμῖν φίλαι.

1055. Keeping the words of the MSS. we must punctuate as in our text (Verrall), for τὰ ἄλλα συμβαίη cannot stand for τὰ ἄλλα ἂν συμβαίη. Markland's ἴσως ἂν πάντα is grammatical, but the sense is feeble. Some editors (e.g. Monk) cut the line out altogether.

1057–8. τἄμ' . . . ἔστιν = ἐγώ εἰμι; the infins. are epexegetic. Editors compare Pl. *Prot.* 313 A ἐν ᾧ πάντ' ἐστὶ τὰ σὰ ἢ εὖ ἢ κακῶς πράττειν where ἐστὶ τὰ σά = εἶ σύ.

The **καί** in 1058 joins the two halves of the second alternative: μηδὲν εἶναι καὶ στερηθῆναι. It does not so much mean 'and' as 'i.e.': cf. l. 1376.

The **καί** of 1057 is suspicious. Köchly reads **ὡς**, which gives much better sense. Note the MSS. ὡς in 1056.

1059. An alternative emendation (see *app. crit.*) is Markland's φίλης τ' ἀδελφῆς φιλτάτου. Paley rejected the whole line.

1061. Cf. E. *Hel.* 329 γυναῖκα γὰρ δὴ συμπονεῖν γυναικὶ χρή.

1064. For the not uncommon and very idiomatic constr. καλόν . . . ὅτῳ see l. 606 and note.

The πίστις of the MSS. was no doubt originally a gloss. Schöne read ὅταν πιστὶς παρῇ (sc. αὐτῇ).

1066. γῆς πατρῴας νόστον; cf. *Od.* 5. 344, 5 νόστου | γαίης Φαιήκων, and E. *Cyc.* 108 πορθμὸν . . . πατρῴας χθονός, and l. 1112 below. The acc. νόστον of our text (= MSS.) is next door to impossible; see *app. crit.* Heath's νόστος should be accepted though not necessarily his μένει. νόστος and θανεῖν are the two alternative aspects of the τύχη.

1069. There seems no reason to suspect σὲ καὶ σέ. Reiske's σεμνῆς and Elmsley's ἱκέτις are utterly unnecessary. The motive underlying their suggestions, as is apparent from the note of Wecklein (who accepts ἱκέτις), is the desire to have Iph. address only the coryphaeus. But (1) πρός σε δεξιᾶς . . . ἱκνοῦμαι, σὲ δὲ . . . παρῃίδος . . . cannot really stand for ἱκνοῦμαί σε πρὸς δεξιᾶς καὶ παρῃίδος. Moreover, τί φατέ; τίς ὑμῶν (1072) makes it clear that she has appealed to more than one person. (2) Why should Iph. *not* address individual members of the chorus? As England remarks 'these customary formulas of entreaty do not necessarily imply that Iph. goes down into the orchestra to touch the limbs, etc., mentioned'. Hermann further points out that, taking **σε** of 1068 as addressed to the coryphaeus, we can suppose the three σέ's of 1069 addressed to the three front-rank members of the chorus arranged κατὰ ζυγά.

1070. Wecklein's suggested γονέων going with **τῶν . . . φιλτάτων** (for γονάτων which goes closely with παρῃίδος) is not unlikely, especially in view of the τε καί. With the reading of our text the punctuation should be παρῃίδος γονάτων τε.

1071. ὅτῳ for ἥτινι is perhaps defensible as having a general reference; cf. S. *El.* 770, 1 οὐδὲ γὰρ κακῶς | πάσχοντι (= πασχούσῃ) μῖσος ὧν τέκῃ προσγίγνεται. Cf. above l. 926 (note).

Monk's εἴ τῳ is certainly more idiomatic. But most editors reject the line, pointing out that the chorus is composed of virgins (l. 130 πόδα παρθένιον). A 'silly-clever' scribe might well compose the line in explanation of τῶν ἐν δ. φιλτάτων.

1072-3. There is little to choose between accepting Musgrave's θέλειν (see *app. crit.*) and explaining as = τίς φησὶ θέλειν ταῦτα ἢ τίς φησιν οὐ θέλειν; and keeping the MSS. θέλει, taking the sentences as = τίς φησίν ('who agrees?'), ἢ τίς οὐ θέλει ταῦτα; In either case φθέγξασθε is parenthetic. Nauck put a mark of interrogation after θέλει and read δῆτα for ταῦτα.

αἰνουσῶν ⟨ὑμῶν⟩.

1075. μόνον is often so used with imperatives; see L & S[9] under μόνος B. II.

1078. ὄναισθε μύθων = 'bless you for those words!'; cf. S. *OC.* 1042, 3 ὄναιο, Θησεῦ, τοῦ τε γενναίου χάριν | καὶ τῆς πρὸς ἡμᾶς ἐνδίκου προμηθίας, and E. *IA.* 1359 ὄναιο τῶν φρενῶν. So εὐδαιμονοίης (without any genitive) = 'thank you' (E. *Ph.* 1086).

1079. Addressed to Or. and Pyl. who now enter the temple (δόμους) leaving Iph. alone on the stage.

1081. Markland's ἐλέγξων should probably be accepted.

1082. Paley's εἴπερ (= if, as is the case) for ἥπερ is attractive.

1083. The double epithet is suspicious; still more the nature of the second. πατροκτόνος = parricidal; here it has to mean 'of a murderous father'. A. *Pr.* 860, 1 Πελασγία δὲ δέξεται θηλυκτόνῳ | Ἄρει (cited by Wecklein), lit. 'with hostility slaying by woman's hand'), is not really parallel.

Herwerden's τεκνοκτόνου would do—supposing that πατρο- (from πατρός, a gloss on τεκν. χερός) had usurped the place of τεκνο-; or Weil's παιδοκτόνου, though he should have printed it *after* χερός and not saddled Eur. with a spondee in the fourth foot of an iambic line. But better than either is Bothe's suggestion ἐκ χερὸς πατρόκτονον ('father-slaughtered'), which has the additional advantage of removing one of the two epithets. It is unlikely that Eur. intended δεινῆς to be taken with Αὐλίδος.

1088. ἔχειν = 'inhabit'; cf. A. *Eu.* 24 Βρόμιος ἔχει τὸν χῶρον (L & S under ἔχω (A 3), 'esp. of tutelary gods and heroes'). There is no need to accept Nauck's πόλλ' for πόλιν.

1089–1151. Second Stasimon.

First strophe: as Alcyone laments the loss of Ceyx, so we lament the loss of Delos.

1090. ἀλκυών: the mythical bird identified with the kingfisher. It is first mentioned by Homer (*Il.* 9. 563 ἀλκυόνος πολυπενθέος οἶτον ἔχουσα, of Cleopatra). For her story cf. Luc. *Halc.* 1 φασὶ γυναῖκά ποτε οὖσαν Αἰόλου τοῦ Ἕλληνος θυγατέρα κουρίδιον ἄνδρα τὸν αὐτῆς τεθνεῶτα θρηνεῖν πόθῳ φιλίας, Κήϋκα τὸν Τραχίνιον τὸν

Ἑωσφόρου . . . υἱόν; cf. further Apollod. 1. 7. 4 and Ov. *Met.* 9. 270 sqq.

1091. If the MSS. οἶτον is right we must take it = 'singest thy fate as a dirge': cf. A. *Ag.* 1191, 2 ὑμνοῦσι δ' ὕμνον . . πρώταρχον ἄτην; S. *Tr.* 49–51 πολλὰ μέν σ' ἐγὼ | κατεῖδον ἤδη πανδάκρυτ' ὀδύρματα | τὴν Ἡράκλειον ἔξοδον γοωμένην. But many edd. accept Barnes' οἰκτρόν.

1092. ξυνετοῖσι (*l*) fits the antistr. better.

1093. We must understand out of ξυνετοῖς ⟨συνιᾶσι γάρ⟩.

The bird's cry "κῆϋξ" was, in the ears of the ξυνετοί, a cry for her dead husband Κῆϋξ.

1094. σοι; the usual compendiary comparison for τοῖς σοῖς.

1096–7. There is nothing suspicious in the words. ἀγόρους (= πανηγύρεις) constantly occurs in Eur.'s lyrics. Artemis λοχία may reasonably be addressed by a chorus of virgins desirous of a return to their homes and of marriage; Nauck's ὀλβίαν, as far as the meaning of the passage is concerned, is quite unnecessary; though with it we should get exact corresponsion with l. 1114.

That the metre does not exactly correspond to that of 1113, 4 need not surprise us, and Weil's early suggestion Ἑλλάνων ἀγόρους ποθοῦσ' | Ἄρτεμιν λοχίαν ποθοῦσ', which would regularize the metre and give almost exact corresponsion, was subsequently abandoned by him. See metrical scheme.

1098 sqq. The chorus here refer to the circumstances of the birth of Artemis (and Apollo) in the island of Delos. The palm and laurel were given by Zeus to support and shelter their mother Leto; cf. E. *Hec.* 458–61 ἔνθα πρωτόγονός τε φοῖνιξ δάφνα θ' ἱεροὺς ἀνέσχε πτόρθους Λατοῖ φίλᾳ ὠδῖνος ἄγαλμα Δίας, and *Ion* 919–22 μισεῖ σ' ἁ Δᾶλος καὶ δάφνας ἔρνεα φοίνικα παρ' ἁβροκόμαν, ἔνθα λοχεύματα σέμν' ἐλοχεύσατο Λατὼ Δίοισί σε καρποῖς. The birth occurred at the foot of Mt. Cynthus, by a circular lake: cf. Theognis 5–7 Φοῖβε ἄναξ, ὅτε μέν σε θεὰ τέκε πότνια Λητώ, | φοίνικος ῥαδινῆς χερσὶν ἐφαψαμένη, . . . ἐπὶ τροχοειδέϊ λίμνῃ.

For the swan which sang on that occasion cf. E. *Ion* 161 sqq. The addition to the story of the Attic olive is doubtless due to some Athenian poet (cf. Call. *Del.* 262 χρύσειον δ' ἐκόμησε γενέθλιον ἔρνος ἐλαίης).

It is not to be supposed that all the women of the chorus come from Delos. They are Greeks, doubtless from different cities, who wish they were back in Greece celebrating the Greek, not the Tauric, Artemis: see Introduction p. xvi.

1099. Musgrave's φοίνικ' ἀμφ' for MSS. φοίνικά θ' (a slight change) would not only secure exact corresponsion with 1116 but also ease the construction. As it is, φοίνικα, δάφναν, θαλλόν, λίμναν are all governed (as well as K. ὄχθον) by παρά.

1102. If the MSS. reading (as in our text) is correct, ὠδῖνα is in apposition to the before-mentioned trees—a very harsh construction. We should almost certainly accept Portus' ὠδῖνι and possibly Musgrave's φίλον; though this latter (referring to θαλλόν) is not so necessary, as φίλαν could apply κατὰ σύνεσιν to θαλλὸν ἐλαίας—and indeed a reference is needed to *all* the trees (? φίλας, an alternative suggestion of Markland's). Λ. ὠδῖνι φίλον = Λατοῖ ὠδινούσῃ φίλον; 'dear to L. in travail'.

1103. εἱλίσσουσαν, lit. 'causing to circulate' (cf. l. 7 above). Eur. supposes that in this circular lake (ἡ τροχοειδής, Hdt. 2. 170; cf. Call. *Ap.* 59 περιηγέος ἐγγύθι λίμνης, and *Del.* 261 τροχόεσσα . . . λίμνῃ) the waters flow round like the stream of Oceanus. κύκλιον (note Seidler's certain emendation) is best taken predicatively or adverbially; cf. E. *IA.* 1055–7 εἱλισσόμεναι κύκλια | πεντήκοντα κόραι γάμους | Νηρέως ἐχόρευσαν.

1106. Weil's λίβες would improve the metre if exact corresponsion is desiderated; though it is true that only λίβα and λιβός are found.

1109. Here a choriambic dimeter corresponds with a glyconic (1092), as at 1096 (= 1113) and 1097 (= 1114). See metrical scheme.

Erfurdt's ὀλλυμένων (bad *present* participle; better *l*'s οὐλομένων) and Elmsley's ἐπί would secure exact responsion. ἔβαν in the sense of 'I was brought', whence the instrumental datives of the next line.

πύργων ὀλλυμένων may be taken either as a gen. absolute or gen. of place whence. If οὐλομένων be read it must be taken as adjectival (= 'from ruined walls'), as this epic form does not seem to be used by the tragedians to form part of a genitive absolute. For οὐλόμενος = 'ruined', rather than the usual 'accursed', cf. *Od.* 18. 273 οὐλομένης ἐμέθεν and E. *IA.* 792 πατρίδος οὐλομένας (so LP: the O.C.T. accepts there Erfurdt's ὀλλυμένας).

1110. I should prefer to put a comma at the end of this line (as Grégoire does), making ἔβαν and ἦλθον parallel verbs in the ἁνίκα clause.

1112. νόστος can mean 'voyage' (cf. E. *IA.* 966, *ib.* 1261, and *Rh.* 427) just as νοστεῖν can mean simply 'to journey' (cf. E. *Hel.* 428, *ib.* 474). νόστον βάρβαρον = νόστον γῆς βαρβάρου; so we get a parallel to γῆς πατρῴας νόστον of l. 1066. Bothe's νᾶσον (is Tauris an island?), Bergk's ναόν (he also read ζάχρυσον), and Kayser's ἐς γᾶν together with various other suggestions are needless.

1115. λατρεύω usually takes the dat.; here (as also at E. *El.* 131 if the MSS. are right) the acc. on the analogy of θεραπεύω, etc.; cf. K.-G. II. i. 293.

For παῖδ' Ἀγαμεμνονίαν cf. τῆς Τυνδαρείας θυγατρός of l. 5 above.

1116. With μηλοθύτας in the MSS. any emendation but Musgrave's τ' οὐ for MSS. τούς is not worth considering, though many have been suggested. Cf. E. *Ph.* 632 θεῶν . . . δεξίμηλ' ἀγάλματα.

1117. 'Those who have always been unfortunate are more fortunate than those who, fortunate at first (like us) have fallen into misfortune'. Eur. was fond of this commonplace: cf. *HF.* 1291–3 κεκλημένῳ δὲ φωτὶ μακαρίῳ ποτὲ | αἱ μεταβολαὶ λυπηρόν· ᾧ δ' ἀεὶ κακῶς | ἔστ', οὐδὲν ἀλγεῖ συγγενῶς δύστηνος ὤν, and *fr.* 285. 15–17 ὁ δ' οὐδὲν οὐδείς, διὰ τέλους δὲ δυστυχῶν | τοσῷδε νικᾷ· τοῦ γὰρ εὖ τητώμενος | οὐκ οἶδεν ἀεὶ δυστυχῶν κακῶς τ' ἔχων, etc. etc.

ἄταν; 'envying misery which is unfortunate all through' is odd, for what else but δυσδαίμων could ἄτη be? Many emendations have been put forward, not a few in violation of the metre; perhaps the best are Köchly's αἶσαν, Tournier's οἶτον and Nauck's αἰῶ—a scribe's ignorance of this short form of αἰῶνα (cf. A. *Ch.* 350) might well cause corruption.

Kirchhoff would make a fresh sentence begin here by reading ζηλῶ δέ; a view for which there is something to be said.

Wecklein desiderating a personal object to ζηλοῦσα takes Greverus' ζηλοῦσα τὸν διὰ π. δ., 'envying the continuously unfortunate man'. Bothe's τάν ('unfortunate *woman*') would keep the actual letters of the MSS.

1119. κάμνεις; the 'ideal' second person is here very clumsy The poet Milton emended to κάμνει and he was almost certainly right. Some of the recent MSS. support him. If Wecklein's τόν (see note on 1117) is right the subject of κάμνει is provided. If the object of ζηλοῦσα is an abstract substantive then the subject of κάμνει must be understood out of this: 'envying the life ⟨of a man⟩ unfortunate throughout; for he ...'

Note that κάμνεις may have arisen from dittography of σ.

1120. It is perhaps a pity that our text (= the MSS.) does not obelize this line, for, as it stands, it is hopeless.

Prinz and Wecklein give 27 proposed emendations most of which are, to my mind, ruled out of court because they retain and try to correct (almost always *contra metrum*) the impossible μεταβάλλει which is palpably a gloss on 1121. *Ex hypothesi* there is *no* change in the case of the character referred to. Of all emendations which treat μεταβάλλει as a corruption, not a gloss, only Nauck's ὃν βάλλει respects the metre and, to a certain extent, the sense. Note further that 'you (or 'he') whom misfortune strikes' helps the subjectless κάμνεις (or κάμνει). Those which consider it a gloss read δυσδαιμονίᾳ (going with σύντροφος ὤν—which is eased by having a dat. of its own instead of having to supply ⟨αὐταῖς⟩ out of ἀνάγκαις), preceded by some conjectured trisyllabic epithet. Of these may be mentioned Herwerden's ⟨θυμαλγεῖ⟩ or Mekler's ⟨ἀσφαλεῖ⟩, and, in another category, Badham's ⟨τᾷ πάλαι⟩ or Wecklein's (better) ⟨ἐξ ἀρχᾶς⟩. Bergk's μεταβάλλειν δυσδαιμονία (= presumably 'change is ⟨the *real*⟩ misfortune') is difficult in itself and ruins ll. 1121, 2 by anticipation, even if we take the δέ of 1121 as = γάρ.

1121. Provided of course that we take εὐτυχίας as acc. plur., Scaliger's εὐτυχίαν is unnecessary. The plur. occurs at Ar. *Ec.* 573.

For the construction—which looks like a confusion of βαρύ

ἐστιν and ὅταν κακῶταί τις . . . βαρὺς αἰών—see notes on ll. 606 and 1064.

1126. This line and the corresponding 1141 as they stand in the MSS. look like epitrites, the first resolved, the second syncopated (◡◡ ◡ — — | — · — —). These come so unnaturally into this system that we might well accept Hartung's and Fritzsche's transpositions and read οὐρείου Πανὸς κάλαμος and ἐν νώτοις ἁμοῖς πτέρυγας.

1127. Pan was to accompany the ship as κελευστής or rather τριηραύλης. κώπαις = κωπηλάταις = ἐρέταις.

Pan was now an Athenian deity with a grotto on the Acropolis (cf. Hdt. 6. 105, E. *Ion* 492 sqq.).

1128. It is the part of a μάντις to forecast the ship's course. So Calchas (*Il.* 1. 71, 2) νήεσσ' ἡγήσατ' Ἀχαιῶν Ἴλιον εἴσω | ἣν διὰ μαντοσύνην, τήν οἱ πόρε Φοῖβος Ἀπόλλων. **ἔχων κέλαδον λύρας** = ἔχων κελαδεινὴν λύραν.

1129. Markland transposed to ἑπτατόνου κέλαδον (cf. 1144). See note on 1126.

For **ἑπτατόνου** cf. E. *Alc.* 446 καθ' ἑπτάτονόν τ' ὀρείαν χέλυν.

1130. Weil suggests μελοποιῶν (Wecklein μελοτυπῶν), regarding ἀείδων as a gloss. This would secure exact corresponsion with 1145.

Paley's πέμψει for ἄξει is tempting.

λιπαράν, the stock but highly prized epithet of Athens ever since Pindar addressed that city (*fr.* 76) as Ὦ ταὶ λιπαραὶ καὶ ἰοστέφανοι καὶ ἀοίδιμοι, Ἑλλάδος ἔρεισμα, κλειναὶ Ἀθᾶναι. 'You have only,' says Dicaeopolis in the Acharnians (639 sqq.) 'to call their city λιπαρά (an epithet suitable for sardines) and you can get anything you like out of the Athenians'. (Cf. E. *Alc.* 452, *Tr.* 803.)

1132–3. These two lines should, but do not in the MSS., correspond with 1147, 8. Endless attempts have been made at securing exact responsion. Either the strophe at this point or the antistrophe must be altered (see *app. crit.*). Our text follows what is certainly the simpler method, that of correcting the antistrophe. But though both pairs now correspond exactly, and yield fair sense, the metre is very strange. We might possibly regularize it by reading in l. 1132 ⟨προ⟩λιποῦσα (Hermann) and transposing to ἐς χαρίτων ἁμίλλας. (It will be noticed that the O.C.T. reading is itself a transposition.) If we do this we get in the strophe a pherecratean (◡◡ — — ◡ ◡ — ◡) and in the antistr. a syncopated choriambic dimeter (— ◡ ◡ — | ◡ — · —). These might well correspond as the pherecratean is in effect a syncopated chor. dim. of which the syncopated chor. has, as it were, got round the unsyncopated one; i.e. — — (— ◡ ◡ —) · —. Cf. the correspondence of chor. dim. with glyconic, e.g. 1096 = 1113; and at E. *El.* 168 we find a syncop. chor. dim. corresponding with a pherecrat. (192).

Weil suggests πλαταν (Wecklein πλάτας (gen. sing.)) on the

ground that the tragedians always use ῥόθιος as a neut. substantive and not as an adj. at all. (Cf. l. 407.)

1134–6. Out of the darkness of these three lines a few clarities emerge: (1) ἀέρι (an awkward causal dat.) may have been a grammatical *marginale* explaining the verb; (2) ἱστία must be retained, for the sails are the only part of a ship which are 'spread out'—τείνειν πόδα doubtless means to haul in the sheet, but ἐκπεταννύναι πόδα cannot (*pace* L & S) mean slack the sheet so as to spread the sail; (3) the nominative πρότονοι is nonsense, because the forestays (whose job it is to hold the mast up against the wind-pressure on the sail of the moving ship) cannot spread anything; (4) κατὰ πρῷραν = 'out over the bows' might be a gloss on ὑπὲρ στόλον = 'beyond the prow'. Comparing E. *Hec.* 111, 2 we know, further, that when the sails of a Greek boat are filled with wind they are pressed against the forestays (ἔσχε σχεδίας λαίφη προτόνοις ἐπερειδομένας—which does *not* mean 'he stayed the ships with their sails already hoisted by means of the forestays' (sails are not so hoisted), but 'pressing their sails against the forestays'). Wecklein accordingly reads ἀέρι δ' ἱστί' ⟨ἐρειδόμεν' ἐς⟩ πρότονον . . . πόδες, i.e. 'the sheets (there was one at each corner of the square Greek sail) cause the sail, pressed by the wind against the forestay, to swell out over . . .' This gives excellent sense but it considerably lengthens the passage and so makes necessary an otherwise unnecessary lengthening of the corresponding passage in the antistrophe. While hesitating to add to a heap of what can but be *ad hoc* emendations, I would propose ἱστία δ' ἐς πρότονον (or προτόνους) . . . πόδες, 'the sheets (i.e. being loose) spread the sails against the forestays over (i.e. so as to belly out over) the bows beyond the prow'. Alternatively we might modify Wecklein's suggestion and read ἀέρι δ' ἱστί' ⟨ἐρειδόμεν' ἐς⟩ πρότον-|ον [κατὰ πρῷραν] πόδ'(ε) ὑπὲρ στόλον ἐκπετάσουσ-|ι νεὸς (Weil) ὠκ. 'the two sheets cause the sails pressed by the wind against the forestay to belly out over the bows of the swift-moving ship'. (This would make 1136 correspond exactly with 1151 as it stands. But ἀήρ = wind is suspicious.)

1137 sqq. The chorus express the wish that they could follow the ship, traversing the heavens like the sun, and arrive at their native city, there to take part in the dances as of old.

λαμπρὸν ἱππόδρομον (see *app. crit.*) gives exact corresponsion with 1123 and might just as well be accepted, as indeed it is by most modern editors.

1141. Cf. note on 1126.

1142. **λήξαιμι θοάζουσα** seems to mean 'may I cease-to-move-fast my wings on my back', i.e. 'may I fold my wings on my back'—as a bird does preparatory to alighting. θοάζειν is here trans. as at E. *Ba.* 65 (πόνον θοάζω) and *Or.* 335 (θοάζων σε). This is quite normal, and few have taken exception to it except Hartung whose θοαζούσας is not likely to win general acceptance.

1143. There is little to choose between the MSS. δὲ σταίην (2nd aor. optat.) and Bruhn's δ' ἑσταίην (perf. optat.); 'may I stand in the dances' (an odd dat.; ? read ἐνσταίην, cf. E. *Supp.* 896). *Not*, as some edd., χοροὺς ἱσταίην which would mean 'may I organize dances'.

1144. If **παρθένος** is right (the strophe at this point, if not corrected, has a tribrach, not a dactyl) we must understand ⟨ἕστην⟩, taking εὐδ. γάμων as descriptive gen. with χοροῖς. Weil's παρθ. εὐδ. γαμ. 'a maiden destined for a noble marriage' is impossible. The construction would be ὅθι καὶ παρθένος ⟨ἕστην καὶ⟩ . . . ἐσκίαζον.

But either Badham's πάρεδρος or Nauck's πάροχος (if πάροχος can mean a 'bridesmaid' as well as a 'best man') should possibly be read instead, in which case these words, and not χοροῖς, are qualified by the gen. εὐδ. γάμων. Paley's πάρος ἐν εὐδοκίμοις γάμοις ingeniously supposes a jumble of letters ΠΑΡΟΣΕΝ to ΠΑΡ-(Θ)ΕΝΟΣ; the construction would be ἑσταίην χοροῖς, ὅθι καὶ πάρος ⟨ἕστην⟩ ἐν εὐδ. γάμοις ⟨καὶ⟩ . . . ἐσκίαζον. Kirchhoff's πάροιθ' is a similar suggestion involving less alteration.

1145. *Not*, as e.g. Seidler and Wecklein 'twining the dances . . . close by my mother' (παρὰ πόδα ματρός). Even if the words could mean this, which is more than doubtful, ἑλίσσειν πόδα is too much of a verbal unity to bear separation: πόδ' ἑλ. . . . θιάσους = foot-dancing revels' (Badham's θιάσοις is unnecessary). παρά with ματρός, 'leaving my mother's side'.

1148. **χαίτας** (in spite of πλοκάμους in 1150) can scarcely be right. Comparing A. *Pr.* 466 ἄγαλμα τῆς ὑπερπλούτου χλιδῆς Markland conjectured χλιδᾶς. We might read χλιδᾶς ἁβροπλούτου (Dindorf: MSS. ἁβροπλούτοιο) ἔριν, supposing the last syllable of ἁβρο. to become short before the ε of ἔριν. With this or with the O.C.T. reading ἔριν is in apposition to ἁμίλλας. (W. Headlam in *CR.* 1902, p. 252, accepts χλιδᾶς. He suggests ἐς ἅμιλλαν χαρίτων | ἁβρο-πλούτοιο χλιδᾶς corresponding with ἐμὲ βήσῃ δὲ πλάταις | ῥοθίοις αὖθι λιποῦσ'. This involves too much rearrangement of words.)

1149. **ὀρνυμένα** (with εἰς ἁμίλλας) = 'setting out for', 'aiming at'. Not elsewhere in Eur., but Soph. uses the word even in senarians (e.g. *OC.* 1320) and there is no need to suspect it. (England ὀρμένα, which necessitates further changes *metri gratia.*)

1150–1. i.e. περιβ. γέννυσι φάρεα καὶ πλοκάμους ἐσκίαζον αὐτὰς αὐτοῖς: the reference is to the veil (φᾶρος) which went over the head and hung down by each cheek (γένυς). She uses veil and curls to shade her cheek.

These lines, too, have been much emended. The only simple but good suggestion is Markland's γένυας. It is just possible that a scribe, overwhelmed with accusatives, and not seeing that the first two went with **περιβ.**, the last with ἐσκίαζον, altered γένυας to γέννυσιν—possibly congratulating himself on having supplied a quite unnecessary dat. for περιβ.

Note that ἐσκίαζον is the only expressed verb of the ὅθι clause.

1153–1233. Fourth Epeisodion, in one scene: Iph. and Thoas.

Thoas appears, entering from the (spectators') right almost simultaneously with the exit from the temple of Iph. bearing the *ξόανον* (1156).

1154. Note Reiske's *ἤδη* for MSS. *ἡ δή*. Elmsley may be right in suggesting *ἆρα* though further from the MSS.; but Monk's objection to *ἤδη* as first word in a question cannot stand in face of A. *Ag.* 1209, *Eu.* 674, and S. *OC.* 385.

1155. λάμπεσθαι πυρί = to shine with fire, not to burn with fire. (The middle is rare, but Verrall's suspicions of it at E. *Med.* 1194 might have been set at rest—had he wanted them to be—by a reference to Ar. *Ra.* 293 (Ἔμπουσα) *πυρὶ γοῦν λάμπεται.*) Many emendations have been proposed, the most likely of which are perhaps Jacob's *δάπτονται* and Verrall's *ἀνάπτονται* (but this passive is not well attested). Rauchenstein would regard *ἤδη . . . πυρί*; as one sentence, reading *σώματ' ἐμπρῆσαι.* This makes good sense, but it is not easy to see how the corruption should have occurred.

1157. ἀκινήτων with a gerundival sense 'that must not be disturbed'. For the plur. *βάθρων* cf. note on l. 997.

1159. The scribe of P, perhaps in ignorance of the somewhat rare word *παραστάς*, has written the dat. of *παράστασις*, a word which does not mean 'vestibule'.

1161. ἀπέπτυσ': the exclamation is called forth not by Thoas' question but by Iph.'s (pretended) horror at the thought of the *μίασμα.* Instead of spitting to avert a sight or remark of evil omen one could *say* '*ἀπέπτυσα*'—the word for the deed. Cf. E. *Hipp.* 614, *Hec.* 1276. *γάρ* explains why she says it. Ὁσίᾳ, κτλ., i.e. I say (do) this for the sake of ceremonial purity, *ὁσία* being personified; cf. E. *Ba.* 370 Ὁσία, πότνα θεῶν.

For similar personifications (very common in Eur.) cf. Τύχη (E. *Hec.* 786), Τυραννίς (*Ph.* 506), Φιλοτιμία (*ib.* 532), Εὐλάβεια (*ib.* 782), Ἔρις (*ib.* 798), Λύπη (*Or.* 398, 9), Ἐλπίς (*IA.* 392), and the curious τῷ Δοκεῖν εὔχου μόνον of *Or.* 782.

1165. πάλιν in the Homeric sense (almost = *ὀπίσω*); turned round from its ⟨normal⟩ position.

A common portent; Wecklein quotes Plut. *Cam.* 6 *ἀποστροφάς τε καὶ καταμύσεις* (cf. l. 1167 below) *ξοάνων, ἃς ἱστορήκασιν οὐκ ὀλίγοι τῶν πρότερον.* For 'historical' instances see Caes. *B. C.* 3. 105. 3 and Tac. *Hist.* 1. 86.

1168. τό: the article is used with reference to the *οὐ καθαρά* of 1163. Dobree's *τι* is unnecessary.

1171. Cf. E. *Ion* 591 *δύο νόσω κεκτημένος*; *Hipp.* 414 *τόλμας . . . κεκτημένας.*

1174. Sc. ⟨*τόδε*⟩, which the MSS. unmetrically read, the word being doubtless a gloss. The object of *ἔτλη* can be easily understood, and it is certainly no improvement to deprive the verb of a subject by writing *τόδ'* for *τις* as Hermann did (cf. E. *Hel.* 97 *ἐπεὶ τίς σωφρόνων τλαίη τάδ' ἄν*). Dobree removed Ἄπολλον and proposed οὐδεὶς ἂν οὐδ' ἐν βαρβάροις ἔτλη τόδ' ἄν—which reads almost like a comment on his own treatment of the line. If any emendation be accepted it should be Weil's neat οὐδ' ἂν (= ἃ οὐδ' ἐν). Possibly Eur. wrote οὐδ' ἂν βάρβαρός γ' ἔτλη τόδ' ἄν.

1179. **ἤλεγχον, ὡς** . . . = 'I questioned them when . . .', or 'I looked into it since . . .'.

1180. ὡς gives, as England says, the reason for Thoas' use of σοφήν: 'clever to see so sharply'. In effect = ὅτι οὕτω; cf. Pl. *Cri.* 43 b πολλάκις . . . σε . . . εὐδαιμόνισα . . . ὡς ῥᾳδίως αὐτὴν (τὴν ξυμφορὰν) . . . φέρεις (K.-G. II. ii, p. 370).

1181. **φρενῶν**: *not* governed by καθεῖσαν as Weil takes it, i.e. let down into my mind, but with δέλεαρ = a bait for my mind; just as at E. *Andr.* 264 τοιόνδ' ἔχω σου δέλεαρ, σου δέλεαρ = a bait for you. καὶ μήν, 'progressive' (cf. Denniston, p. 352). Paley suggested καὶ [μὴν] ⟨συγ⟩καθεῖσαν—the συγ- meaning that with their answer about the φόνος they gave her this good news. For καθιέναι = to dangle (of bait) cf. Ar. *Vesp.* 174 οἵαν πρόφασιν καθῆκεν, to which Bdelycleon answers ἀλλ' οὐκ ἔσπασεν (catch) ταύτῃ γε.

1182. **τῶν Ἀργόθεν** = τῶν ἐν Ἄργει; cf. l. 540 and note; and add τὰς ἐκεῖθεν σημανῶν (l. 1410), and E. *Med.* 506 τοῖς . . . οἴκοθεν φίλοις. Thoas changes the metaphor from a *bait* to a *charm*. φίλτρον should be taken as in apposition to τι. F. W. Schmidt proposed τι φίλιον.

1186. **ἐξένευσας** from ἐκνεύω, not ἐκνέω. 'And you naturally inclined to the side of the goddess.' (Cf. E. *Ph.* 1268 ἐς θάνατον ἐκνεύοντε and l. 1330 below.)

1190. **ἐν ἔργῳ** = 'ready for action'.

1192. **ὑδάτων** = sweet)(salt) water. Usener's νασμῶν is unnecessary.

For the lustral use of sea-water cf. *Il.* I. 314 οἱ δ' ἀπελυμαίνοντο καὶ εἰς ἅλα λύματ' ἔβαλλον; A. *Pers.* 201, 2 χεροῖν καλλιρρόου | ἔψαυσα πηγῆς (Atossa, after her dream); S. *Aj.* 654–6 ἀλλ' εἶμι πρός τε λουτρὰ καὶ παρακτίους | λειμῶνας, ὡς ἂν λύμαθ' ἁγνίσας ἐμὰ | μῆνιν . . . ἐξαλύξωμαι θεᾶς; A. R. 4. 663 ἁλὸς νοτίδεσσι κάρη ἐπιφαιδρύνουσαν.

1195. An effective *double entente*: Iph. appears to refer to her functions as priestess; actually she refers to her projected escape.

1201. '⟨It has;⟩ for ⟨otherwise⟩ I should not have . . .'

1202. Note the rare fem. δίκαιος (cf. E. *Heracl.* 901 ὁδὸν . . . δίκαιον). The word here means 'right and proper'. ἡ = your.

1203. **οἶσθα . . . ἅ . . . γενέσθω**: cf. the common οἶσθ' ὃ δρᾶσον. In Greek an imperative can stand in a relative clause. Even in English we can say 'which do at your peril'; cf. note on l. 759.

1207. **κρᾶτα**, sc. τῶν ξένων.

πρόσθεν = 'before', 'as a protection for'. The pure rays of the sun were to be protected from the impurity of the ξένοι. Heracles, after the murder of his children, asks Theseus τί δῆτά μου κρᾶτ' ἀνεκάλυψας ἡλίῳ; (E. *HF.* 1231); so, too, Creon to

Oedipus (S. *OT.* 1425–7) τὴν . . . πάντα βόσκουσαν φλόγα | αἰδεῖσθ' ἄνακτος Ἡλίου, τοιόνδ' ἄγος | ἀκάλυπτον οὕτω δεικνύναι; and the chorus in E. *Or.* (819–21) οὐ καλόν . . . μελάνδετον . . . φόνῳ ξίφος ἐς αὐγὰς ἀελίοιο δεῖξαι.

1209. **πόλει** with σημανεῖ, not πέμψον. **τύχας** is certainly odd and many alternatives have been suggested: Elmsley's ποίους λόγους, Hermann's ταγάς (but ταγαί = 'commands' is otherwise unknown in tragedy), Rauchenstein's ποῖόν τι δρᾶν. Weil thinks that ειποιας may hide the word ἐντολάς and proposes καὶ πόλει τὸν σημανοῦντα πέμψον—ἐντολὰς τίνας; a most improbable theory.

1210. **συναντῴεν**: the optat. because the intention with which Thoas credits Iph. was already in her mind; cf. Ar. *Ra.* 23, 4 τοῦτον δ' ὀχῶ | ἵνα μὴ ταλαιπωροῖτο (K.-G. II. ii, p. 382). Elmsley wrongly altered to συναντῶσιν.

1211–14. I can see no reason for either transposition or excision in this passage. In 1214 Iph.'s answer is lost; it may have been εὖ λέγεις (Herwerden) or εἰκότως (Köchly, who rather unnecessarily continues Θο. ὡς κάρτα καὶ σέ, κτλ.). Nothing is to be gained from a general reshuffle of the lines or the rejection of στεῖχε . . . πελάζειν (Wecklein) on the ground that it is a variant of 1210. England excises both 1210 and 1214.

Markland put 1214 after 1202, giving it to Thoas. This spoils the stichomythia of that passage and creates an abrupt transition between 1213 and 1215.

1213. i.e. καὶ φίλων γε ⟨τούτους κηδεύω⟩ οὓς . . . She refers to Or. and Pyl., but Thoas takes the reference as being to himself.

The MSS. οὐδείς is hopeless. The scholarly Markland must for once have been nodding when he suggested that πελαζέτω was to be understood.

Badham's οὓς δεῖ may be called palmary (though he unwisely combined it with φιλῶ for φίλων).

1216. i.e. ὡς πάλιν μόλῃς ⟨εἰς αὐτὸ (sc. τὸ μέλαθρον) ἤδη⟩ καθαρὸν ⟨ὄν⟩. For such lustration (done by means of sulphur) cf. Odysseus' of his home after the killing of the suitors (*Od.* 22. 481 sqq.), and E. *Hel.* 865 sqq. Reiske's πυρσῷ for MSS. χρυσῷ may be considered certain, though other suggestions have been made: e.g. Hermann's κύκλῳ and Bergk's κρωσσῷ (water-pail).

1218. **παλαμναῖον**: here the neut. of the adj., sc. τι. It is used like φόνος at ll. 1177 and 1230 = stain of murder. Some edd. take it as masc. citing Xen. *Cyr.* 8. 7. 18. No doubt the adj. can be so used (= demon of pollution), but not with λαμβάνειν. W. Bauer, taking the word as masc., proposed βλέπω.

1219. **τοῦδε** = τοῦ χρονίζειν. **ὅρος** may have here the sense of *aim* or *object*: 'what am I to think (μοι) the object of *that* (τοῦ χρονίζειν) to be?'; or, more naturally, mean *limit*: 'what am I to take as the limit of that (τοῦ χρονίζειν)?'; or again it may signify *means of determining*. Either of the latter two would accord better with σχολή of the next line.

1220. If ἐπί is the reading of the MSS. (see *app. crit.*) we must take Schäfer's σχολῆς = at your leisure.

1223. κόσμους (Bothe κόσμον) though often suspected, is probably right. The trappings and adornments of the statue are referred to; cf. A. *Ag.* 1270, 1 ἐποπτεύσας δέ με | κἀν τοῖσδε κόσμοις καταγελωμένην μέγα. Wecklein's μόσχους is possible. If it be read then with θεᾶς it means the flocks and herds belonging to the goddess' temple. Kirchhoff's ὧν (taken with φόνῳ) for ὡς is very plausible.

1227. Iph. mentions particularly three types of visitor likely to approach the temple: (1) those who would devote themselves to temple service [πυλωρός I take as = ὡς πυλ., or ὡς πυλ. γενησόμενος. This is, I think, better than taking the reference to be to those who are already consecrate, as Weil does. The pres. tense ἁγνεύει is against this]; (2) those who come to offer sacrifice preliminary to marriage (προτέλεια: cf. E. *IA.* 718, where Clytemnestra asks Agamemnon προτέλεια δ' ἤδη παιδὸς ἔσφαξας θεᾷ;); (3) those who come to pray for safe delivery in child-birth.

Herwerden thought these three lines spurious as being inconsistent with the ἅπαντας of 1210—a very insufficient reason. Nauck's suspicions of 1227, 8 seem to me equally baseless.

1229. ἐξίστασθαι seems to be a technical term in ritual; cf. Ar. *Ra.* 354, 5 εὐφημεῖν χρὴ κἀξίστασθαι . . . ὅστις ἄπειρος τοιῶνδε λόγων.

1231. οὗ, 'where'. Another *double entente*: Iph. means 'in Athens', Thoas takes her as meaning 'at a suitable place on the sea-shore'. He also supposes the object of θύσωμεν to be τούσδε (understood from τῶνδε); Iph. uses the verb absolutely. So, too, with δόμον which Thoas understands as the former temple, now purified, whereas by it Iph. really means a temple in Greece unpolluted by human sacrifice.

1232. τἄλλα: cf. S. *El.* 657, 8 (Clytemnestra) τὰ δ' ἄλλα πάντα καὶ σιωπώσης ἐμοῦ | ἐπαξιῶ σε δαίμον' ὄντ' ἐξειδέναι.

1233. τὰ πλείονα: the Greek idiom; we should expect simply πλείονα, the meaning being πλείονα τῶν βροτῶν. Cf. E. *Hipp.* 471 τὰ πλείω χρηστὰ τῶν κακῶν ἔχεις, *fr.* 417 ζητῶν τὰ πλεῖον', εἶτα πάντ' ἀπώλεσεν, and *Med.* 609 τῶνδε . . . τὰ πλείονα (in spite of Verrall's note). Monk's τε for τά was singularly ill-advised.

[Soph. constantly uses a, to us, redundant article with πλείων; e.g. *Ant.* 313, *Tr.* 731, *Ph.* 576, *OC.* 36, *ib.* 796.]

1234–1282. Third Stasimon. A triumphant song to Apollo no doubt motived by Orestes' previous want of faith in that divinity. The strophe tells how Apollo slew the dragon, Pytho, and took over the shrine of Delphi; the antistrophe describes the successful defence of his acquisition against the dreams and visions which up to that time had been mankind's only form of prophesy.

1234. εὔπαις: here somewhat unusually of the child; not of the parent. Cf. E. *HF.* 689 Λατοῦς εὔπαιδα γόνον; *Or.* 964 Περσέφασσα καλλίπαις θεά; *Alc.* 906 μονόπαις (= only child), and *Ba.*

520 εὐπάρθενε Δίρκα (= Dirce, 'lovely maid'). For the commoner meaning cf. E. *Hec.* 810 εὔπαις ποτ' οὖσα, νῦν δὲ γραῦς ἄπαις.

The construction is εὔπαις ⟨ἐστίν⟩ . . .

1235. Δηλιάς: i.e. Leto—but it is awkward after the Λατοῦς of l. 1234, nor can the goddess well be called a Delian woman because she gave birth to Apollo and Artemis in Delos. Most edd. (rightly) accept Seidler's Δηλιάσιν [ἐν]. For this combination of feminine (in form) adj. with neut. substantive cf. E. *Hel.* 1301 δρομάδι κώλῳ, *Or.* 270 μανιάσιν λυσσήμασιν, *ib.* 837 δρομάσι βλεφάροις, *Ph.* 1024 φοιτάσι πτεροῖς, and in Latin Virg. *Aen.* 3. 54 victricia arma. The subject (Λατώ) is easily understood from Λατοῦς.

καρποφόροις is difficult, as Delos was notoriously barren. Some edd. accept Jacob's κουροτρόφοις (cf. Call. *Del.* 276 ⟨Delos⟩ 'Απόλλωνος κουροτρόφος). Weil reads καρποφόρος—an epithet proper to Demeter, and not (even metaphorically) suitable to Leto. Wilamowitz' καρποφόρει supplies a needed verb, but καρποφορεῖν = τίκτειν is elsewhere unknown.

1236. ἔτικτε. If the ⟨δ'⟩ of 1238 be read we need a main verb. Kirchhoff's ἔτικτε gives the sense; Mekler's ὤδινε would both give the required sense and correspond more exactly to 1261. Edd. who in 1238 read φέρεν take Markland's τεκοῦσα.

The MSS. φοῖβον is clearly a gloss, though if καρποφόρει be read in 1235 something like Φοῖβόν τε must be retained (before χρυσοκόμαν) for metrical reasons. But Φοῖβον is awkward after τόν.

1237. ἅ τ' = ⟨Ἄρτεμίν⟩ θ' ἅ. The reference to Artemis is unexpected since the whole ode deals with Apollo, and the conjunction of the understood substantive with the previous relative (τόν) is grammatically awkward, though parallels can be found; e.g. E. *Med.* 496, 7 ἧς σὺ πόλλ' ἐλαμβάνου καὶ τῶνδε γονάτων, and *ib.* 503 οὓς σοὶ προδοῦσα καὶ πάτραν. Most modern edd. accept Weil's simple ᾇ τ', i.e. σοφὸν ἐν κ. καὶ ἐν ἐκείνῃ ἐφ' ᾇ γάννυται εὐστοχίᾳ; cf. the words of the infant Apollo in *h. Ap.* 131 εἴη μοι κίθαρίς τε φίλη καὶ καμπύλα τόξα.

1239–44. Literally: 'And she his mother, leaving the famous birth-place, brought him from the sea-reef to the summit of Parnassus with the abundant torrents revelled over by Dionysus.' The νιν of the MSS. suggested to Kirchhoff the emendation φέρε ⟨δ' ἶνιν⟩ 'her son' (cf. E. *HF.* 354) which may be right. But any completion of the lacuna must be tentative, especially in view of the metrical uncertainty of the corresponding lines in the antistrophe. It may, however, be urged that Professor Murray's αὐτή is (1) redundant, and particularly so in a text which retains Δηλιάς and μάτηρ, and (2) not corresponsive with the end of l. 1263. Grégoire's ⟨δ' αὐτίκα⟩ would be better in both these respects.

δειράδος: 'ridge of a chain of hills' (L & S). The more usual word for Delos is χοιράς ('reef', 'hogsback'); cf. A. *Eu.* 9 Δηλίαν . . . χοιράδα, E. *Tr.* 89 Δήλιοι . . . χοιράδες.

μάτηρ is possible though redundant, and many edd. reject the nominative for the acc. (cf. *app. crit.*), taking *ματέρα* in apposition to *κορυφάν*; e.g. Weil's *ἀστάκτων ματέρ' ⟨εἰς⟩ ὑδάτων*. This gives an easier construction to the gen. *ὑδάτων*. Taking the reading of our text *ἀστ. ὑδ.* is a descriptive gen. going with *κορυφάν*. For Mt. Parnassus as 'mother of abundant waters' cf. E. *Hec.* 452 where the Apidanus is called *καλλίστων ὑδάτων πατέρα*, and Pi. *P.* 1. 20 where Etna is *χιόνος ὀξείας τιθήνα*. So, too, at E. *Tr.* 222 the chorus sings of Etna as *Σικελῶν ὀρέων ματέρα*. Wecklein[3] proposed *λιποῦσ' ἀστάκτων μάτειρ' ὑδάτων* = 'leaving ... in search of abundant waters'. Hesych. gives *μάτηρ· ἐπίσκοπος, ἐπιζητῶν, ἐρευνητής*. *μάτειρα* is supposed to be the feminine form; cf. *σωτήρ : σώτειρα*. *μάστειρ'* (see *app. crit.*) would have been safer. This word occurs at A. *Supp.* 163 and the masc. form is found with the gen. at S. *Tr.* 733 *μαστὴρ πατρός*.

ἀστάκτων: cf. Hesych. *ἄστακτον· οὐ καταστάζον, ἀλλὰ ῥύδην*. The epithet is a good example of *litotes*: 'not falling in drops', i.e. 'torrential'. Cf. the adv. *ἀστακτί*, e.g. S. *OC.* 1250, 1 *δι' ὄμματος | ἀστακτὶ λείβων δάκρυον*.

βακχεύουσαν should not be 'corrected'—as it was by Dobree —to *βακχευθεῖσαν*. The mountain is said to take part in the revels held on its summit. For this verb used actively of places cf. A. *fr.* 58 *ἐνθουσιᾷ δὴ δῶμα, βακχεύει στέγη*, and E. *Ba.* 726 *πᾶν δὲ συνεβάκχευ' ὄρος*. For Bacchic revels on Mt. Parnassus cf. E. *Ion* 713–17 *ἰὼ δειράδες Παρνασοῦ πέτρας . . . ἵνα Βάκχιος . πηδᾷ . . . ἅμα σὺν Βάκχαις*, and S. *Ant.* 1126 sqq.

Grégoire's attempt to keep the MSS. order of words (see *app. crit.*) causes metrical confusion and necessitates changes in the antistrophe which, except for metrical reasons so caused, are uncalled for.

1245. The first possessor of the Delphic oracle was Earth herself; then her daughter, Themis; cf. A. *Eu.* 2–4 *ἐκ δὲ τῆς* (= *Γαίας*) *Θέμιν, | ἣ δὴ τὸ μητρὸς δευτέρα τόδ' ἕζετο | μαντεῖον*. The Python, also a child of Earth, defended the shrine for his mother and sister.

1246. For **κατάχαλκος** cf. E. *Ph.* 110, 1 *κατάχαλκον ἅπαν πεδίον*. Here the word, taken by itself, might mean 'covered with brazen scales', but this meaning accords ill with the datives which would have to be taken in a locative sense, i.e. 'under the laurel'. To take them as instrumental and translate, as Grégoire does, 'couvert, ainsi que par une cuirasse, du laurier', is simply impossible. Most edd. have supposed *κατάχ.* a misreading for some adj. meaning 'hidden' or the like and suggested e.g. *κατάφρακτος* (Monk), **κατάχαιτος* (cf. *κατάκομος*, E. *Ba.* 1187) (Housman). It is possible, however, that the word derives not from *χαλκός*, bronze, but from *κάλχη*, the murex. Hence Verrall's *κατάκαλχος* = *ἑλικτός* (see *app. crit.*), i.e. coiled like the volutes of a shell. Better is Prof. Murray's suggestion that not the shape of the murex but the dye extracted from it is referred to. Thus κατάχ. would mean 'purpled over', i.e. 'darkly shaded'. This gives admirable sense with the datives. We need not alter to κατάκαλχος as κάλχη appears in the MSS. of Nicander in the form χάλκη. That Nicander is the earliest authority for this word need not disturb us; the fifth-century Greeks must have known of it from their use of the derivative verb καλχαίνειν. Eur. may well, however, have written κατάκαλχος. This would not unnaturally be changed to κατάχαλκος by a scribe ignorant of the rarer adjective. Badham suggested σκιερὸν κάτεχ' ἄλσος (with ἀμφέπον in l. 1248)—in which case the dative would be descriptive.

1248. With a full stop at **Χθόνιον** the sense is complete. The uncertainty of the reading of the corresponding line in the antistrophe (see note on 1273) makes any alteration here risky. If ∪ — — is wanted either Köchly's φυλάσσων or Bergk's Θέμιστος (gen. of Θέμις) would do.

1249. **ἔτι μιν:** μιν is not tragic; a connexion is wanted; the first ἔτι is pointless. We should probably read with Nauck σὺ δέ νιν.

1255. **θεσφάτων** should be taken substantivally as a gen. of definition with μαντείας (acc. plur.) as it is in l. 1282 with ἀοιδαῖς, though some edd. regard it as adjectival with ἀδύτων.

1256. **ὕπο** = ὑπέξ, 'up from out of': so commonly in Homer; rare in tragedy, cf. E. *Hec.* 53 περᾷ γὰρ ἥδ' ὑπὸ σκηνῆς πόδα, *Andr.* 441 ὑπὸ πτερῶν σπάσας, and *HF.* 296 ἥξειν . . . γαίας ὕπο.

μέσον: for Delphi as the centre of the world cf. E. *Ion* 5, 6 Δελφῶν τήνδε γῆν, ἵν' ὀμφαλὸν | μέσον καθίζων Φοῖβος . . ., *ib.* 461, 2 Φοιβήιος ἔνθα γᾶς μεσσόμφαλος ἑστία, *Med.* 668 ὀμφαλὸν γῆς θεσπιῳδόν, *Or.* 331 ἵνα μεσόμφαλοι λέγονται μυχοί, etc.

1259–62. **ἰών** = 'on his arrival' is weak, if not impossible. We should probably read Bruhn's **Γαῖαν** for γᾶς ἰών. Some edd., desiring a more clearly expressed subject, read παῖς for παῖδ' and complete the lacuna by ἀπενάσσαθ' ὁ ⟨Λατῷος⟩ (Mekler), or ἀπένασσεν ὁ ⟨Λατῷος⟩ (Nauck), or ἀπένασσεν Ἀπόλλων ἀποπρὸ ζαθέων (Housman). We should certainly expect the active of ἀποναίω in the sense of 'send away' rather than the middle (which is not elsewhere used transitively), but the text is probably in this matter sound as it stands. From the point of view of the sense, indeed, the middle is the voice we want: 'sent away in his own interest'. It is quite clear that Phoebus is the subject of ἀπενάσσατο, and παῖδ' should not be altered.

For Earth, the mother of dreams, cf. E. *Hec.* 70, 1 ὦ πότνια Χθών, | μελανοπτερύγων μῆτερ ὀνείρων; and for Θέμις, daughter of Γῆ, cf. A. *Eu.* 2. At A. *Pr.* 212 the two are identified—πολλῶν ὀνομάτων μορφὴ μία.

1263–7. **τά τε πρῶτα, τά τ' ἔπειθ', ὅσσα τ' ἔμελλε:** Eur. seems fond of this turn of phrase; cf. *Supp.* 550, 1 εὐτυχοῦσι δὲ | οἱ μὲν τάχ', οἱ δ' ἐσαῦθις, οἷ δ' ἤδη βροτῶν, *Ion* 6, 7 Φοῖβος ὑμνῳδεῖ ... τά τ' ὄντα καὶ μέλλοντα, *Hel.* 13, 14 (Theonoe) τά τ' ὄντα καὶ μέλλοντα πάντ' ἠπίστατο, *ib.* 922, 3 πάντ' ἐξειδέναι | τά τ' ὄντα καὶ μέλλοντα.

Comparing this passage with Pl. *Prm.* 152 C τοῦ τε νῦν καὶ τοῦ ἔπειτα, and S. *Ant.* 611 τό τ' ἔπειτα καὶ τὸ μέλλον (where, according to Jebb, τὸ νῦν is understood), it seems best to take τὰ πρῶτα not of the past (as many edd. have done) but of the present or immediate future. Wecklein suggested ἃ πέπρωτο with τά τ' ... ὅσσα τ' in apposition. We might possibly read τὰ πρωτά (= τὰ πεπρωμένα; for which word see Hdn. Gr. I. 215).

Keeping the MSS. reading we can take τά ... τά either as articles or relatives with verbs understood. For τά (= ἅ) ... ὅσσα τε cf. E. *Tr.* 499 οἵων ἔτυχον ὧν τε τεύξομαι.

If l. 1240 is metrically correct Musgrave's ὅσσα τ' must be accepted as producing correspondence, the initial iambus of the antistrophe (ἔπειθ') answering to the tribrach of the strophe (νιν ἀπό). Burges' ὅσ' is metrically unsatisfactory, and 'the future (lit. "the next" or "the then"), whatever it is going to prove' (1) gives very poor sense; (2) involves taking ὅσα = οἷα.

Instead of οἷ many edd. accept Hartung's οἷς (instrumental dat.) ... ἔφραζεν, 'by means of which she (Earth) told to many mortals', though this makes Γαῖα (l. 1267) (= Χθών) redundant.

1266. Our text keeps the MSS. reading, changing only δνοφερᾶς to δνοφεράς = 'throughout the dark earth-beds of sleep'; i.e. during the darkness of night when they (the μέροπες) were asleep. Dream-oracles were consulted by clients sleeping on the ground at the shrine: Gk. ἐγκοίμησις, Lat. *incubatio.* The gen. γᾶς is very difficult, and the line has been variously emended. Linder's χαμεύ-|νας (a gloss on which would probably contain the words γᾶς and εὐνάς) is very probably right. Incidentally, to read it would give us a better correspondence with 1241, though in view of the uncertainty of the reading of that line little stress can be laid on this fact.

1267. δέ = 'and thus'.

1268. μαντεῖον is here (as at E. *Ion* 130 μαντεῖον ἕδραν) fem. Seidler's μαντείων is worse than useless.

ἀφελ. τιμὰν Φοῖβον = 'deprived Ph. of the privilege'.

1269. φθόνῳ θυγατρός, i.e. in jealous championship of her dispossessed daughter, Themis.

1271. χέρα ... ἕλιξεν ἐκ ... θρόνων = χέρα ἑλίξας περὶ θρόνους ἤρτησεν ἐκ θρόνων. This is good and not particularly difficult Greek, and such 'emendations' as Badham's ὄρεξεν εἰς Δῖον θρόνον are no more than a rewriting of Euripides. The only alteration that is conceivably necessary is that of Διός (◡ –; cf. – – in 1245) to Seidler's Ζηνός (but what caused corruption?) or more probably to Wecklein's Δίων (adj. = 'of Zeus': cf. l. 404 above (note), also E. *Ion* 200 Δίῳ παιδί, *Ba.* 245 Δίους ... γάμους; also

Barnes' metrically necessary Δίου πυρός (MSS. Διός), *ib.* 8, and Nauck's Δίοις (MSS. Διός) μελάθροις, *Or.* 1684).

1273. **χθονίαν . . . μῆνιν θεᾶς**, hypallage for χθονίας (which Nauck would read) μ. θ. The MSS. have θεᾶς μῆνιν. Wilamowitz' transposition is not satisfactory, as the cretic -νιν θεᾶς does not correspond with the choriambus of the strophe (-ον χθόνιον). For this we need Hartung's μή-|νιμα θεᾶς for θεᾶς μῆνιν, which is especially good as Apollo wished for the removal rather of the *cause of anger* than of the anger itself. We *must* in this case read χθονίας for metrical reasons, for χθόνιŏν (μήνιμα) would not scan. The meaning would be: 'begged . . . to take away from the Pythian shrine the cause of his quarrel with the goddess'—i.e. the prophetic dreams.

Wecklein boldly suggests θεᾶς (monosyllabic) | μαντοσύναν.

The infin. ἀφελεῖν is due to the fact that χέρα ἕλιξεν implies ⟨λισσόμενος⟩ or the like. Cf. E. *Suppl.* 285 γούνασιν ὧδε πίτνω τέκνοις τάφον ἐξανύσασθαι.

νυχίους τ' ἐνοπάς is redundant both to sense and metre. It may well have been (without τ') a gloss on μήνιμα introduced into the text with the addition of τ' to complete the construction. The simplest plan is to remove it altogether. If, however, it is held that ἐνοπάς only is corrupt we can read with Seidler μῆ-|νιν [θεᾶς] νυχίους τ' ὀνείρους, regarding θεᾶς as a gloss on χθονίας, and adding a hypobacchius to l. 1249 (see note on that line). Supposing that νυχίους τ' ὀνείρους *was* the original reading we should get a reason for the corruption, if corruption it be, of νυχίους ἐνοπάς to νυχ. ὀνείρους in l. 1276 (see *app. crit.*).

1274. **γέλασε**, sc. Ζεύς.

1275. The practical monetary value of the Delphic oracle was recognized as early as Homer (Il. 9. 404): cf. S. *OT.* 152, 3 πολυχρύσου Πυθῶνος; E. *Andr.* 1093 χρυσοῦ γέμοντα γύαλα, θησαυροὺς βροτῶν.

1276. **νυχίους** is awkwardly near νυκτωπόν and Bergk's μυχίους ('subterranean') may be the right reading.

παῦσαι, as ἐπέσεισεν κόμαν = ἐκέλευσεν. This is idiomatic enough Greek (see note on ἀφελεῖν in l. 1273), but Musgrave's ἐπὶ δὲ σείσας κόμαν παῦσεν (see *app. crit.*) gives good sense and is equally near the MSS.

1277. The MSS. λαθοσύναν (presumably = λήθην) makes nonsense, though it was defended by Wilamowitz (*Herakl.* ii. 68), and though Weil retains it, thinking it refers to the trance into which those visited by the νύχιοι ἐνοπαί would be thrown. Many suggestions have been made, of which may be mentioned Markland's δὲ μαντοσύναν (fair sense, but not very near the MSS.), Weil's δ' ἀλαμοσύναν (i.e. ἀλημοσύνην = 'mental wandering'), and Hoffmann's δ' ἀδαμοσύναν (i.e. ἀδημοσύνην = 'mental distress')—both good palaeographically, but neither substantive has good authority and neither gives the required meaning. Much the simplest and most satisfactory is Nauck's ἀλαθοσύναν, though this is a rare word, found only at Thgn. 1226. Zeus removed from mortals not dreams but prophetic truth as given by dreams. Apollo is to have the monopoly of ἀληθοσύνη.

As ἀπό must be taken by tmesis with ἐξεῖλεν, and as verbs compounded with ἀπεκ- are, with the single exception of the Homeric ἀπεκλανθάνομαι, not classical, Wecklein reads ὑπό.

1281–2. 'Restored to mortals their confidence in the verses of oracles (see note on l. 1255) ⟨chanted⟩ at his throne thronged by crowds of visitors.'

ἀοιδαῖς, as the oracles were given in hexameter verse. Weil adopts Tournier's ἀοιδάς, in which case θάρση becomes predicative: Zeus restored ⟨Apollo's⟩ prophecies as things in which mortals could feel confidence.

1284–end : Exodus.

(*a*) Messenger and Chorus, 1284–1306.

(*b*) Messenger and Thoas, 1307–1434.

(*c*) Thoas and Athena *ex machina*, with a short choric song in completion, 1435–99.

1284. The messenger shouts to those within the temple. He takes no notice at first of the chorus; hence their designation of themselves as μὴ κελευσθεῖσαν (l. 1288). Failing to grasp this point Lenting foolishly suggested, and Hermann accepted, εἴ με χρή for εἰ χρὴ μή.

1285. **βεβώς** being a participle of motion we might have expected ποῖ for ποῦ, but Greek shows considerable latitude in this respect (cf K.-G. II. i, p. 545), and ποῦ and ὅπου are often found with the *perfect* tense of verbs of motion; cf. S. *Tr.* 40, 1 κεῖνος δ' ὅπου | βέβηκεν οὐδεὶς οἶδε. Cf. below l. 1296 (note).

1291. **φεύγοντες**—*not* φυγόντες (Markland); they are still in flight though possessed of the image (λαβόντες).

1296. ⟨ἐκεῖσε⟩ . . . ὅπου; cf. Th. 2. 86. 1 παρέπλευσαν . . . οὗπερ . . . ὁ στρατὸς . . . προσεβεβοηθήκει (K.-G. II. i, p. 545).

1299. **μέτεστι** seldom has a personal subject and attempts have been made to oust μέρος, presumably as a gloss (?) Hence Nauck's ⟨τῶνδε⟩ τῶν πεπραγμένων [μέρος], and Wecklein's σαφῶς for μέρος. But if Herodotus can write ὁκόσον δέ τι μοι μέρος μετῆν (6. 107), and Thucydides μέτεστι δὲ . . . πᾶσι τὸ ἴσον (2. 37. 1), Euripides can presumably say μέτεστι . . . μέρος. The messenger's accusation is just. The chorus tries to send him on a wild-goose chase to give more time for the conspirators' escape.

1302. With the MSS. reading τόδε (referring to the next line) we must suppose that the ἑρμηνεύς was some otherwise unknown official connected with the temple like the κληδοῦχος or πυλωρός. Prof. Murray's ingenious ὅδε suggests (see crit. note) that at this point the messenger blows a blast on his trumpet or uses the door-knocker. But even so the word ἑρμηνεύς is scarcely what we should expect.

1306. Cf. E. *Hec.* 105, 6 ἀγγελίας βάρος . . . μέγα. Weil thinks ἀγγέλλων a gloss and would read εἰσάγων (cf. E. *Ba.* 650 τοὺς λόγους . . . εἰσφέρεις καινούς), a verb which certainly fits the metaphor better.

1307. Tournier's ὅδ' (see *app. crit.*) may well be right; cf. E. *Supp.* 395 λόγων τίς ἐμποδὼν ὅδ' ἔρχεται; βοὴν ἱστάναι (Eng. 'raise a shout') is the regular idiom; cf. A. *Ch.* 885 τίνα βοὴν ἵστης δόμοις; S. *Ph.* 1263 τίς . . . θόρυβος ἵσταται βοῆς; E. *Heracl.* 128 βοὴν ἔστησε, etc.

1308. The Aldine ed. has φόβον—an interesting variant.

1309. The MSS. ψευδῶς ἔλεγον αἴδε is unmetrical. Three lines of emendation have been followed: (1) considering ἔλεγον as corrupt to read (e.g.) ψευδῶς λέγουσαί μ' αἴδ' (Pierson); (2) regarding ψευδ. ἔλ. as a gloss to read ἔψευδον αἴδε (Heimsöth. Herwerden's objection to this use of the active cannot stand in the face of S. *OC.* 628), or simply ψευδῶς ἄρ' αἴδε (Matthiae, taking only ἔλεγον as a gloss and translating καί as 'actually')—but ὡς ἐκτὸς εἴης = 'on the ground that you were outside' is scarcely possible; (3) taking ψευδῶς as corrupt to accept some such correction as that of our text (see *app. crit.*).

1312. **αὖθις** = 'later'; cf. ll. 377 and 1432.

1317. **πνεῦμα συμφορᾶς**: πνεῦμα is here used = 'influence' as e.g. πνεῦμα λύσσης (A. *Pr.* 884), θεοῦ πνεῦμα (E. *HF.* 216), while συμφορά has a subjective meaning, almost = 'defect of character' (as in Th. I. 122. 4). Much ingenuity has been needlessly spent in 'emending' the line; e.g. Burges's τί βούλευμ' ἐν φρεσὶν κεκτημένη;

1319. Thoas' knowledge of who Orestes is saves, as Hermann pointed out, a long, and to the audience boring, explanation; nor is such knowledge on his part strange considering the length of Iph.'s sojourn in his country.

1321. **τύχω** here = 'am I to hit the mark?' Cf. A. *Ag.* 1232, 3 τί νιν καλοῦσα δυσφιλὲς δάκος | τύχοιμ' ἄν; *Ch.* 14, 15 ἢ πατρὶ τῷμῷ τάσδ' ἐπεικάσας τύχω | χόας φερούσας . . .; *ib.* 418 τί δ' ἂν φάντες τύχοιμεν; E. *Hipp.* 826, 7 τίνα λόγον, τάλας, τίνα τύχαν σέθεν | βαρύποτμον, γύναι, προσαυδῶν τύχω; But σε is odd, and we should expect not so much 'what *more* can I call it (lit. "you")?' as 'what *less* . . .?': cf. E. *Hel.* 601 θαῦμ' ἔστ', ἔλασσον τοὔνομ' ἢ τὸ πρᾶγμ' ἔχον. Mekler's πῶς δ' ὃ μεῖζον would avoid the first difficulty, while Markland's σε μεῖον would settle the second. Wecklein's πῶς ὀλείζον would solve both. (This form of the comparative is found in Homer and later in the Alexandrines. Its existence in the classical period is vouched for by inscriptions (Meisterh., p. 151), though it is not found in literature.) We might perhaps accept Markland's μεῖον and alter σε to γε. (For γε with the interrog. cf. Denniston, p. 124.)

Alternatively we might read μῶν σε (? or γε) μεῖζον, i.e. τοῦ προσήκοντος ὀνόματος: i.e. surely I have not used too strong a word? In this case ὀνομάσας τύχω would = simply ὠνόμασα.

1322. **'νταῦθα**, thither, i.e. to the search for the *mot juste*.

1324. Either Hermann's *διωγμὸν ὅστις* or Monk's *ὅστις διωγμός* would be more natural Greek.

1325. **ἀγχίπλουν πόρον**: lit. 'they do not flee a near-by-sea journey'. *πόρον* is internal acc. Th. means that though the fugitives may have the start of him he cannot fail to overtake them, such being the length of the voyage to Greece. Hesych. has a gloss *ἀγχίπους· εὐδιακόμιστος, καὶ ὁ παρεστὼς καὶ σύνεγγυς. Εὐριπίδης Ἰφιγενείᾳ τῇ ἐν Ταύροις*, with reference to which some edd. have wished to read here *ἀγχίπους*. *ἀγχίπους* (lit. 'near the foot', i.e. 'near'; Lyc. 318 *ἄτην ἀγχίπουν* = approaching doom), however, is scarcely the right word in this passage and it is better either to correct Hesych. to *ἀγχίπλους* or to suppose a confusion of two glosses in his text.

1326. **δόρυ** here probably = ship; cf. A. *Pers.* 411, E. *Cyc.* 15 and 19, *Hel.* 1268, 1568, and 1611, etc., where it is used without the usual epithet *νήϊον*.

1331. **φλόγα . . . καὶ καθαρμόν** = *φλόγα καθάρσιον*. Cf. E. *HF.* 936, 7 *θύω . . . καθάρσιον πῦρ*. The pres. part. *θύουσα* (Reiske *θύσουσα*) is used conatively like *σῴζουσα* in l. 1318 (where Markland proposed to read *σώσουσα*).

1332. **μετῴχετο** here used rather oddly (as though it were *μετήρχετο*) with an acc. of the *thing*, not the *person*.

1333. **αὐτή** here probably means 'alone', i.e. 'without us' (see L & S, *αὐτός*, i. 3). Nauck's transposition (see *app. crit.*) would give a much more natural order of words. Eur. may have written *αὕτη δ'* (cf. *ἡμᾶς μέν* of 1329).

1336. **χρόνῳ** ⟨*ὕστερον*⟩. *πλέον* not, I think, as England, 'to do something *special*', but = the idiomatic *πλέον ποιεῖν* = 'to do some good', 'to effect something'. Iph. is the subject of *δοκοῖ*.

1337–8. **βάρβαρα** = unintelligible. *μαγεύουσα* (observe the correction) is used absolutely, *μέλη* being governed by *κατῇδε*.

1339. **δαρὸν . . . χρόνον**; so at A. *Supp.* 516, though *δαρόν* is generally used alone adverbially.

1340. **ἐσῆλθεν**, impersonally, 'it occurred to us'. Followed by *μή* as *φόβος* is understood. Prinz' *ἥμενοι, φόβος* is quite unnecessary.

1341. **κτάνοιεν** 'might kill', not 'might have killed' (England) which would demand a perf. or pluperf. indic.

1342. The infin. **εἰσορᾶν** depends on **φόβῳ** (= *φοβούμενοι*), as, below, does *στείχειν* on *πᾶσιν . . . λόγος* (= *πάντες ἐκέλευον*). Cf. S. *fr.* 953 *θανόντι κείνῳ συνθανεῖν ἔρως μ' ἔχει.*

1344. **οὐκ ἐωμένοις**; closely together = 'forbidden'.

1345. Cf. E. *Cyc.* 85 *ναὸς Ἑλλάδος σκάφος.*

1346. 'Winged as to its sweep of oars with blade made ready' is very odd, nor does Barnes's *κατῆρες* (going closely with *σκαφὸς ταρσῷ*, with *πίτ. ἐπτ.* in apposition) help matters much. The best emendation is Dobree's *ταρσῶν κατήρη*. But better still is Hermann's transposition of the line after 1394 (see note there).

κατήρης seems a variant for the commoner εὐήρης as at 1050 (cf. Od. 23. 272 εὐήρε' ἐρετμά, τά τε πτερὰ νηυσὶ πέλονται). Hdt. (8. 21) has πλοῖον κατῆρες.

1349–53. A very vexed passage. Our text, except for the necessary corrections of ἀγκύρας (1351) and τὴν ξένοιν (ξένην) (1353) (see *app. crit.*) sticks to the MSS. This involves three difficulties, one, as I believe, insuperable. (1) πρύμνηθεν ἑστῶτας. It is quite clear from what follows that Or. and Pyl. are not yet aboard. We must therefore regard this phrase as = 'standing on ⟨shore by⟩ the stern of the vessel'. This is, to say the least of it, a strained interpretation of the words. (2) κοντοῖς δὲ . . . εἶχον must be taken as = καὶ οἱ μὲν κοντοῖς, κτλ. This, in spite of δέ, is possible. Edd. cite E. *Hec.* 1160–2 κᾆτ' . . . λαβοῦσαι φάσγανα . . . κεντοῦσι . . ., αἱ δὲ . . ., and *HF.* 636 ἔχουσιν, οἱ δ' οὔ (= οἱ μὲν ἔχουσιν, οἱ δ' οὔ). More to the point, as containing an initial δέ, are E. *Hel.* 1604, 5 σπουδῆς δ' ὕπο | ἔπιπτον, οἱ δ' ὠρθοῦντο, τοὺς δὲ . . ., and *Or.* 1489 νεκροὶ δ' ἔπιπτον, οἱ δ' ἔμελλον οἱ δ' ἔκειντο. (3) The same sailors cannot at one and the same time 'hastily prepare and lower ladders' and 'haul in the stern cables'; nor, if they could, could a statement to the effect that they were occupied on the first of these two operations be bisected, as it were, by the statement that they were employed upon the second.

We must either follow Bergk and excise l. 1352, or else with Köchly transpose it after 1349. The second course involves the divorce of ἑστῶτας from νεανίας and its correction to ἑστῶτες—a change which, in and for itself, is, as we have suggested, for the better; for, though Or. and Pyl. were still on shore, the *sailors* were standing πρύμνηθεν. We may then either put a full stop at ἐλευθέρους, and, removing the stop after νεώς, suppose a new (asyndeton) sentence to start with πρύμνηθεν (as does, e.g., England); or, with Weil, postulate a lacuna between ἐλευθέρους and πρύμνηθεν. The latter seems to me preferable. We may further suppose this lacuna to have contained the words οἱ μέν and take the δέ after κοντοῖς as introducing a second activity of the same set of sailors: i.e. ⟨some⟩ standing on the vessels stern were hastily hauling in the stern cables and holding the ship with quants (i.e. preventing the now unattached vessel from floating off), others were weighing anchor, others lowering ladders. If this solution be accepted we must further accept Kirchhoff's διδόντες in 1353 for the MSS. δὲ δόντες, an easy change and one which gives us a suitable present, for a very unsuitable aor., participle. This change must be made also if, with Bergk, we cut out l. 1352 altogether. The two datives of l. 1353 are certainly awkward and Rauchenstein's κάτω for πόντῳ may well be right.

(Kirchoff's suggestion (see *app. crit.*), while arbitrarily introducing ἤ and καί, fails to solve the πρύμνηθεν ἑστῶτας difficulty.)

The ladders may have been rope ladders (cf. Aen. Tact. 38. 7 ταῖς ἐκ τῶν σχοινίων κλίμαξι πεποιημέναις. I owe this reference to Prof. Murray). So also may those have been that are mentioned at E. *Rh.* 73.

As to details: **νεώς** (in our text) is a partitive gen. with πρύμνηθεν (= ἐν πρύμνῃ); cf. ποῦ γῆς;

κλίμακας: plur. for sing. as at E. *Ph.* 104 (there is no need to accept Kirchhoff's κλίμακα). The technical term for this was ἀποβάθρα (S. *fr.* 415). For the whole passage cf. Polyaen. 4. 6. 8 ἄλλοι μὲν ἀνέσπων τὰ πρυμνήσια, ἄλλοι δ' ἀνεῖλκον τὰς ἀποβάθρας, ἄλλοι δ' ἀγκύρας ἀνιμῶντο. **ἄγκυραν ἐξανῆπτον** = 'were suspending the anchor from the cat-head', i.e. were hauling up the anchor.

1354. **ἀφειδήσαντες**: not 'not sparing ourselves', i.e. energetically, but 'no longer respecting Iph. as a priestess'.

1356. The cables, though detached from their moorings on shore, were seemingly not yet completely hauled aboard. The εὐθυντηρίαι were two holes in the stern bulwarks, one on either side, through which the rudder-oars (οἴακες) passed: these rudder-oars were like the ordinary propellent oars attached to the tholes (σκαλμοί) by means of leathern loops (τροποί or τροπωτῆρες).

1357. **ἐξῃροῦμεν** is conative.

1358. **λόγοι . . . λόγῳ**: awkward but not un-Euripidean. Cf. note on l. 139.

λόγῳ = excuse, justification (cf. l. 998).

1359. The plurals (see crit. note) are half humorous: cf. E. *Heracl.* 950 ὕδρας λέοντάς τε. So, too, ἀπεμπολᾷς (l. 1360) = 'smuggle out of' as though to sell her as a slave.

1360. Notice the idiomatic Greek double question. **τίνος**; the Greeks had no surnames.

1366. **τά** is demonstrative here = τάδε. **ἦν**; as in English we might say 'that's how I got . . .' His wounds, though they show in the present, were received in the past.

1367. i.e. οὔτ' ἐκεῖνοι οὔθ' ἡμεῖς εἴχομεν σίδηρον; cf. A. *Th.* 399 λόφοι δὲ κώδων τ' οὐ δάκνουσ' ἄνευ δορός, and below, ll. 1477, 8.

1368. δ' for MSS. τ' dates back to the Aldine ed. and should almost certainly be adopted. Badham's ᾖσσον, 'were darting forth', is attractive.

1369. Bergk suggested θάμα for MSS. ἅμα.

1371. **ξυνάπτειν** must be taken absolutely (as at Ar. *Ach.* 686), for though one can συνάπτειν μάχην and even ἀλκήν (E. *Supp.* 683) one cannot συνάπτειν μέλη in the sense of joining combat. The MSS. reading ὥστε ξυνάπτειν, κτλ., has been taken as = ὥστε τὸ ξυνάπτειν συνεῖναι τῷ μέλη ἀποκαμεῖν; i.e. so that as soon as we had joined battle we were tired out. This seems to be the required meaning, but we can scarcely extract it from the Greek without Hermann's ὡς (= ὥστε) τᾷ, accepted in our text. Paley arbitrarily excised the line. Other possible emendations are Markland's ὡς ξύν τ' ἀπειπεῖν or ὥστε συναπειπεῖν (the latter metrically objectionable): i.e. so that our crying off and our getting tired were simultaneous.

1372. **ἐσφραγισμένοι**: Weil compares Verg. *Georg.* 4. 15 et manibus Procne pectus *signata* cruentis. Cf. also Peithetairus' question to Iris (Ar. *Av.* 1213) *σφραγῖδ' ἔχεις παρὰ τῶν πελαργῶν;*

1373. **κρημνόν**: the cliffs behind the beach = *ὄχθοις* of l. 1375.

1375. A few adverbs sometimes form their comparative in **-ως** instead of the normal **-ον**; cf. Jannaris, *Hist. Gk. Gram.* § 520.

1376. **καί** is here used in further specification of what has been already stated by the preceding verb and adverb; cf. l. 1058 and note.

Paley's *πέτροις* would give *ἐβάλλομεν* its normal construction. The Greeks said *βάλλειν τινά τινι* not (as a rule) *βάλλειν τινί τι.*

1378. **ἀναστεῖλαι** = to check. A military use; cf. Th. 6. 70. 3 *οἱ ἱππῆς . . . εἶργον, καὶ ἐσβαλόντες . . . ἀνέστελλον.*

πρόσω = ⟨and keep us⟩ at a distance.

1380. See critical note. *l*'s *ὥστε μή* with the infinitive after *φόβος* is scarcely grammatical (cf. K.-G. II. ii, p. 398). Some dat., too, seems called for to complete the lacuna. The corrector of P had little knowledge of Greek accidence and less (we hope) of Greek sailors.

That a similar lacuna occurs at l. 1404 suggests that our MSS. derive from an archetype which had 24 lines to the page.

1381. **λαβὼν . . . ὦμον** = 'hoisting ⟨his sister⟩ upon his shoulder'.

1382. MSS. *ἐπὶ κλίμακος* = 'on the ladder'. We should probably accept Wecklein's *κλίμακας* (plur. as in l. 1351) = 'up the ladder'. Cf. E. *Cyc.* 352 *ἐπὶ κινδύνου βάθρα.*

1383. **εὐσήμου.** The word ordinarily means 'conspicuous', occasionally 'of good omen'. Neither meaning fits here. In E. *IA.* 254, 5 we read of *πεντήκοντα νῆας . . . σημείοισιν ἐστολισμένας*, i.e. 'decked with ensigns', and it may be that in this passage *εὔσημος* has the sense of 'fair-ensigned'. Most edd., however, accept Pierson's *εὐσέλμου*—a Homeric epithet used by Eur. at *Rh.* 97.

1384. For this ablatival gen. cf. E. *Tr.* 1121 *πύργων δίσκημα* = a thing (Astyanax) thrown from the walls.

1386–7. The MSS. reading accepted by our text is scarcely possible; (1) 'sailors of the Grecian land' is at least dubious Greek; (2) 'lay hold of the ship with oars' is even more unlikely. (It does not ease matters to reject the comma after *ναῦται* and take *γῆς . . . νεώς* as a double genitive, as Wecklein does. This further necessitates emending *κώπαις* to *κώπης*, 'lay hold of the oar'.) Kviçala may be right in rejecting l. 1386 altogether. He further puts a full stop at *νεώς* (l. 1383); keeps the MSS. *δ'* in l. 1384, not supplying Markland's ⟨*δ'*⟩ in l. 1385, and so makes *ἄγαλμα* the subject of *ἐφθέγξατο.* *βοή τις* (or *βοήν τινα*, the reading of the Aldine ed.), may, he thinks, have been a gloss, expanded later into a line. The objection to this view (which also involves the accepting of Reiske's κώπης) is that it involves the omission of any account of the shipment of the ξόανον.

Retaining l. 1386 we can either (*a*) suppose corruption and emend (1) γῆς to τῆσδ', removing the comma at ναῦται (so Markland), or (2) ναῦται, νεώς to ναύτης λεώς (so F. W. Schmidt—for ναύτης as adj. cf. E. *Hec.* 921 ναύταν . . . ὅμιλον); or (*b*) regard ναῦται, or ναῦται νεώς, as a gloss and take Nauck's νεανίαι or Köchly's νεηλάται—preferably the latter, as being a word more in need of glossing and more accurately glossed by ναῦται νεώς.

Reiske's κώπης may be taken with any of these. κώπαις indeed can only be kept on the supposition that what Eur. wrote was something like ὦ γῆς Ἑλλάδος λεώς, ἁλὸς λάβεσθε κώπαις (Musgrave).

The new ed. of L & S persists in its error of translating ἐκλευκαίνειν 'dash the white spray off the oar'. The ἐκ is simply intensive. Cf. E. *Cyc.* 16, 17 ἅλα | ῥοθίοισι λευκαίνοντες.

1392. With this punctuation we must translate 'went ⟨straight for⟩ the harbour mouth'. It is, however, perhaps better to put a comma after ἐχώρει. Eur. not infrequently puts δέ third word (see Denniston, p. 188), especially where, as here, the two words give a combined sense, e.g. *IA.* 1006 ψευδῆ λέγων δέ. ἐχώρει in this case is used absolutely = 'made progress'.

Prof. Murray's suggested emendation (see *app. crit.*) is particularly attractive in view of the fact that στόμιον is not elsewhere used of the mouth of a harbour. For στόμα in this sense cf. Ar. *Ec.* 1107 ἐπὶ . . . τῷ στόματι τῆς ἐσβολῆς.

Badham's στόμια δ' ἐκπερῶσα δή deserves mention.

1393. Many 'corrections' of ἠπείγετο have been suggested, of which the most plausible perhaps are Pierson's ἐπείχετο and Earle's ἀπείργετο, but in view of *Od.* 23. 234, 5 νῆ' . . . ἐπειγομένην ἀνέμῳ καὶ κύματι none is needed.

ἐπείγειν here = 'laborare'.

1395. Kirchhoff's ὠθεῖ may be right, though I see little reason to suspect the imperf. of the MSS. which sorts better with the surrounding imperfects. ὤθει, Ion. and epic. form of ἐώθει, is found in the MSS. at Pl. *Chrm.* 155 C; and in any case the unaugmented form is not unnatural in a ῥῆσις.

The MSS. πάλιν πρυμνήσι' is nonsense. Mekler's παλίμπρυμν' ἱστί' gives admirable sense: 'forced the sails (*synecdoche* for "the ship") astern'. Hermann's παλιμπρυμνηδόν (a word he took from Hesych.—as did Mekler his παλίμπρυμνα) is also good, though it involves either correcting νεώς to σκάφος (νεώς would on this theory have been a gloss), or introducing l. 1346 after l. 1394. This latter transposition appears the more likely when we remember that the two lines are 48 lines apart and that the archetype probably had a page of 24 lines. (See note on l. 1380.)

1396. πρὸς κῦμα λακτίζοντες: an adaptation of the proverb *πρὸς κεντρα λακ.* (E. *Ba.* 795). Nauck, with singular lack of taste, proposed reading *κέντρα* here. As Wilamowitz says (*Herakl.* l. 729): wenn *κέντρα* statt *κῦμα* überliefert wäre, müsste man ändern.

1404. For the possible cause of the lacuna cf. note on l. 1380. Suggestions for its completion have been made in plenty, but none deserves attention that does not retain at least *ἐπωμίδας*, a rare word and unlikely to be corrupt. This limits us to (1) *p*'s *χερῶν*; (2) Nauck's [*ἐκ*] *εὐχερῶς*, and (3) Markland's *πέπλων*. Of these (1) has been interpreted in two ways: (*a*) 'applying shoulders bare from the hands', i.e. rowing with arms bared from hand to shoulder; (*b*) 'fastening the oar-handle under the armpits having let-go with the hands.' To this second interpretation, however, it may be objected (1) that *ἐκ χερῶν* cannot really be made to yield this sense; (2) that *ἐπωμίς* does not = *μασχάλη*; (3) that no sane man tucks the handle of his oar under his arm in a heavy sea in order, apparently, to sing a paean.

Reading, as our text does, ⟨*πέπλων*⟩ we get to *γυμνὰς ἐκ π.* an exact parallel in 1348, 9 *ἐκ δεσμῶν . . . ἐλευθέρους*; cf. also E. *Ion* 1208 *γυμνὰ δ' ἐκ πέπλων μέλη*. This seems to me much the most satisfactory conclusion—unless, indeed, we suppose with Wecklein that the two lines have got in from some other play, *παιᾶνα* being unnecessary to the construction. Another line of emendation deserves notice: it is to alter *ἐπωμίδας* to *ἐπωμίδος* and read for *ἐκ* ⟨*πέπλων*⟩ e.g. Hartung's *ὠλένας*. *ἐπωμίς* besides meaning 'shoulder' can mean 'tunic sleeve' (usually of a woman's garment (as at E. *Hec.* 558) rather than a man's; but of a man's at e.g. Plut. *Eum.* 7).

1405. ἐκ κελεύσματος: in accordance with the chant of the *κελευστής*. The expression occurs again at A. *Pers.* 397.

κέλευμα is the older form (see L & S[9]), and *κελεύματος* should probably be read here.

1406. For **μᾶλλον . . . μᾶλλον** cf. Ar. *Ra.* 1001.

1407. For **ὃ μέν τις** cf. E. *Med.* 1141 *κυνεῖ δ' ὃ μέν τις . . . ὃ δέ . . .*, *Hel.* 1597, 8 *ὃ μέν τις . . . ὃ δέ . . .* This and the next line used to be understood of the Greeks, on whose part such actions are really inexplicable. Actually they refer to the Taurians, who dashed into the water carrying with them ropes the other ends of which others had attached to (*ἐκ*, as usual) trees or rocks, their object being to secure the labouring vessel. Grégoire takes it as = lasso the vessel (*accrocher des lacets*).

Rauchenstein's *χηλῶν τις* would make this clearer, but it is unnecessary.

ἀγκύλη here = looped rope.

1410. ἐκεῖθεν: cf. notes on ll. 540 and 1182.

1411. ἀλλά, probably of exhortation (Denniston, p. 14)—though it may answer the otherwise *solitarium μέν* of 1409. But *μέν, . . . ἀλλά* is a rarity (cf. S. *OC.* 1615).

1414–15. For Poseidon's friendship for Troy cf. E. *Tr.* 6, 7 οὔποτ' ἐκ φρενῶν εὔνοι' ἀπέστη τῶν ἐμῶν Φρυγῶν πόλει, etc.

'**τε . . . δέ.** δέ is often unnecessarily emended by editors' (Denniston, p. 513); cf. l. 387 (note). Here the MSS. Πελοπίδαις δ' is quite possibly right, in which case the καί of 1416 = even (see Denniston, p. 319)—Kirchhoff's ὤν for καί is quite unnecessary.

1414–19 is rejected altogether by England. Certainly the lines require some doctoring, and even then the result is scarcely worthy of Euripides. Mr. Page (*Actors' Interpolations*, p. 78) suggests that ll. 1414, 5 may have been put in by some one ignorant of the impersonal use (as at E. *El.* 1080) of παρέχειν. They come in oddly, as he says, in the messenger's speech.

1418. The MSS. τ' ἀδελφήν, i.e. παρέξει . . . γόνον . . . ἐν χεροῖν ⟨λαβεῖν, ἐν χεροῖν⟩ λαβεῖν τ' ἀδελφήν is scarcely defensible on the analogy of A. *Ch.* 130, 1 ἐποίκτειρόν τ' ἐμὲ | φίλον τ' Ὀρέστην. Musgrave's ἀδελφήν θ' must be accepted.

1418–19. These lines as they stand in the MSS. (kept in our text) are grammatical but nonsensical. We must accept Markland's ἀμνημόνευτος (here = ἀμνήμων, 'unheedful of') and Badham's θεάν with genitives—better singular (φόνου τοῦ 'ν) than plural—see *app. crit.*

The messenger means that Iph. in carrying off the ξόανον is showing ingratitude in forgetting her threatened sacrifice in Aulis ⟨and the goddess's rescue of herself therefrom⟩.

1423. **εἶα** is normally used with imperatives, but, as οὐ . . . δραμεῖσθε; = τρέχετε, εἶα is quite natural. Cf. E. *Hel.* 1597 οὐκ εἶ' ὁ μέν τις . . . ἀρεῖται δόρυ;

1424. **παράκτιοι** = παρὰ τὴν ἀκτήν. The Greeks used adjectives denoting place and time where we should use adverbs or adverbial phrases; cf. χρόνιοι in l. 258 above. ἐκβολάς *v.* = wreckage.

1427. **οἳ δέ** (vocative), as though οἳ μέν had preceded; cf. note on 1349.

1428. I.e. ἐκ θαλ. ⟨διώγμασιν⟩. **ἱππεύμασι**, as it is, has to do duty for both. Wesener wished to read θηρεύμασι

ἐκ θαλάσσης ἔκ τε γῆς = 'by sea and land a rare use of the preposition; cf. such expressions as ἐξ ἀριστερᾶς, ἐκ δεξιᾶς.

1430. Edd. point out that while κατακρημνισμός was a recognized Greek punishment σκολοπισμός was not; the latter being one of those things τὰ πρέπει μᾶλλον βαρβάροισι ποιέειν ἤπερ Ἕλλησι (Hdt. 9. 79). Apollo is made to refer to this punishment as barbarous in A. *Eu.* 189, 90. Orestes, however (at E. *El.* 898), suggests to Electra such treatment for Aegisthus—πήξασ' ἔρεισον σκόλοπι.

1432. **αὖθις** as at ll. 377 and 1312 = on a later occasion.

1433. If **τήν** is right it must mean 'this' (cf. l. 1366), but Barnes' τῶν προκειμένων is very attractive; for σπουδὴν ἔχειν + gen. cf. E. *Alc.* 778 = 1014 (θυραίου πήματος σπουδὴν ἔχων).

1435. Athena appears as *dea ex machina* on the θεολογεῖον. For her dramatic justification see Introduction, p. xviii. A poet who writes ἴχνος (l. 266) and πόδα (l. 936) πορθμεύειν should not awake distrust in using the phrase διωγμὸν πορθμεύειν. Nauck's πορσύνεις, therefore, and Wecklein's τόνδ' ἐπευθύνεις are needless.

For **ποῖ ποῖ** cf. E. *Or.* 278; *ib.* 470 and E. *El.* 487 ποῦ ποῦ.

1436. The normal voc. form is Θόαν; cf. *Il.* 13. 222 (K-G. I. i. 415). At E. *Supp.* 1183 we find ἄκουε . . . τούσδ' Ἀθηναίας λόγους.

1437. **ῥεῦμα,** 'lit. 'the flood of your army', a common and, to a Greek, a natural metaphor. The exact phrase is to be found in A. *Pers.* 412 ῥεῦμα Περσικοῦ στρατοῦ.

1438. The impossible dat. plur. (πεπρωμένοις) of the MSS. may be emended either to this (personal) nominative or to the acc. sing. (Monk), in which case we have an impersonal acc. absolute. For the personal use of the participle cf. E. *Tr.* 340, 1 τὸν πεπρωμένον . . . πόσιν. πεπρωμένον does not seem to occur in the absolute use, but on the analogy of εἰρημένον, γεγραμμένον, etc. (cf. K.-G. II. ii, p. 88), it is not impossible.

1440. England calls attention to the ambiguity in Goethe's *Iphigenie* of Apollo's command to Or. to bring back from Tauris *die Schwester*, words which Or. interprets as *Apollo's* sister, Artemis, not his own. There is, however, no ambiguity here; for, though ἀδελφῆς might mean either Apollo's or Orestes' sister, δέμας cannot = ἄγαλμα (England's citation of E. *Alc.* 348 is merely misleading), and, while Iph.'s goal was Argos, the statue's was Athens (ἐμὴν . . . χθόνα). In this case, too, l. 1441 would be redundant.

1441[b]. This line is missing in P and in all the old printed editions. It is true that it in part resembles E. *Hipp.* 600 (τῶν νῦν παρόντων πημάτων ἄκος μόνον) and in part E. *Supp.* 615 (κακῶν . . . ἀναψυχάς), but these are not sufficient grounds on which to reject it. ἀναψ. is in apposit. not to ἄγαλμα but to the preceding clause.

1442. **ἀποκτενεῖν δοκεῖς**: 'expect to kill' rather than 'intend to kill'.

1444. When used with personal pronouns χάριν (= 'for the sake of') takes the adjectival form in agreement, not the genitive of the substantival. An extension of this use may be seen at E. *Heracl.* 241 where πατρῴαν χάριν = πατρὸς χάριν.

At S. *Tr.* 485 we get a combination: κείνου τε καὶ σὴν . . . χάριν.

1445. Some edd. (e.g. Hermann) keep the MSS., apparently regarding τίθησι πορθμεύων = τιθεὶς πορθμεύει. This is really impossible. We can either, with Badham, alter πλάτῃ to πλάτην: i.e. '⟨for him⟩ Poseidon makes the sea smooth, causing the ship (*lit.* oar) to pass over it'; or accept (as our text does) Tyrwhitt's correction. In this case the sentence can be construed in two ways: (1) '⟨him⟩ P. is at this moment (ἤδη) causing to voyage in his ship over a waveless sea . . .'; (2) '⟨for him⟩ P. is at this moment making the sea's surface smooth so that he may voyage . . .', i.e. ⟨ὥστε⟩ πορθμεύειν.

Of these the second is preferable, though the acc. of 'motion over which' involved in the first is not impossible cf. E. *Andr.* 1228, 9 λευκὴν αἰθέρα πορθμευόμενος), and such a constr. of τίθημι is not (as England tries to make out) confined to cases where compulsion rather than enablement is expressed (see, e.g., E. *Med.* 717, 8 παίδων γονὰς | σπεῖραί σε θήσω, where the verb means 'I will enable', not 'I will force'. So, too, E. *HF.* 311 ὃ χρὴ γὰρ οὐδεὶς μὴ χρεὼν θήσει ποτέ).

Weil suggests τίθησ' οἱ, unnecessarily. A datival antecedent to ὅν can be easily understood.

1447. There is something to be said for ending the parenthesis at παρών and taking θεᾶς with ἄγαλμα (so Bruhn).

For divine telephony unaccompanied by television cf. E. *Hipp.* 85, 6 σοὶ καὶ ξύνειμι καὶ λόγοις ἀμείβομαι, | κλύων μὲν αὐδήν, ὄμμα δ' οὐχ ὁρῶν τὸ σόν; cf. also S. *Aj.* 14, 5.

1449–50. ὅταν . . . χῶρός τις ἔστι: cf. note on l. 260 above.

1451. Halae Araphenides (so called to distinguish it from Halae Aexonides) was in the east of Attica, on the coast of the Euboeic Gulf opposite the δειρὰς Καρυστία = Ὄχη, beneath which mountain lay the town of Carystus in the south of Euboea (cf. Str. 10. 1. 6. Κάρυστος δ' ἐστὶν ὑπὸ τῷ ὄρει τῇ Ὄχῃ . . . ὅθεν διάπλους εἰς Ἁλὰς τὰς Ἀραφηνίδας). See Introduction, p. vii.

1455. Eur. uses the verb περιπολεῖν for the sake of the syllable πολ in his punning derivation of the title Ταυροπόλος.

1456. οἴστροις, instrumental dat. as though περιπολῶν had been a passive participle.

For Ἐρινύων trisyllabic see l. 931 and 970.

1457. Attempts to avoid the anapaest in the fifth foot by reading Ταυροπόλον εἰς τὸ λ. ὑμν. δή (Weil) or Ταυροπόλον ὑμν. εἰς ἀεὶ θεάν (Nauck) will seem unnecessary when we consider the comparative frequency of this metrical licence where proper names are concerned; cf. above l. 825.

1458. ἑορτάζῃ ⟨τῇ Ἀρτέμιδι⟩.

1459. ἄποινα is in apposit. to the sentence which follows.

σφαγῆς refers to the attempted sacrifice of Or. by the Taurians.

With ἐπισχέτω and ἐξανιέτω we must understand ὁ ἱερεύς: cf. the ἀναγνώσεται ⟨ὁ γραμματεύς⟩ so common in Demosthenes.

1460. δέρῃ πρός = πρὸς δέρῃ. The anastrophe is eased by the following genitive. A not uncommon word-order in Eur.: cf. *HF.* 527 ὄχλῳ . . . ἐν ἀνδρῶν, *ib.* 863 στέρνον εἰς Ἡρακλέους, *Ph.* 24 λειμῶν' ἐς Ἥρας, *Rh.* 660 εὐνὰς . . . πρὸς Ἕκτορος, and ναῦς ἐπ' Ἀργείων *ib.* 150 (and in five other lines of the play: 155, 203, 221, 502, 589).

1461. ὁσίας ἕκατι looks back to σφαγῇ ἄποινα, but the rest of the line suggests another motive: compensation to Artemis for the loss of her Tauric sacrifices.

Actually the ritual of Artemis Tauropolos contained traces of much earlier human sacrifice. This false aetiology is a conscious attempt to clear the Greeks by attributing such sacrifice to the barbarians; see Introduction, p. ix.

1462–3. κλίμακας seems to have here the meaning (ignored in L & S) of 'terraces' (cf. D.S. 19. 21, and Str. 12. 2. 6 (κλιμακώδη)).

On Pierson's suggested λείμακας (a word which the tragedians, except at Pseudo-Eur. *IA.* 1544, use only in lyrics) Hermann's comment is: temerarium est descriptiones tentare locorum quos quis non ipse viderit. βάθρα (which can mean 'rungs of a ladder' as at E. *Ph.* 1179) seems to be used in this sense at E. *IA.* 81 Αὐλίδος βάθρα, *ib.* 705 Πηλίου βάθρα, and *Ph.* 982 Δωδώνης βάθρα.

Βραυρωνίας. Faced with the difficulty that similar rites occurred both at Halae and Brauron Eur. places the ξόανον in the former, sending Iph. to the latter. In this Strabo (9. 1. 22) follows him, as also Callimachus (*Dian.* 173).

Weil keeps the almost impossible gen. τῆσδε . . . θεᾶς, but κληδουχεῖν cannot = κληδοῦχον εἶναι.

1465. It is best to take εὐπήνους ὑφάς with πέπλων and ἄγαλμα in apposition. The subject of θήσουσι is left vague. The garments of such as died in child-birth were dedicated to Ἄρτεμις λοχία. Clearly Iph. is here identified with this goddess. Pausanias (2. 35. 1) speaks of a goddess Ἄρτεμις-Ἰφιγένεια as worshipped at Hermione and elsewhere (Introduction, p. viii).

1467. τάσδε = the women of the chorus.

The older edd. regarded the addressee of this sentence as Thoas. This is difficult for four reasons: (1) the absence of a vocative; (2) the fact that Athena seems to have finished with the king at l. 1445; (3) it would be necessary to postulate a long lacuna in which Athena would end her new instructions to Thoas and recommence those addressed to Or. (ἐκσώσασα δέ, κτλ.); (4) the change of addressee in the middle of a line. That at l. 1482 Thoas says πέμψω . . . τάσδ' does not preclude the possibility that here, as at E. *Hel.* 1427, ἐκπέμπειν = 'escort out of', not 'send out of', see l. 171 n. above. It is better, therefore, to suppose that Athena addresses Or. and his sister throughout.

But though γνώμ. δικ. οὕνεκ' and ἐκσώσασα are *grammatically* possible as expressing two reasons for Athena's command, they are not *logically* so, and most edd. have supposed a lacuna starting either after οὕνεκ' or after ἐξεφίεμαι. If the former, then the γνώμη δικαία was the chorus' when it decided to help Iph.; if the latter, then it is Or.'s as shown in his coming to Tauris, and may have been preceded by some such remark as '⟨I save thee now⟩ because of . . .' In this case we may adopt the reading preserved in the Aristophanic scholium (see *app. crit.*) ἐξέσωσα δέ.

It is possible to translate the text as it stands (accepting the scholiast's reading) without postulating a lacuna. In this case not only a new sentence but a new paragraph starts at ἐξέσωσα δέ. Athena, after enjoining on Or. the duty of rescuing the chorus, bids him see to it that in future in matters legal the principle of 'the benefit of the doubt' holds good, citing his own case as a precedent. There would be only a comma after Ὀρέστα, and καί (l. 1471) would mean 'and therefore'.

On the whole, however, it is best to postulate a lacuna after οὕνεκ'. Grégoire ingeniously suggests that this lacuna may have contained Athena's instructions for the establishment of the chorus in Delos, an island for which they express their admiration in the strophe of the second stasimon of the play (ll. 1089 sqq.). We know, and Eur. must have known, that the Hyperboreans were somehow connected with Delos and the worship there of Apollo (cf. Hdt. 4. 32 sqq., Pi. *P.* 10. 30, *O.* 3. 16), and in this passage Eur., identifying the chorus with the Hyperboreans, may have given an 'explanation' of the connexion between these and the island of Delos parallel to that of the connexion of Iph. with Attica. (Cf. further Call. *Del.* 281.)

1470. **ἴσας**; cf. l. 965.

Ἀρείοις ἐν πάγοις, cf. E. *Or.* 1651 πάγοισιν ἐν Ἀρείοισιν.

1471. Markland's emendation (see *app. crit.*) is easy. Without it we must, with Hermann, suppose a lacuna after l. 1471.

1476. **ἄπιστος** here = disobedient. Hesych. has the gloss: ἄπιστος· ἀπαράπιστος, ἀπειθής. Σοφοκλῆς Τρωίλῳ (*fr.* 627). The adj. is so used also by Aeschylus (*Th.* 842 βουλαὶ . . . ἄπιστοι Λαΐου; cf. *ib.* 1036); cf. the not uncommon use in tragedy (and in Plato) of ἀπιστεῖν = ἀπειθεῖν.

1477–9. **τε . . . τε . . . οὐχί** may be all right (cf. l. 1367), but England's ἀδελφήν τ' (i.e. φέρων βρέτας θ. ἀδελφήν τε) is not unlikely. In this case the τ' after Ὀρέστῃ is answered by the δέ of l. 1482 (see note on l. 1415).

τί . . . καλόν; lit. 'in what way is it a good thing to . . .?'

Bruhn's emendation (see *app. crit.*) has much to be said for it. Alternatively we might accept Stadtmüller's πλέον for καλόν. Weil thinks θεούς may be a gloss which has got into the text and suggests: τί γάρ; | πρὸς τοὺς σθένοντας πῶς ἁμ. καλόν;

1480. **ἴτωσαν**: this 3rd per. plur. imperat. is a late form. Only one example is known from inscriptions as occurring before 300 B.C. and that dates to the year 352 (Meisterhans, p. 168). Several occur in the MSS. of Thucydides, but these may well be 'corrections' of the early -ων form. In fifth- and fourth-century verse the only instance besides this seems to be ἔστωσαν in E. *Ion* 1131. Both should probably be emended. We might here read Elmsley's εἰς σὴν ἰόντων, Herwerden's ἴοιεν εἰς σήν, or Wecklein's ἴτων νυν εἰς σήν.

1486. There seems no reason to suspect χρεών. It is used substantivally at E. *HF.* 21, *Hel.* 1636, and *Hipp.* 1256 (where it is a disyllable). The synizesis (see note on l. 647 above) is not unusual; cf. E. *fr.* 734 τὸ γὰρ χρεὼν μεῖζον ἢ τὸ μὴ χρεών. But σοῦ τε καὶ θεῶν meaning 'not only you but also the gods' is strange (S. *Tr.* 443, 4 οὗτος (sc. Ἔρως) . . . ἄρχει καὶ θεῶν . . . κἀμοῦ γε is different), and the truism (Simonides' ἀνάγκᾳ οὐδὲ θεοὶ μάχονται) comes in rather frigidly. Nauck rejected the line.

1490. 'Go in your good fortune, happy ⟨as⟩ being of the number of the saved'. μοῖρα here means 'section' or 'division'; cf. E. *Med.* 430 ἀνδρῶν . . . μοῖραν = 'the male division of mankind'.

1497–9. E. *Or.* and *Ph.* have a similar ending, just as five other of Euripides' plays have a common conclusion. The chorus, in the person of the poet, prays for a dramatic victory.

METRICAL SCHEME AND NOTES

ll. 1–122 iambic senarians.

ll. 123–235 (except 126, 7) anapaests.

(Mostly, as is usual, acatalectic and catalectic dimeters; spondaic, as being 'anapaesti lugubres'.)

126, 7 dochmiac monometers.

130 normal if we read *ὁσίας ὅσιον πόδα π.* (*see* notes).

183 first anapaest resolved.

188 *πατρῴων* | *οἴκων* (⏑ ⏑– | – –) (if text correct: *see* notes).

194 second anapaest resolved.

197 ⏑ ⏑ ⏕ | ⏑ ⏑ ⏕ | ⏑ ⏑ ⏕ | ⏑ (*φόνῳ̆ . . .* ⟨*τ' ἐπ'*⟩ *ἄ̆χεσιν*: *see* notes).

213 reading ⟨*θεοῖς*⟩ *ἔ̆τεκεν* . . . catalect. dim. with second anapaest resolved.

215 *see* notes.

216 *νύμφαιον* (– ⏑ ⏑).

220 ? resolved anapaestic tripody (*see* notes). [Wilamowitz (*Griech. Versk.*, p. 267) strangely takes this line, as also 197 and 232, as trochaic].

230 read *δμαθέντ' ἀγκλαίῳ* (*see* notes).

231 second anapaest resolved. For apparent final tribrach see notes.

232 reading ⟨*σύγγονον*⟩ *ἔτι βρέφος* . . . acatalect. dim. with all but first foot resolved.

ll. 236–391 iambic senarians.

392 = 407 – ⏑ ⏑ – | – ⏑ ⏑ – = choriambic dimeter.

393 = 408 ⏑ ⏑ – | ⏑ – – ⏑ – = ? anap. + doch.[1]

394 = 409 ⏕ ⏑ ⏕ ⏑ – ⏑ ⏑ [–] = lecythion. (Reading *νότια* for *πόντια* in 409, *see* notes.)

395 = 410 ⟨–⟩ ⏑ ⏑ | ⏑ – | ⏑ ⏕ | ⏑ – | ⏑ – | · – = syncopated iambic trim. (*see* notes.)

396 = 411 ⏑ ⏑ – ⏑ ⏑ – ⏑ = Reizianum.

397 = 412 – – – ⏑ ⏑ – – = pherecratean.

[2] 398 = 413 ⏑ – | ⏑ ⏑ ⏑ | ⏑ – | ⏑ – | ⏑ ⏑ ⏓ | ⏑ ⏑ = iambic trim. (*see* notes).

400 = 415 ⏑ – | ⏑ – | – – | · – = syncopated iamb. dim.

401 = 416 – ⏑ ⏑ – | ⏑ – · – = syncopated choriamb. dim.

[1] A suspiciously odd combination. The lines may be (as Mr. Denniston suggests in his article in 'Greek Poetry and Life', p. 139) syncopated iambic dimeters with *Doppelsenkung*, i.e. ⏑ ⏑ – | ⏑ – | ⟨⏑⟩ – | ⏑ –.

[2] Where two marks of quantity are given in an antistrophic system the top one refers to the strophe, the bottom to the antistrophe.

402 = 417 ⏑–⏑⏑–⏑⏑–⏑|–⏑–⏑–– = Archilochean dicolon.
403 = 418 ––|–– = double spondee.
405 = 419 –––⏑⏑–⏑– = glyconic.
406 = 420 –––⏑⏑–⏓ = pherecratean.

421 = 439 ––––|–⏑⏑– = choriamb. dim.
422 = 439 (b) ––⏑⏑–⏑– = telesilleion or syncopated glyconic (= –·–⏑⏑–⏑–).

423 = 440 –––⏑⏑–– = pherecrat.

424 = 441 ⏑⏑⏑⏑ [antist.? Τρῳάδα].[1]
425 = 442 –⏑⏑⏑⏑|–⏑– = resolved choriamb. + cretic.
426 = 443 –⏑⏑–|⏑–·⏓ = syncopated choriamb. dim.
427 = 444 ⏑––⏒|–⏑⏑– = choriamb. dim.
428 = 445 –·––|–⏑⏑– = syncopated choriamb. dim. (*see* notes).
429 = 446 –·–⏓|–⏑⏑– = syncopated choriamb. dim.
430 = 447 –·–⏓|–⏑⏑– = syncopated choriamb. dim. (*see* notes).
431 = 448 ––––⏑⏑–– = paroemiac.
432 = 449 –·––|–⏑⏑– = syncopated choriamb. dim.
433 = 450 ––|–⏑⏑– = spond. + choriamb.
434 = 451 –·–⏓|–⏑⏑– = syncopated choriamb. dim.
435 = 452 –⏑⏑–|–⏑⏑– = choriamb. dim.
436 = 453 –⏒–⏒|–⏑⏑– = choriamb. dim.
437 = 454 –⏓––|–⏑⏑– = choriamb. dim.
438 = 455 –––⏑⏑–⏓ = pherecrat.

ll. 456–66 anapaests.

ll. 467–642 iambic senarians.

643 ⏑⏑⏑–⏑–|⏑––⏑– = dochmiac dim.
⟨644⟩ ⏑⏑⏑⟨–⏑–⟩ = doch. monometer (*see* notes).
645 ⏑⏑⏑⏑––– = doch. monometer
646 iambic trimeter.
647 ⏑⏑⏑–⏑–|⏑–⏑–⏑– = doch. dim. (*see* notes).
648 ⏑⏑⏑–⏑– = doch. mon. (*see* notes).
649 ⏑⏑⏑⏑––– = doch. mon.
650 iamb. trim.
651 –⏑⏑––– = doch. mon.
[652, 3 *see* notes]

[1] Four shorts in isolation is very strange and the following choriamb. + cretic unusual. We might take 424–6 (= 441–3) together, dividing them respectively at -*τας* and -*τᾳ*. This would give us a syncopated iambic trimeter (with initial tribrach in stroph. = initial dactyl in antist.) followed by a Reizianum.

655 ⏑⏖–⏑⏖|⏑⏖⏖⏑– = doch. dim.
656 ⏑⏖–⏑–|⏑––⏑– = doch. dim.

ll. 657–826 iambic senarians.

827, 8 iamb. trim.
830 –⏑⏑–⏑– = doch. mon.
831 iamb. trim.
832 ⏑⏑⏑|⏑⏑⟨⏑|⏑⏑⏑⟩|⏑⏑[⏑]⏑|⏑⏑⏑|⏑– = resolved iamb. trim. (*see* notes).
833 iamb. trim.
834 ⏑⏖⏖⟨⏑⏖⟩ = resolved doch. mon. notes).
835 ⏑⏑⏑–⏑–|⏑⏑⏑–⏑– = doch. dim.
836 ⏑⏑⏑–⏑– = doch. mon.
837 iamb. trim.
838 [––]⏑––⏑– = doch. mon. (*see* notes).
840 ⏑––⏑–|⏑–⏑⏑⏑– = doch. dim.
841 iamb. trim.
842 ⏑⏑⏑–⏑–|⏑⏑⏑–⏑– = doch. dim.
843 iamb. trim.
844 –⏑⏑–⏑– = doch. mon.
845 iamb. trim.
846 ⏑––⏑– = doch. mon.
847 ⏑⏑⏑–⏑–|⏑⏑⏑–⏑– = doch. dim.
848 ⏑⏑⏑–⏑–|⏑⏑⏑–⏑⟨–⟩ = doch. dim. (*see* notes).
849 [–]⏑––⏑– = doch. mon.
850, 1 iamb. trim.
852 ⏑––⏑⏖|–⏑⏑–⏑– = doch. dim.
853 ⏑––⏑–|⏑⏑⏑–⏑– = doch. dim.
855 iamb. trim.
856 ⏑⏑⏑–⏑–|–⏑⏑–⏑– = doch. dim.
857 –⏑⏑––– = doch. mon.
858 ⏑⏑–⏖⏑– = doch. mon. (*see* notes).
860 ⏑⏑⏑–⏑–|⏑⏑⏑–⏑– = doch. dim.
861 –––⏑–|[–]⏑–⟨–⏑–⟩ = doch. dim. (*see* notes).
862 iamb. trim.
863 ⏑⏑⏑|⏑⏑⏑|⏑⏑⏑|⏑⏑⏑ = resolved iamb. dim.
865 –⏑–––⏑– = lecythion.
867 –⏑–⏑–⏑⏑ = lecythion.
866 iamb. trim.
868 –⏑⏑–––|–––⏑– = doch. dim.
869 –⏓–––|–⏖⏖⏑⏖ = doch. dim.
871 ⏑⏖⏖⏑⏖|⏑⏖–⏑– = doch. dim.
872 ⏑––⏑– = doch. mon.
873 ⏑⏑⏑|––[⏑]|–⏑|–– = trochaic dim. (*see* notes).
874 –⏑|––|–⏑|–– = trochaic dim. (*see* notes).
875 ⏑⏑–|⏑⏑–|⏑⏑–|⟨––⟩ = anapaestic dim. (*see* notes).

876 ⏑⏑⏑⏑⏑⏑ ⏑–|⏑⏑⏑⏑–⏑– = doch. dim. (*see* notes).
877 ⏑⏑⏑––– = doch. mon.
880 ⏑⏑–|⏑⏑–|⏑⏑–|⏑⏑– = anap. dim.
881 ⏑⏑⏑⏑⏑|–⏑⏑––– = resolved cretic + doch. (so Schröder).
882 ⏑⏑⏑––– = doch. mon.
883 ⏑⏑–|⏑⏑–|⏑–|⏑–|⏑ ⟨–|⏑–⟩ = anap. mon. + iamb. dim. (*see* notes).
885 –⏑⏑––– = doch. mon.
886 ⏑⏑–|⏑⏑–⏑⏑–⏑⏑–⏑ = anap. + paroemiac.[1]
887 dactylic hexameter.
890 ⏑⏑⏑–⏑–|⏑⏑⏑–⏑– = doch. dim.
891 ⏑–––– = doch. mon.
892 ⏑–⏑⏑–⏑ = Reizianum.[2]
895 ⏑⏑–|⏑⏑–|⏑⏑–|⏑⏑– = anap. dim.
896 ⏑⏑–|––|–⏑⏑|–– = anap. dim. (*see* notes).
897 ⏑⏑–|⏑⏑– = anap. mon. (*see* notes).
898 ⏑––⏑–|–––⏑– = doch. dim.
899 ⏑––⏑– = doch. mon.

ll. 900–1088 iambic senarians.

1089 = 1106 –––⏑⏑–⏑⏑⏑ = glyc.
1090 = 1107 –⏑̄–⏑⏑–⏑– = glyc.
1091 = 1108 ⏑⏑⏑–⏑⏑–– = pherecr.
1092 = 1109 { –⏑⏑–⏑⏑ – ⏑ – / ⏑⏑⏑– – |–⏑⏑– } = { glyc. / chor. dim.[3] (*see* notes).
1093 = 1110 ⏑⏑⏑–⏑⏑–⏑–|–– = glyc. + spond.
1094 = 1111 ⏑––⏑⏑–⏑– = glyc.
1095 = 1112 –––⏑⏑–̆ = pherecr.
1096 = 1113 { ⏑–––| –⏑⏑– / –⏑–⏑⏑– ⏑ – } = { chor. dim.[3] / glyc.
1097 = 1114 { ⏑––⏑| –⏑⏑– / ⏑––⏑⏑– ⏑ – } = { chor. dim.[3] / glyc.
1098 = 1115 –⏑⏑–⏑⏑–⏑– = glyc.
1099 = 1116 –––⏑̲|–⏑⏑– = chor. dim. (*see* notes).
1100 = 1117 –·––|–⏑⏑– = syncopated chor. dim.
1101 = 1118 –––⏑|–⏑⏑– = chor. dim.
1102 = 1119 ––––|–⏑⏑– = chor. dim.
1103 = 1120 ––––|–⏑⏑– = chor. dim. (*see* notes).

[1] The single anapaest is strange; cf. l. 393.

[2] For Reiziana in dochmiac surroundings cf. A. Ag. 1080 sqq. We may, however, regard these lines as themselves dochmiac.

[3] The glyconic may be considered as a chor. dim. (∘∘∘•|–⏑⏑– or –⏑⏑–|∘•∘∘) of which the definite choriamb. has split the polyschematic one (∘∘|–⏑⏑–|∘∘); so the correspondence of glyc. and chor. dim. is in no way surprising. Similarly a pherecratean (= a syncopated glyconic) may correspond with a syncopated chor. dim.

1104 = 1121	⏑⏑⏑–⏑⏑–⏑–	= glyc.
1105 = 1122	–––⏑⏑––	= pherecr.
1123 = 1137	–⏓–⏑⏑–––	= glyc.
1124 = 1138	–––⏑⏑–⏑––	= hipponacteion.
1125 = 1140	–––⏑|–⏑⏑–	= chor. dim.
1126 = 1141	––––|–⏑⏑–	= chor. dim. (*see* notes).
1127 = 1142	––⏑⏑––⏒	= telesilleion.[1]
1128 = 1143	⏑––⏓|–⏑⏑–	= chor. dim.
1129 = 1144	⏓⏑⏑–⏑⏑–⏑–	= glyc. (*see* notes).
1130 = 1145	⏑⏔––|–⏑⏑–	= chor. dim.
1131 = 1146	–⏑–⏒|–⏑⏑–	= chor. dim.
1132 = 1147	⏑⏑––⏑⏑–⏑ } –⏑⏑–|⏑–·– }	= { pherecr. { syncopated chor. dim.[2] (*see* notes)
1133 = 1148	––⏑⏑–⏑⏑⏒	= prosodiac.
1134 = 1149	–⏑⏑|–⏑⏑|–⏑⏑|–⏑⏑	= dactyl. tetram. (*see* notes).
1135 = 1150	–⏑⏑|–⏑⏑|–⏑⏑|–	= dactyl. tetram. catalectic.
1136 = 1151	⏔⏑–⏑––	= ithyphallic.

ll. 1152–1202 iambic senarians.

ll. 1203–33 trochaic tetrameters.

1234 = 1259	⏒–|⏑–|–⏑–	= diiamb. + cretic.
1235 = 1260	–⏑⏑–⏑⏑–|–⏑⏑–⏑⏑–	= two hemiepes.
1236 = 1261	⏓·–⏑|–⏑⏑–	= syncopated chor. dim.
1237 = 1262	–⏑⏑|–⏑⏑|–⏑⏑|––	= dactyl. tetram.
1238 = 1263	–⏑⏑|–⏑⏑|–⏑⏑|–⏑⏑	= dactyl. tetram. (*see* notes).
1240 = 1265	⏑⏓⏓–⏕|–⏑⏑–	= ? resolved chor. or polyschematist dimeter.
1241 = 1266	⏑–|⏑–|⏑⏑–|⏑–	= ? iamb. dim. with *Doppelsenkung* (*see* notes).
1242 = 1267	–⏒––|–⏑⏑–	= chor. dim.
1243 = 1268	–·–⏔|–⏑⏑–	= syncopated chor. dim.
1244 = 1269	–––⏑|–⏑⏑–	= chor. dim.
1244 (b) = 1269 (b)	⏑⏑–⏑⏑–⏑–	= telesilleion.[1]
1245 = 1270	––|⏑–	= diiamb.
1246 = 1271	⏑⏑–⏑⏑–⏑–	= telesilleion.[1]
1247 = 1272	⏒–|⏑–	= diiamb.
1248 = 1273	–⏑–|⏑–⏑⏑–⏑⏑––	= cretic + paroem.
1249 = 1274	–⏑⏑⏓	= choriamb. (*see* notes).
1249 (b) = 1274 (b)	⏑⏕|⏑⏕|⏑⏕|⏑–	= iamb. dim.

[1] Cf. l. 422 (= 439 b): a telesilleion may be regarded as an acephalous or a syncopated glyconic.

[2] See note 3 on p. 184.

1250 = 1275 ⏑ ⏑ – ⏑ ⏑ – ⏑ – | ⏑ – – = telesilleion + bacchius.[1]
1251 = 1276 ⏖ ⏑ – | – ⏑ – – | – ⏑ ⏑ – ⏑ ⏑ – = cretic + dactylo-epitrite.
1252 = 1277 ⏑ ⏑ ⏑ – ⏑ ⏑ – – | – ⏑ – – | – ⏑ – = pherecr. + epitrite + cretic.
1255 = 1280 – – | · – | ⏑ – | · – | ⏑ – | ⏑ – = syncopated iamb. trim.[2]
1256 = 1281 ⏑ ⏑ – | ⏑ ⏑ – | ⏑ ⏑ – | ⏑ ⏑ – | – – | ⏑ – = anap. dim. + diiamb.
1257 = 1282 – ⏑ – ⏑ – – = ithyph.

ll. 1283–1489 iambic senarians.

ll. 1490–9 anapaests.

[1] This odd type of line is found also at E. *Alc.* 437, *Med.* 648, *Hec.* 655, 927, *Ion* 457, 1458, *Rh.* 462, 900, 901, and Ar. *Av.* 1411, 1415.
[2] We might alternatively take this as – – – ⏑ – | – ⏑ – ⏑ –; i.e. a dochmius + a hyperdochmius; though dochmiacs seem out of place in this system.

PRINTED IN GREAT BRITAIN
AT THE UNIVERSITY PRESS, OXFORD
BY VIVIAN RIDLER
PRINTER TO THE UNIVERSITY